Eternally Naïve

A Reluctant Autobiography

T. R. Robinson

Anickto Publishing

Anickto Publishing

(www.anickto.com)

Copyright © 2023 T. R. Robinson

All rights reserved.

The right of T. R. Robinson to be identified as the author of this work has been asserted by her in accordance with the Copyright, Designs and Patents Act 1988.

No part of this publication may be reproduced, stored in a retrieval system, or transmitted, in any form or by any means without prior written permission of the publisher, nor be otherwise circulated in any form of binding or cover other than that in which it is published and without a similar condition being imposed on the subsequent purchaser.

ISBN 978-1-7385435-3-3

In order to protect those still living, the descendants of those referred to and my own family, names of people and places have either been changed or omitted.

Contents

Dedication	VI
Prologue	VII
1. Origins	1
2. Bliss	13
3. Mama	25
4. Bereft	35
5. Lust	55
6. Occupation	69
7. Devastating	85
8. Darkness	103
9. Emergence	119
10. Reunited	135
11. Resolution	149
12. Transition	167
13. In-Laws	181

14.	Surprise	195
15.	Advent	217
16.	Desperation	229
17.	Flight	243
18.	Arterial	257
19.	Divorce	271
20.	Jurisdiction	281
21.	Bullies	297
22.	Discovered	317
23.	Income	331
24.	Nightclub	353
25.	Catwalk	369
26.	Nightingales	381
27.	Society	393
28.	Misstep	409
29.	Crushed	425
30.	Niece	435
31.	Predators	449
32.	Disappointment	455
33.	Finally	465
34.	Ransom	477

35.	Duped	487
36.	Cheated	499
37.	Menacing	521
38.	Despicable	543
39.	Endless	561
40.	Penned	571
41.	Memorial	587
42.	Malicious	597
43.	Shadows	609
44.	Closing	617
Epilogue		621
Other Books		627

DEDICATION

For my beloved Mama

with whom I enjoyed far too little time.

Prologue

I have described this chronicle of my life as a reluctant autobiography. That is because I am essentially a private person and, as you will see, dislike public exposure. It is also because I am ashamed of those events that reflect negatively upon some relatives. I am also ashamed of what was done to me, and of my weak timidness in the earlier part of my adult years. However, I do not think it would be right to depart this life without leaving some sort of record of my experiences. It has been difficult to write because it has stirred innumerable sad, painful, and hurtful memories, though many have never been far from my thoughts. I do not feel the book really does justice to all I have endured, nor does it truly convey the full strength of the emotions and fears. Nevertheless, I have done my utmost and believe it is the best record I could compose. I have intentionally omitted some details and events. There is no justification for unnecessarily traumatising readers beyond what is required to make sense of some situations. The rest will pass into eternity with me. I must clarify, though much was difficult, there have been lighter amusing moments and events, which I also share with you as I recount my tale. My primary aim, besides that of providing a history of my life and the times I have lived through, is to try to help and inspire those who, by whatever means, have suffered, or are suffering, in their lives.

A couple of minor points before you continue. I have used British English throughout. When I refer to 'in this country' or similar, I mean England, United Kingdom. As stated on the copyright page, in order to protect those still living, the descendants of those referred to, and my own family, I have either changed or omitted the names of people and locations.

1

ORIGINS

So you would like to know about me and my life. Well, the first thing to say is my story is not just a case of I was born, I lived, I aged and I will die. It is far more. Now where to begin? I suppose logically it should be with my earliest memories, though chronology may well go a little awry thereafter.

I recall those early days vividly. When my sisters had gone off to school, mama would carry me out with her to feed the chickens and our other livestock. I was not yet old enough for school nor, in fact, was I walking. I should explain I was the product of my parent's later years. People commonly referred to me as my parents 'love child'. A term that has a far different meaning these days. I would squeal with delight as the tan, white and black feathered chickens, clucking loudly, ran with their seesaw gait to mama in anticipation of the food she would give them. At how they scrambled and pushed each other to get at the seed or corn. At how the handsome cockerel would stretch to his full height and crow over his harem. Of course, I did not know what a harem was then. After this, he would also push in, determined to get his fill and woe betide any hen who got in the way. When I could stand on my own feet, mama let me throw some of the seed. The geese, with their loud cries and tendency to push hard, frightened me at first. But once we got to know each other I was fine and quite happy for them to press up against my legs while they attempted to grab food from my hand. I was fortunate never to suffer from nipped fingers.

Over time, mama developed my play teaching me how to care for all our animals. I loved each one and eventually made pets of them all. My attachment to them was to cause a few problems for papa. Mother also showed me how to plant and care for a variety of vegetables, flowers, and fruits. There is no doubt in my mind I get my love for nature from her. She was such a gentle and loving woman. I was so happy and never dreamt of any other life. Mama, papa, my sisters and grandma, who lived nearby, together with our animals, were all I could ask for. I did not know then how my life would soon change. Nor how cruel and unkind life could be.

I think we were all very happy in those days. Admitted father could sometimes be a little difficult. That did not mean we did not love him or he us. He was very much a man of his generation, a 'man's man'. For example, he was a carnivorous eater, whereas mama, because of her love of all things living, was vegetarian. Though fully aware of this, he still insisted on having meat for most meals. To keep the peace, mother would put a small pile of bones on her plate and pretend to chew meat from them. In truth, she ate no meat. Having made pets of all our livestock, I would allow none to be harmed therefore papa had to turn elsewhere to find the meat we ate. Thankfully, with his genuine love for us all, he knew and accepted the validity of my affection. Most may well have considered it childish, and a passing phase or fancy to be ignored. But for me it was not. He respected that. In my innocent and naïve way, it never crossed my mind where our dinner table meat came from. All I knew was my friends were all safe. My sister has since explained the pork on our table had been wild boar papa and his friends had hunted in the forests above the village. Sadly, these, along with many other specious, have been hunted to extinction, in our area at least. I do not know where the chicken, lamb, etc., that regularly adorned our table came from.

In some ways my parent's marriage appeared incongruous with mama's sensitivity and papa's robust masculine attitudes. Mama never spoke about how they met and it was to be many years later before I learnt anything about it. It was round the end of the nineteenth and the beginning of the twentieth centuries, when cultural and social acceptances were very different. Generally, and especially in families like ours, girls were not permitted direct contact with the opposite sex other than fathers and brothers. Conversation with other men was definitely out and when away from home, the expectation was for girls to be chaperoned. Our national church, along with its strict teachings, was then an integral part of society. Apparently it was while walking to a service with her mother, my grandmother, that papa first set eyes upon her. And, as far as I understand, was immediately captivated. From an early age, mama's beauty was renowned throughout the district. She was a tall, elegant woman with exquisite aquiline features and wonderful eyes. I can never forget those warm golden hazel eyes which she would lovingly turn upon me. If eyes are the windows of the soul, then what a truly wonderful soul I looked upon. Anyway, as said, father's captivation was immediate. I believe mama, though aware of his stare, had kept her eyes modestly cast down as expected from a young unmarried woman at our social level. Ours was an important influential family within the district.

I understand father then made enquiries and started visiting my grandparent's home with the clear hope of seeing mother. He came from a well-to-do family, though not quite on the same social level. While remaining politely friendly, grandma did not encourage him in his visits. Of course, she had comprehended well his sudden interest in the family. There was mama's beauty to start. In addition, as grandmother's last living child, she would receive the substantial family inheritance. That made it necessary to protect her from fortune hunters. Ignoring what was more than obvious to all, father persisted in his visits until he eventually asked for mother's hand in marriage. Normally, it would have been the senior male in the family who would deal with such requests. However, as grandfather had died[1] and there was no son and heir, he had to address his request

---

1. *Grandfather's death is another story and is the subject of my novel Peter.*

to grandma. She was reticent. He had spent most of his adolescent years and early twenties overseas. Particularly in the United States of America, and had the reputation of being a playboy, at which he apparently excelled. His stability and suitability were therefore questionable. There was also the added concern he may squander the family wealth in carousing and gambling. These were the days when a wife's wealth automatically became the husband's property upon marriage. His slightly lesser social standing also played a factor. Not that our family was ever snobbish. It was just the way of society then. She refused.

Papa not accustomed to being thwarted took offence. However, he controlled his indignation and continued to call at the house. Grandmother appreciated he was not an evil man but remained perturbed about his suitability and whether he would squander mother's inheritance. She therefore continued to decline his frequently repeated proposals.

Now I do not know how the following came about. Obsessed by the idea of marrying mama and incensed by grandmother's continuing refusals, father somehow abducted the object of his desire. I would love to know how he managed this. I may only surmise. Grandmother and mama were both very caring people. They consistently visited and assisted families in the district, especially those who were sick or lacked means. It did not help that the poor were mostly uneducated and therefore also required instruction in some of the most basic matters. Schooling was not compulsory then. Grandmama was a qualified nurse, having got her degree in Vienna, where both my grandparents studied. Grandfather was a qualified doctor. It was where they met. Mama, having shown an aptitude for medicine when helping her father in his clinic, had also studied in the academies of Vienna. It housed the best medical institutes available then. This was unusual. For a woman to study a profession was almost unknown. Unlike these modern days, people did not consider nursing a profession in the same way as a doctor. As his only son was no longer and there was no one else in the family suitable, grandpapa, who held a deep respect for mama, agreed to her being the one to carry on the family's medical expertise. She successfully obtained a doctor's degree. Therefore, the two of them, grandmother and mama, could provide excellent care for the villagers. Besides her nursing degree, grandmama also had considerable knowledge and experience of the old effective family remedies. I may only assume it was whilst on one of these mercy trips, father abducted her. Not fearing any danger or untoward inappropriate contact with men, grandmother allowed her daughter to go on these trips alone.

Later that day, he presented grandmama with an ultimatum. Either she gave her permission for the marriage or he would kill her daughter and himself. Grandmother was, naturally, horrified. No amount of pleading or trying to talk sense into him had any impact. She subsequently asked some friends and acquaintances to help search for her daughter. All to no avail. No one could find her. Apparently, father constantly and unequivocally stated his love for mother. I have to say there was never any doubt in my mind or that of other family members that he really loved her with all his heart. Despite that love, he would not concede to grandmother's pleas to return her daughter to her unharmed. He clearly meant the threat. Obsession can be an ugly and dangerous thing. Ultimately, grandmama felt she had no choice. Still, and understandably, holding deep reservations, she conceded to the marriage. The alternative too horrific to contemplate. Of course, they could have rescinded once mama was safely back. However, those were the days when people kept their word. Anyway, if they had gone back, there was no certainty mama would remain safe. He was a determined man.

No one could understand their inability to locate mother. After all, this was a rural community with, despite the forests, not that many unknown places in which to hide someone. All mama could tell was it had been a reasonably extensive property that sported stained glass windows. Father had never allowed her to see the actual location, having covered her eyes when taking and removing her. Stained glass was an expensive luxury, so people assumed it must have been a property owned by his family. That theory however, never helped. To this day, none of us has any idea where it is.

They were married. I think mama remained apprehensive for a while, especially in view of their different outlooks. As mentioned, her love of all things living had led her to being a vegetarian while papa loved his meat. In addition, father, whenever he perceived someone had done something wrong, had a volatile temper. He was a very just man. Thankfully, he never hit mama, my sisters or me. But he insisted when someone, no matter who they were, had done wrong, they paid the price whether by immediate punishment, imprisonment or fine. Nonetheless, with time it became more than evident a loving man existed under the fierce exterior. I have to admit when angry, he sometimes frightened me even though I knew without doubt how much he loved us. He certainly held the villagers in terror of ever crossing him. Even now mention of his name brings fearful respect from those old enough to remember.

As said, I was the product of my parent's later years. Helen, the serious one, Anna, by far and away the most mischievous, and George, who died before I was born, had preceded me. I was definitely the naïve and innocent one.

Before continuing, I would like to make clear our parents loved and treated us equally. They always ensured we had time with them as individuals and as a family unit. It would have been easy for Helen and I to think Anna the favourite because she had a medical condition that regularly resulted in high temperatures. Consequently, she needed constant monitoring. However, there was never any question of her receiving privileged treatment. Helen told me that even George, their only son, never received preferential treatment or attention. It is hard to relate in words not only the knowledge of being loved but also the feeling of being loved.

It did not take me long to note mention of George was rare and when there was an awkwardness pervaded. This intrigued me so I asked mama to tell me about him. She would simply say there was really nothing to tell and change the subject. But I now had the bit between my teeth and was more than just a little curious. Helen and

Anna, when I asked them, could tell me nothing much except he had fallen ill and died shortly after. Realising there was something behind it, I continued to pester mama on an almost daily basis. Eventually, she conceded. I suspect my continual niggling had worn her down. It must have been clear I was not about to give up asking. Mind, in the end, I wished I had.

When grandmother no longer felt up to undertaking the daily running of our estates, she handed full control over to father. He had in practice already been doing much of the work. However, she was not one to sit idle and, though not capable of much physical activity, wanted an occupation. She therefore opened a haberdasher in the village's commercial centre. A grand term for what was basically the gathering of a few small suppliers. There was the baker. Back then, there had been no such thing as household electricity and gas supplies. People had to constantly prepare and light outside clay ovens, which was tedious. As a rural society, virtually everyone worked in the fields from morning to dusk, including grandparents and children. Time for domestic cooking was therefore limited and most bought their bread from the baker. The delightful aroma of fresh baked bread filled the village in the mornings, followed later by a variety of other mouth-watering scents. For a tiny charge, the baker would accept ready prepared meals for cooking in his already heated ovens. The general store was always one I delighted looking round. To me it was like an Aladdin's cave with its mixture of goods, buckets, mops, soap, lamps, dried foods, oil, pictures, crockery, and so on. You never quite knew what would be round the next corner or in a dark alcove. And, of course, there was the ubiquitous café where the men of the village would gather to have heated discussions of politics or commerce. My people are demonstrative and I remember frequently, while still very young, being frightened by their raised voices and gesticulating antics. There was never any real harm in them and they usually ended up clapping each other on the back and enjoying a drink together. Besides the coffee, cafes also served locally made wines and fermented spirits, all of which were consumed in small amounts. Drunkenness was not generally heard of as the men tended to enjoy a mixture of small hors d'oeuvres with their drinks.

Grandmother's choice of haberdashery made a lot of sense. Embroidery, lace making, and crochet were daily occupations for women, both young and old. In our rural community, life was always busy, especially for women. Besides helping with crops, the women managed their homes and helped the community with tasks like caring for the sick and acting as midwives. Being used to constant activity, they found it difficult to sit with idle hands and were therefore pleased to have the skills mentioned and others, dressmaking and knitting among them. In the evenings we would gather with neighbours, friends and relatives often, with the mainly warmer climate, outside on terraces or balconies. These were our social times when we could catch up with village and family events. I say we but for most of the time we younger ones usually sat quietly listening, hopefully picking up knowledge and wisdom from our elders, who also taught us the skills needed for these crafts. However, these were not just social times they were also culturally important. When a girl married she was expected to have a substantial 'bottom draw'. An old-fashioned term that essentially meant she had a ready selection of bed linen, tablecloths and runners, cushion covers, ornamental side table napkins, and more. Unlike modern days, where plain tends to be favoured, these were all expected to be embroidered or crocheted with pleasing designs. Along with floral decorations, there were also images of national costumes, historic places, fruits, and more. Each piece would be boarded with designs peculiar to our nation or district. Many were so skilled with their embroidery that it was often difficult to know which way up was correct. They looked the same from both sides. Older women still practice these skills but, sadly, many of the younger generation cannot be bothered with the intricacies involved. We live in an impatient age. The 'bottom draw' concept helped young married couples who did not have the opportunity or resources to purchase items, to set up their homes with a little more comfort. Even if they had the means, shops for such luxuries only existed in major cities, not in villages or even district towns.

Still holding the legal rights to everything grandmama sometimes needed to attend to other business. On those occasions or when she required a rest, we children would look after the shop in her absence. I well remember feeling very proud and adult when I first took my turn, even though I could barely see over the counter. One day, when George was in charge, mother asked him to take some money from the till when closing and buy bread for the family lunch on his way home. Father, unaware of her request, saw George with the money and concluded he had stolen it. George tried to explain. But to no avail. Regrettably, when papa's temper was roused, he had a tendency not to listen. No one is sure, but it is possible he may have struck his son, though I would query the thought. Papa never, not once, raised a hand to any of us, Mama, Helen, Anna or I. Anyway, George, who I understand was a sensitive soul, ran off into the forest. To this point there had been warm sunshine, but now, as the afternoon progressed, strong cold wind and rain arrived. Mother explained to father his error. Both then went looking for their son. They found him soaked through and shivering from the cold. He died shortly after. Though I never knew my brother, I remember feeling as if there were some sort of connection between us. I often found myself crying for him. Mama told me she thought we would probably have been kindred spirits had he lived. It is a shame I will never know.

2

Bliss

Well, enough of them for the present. After all, this is supposed to be my autobiography. Now, knowing what this autobiography should encompass and what to omit is a bit of a problem. Neither you nor I would want this to become an eight-hundred page doorstop. What would you be interested in, I wonder? Not the boring day-to-day routine, I suspect. Though a few will need to be referred to if some events are to be put into context. I shall do my best to avoid the more laborious accounts and confine myself to those moments that define my life and who I have become. Those of you who have read my previous memoirs, and some of the short stories, will recognise some details, events, and experiences have been omitted from this more formal account of my life. As said, I do not want this to become a wearying missive, though I hope I have forgotten nothing of import.

I loved where we lived. The vast open valley dominating the district, with its different coloured fields and the river running through its centre, remains a delight to look upon. Our ancestral home is located upon higher slopes. Then there are the surrounding forest-covered mountains, native wildlife, and domestic pets and livestock. Added to which were my loving family, my friends, and the simple rural provincial society. These all combined to make me happy. I could not dream of any better life. In all honesty, I may say those were blissful days. Those were the days when I felt loved and there was no danger threatening me. Happy, innocent, carefree days. I was totally unaware of how, within a brief time, things were to change. How a blissful life may quickly become disappointing, hurtful, and worse. How life would never be the same again. How there would not even be a trace of those happy days except in the memories I would call upon in later life. Memories I am now sharing with you.

Let us go back to those precious days. Unlike most properties of the time, ours was a large two-storey house constructed, as the majority were, from local hand hewn rock. In the bright sun, the red and sienna shades, incorporated within the stone, would sparkle delightfully. We primarily reserved the lower floor for the storage of dry goods, animal feed, wine, oil and such items. The upper comprised our living quarters, including our opulent salon and dining room. My parents had decorated each with exquisite gilt furniture and ornaments they had collected during their travels. Remember, my grandparents and mother had spent much time in Vienna. Father had also travelled extensively, especially to the United States of America. The kitchen, pantry and bathroom facilities were within the domain of a smaller building constructed in the lower garden.

This was normal for homes like ours. We did not want all the 'aromatic' scents of the utility rooms permeating the main house. The smaller building was also where my sisters and I did our homework, that is of course once I started going to school. I will explain in a moment. On cooler evenings there was always a lovely roaring fire. Thanks to my mischievous sister, Anna, I have cause to remember one of those homework evenings. At the time we used nib pens, biros were yet to come. I suspect you are guessing what will follow. Impish Anna got hold of a straw into which she inserted a pen nib. Then, using it as a dart, my sister threw it across the room. It turns out at me. I had been sitting with my back to her but for a reason I do not recall, turned just at that moment. The dart went straight into the bridge of my nose. With so little flesh there, it penetrated right to the bone causing me to cry out in pain, let alone surprise. Anna rushed across to quieten me, fearful my cry might attract mama. You will see her mischievousness often resulted in a gentle reprimand, and she did not want another. She quickly pulled the weapon out and wiped the blood from my nose. We were both quite shocked when realisation dawned that if it had missed my nose it could have blinded me. In later years we often laughed about the incident. Anna, unfairly, still insisted it was my fault for turning my head. I need to make clear, my sister never behaved badly, it was just her mischievous nature. Even in later life she was still the same, but a little wiser about the things she did or said.

All this, for me, was enchanted further by my vast collection of pets. As said, I made pets of most of our household livestock, though as with any multiple relationships there were those with who a greater affection existed. Perhaps that is unfair. It is probably more accurate to say with who a more intimate connection existed. An uncontrived connection that we sometimes experience between souls, assuming animals have souls. I think they must. It was quite the menagerie. Pony, horses, geese, ducks, chickens, cats, dogs, rabbits, pigs and goat. I must tell you about my pet goat. He was such a character and always playful. White with a little beard, he had a remarkable sensitivity. Even before I appeared over the breast of the hill, when returning from school or an outing, he would start jumping about and bleating his friendly, excited greeting. Somehow or other he knew I was on my way. Each time I immediately, even before greeting mama or any other family member, went and hugged his little neck while he nuzzled me with genuine affection. I know it sounds a little childish and I suppose it was, but we really did care for each other. I have to say, I unashamedly remain the same with any animal I become acquainted with.

I should mention here, even though I was too young for school, I missed my sisters so much that I asked to join them in class. Both mama and teacher had been reticent. However, seeing how distraught I was becoming by their absence, eventually agreed on condition I remained quiet and did as I was told. Thankfully, I was an obedient child, so the condition did not prove too arduous for me. It is as well I went because with the changes my life was to encounter, I would receive minimal further education. It still amazes me I can read, write and converse fluently in two very diverse languages. Even my son, who received education within the British system, admits that my spelling is much better than his. He has a bit of a blind spot with spelling the reason for which even he cannot fathom. Just one incident from those short school days that bears mentioning. As said, I was never a naughty child. This is not an attempt to present myself in a preferential light, it is simply the truth. It never occurred to me to be otherwise. That said, there were odd occasions when I thought I had done something wrong. I would then go and stand in a corner facing the wall. When she discovered me, mama would say that if I did ever do something wrong, she would tell me, and I should not just go and stand in a corner of my own volition. In class one day, my best friend and I, we had adjoining desks, decided it would be fun to marry our dolls, which we did under our desks. It was an innocent decision, with neither of us thinking it wrong or disobedient. Unfortunately, the teacher took a different perspective. We received a caning across the palms of both hands. This was a complete shock to my system. No one had ever struck me before. Mama disciplined us, when necessary, through question, answer and explanation. I returned home with open palms held high. Mama consoled me and applied soothing ointment. So far, so good. It was not until mother told papa we had cause to become anxious. He flew into an immediate rage and stormed out. We remained back, terrified of what he was about to do. As already explained when roused, he had a vociferous temper and, quite honestly, was capable of anything when in that state. Would he beat or worse the teacher? I cannot possibly convey how mama and I felt. Thankfully, father had controlled his anger restraining himself to simply, though I doubt it came across as simple to the teacher, informing her 'No one touches my children! If there's any discipling to be done, I'll do it!' We all released our long held breath in relief once we heard. Such an occurrence never arose again, the teacher having subsequently ensured we all understood what was, and was not, acceptable. I think she accepted she had been over zealous and had moved beyond the proper bounds. Also that there had been nothing malicious or intentionally disobedient in our actions.

Earlier, I mentioned Anna's mischievousness and mama's, non violent, discipline. My sister had a sweet tooth and often sneaked to the press, where mama kept the homemade preserves, biscuits, cakes, and sweets. Doing her best not to disturb the trays, my sister would use two finger tips when lifting a delicacy that had taken her fancy. That did not fool mother, who always knew. Along with the rest of us she also knew who was responsible but never pointed an accusing finger. Rather she asks who has been at the press. Because I was the youngest and most timid, Anna always tried to imply it was me. Mama, even though we knew she was not really very cross, tells Anna off, but in gentle tones. She tells her how wrong it is to blame other people for something she has done. And, to all of us, highlights how honesty is the best policy in all circumstances. A lesson we never forgot. All three of us grew up to be responsible citizens.

In addition to our lovely home and lands, we had estates in the upper regions. These had belonged to papa's family. Because of the altitude, harvests there are later than in the valley where our other estates reside. Whenever they occurred we would all help with the various harvests. I remember us making our way up through the forests. While the others walked, I was made to ride our donkey. It annoyed me because I wanted to be just like the adults and also walk, but they considered it too far for me and that I would tire before arriving. We only had a wooden slat saddle for the donkey that, if it had not been for mama's care, by ensuring there was a thick padded cover, would have chaffed me terribly even though I rode sidesaddle. The sunbeams penetrating the high cypress and pine arches would create a son et lumière effect that gave the forests a fairytale world feel. I was still very young and would try to see if I could spot any of the imaginary creatures I heard about in stories, hiding behind trees or under bushes.

Our home in the upper estates had been built on a large, slightly elevated, rock outcrop in the midst of everything. The panoramic views were breathtaking. The surrounding land was dominated by olive groves, vineyards, and a variety of orchards. All enhanced further by the magnificent forests and mountainous backdrop. You may have noticed I am using the past tense. Sadly, the house no longer exists, the only signs of it being small random piles of stone. Many of the orchards have also disappeared. Some of the olive groves are still there but are unkempt. The wonderful estates are now mostly wild grasses and brambles. Even the lovely trees my sisters and I used to enjoy sitting in have gone, cut down by an unscrupulous distant relative to sell for firewood. He was always looking for ways to finance his lazy, drug imbibing, lifestyle. But, I want to return to those original days when it still retained its glory and we all delighted in it.

Papa's grandfather had set out the vineyard in the shape of his initials. A true novelty that, as far as I am aware, has never been repeated. The approach road rises above it at one point which is when a traveller gets the full benefit of the outlay. The grapes were a wonderful rosé colour that comes through in the eventual wine. My sisters and I had great fun when it came to pressing the grapes. This was always done by foot until more recents days. A large, slat bottomed crusher was placed in an elevated position with some sort of bowl beneath. The men then climbed in whilst us smaller ones had to be lifted in. Crushing the grapes was a time of laughter, fun, and anticipation, we would all be enjoying the wine the following year. We did not mind that our legs would remain stained for days. I remember the first impression of standing on the cool, slightly firm but moist mixture. Within short time this was replaced with a squishy, wet compound. The consequence of us all moving our legs up and down, as if we were marching. The resulting liquid would pour through the slats into the bowl and then along a small channel to be collected for siphoning into barrels. These were then sealed and placed in cool storage until the following year. The remaining residue would be boiled and fermented to produce a powerful apéritif. So powerful that it was, and still is, only possible to drink a very tiny amount and that usually accompanied by hors d'oeuvres. This was usually kept for special occasions.

The trees I mentioned, that my sisters and I loved sitting in, were large cherry trees. They were truly magnificent with large upward sweeping branches which acted as seats for us. Sadly, the uncouth distant relative has also cut these down. The cherries were amazing, large and succulent. I have not tasted the like since. Sitting on those branches, we would sing together and became known as the singing nightingales. We had not realised people were listening. This was also the place in which we shared our, all important, little secrets. We were also a little bit naughty in that, hidden from the others by tree leaves, we would read comics. These, along with makeup, were forbidden in our morale, church immersed society. As indeed they were in many other cultures of the time. I had not wanted to participate at first, but when I saw Helen and Anna apparently unperturbed, I, in my young mind, thought it okay to join in. We particularly loved the ones with tales of Zoro. He was our hero and we daydreamed of us being princesses he would rescue. My sisters would sometimes, daringly, replace him with boys they knew. I still enjoy Zoro stories and films. This was also the place where mischievous Anna would lead us further astray. As said, makeup was also a taboo. My sister discovered by stripping away the outer layer of a wild plant root a deep red interior would be revealed. She would then break the end off and apply the remaining stalk to her lips. It was just like the ladies in the Zoro comics. Of course, we made sure to wipe the colour away before returning to the house.

So far I have not told you my first action upon arriving in the upper estates was to run to our large pond and greet our enchanting swans who lived there. I would also look round for the foxes and hawks that then populated the district. Because it was a more remote area there were fewer people. Sadly, the foxes have been hunted to extinction and there remain few hawks. Through the years of my and my son's visits, we have only spotted one most of the time, though a second will occasionally make an appearance. Two after the many we used to see is a depressing sign of the times.

It was just as well crops ripened at different times. We would never have coped otherwise. Grains in the summer, grapes and wine making in early autumn, and olives and oil in the winter. Of course, there were other in-between crops such as various fruits, but the three mentioned were the most time consuming.

December is the normal time for the olive harvest. If the weather is really bad, and I mean really bad, harvesting may be delayed, but that is very unusual. Everyone helps. Before starting we would lay sheets beneath each tree. With our large estates you may imagine how long just that simple task took. Once they were down, the stronger adults would shake the trunks and lower branches to dislodge the ripe, full-blown olives. Others used long sticks to strike the higher branches. Olive trees are hardy so little, if any, damage results from what sounds like brutal treatment. We younger ones, along with the frailer older generation, were responsible for collecting those olives that escaped the sheets and for packing the lot into sacks. Again, as it was with the wine making, this was a joyful time with laughter and lighthearted chatter. It is again a time for celebrating a good harvest. These olives were then ground between two heavy millstones to extract the delicious olive oil. Of course, this is now done by machinery. Besides the large groves of oil producing trees, we had some smaller ones with a few different varieties. These produced eating olives. Preparing eating olives is a slow business. Each olive should have its stem removed and then, for the best taste, have its sides gently sliced. They are then marinated in a carefully prepared liquid, ensuring the correct combination and measurements of ingredients have been put in. Too much, or too little, of one can spoil the eventual taste.

As you see, it was a busy life but one of great happiness and joy. Who could want anything else? Loving family, wonderful pets, stunning scenery, comfortable home, glorious fresh air, safe environment, and a caring society. And, in the middle of it, was my mama quietly holding everything together. How could all this change to the horror that would become my life?

3

Mama

Now we come to the start of events that would change my life forever. Events that would throw me, at the tender age of five, into a cruel, dark world where sadism, licentiousness, self-indulgence, mean spiritedness and even more dark characteristics reigned.

As mentioned, my mother was a very loving, caring person who always sought to help those in difficult circumstances. She never refused a call for help and would venture out at all times, day or night, and in all climates, wind, rain, snow. One late evening, when I was watching the first snow I had ever seen cascading past our window, mama suddenly asked, 'What was that?' My sisters, who were watching with me, and I turned to enquire what she meant. Besides the thuds of heavy snow deposits falling from tree branches, there was also a powerful wind. The sound of it rushing through any crack or crevice it could find had been quite deafening. 'A baby's cry.' We looked at her, dumbfounded. How could she possibly think she had heard a baby, especially in such weather and through the resounding crashes of snow and wind? And we said so. 'No, that was definitely a baby's cry.', was her unhesitating response. Knowing mama never told untruths, we pressed our ears to the window and listened for ourselves but could hear nothing more than the wind and snow. Nevertheless, she was insistent, deciding she would investigate. We were concerned about her going out into the inclement conditions. However, we could not persuade her to abandon the idea or to at least wait for the worse to pass. I have to admit, we started to wonder if she had really heard something because, with her sensitive, caring nature, she often detected things neither we nor anyone else for that matter could. 'Wait here inside. Inside, remember. I will not be long. Make sure the door is properly closed behind me Helen.' As the eldest, Helen was the stronger, which was just as well with the strength of the ferocious wind seeking to blow the door further open after mama had exited.

We watched with bated breath as her retreating figure disappeared from view into the whirling snow. Then there had been nothing. Tense as we were, we heard every stroke of the mantel clock. Time slowed to a snail's pace. Each ticking second resounding as if it would be the last we would hear. Anna and I watched through the main window while Helen stayed by the door, observing through a small side window. We waited and waited. Her delayed return causing us to worry she may have fallen, or worse. A mix of scenarios ran through our childish imaginations. I am unable to convey the relief we felt when we spotted a dark form heading back toward the house. Of course, we could not see clearly and could not really be sure, but something inside told us the dark shawl covered figure was mama. As with any such situation, it could have just been wishful thinking. Thankfully, it was not and our assumption proved correct.

Helen quickly fastened the door while mama headed straight toward the fireside. Sitting in a chair facing the roaring flames, she undid the shawl that had been wound tightly round her head and torso. There, in her arms and much to our surprise and wonder, lay a small bundle. What was it? What had she found? Then a tiny weak cry alerted us to the fact it was a baby! Mama had been right! We could hardly believe our ears or eyes. How had a baby come to be out in this weather? Where had mama found it? Our questions tumbled out like an avalanche of the outside snow. Mother held her hand up to stop us. 'Before I explain we need to get this poor little soul warm, give him some nourishment and find him some clothes. The poor thing is a naked as the moment he was born. Helen, please fetch some milk in a pan. Anna, please get the old baby bottle from the dresser draw. You know the one I mean?' Anna confirmed she did. What should I do? I wanted to help as well. 'You stay with me and help me look after the baby.' I wanted to ask where she had found him and why he had been outside in the snow but knew better. Mama would explain when she thought it right to do so. I knew she always kept her word and never deceived us. If she said she would do something, she always did. So I knew an explanation would eventually be forthcoming.

A factual explanation, however, proved elusive. Mother spent the next few days asking round the village, to no avail. No one laid claim to the baby or provided any idea of where he may have come from. In the end, mama could only surmise he had been an illegitimate birth, a very serious matter in those days, who the mother had abandoned. Alternatively, he may have been one too many for a family already straining to provide for themselves. There were many poor families who struggled to find work and an income, especially in the winter months. It was not unheard of for babies to be abandoned. It is horrible to think, whatever their situation, whoever left him had probably intended, or at least expected, him to die. They had hidden him under a snow-covered bush that had not really provided any shelter. The snow had also covered him. If it had not been for his cries and mama's acute sensitive ear, she would never have found him. The realties of life can often be very cruel.

Naturally, exposure to those extreme elements, naked as he had been, impacted the poor little creature's health. Over the following weeks, mama used all her medical knowledge and skill to care for him. She allowed us to help now and then, when home from school, but insisted we did not fall behind with our homework and education. We had wanted to stay home with her to look after the baby. It was still winter and I think the worst times were at night when he seemed to suffer the most and often cried. Mama spent many a long night sat with him getting little or no sleep herself. She never complained nor became impatient or irritated with us. Mother was indeed a remarkable woman. However, we all grew concerned at how drawn and tired she became. You may wonder where papa was while all this was going on. He was there and though he could be an uncompromising man, he also had a sense of right and fairness and a complete understanding of mama's caring nature. He knew it pointless to ask her to pass the child onto what, in those days, stood in for an orphanage. Awful places at the time.

Eventually, the sitting up during cold winter nights, lack of sleep, worry for the child's health as well as continuing to fulfil all the requirements of running a family home took a toll. Mother fell ill. However, no one informed me of the fact. One day, when I returned home, I cannot remember if I had been at school or visiting a friend, though likely the latter, Helen met me at the door. In itself unusual, she was courting at the time and would normally visit her fiancé's family home at that time of day. She, abruptly, told me to go to my room and pack a bag because I was going to stay at my friend Helen's house (another Helen, of course). I asked why, because we had not made any such arrangement. Something was definitely off. I may have been young, but I was no fool. My sister's belligerent, no argument, aggressive attitude had not helped. Evidently, something was amiss. I would ask mama. I sidestepped my sister and rushed to the kitchen where mother would be well into preparations for the evening meal. An empty room greeted me. Now I knew something was wrong. Where was my mama? I turned and asked Helen who had followed me. All she would tell me was mama was not feeling well, was resting in her room, and we were not to disturb her. I was not having any of that and demanded to see her. Helen's aggressive response was simply to tell me I could not and to hurry and get ready. I continued to demand until she unkindly shouted, 'Get ready!' I am a sensitive soul and have to admit her attitude upset me. Of course, it did not help that I was now certain something was seriously wrong. I knew better than to argue when my sister was in such a mood so, reluctantly obeyed and collected a couple of things into a small bag. I had no intention of staying with my friend for more than one night or perhaps two.

Helen, my friend, and her parents could not have been more welcoming. They were a nice family who I usually enjoyed staying with, but not this time. I wanted my mama and determined, somehow or other, I would get to see her. The formal greetings over, my hosts suggested their daughter and I play while they talked to my sister. I wanted to listen, but they waited until Helen and I had gone upstairs.

My friend's parents could not have been more hospitable or caring. Nevertheless, they constantly sidestepped my questions about mama and what they knew. Undoubtedly they, because of my young age, I was barely five, considered it would not be suitable to tell me what was going on. Of course, this did not fool me. I knew something was wrong and that it had to do with mama. Rather than helping this avoidance just made me more anxious, to the point, on the second night of my forced stay, I decided to do something about it. I waited until I was sure Helen was asleep, we shared her bedroom, before putting my plan into action. I slipped my day dress on and, barefooted, headed out of the room and down toward the rear of the house. Negotiating the stairs was a bit of a heart-in-mouth moment as I was aware one of them creaked. Gratefully, I made it to the back door without disturbing the sleeping occupants. Once in the courtyard, I headed to the stable where their grey mare resided. I had been concerned she may make a fuss but we had got to know each other over time and all she did was nuzzle my shoulder and greet me with a gentle whinny. I led her out and jumped on to her bare back. Then, holding onto her mane, directed her head toward my home. Unfortunately, we disturbed the cockerel who immediately crowed at the top of his piercing voice. Undoubtedly, that would disturb the people within. I pressed my heals into her flanks to indicate she should gallop as fast as she could. Thankfully, there was a full moon helping us not to fall victim to the numerous potholes and small rocks with which the rough track was strewn.

Though the distance between our homes was short, the trip felt interminable. Finally, we came into sight of my beloved home. To my surprise, considering the late hour, there was an unusual amount of activity, not to mention every room seemed to be lighten up. I also noticed soft lighting under the veranda that circumvented the entire building. Groups of darkly clad figures stood or sat beneath in apparent subdue conversation. This was definitely odd.

My intent had been to head immediately for mama's room. However, after my sister's attitude, I was afraid people would not let me in. I had to stop and think.

I alighted while some distance from the house and crouched so as not to allow the bright moonlight to silhouette me against the midnight blue backdrop. I whispered to the mare to go home. She understood and obediently trotted away with minimal sound. Most horses have a wonderful instinct for their homes. It still surprises me a little to think I had such presence of mind at such a time and at such an age. Mama really had taught me well. How was I going to get in undetected? Now certain those standing about would try to prevent me from doing so. Perhaps I was being paranoid, but something told me otherwise.

Slowly, as I imagine a marine commando would, I moved from bush to bush, tree to tree, grass clump to grass clump, ensuring all the time I remained small and in shadow. Thankfully, at that age, my knees were strong and supple. I would hate to try it now. As I got closer, though I could not discern the actual words, I could hear the varied subdued, sad toned conversations. A lightning rod pierced my being. I had been right, something was wrong. Now sure it had to do with mama. Breath caught in my throat as I tried to bring the resulting trembling under control. I knew I had to be strong if I was going to get through the throng of people. Glancing up, I gratefully noted the moon had moved to the further side of the building, providing lengthening deeper shadows on my side. Using any shelter available, I stealthily drew closer. Eventually, I found myself opposite the base of one staircase. As mentioned, with all larger homes of the time, residential rooms were on the upper level. The lower ones being reserved for storage of dry crops such as corn, barley and wheat, as well as wine, oil, animal feed and other such necessities for a rural life.

Now what? Should I just make a run for it? Perhaps not the best idea. Taking further advantage of the dark and hoping people would be so engrossed in their conversations they would not notice, I took what remaining courage I had in my hands and made a quick dash across the open ground laying between me and my goal. I made it. I rested against the darkened wall for a moment to catch my breath. Cautiously, I put my head round the corner and, much to my gratification, found the staircase devoid of people. Thank you Lord. Again crouching to keep my body small, I quickly ascended, stopping behind one of the thicker supporting balustrades at the top. My vantage point afforded me a clear view of mama's bedroom door. However, to my anguish, people crowded round it. How was I going to get through? The atmosphere had been eerie, not exactly silent, neither still. Subdued conversation emitting from the small gathered groups, mostly in twos or threes, reached my ears. There could be no doubting, something was amiss and, whatever it was, it involved mama.

Taking a couple more minutes to consider if there was any alternative route, of which I quickly concluded there was not, I made my decision. I would have to make a run for it. Drawing in a further deep breath, I gathered my wits and made my dash. My presence to this point undetected, the sudden appearance of my little body surprised all. It appeared to momentarily freeze them to the spot. Or at least that is how it seemed. Whatever it was, it provided enough time for me to run between and underneath their legs. Remember, I am still barely five and therefore of small stature. Making it through the open door, I made a beeline for mama's bed where I had speedily ascertained she lay. I sensed hands reaching out to grab, but thankfully, as a fairly agile athlete, had been too fast. Diving to the floor, I wormed my way beneath the mosquito net and clambered onto the bed. Gasps of surprise filled the air as mama and I embraced. Though in a weakened state, the sudden activity and no doubt weight of my landing on the bedclothes had made her aware. 'Darling, you have come at last.' A soft, barely audible voice that had made my heart sick. Further gasps from round the room penetrated through the net. 'Oh.' 'Look.' 'Ah.' One whispered, 'She must have been waiting for her.' Recalling this still brings tears.

A quick aside to give you some further insight into my mother's character. Mama's belief in God was strong and sincere. A belief I share. When first confined to bed she noted a button had come off from the top of her nightdress. Asking for thread and needle mama had insisted upon sewing it back on herself, stating 'I cannot go to my maker like this.'. Propriety without hypocrisy was an important principle to her and one she bred into us.

4

BEREFT

This is a difficult chapter for me to write. Nevertheless, it is an essential one because the consequences of the following events changed my life forever.

As best as she could, mama tightened her embrace, telling me 'I love you very much. Now you must be a good girl and remember all the things I have taught you.' Her voice growing softer and weaker all the time. 'God be with you my darling. I love you very much.' With that, a last deep gurgling breath escaped. The hand that had been caressing me went limp and fell away. 'No! Please don't go! Please don't go! I love you mama. I will be ill for you. You stay and I'll be ill. Please don't go!' I may have been young and may well have not fully perceived yet somehow, somewhere within, I understood mama was no longer with us though, of course, I had not really comprehended where she had gone. I remember feeling as if floating in an ethereal mist. 'Mama! Mama! Speak to me! Talk to me!' My soul was in shreds. Again I heard someone whisper, 'She must've been waiting for her.' Another responded, 'Yes, she's been hanging onto life by a thread these last days. Did you see how she let go once she saw her?' 'Yes, may God bless her. She was such a lovely woman.' Though conscious of their voices and words, my anguished thoughts were otherwise engaged. Inwardly, I asked God to bring her back. Asked her to hug me again. Asked to feel her arms round me. But, of course, there had been no response. My anguish deepened to the point of feeling as if a volcano was erupting within me. 'Mama! Mama! Mamaaa!'

I had been so distracted, my attention being fully and solely on mama, I failed to notice my sister drawing the mosquito net aside until she tried to pull me off the bed. 'No! I am NOT leaving mama!' Despite my obvious need and pain, she continued to pull, but I was not having it. I clung tighter to mama's still form. Silently I spoke to her. I will not leave you. I will stay with you. My sister persevered, eventually loosening my grip on my beloved mama. I grasped the bedding. She carried on pulling. 'No! No! Let go of me!' But in the end she had been too strong. My heart broken, I sobbed and sobbed. Tormented darkness oppressed my soul. This became the first time I experienced fear, genuine fear. There had been things I had not liked, such as snakes and scorpions, but mama had explained they were simply another form of life that did not deserve to be harmed. As a result, I never feared them. But the anguish and emptiness I now felt was new. It was terrible, it was painful, it scared me.

It is hard to explain my subsequent emotions. Perhaps, if someone had bothered with me, bothered to explain a bit more, bothered to put a loving arm round me, bothered to allow me to cry with them, bothered to let me say what I felt, and so on, I may not have felt so barren, destitute and alone. But they did not. More often than not, they pushed me aside and harshly accused me of supposedly getting in the way. I should mention mama had previously warned, should she not be around, to be careful of my eldest sister because she could be impatient and, if annoyed, might lash out. Glad to say she never did with me, though she could be unkind in words and actions. I like to think this had more to do with her being engrossed in her ongoing courtship and consequently resenting an underage sibling's presence than any actual malicious tendency toward me. Neither of us knew at the time we would soon to be parted and many years were to pass before we would see each other again. I am grateful to tell you, when we did re-establish contact, in later life, we were on very good terms.

Anna, my middle sister, the brightest and most intellectual one, had naturally been recalled from university in the metropolis. These were the days when few universities existed and those that did were mostly based in capital cities. I was so glad to see her and rushed into her arms. She was far more accommodating. Almost as distressed as I, she wept along with me. We just could not fathom the idea of life without mother. I asked her if she knew where mama had gone. I still did not really understand. She explained, when people like mama die, they go to heaven, that it was a nice place, and therefore that must be where our precious mama is. In my innocence, I asked if we could go there and be with her. 'Only when we also die.' This engaged my mind. I looked at Anna and in the pursuing silence knew she understood my thoughts. It was almost telepathic the way we took each other's hand and moved to the further side of the veranda. Being consistently pushed out of the way, I had taken refuge up there, in a remote corner. In retrospect, I am surprised Anna went along with me. She was older and more stable in herself and under normal circumstances not expected to be subject to the same emotions as I. Once at the back and out of sight, or so we thought, we looked over the railing assessing whether it would be high enough. Silently, we must have concluded it was because, without hesitation, both of us stepped forward. We were about to launch ourselves when I felt a firm grip round my waist, pulling me back. 'What do you two think you are doing?' It was papa's voice. Instinctively I shouted for him to let go and that I wanted to go to mama. It turned out he had been observing Anna and I whispering, and realising something was afoot had followed us. I confess, though I loved papa, my annoyance with him and the fact he did not appear to understand was extreme. However, turned out I was wrong. Embracing both of us, he assured us he understood our distress and that he also missed mama. A point confirmed by the deep, powerful sobs we could sense vibrating within him. What would he do if we also left him? This must have brought us back to our senses. Up to then I, and I suspect Anna, had felt as if we were on our own, that no one cared and besides wishing to be with mama, we would be better off by leaving. Father's declaration now helped us appreciate we were not alone and that at least he needed us.

Our house was a hive of activity the following morning. Tradition and practical considerations, my homeland is hot for most of the year, mean we usually conduct funerals on the day after death or at most the second day. Though I still think I did not really fully comprehend, I had wanted to be involved in the preparations. Mother had always allowed me to help when an event was due, whether it be a party, a church feast, or a day of national celebration. Regrettably, yet again, people pushed me away and told me to get from under their feet. Not a kind word from anyone. I ended up sitting alone, brokenhearted, in a dark corner with only my troubled, anguished thoughts for company. Anna could not come to my aid. Presumably because of her being that much older, they had roped her into helping. Later, without ceremony or a by-your-leave, I was dragged off and, from head to toe, dressed in black, even down to long black socks. Goodness knows what I must have looked like. Remember, I was not quite five years old. I appreciate others also had to deal with their own grief, but would it have been so hard to have given me a considerate word or to enquire how I was? But it was not to be.

The funeral was awful, well it was for me. I am not sure how the others saw it. A sad occasion obviously, but whether they felt more deeply, I shall never know. When it was time, Helen clamped a vice like grip upon my wrist and led, or rather dragged, me through the house. I suspect, besides the fact she was the eldest and therefore the chief mourner, she had decided not to tolerate any more of my 'nonsense'. She also probably did not consider she could trust anyone else to control me. I have to say it felt very brutal, though in retrospect I am, to a degree, able to understand her motivation. The first thing I saw when exiting the house was the hearse. An immediate surge of bile travelled from my stomach into my throat. I had the good sense to control it because I knew any such display would bring further admonishment. It still amazes me how one so young can be so apprehending of others' attitudes. Helen's appearance through the front door was the cue for the procession to commence. As you may imagine, my emotions were in turmoil. I understood this was to do with mama but do not think I still truly comprehended. There was no releasing of the grip on my wrist as I dutifully walked alongside my sister following the slow-moving vehicle. Despite the confusion within and consequent blurring of my vision, I still noted that most, if not all, of the village had turned out. As previously mentioned, mama had been a very caring, loving, compassionate, understanding, unbiased person. Many then, and subsequently, acknowledged without her ministrations and teaching they would probably not have survived nor gone on to live the quality lives they had.

The strain upon me grew moment by moment until I really was not there. Penetrating through the nauseous bewilderment and confused mass, a kaleidoscope of clashing blurred images paraded. Images of mama laughing, us together making spring flower wreaths, playing games, chickens running for the feed in her hand, mosquito net, combing her floor length auburn hair, brilliant loving eyes, crosses, black armbands, black dresses, marble headstones, angels, more flowers, tears, and so on. Somehow, I kept putting one foot in front of the other. Probably more to do with Helen firmly pulling me along than anything else. My state became so bad that I do not even remember entering the church, or the service. When I came round, I found we were in the cemetery. Before my eyes, in utter horror and disbelief, I saw men about to lower the awful box supposedly holding my mama within, into the ground. 'No!' I ripped my hand free and threw myself across the coffin, crying out, 'Mama! Mama!' I could not be seeing what I was. After a few moments, when I suspect my unexpected action had frozen people, several moved forward and tried to lift me away. But I was having none of it. I wanted to be with mama. Not prepared to let her go, I firmly griped the carved edge of the lid and clung on for dear life. I would not leave my mama to go into that hole. Inwardly, I cried for her to stay and I would go for her. Did I understand what I was saying? Not really. Initially without success, a few tried to prise my fingers away. It was not until one of the more robust men took charge did they, or rather he, achieve their goal. I screamed and screamed. I have tried to find further words to describe my feelings, emotions, thoughts and torn heart. I have failed and must therefore submit to your imagination or perhaps personal experience to discern.

My distress did not subsequently decrease. I was utterly distraught, unable to eat or sleep or to cease crying. Though it felt as if a great dark vacuum had replaced my heart and soul, there had also been an extreme, excruciating pain. The combination had been utterly destroying. It was as if I had floated off to a different universe.

Despite my love for them, I neglected my many wonderful pets. All I wanted was mama. It got so bad I started searching everywhere. In every room, behind doors, under beds, in cupboards, in all the outbuildings, behind bushes and trees, in the fields and orchards, anywhere and everywhere. My mind and heart had been telling me mama was somewhere in the house or out on the estate and I would find her any moment. I realise some of this may sound bizarre, but it is the truth and exemplifies the awful condition I was in. I think I may safely say the balance of my mind had been in real danger. Something with which the medical profession would ultimately agree.

I became weaker and weaker by the day, rapidly losing weight to the point my clothes hung on, or rather off, me as if I were a thin wire hanger. My eyes sunk into their sockets and my cheek bones became so pronounced it appeared they would break through my flesh like some horrible creature from Alien. No distraction invented nor any chore allocated turned my thoughts away from mama and where she was. Nor did either help in getting me to eat or sleep. Naturally, papa, my sisters, extended family and friends became concerned. Nothing they tried helped. They finally summoned the family doctor. His conclusion had been I would be unlikely to recover while I remained in our home where there were so many reminders of mama. If I stayed, he thought it likely I would suffer a severe mental breakdown that could easily lead to insanity or even death. He apparently reckoned the latter two more than probable if they did not move me away, straight away. A change of environment was what I needed if there was to be any hope. Though effectively living in an ethereal, unreal world, I had been dimly aware of the doctor's presence. Voices and words penetrated through the fog, though I had absolutely no comprehension of what was really going on or that it was all about me. It would be sometime later, when papa explained, I would know.

What followed the doctor's visit upset and angered me, as much as a child of my age can be angered. Papa had taken me to one side and, having accepted nothing else was likely to work, told me of his decision to follow the doctor's advice. He would take me away to stay in the small convent above our village. I objected loudly at the prospect of being taken from where my mama should be. However, papa would not concede. He simply said it would be good for me and would help me recover my health. What did I care about my health! It was mama I wanted! My protestations went unheeded, though I now understand the situation must have also been painful for him. Still young and therefore of small stature, I was unable to fight him as he physically picked me up and carried me away. With each step it had felt as if even more of my soul was being ripped out, piece by piece. The jagged ends of what was left hurt terribly. I continued to protest as tears cascaded down my cheeks, distinctly moistening the dry dirt track behind us. Normally, I enjoyed the panoramic views afforded through gaps in the dense forest, but on this occasion had been too upset and distracted by thoughts of leaving mama to even notice.

They had built the convent on a plateaued outcrop that breaks through the dense forest foliage. It commands views over village rooftops into a fertile valley beyond. The multicoloured fields, guarded by occasional sentinel walnut, fig, plane and cypress trees, combined with the refreshing blue of a reservoir and backdrop of purple hued mountains remain a beautiful sight. One I continue to enjoy to this day, though at the time it had little impact upon me. The mother superior, who had originally built the church and then overseen its extension into a convent had greeted us. I would, in time, become fond of her, but at that moment, she was just another 'enemy' who wanted to take me away from my mama. Though my reluctance and antagonism had been evident, she could not have been kinder. Crouching to be on eye level, papa having returned me to the ground to stand upon my own two feet, she quietly welcomed me. I had been in no mood for friendliness and ignored her. It hurts to think I could have been so rude to someone who was simply trying to be considerate and kind. She had then summoned a sister requesting she take me to my room. It was actually one of the nuns basic cells. They had clearly been forewarned because, unlike their own rooms, they had decorated this one with bunches of beautiful flowers. Not that I really noticed. I just wanted to go back to where mama would, should, be. Papa had then come to see and attempted to cheer me with observations of how nice the place looked. My only response had been that I did not want to stay! He replied, a little sharply, my behaviour clearly frustrating him, I would be staying! He then announced it was time for him to go. I had clung tightly to him, trying to prevent him from departing without me. It had felt as if I was also losing him, though I was not sure he fully understood. He gently prised my arms away while assuring he would be back to see me soon. He then left me to the loneliness and quiet of the cell, my prison cell as it felt. My heart and soul broke further. Weeping I threw myself upon the bed. I wanted mama. I wanted papa, who it now felt had deserted me. Why? Why would he leave me here? Why did he not love me anymore? My tears continued for many a day. My despondency a lot longer.

The nuns could not have been kinder. But I simply did not want to be there. All I wanted was mama and to be where she should be. I know I keep repeating myself, but it had constantly been the overriding, ruling factor to my existence. Nothing else truly mattered. It seemed papa had informed mother superior of my affinity with nature and love of all things living. After having left me to cry a little, the sisters attempted to get me to join them in the garden and in caring for their livestock. However, I had no heart for either and asked they leave me alone. I fear I was a little abrupt at times. But they were not about to acquiesce and continued to encourage me to join them every day. Mother taught us to have respect for everyone and it came to the point where I realised I was bordering upon being rude to these kind, well meaning, people. I could not do that. Mama would have not liked it. Consequently, I eventually submitted and went along with them. Each nun had their allocated responsibilities. Some in the garden where they grew a variety of glorious flowers, herbs and vegetables. Others with the livestock of chickens for eggs and goats for milk. Each would invite me to help. In normal circumstances such activities would have delighted and given me great pleasure, but not now. No matter what distraction they invented, my thoughts remained upon mama. Nevertheless, it was hard to ignore the delightful creatures who had a tendency to snuggle up. I have always thought animals sensitive and suspect these detected my sorrow. I subconsciously fell into the habit of helping the sisters. Despite this, I do not think I ever truly connected with reality. I felt despondent, abandoned, rootless, bewildered, forlorn, and unloved. Why else would papa have left me here? I still did not really eat or sleep. The fundamental state of my mind never changed.

Mother superior had obviously been keeping an eye on me. She, appreciating I had not been getting any better, and in fact, was deteriorating, summoned papa. In her opinion, the convent was in too close a proximity to our home for me to forget or come to terms with what had happened. Unless moved further away, my pinning would get worse with consequent results. She had been upset my stay with them had not helped as she had originally hoped, but it was clear the trauma I had suffered was deep and severe. In the end all concluded, that is papa, mother superior, the rest of the family, and the doctor who they had consulted again, I needed to be removed from the area completely. Of course, I knew none of this at the time. I do however, remember the sorrow and disappointment in mother superior's eyes when we made our last farewells.

Before I continue, I feel it incumbent upon me to confess. While at the convent I became attached to a small icon of the Virgin Mary.

It gave me comfort and I never wanted to be parted from it. I think it reminded me of mama. So accustomed to having it with me while there, I failed to realise it was still in my pocket when I left. It has bothered me for years because, although done unconsciously, I feel as if I have stolen it. I wanted to confess and ask forgiveness, but when I finally returned, the convent had closed, mother superior had died, and the sisters had dispersed elsewhere. Knowing how attached I had been to it, they probably realised, but being neither materialistic nor possessive, I doubt minded. Regrettably, I no longer have the icon. It was among items stolen from me in later years. I have confessed in prayer and asked forgiveness that I believe I have received. I have subsequently had opportunity to gift an icon that also depicts the Virgin Mary to the still existing convent church.

Papa left me at the convent while he made arrangements. I got excited when he finally came for me, anticipating my return home. You may therefore comprehend my disappointment, or rather infuriation, when we sailed past our home and estates. In response to my demand to know why, papa simply told me we were going to stay with my sister in the metropolis. That is Anna, who had returned to her university studies. And that it was to help me get better. I am unable to find words to describe the clashing emotions that assailed me. I could not believe he was being so cruel, that I would not be going to our home, and I would not be going to see mama. My heart and soul were being torn apart all over again.

Once I regained some composure, in part, I questioned papa about the wisdom of going to stay with Anna. She had been away from home for a while and had developed her own life in the city. Would she really be pleased to have a young, immature sibling staying? Papa did his best to reassure me, stating he was sure Anna was looking forward to seeing me. I had not been so sure. He added he would also be staying. That helped a little because at least I would not be completely on my own, though his recent desertion of me at the convent remained a concern. Would he leave me again?

I had never left our home territory before. The furthest I had ever travelled was to the next village, where we had relatives, and to our estates in the mountains, a forty-minute donkey ride. Other family members had been to the district market town that also acted as the municipal centre. Even today it takes approximately half an hour by car. In those days, it was either on horseback or by pony and trap, so you may appreciate it was not a journey undertaken lightly. Of course, papa had journeyed further as mama had also when attending the academy in Vienna. Other than that, we, along with most others in the village, lead a very parochial life. Under normal circumstances, I would undoubtedly have been intrigued and excited at the prospect of seeing other places, but my spirit and soul were in no condition to appreciate the impending trip. Dark clouds of despair and sorrow continued to blur my mind and keep me introspective with thoughts of mama.

We had gone directly to the railway station situated in the valley basin where my sister Helen was waiting to see us off with a packed lunch. She also had some fresh produce and wine for us to give to Anna. It still brings tears to my eyes to recall how, except for this one occasion, Helen had virtually abandoned me. She never came to see me at the convent, nor subsequently. It would be decades before I saw her again. The train's arrival had startled me with its huffing, puffing, hissing, steam, and smoke. It reminded me of those dragons often encountered in children's stories. When it came time to board, papa had to reassure me it was safe. I had never been on a train and had been rather apprehensive. There was also the distress of knowing this iron beast was about to take me away from mama. Would I ever be able to forgive papa or Helen? In time, perhaps. Despite my disconsolate state, the scenery we journeyed through gained my attention. Though much had been like our own, we occasionally went through parochial towns where, to me, the buildings were immense. The church in our village had been the largest edifice I had ever encountered in my young life. Colossal as it should be for a place representing God. But I was now confronted by constructions which would dwarf it as well as by broad crowded streets the like of which I had never seen before. I wondered how all those people and vehicles avoided bumping into each other. A mix of items, cans of oil, boxes and baskets of fruit, vegetables and eggs, paper packages containing freshly butchered meat, cheeses and whatever cluttered our carriage. There were even live chickens thrust up by their feet. All were gifts passengers were taking to their relatives in the city. Our fellow travellers had been friendly and, our society being a fairly relaxed one, had automatically conversed. Friendships often commenced this way. I had been too shy and too disconsolate to participate, but papa had held up his side.

Seven or eight hours later we finally entered what I now know to be the metropolis suburbs. I have to confess my fear at the sight of those immense tall buildings crowded close to the track. After the open countryside I was accustomed to, it felt claustrophobic, airless, and suffocating. Papa had obviously registered because he held me close. In response to my enquiries about how the buildings did not fall down, he assured me it was all quite normal and safe. He explained, because there was insufficient land in the city for everyone to have their own house, they had built these apartment blocks. It sounded terrible. I had sincerely hoped Anna did not live in one. Matters did not improve for me when we alighted. The platform had been jam-packed with people, cases, and packages. No one appeared to be concerned about anyone else as they selfishly pushed and shoved their way through. Remember, I was still barely five and consequently found myself in a forest of legs. Papa told me to keep a firm hold of his hand. He could not pick me up because of the packages we had brought for Anna and the small suitcase containing our personal items. His iron grip had been painful however, I dreaded losing him in the crowed and therefore put up with it. We eventually beat our way through to the main station concourse. Someone called papa's name in response to which he had beaten a path through the crowds toward a tall, elegant man. I vaguely remembered his face, but could not place who he was. He turned out to be one of father's brothers. After greeting us both and embracing papa, he took some packages and led the way out to where his car sat waiting. I was only used to horses, ponies and the carts and carriages they pulled, which made this car an anomaly. How could it move if there were no horses? Again papa reassured me it was safe and did his best to explain how the vehicle worked, not that I really understood.

The reverberations from the car engine combined with the crowded streets and immense buildings we drove past continued to unsettle me. I really dreaded the thought of having to live in one of those 'apartments'. However, as we journeyed further the streets became less crowded and the surrounding scenery opened up. I felt I could breathe again and had been delighted to see trees, bushes and plants reemerge into the view. Though my heart and soul still ached, the intrigue of now seeing new vistas numbed the pain a little, at least for a while. After all the noise and claustrophobia of the city, you may imagine my delight when we pulled up outside a pleasant two-storey house set in its own grounds. I immediately knew this was the place we were going to stay. Anna, looking radiant with her beautiful auburn hair falling in a natural curl upon her shoulders and dark mischievous eyes glinting, stood on the threshold. My nervous apprehension returned but soon dispelled when she embraced and kissed each of us. She seemed genuinely glad to see us both. Anna had then led us to the drawing room where she had refreshments ready. While we enjoyed these, she quizzed papa about relatives and friends, who was seeing who, how the harvests were doing, and so on. Papa did his best to answer but could not really satisfy Anna's curiosity. Other than the estates, business and politics, he had no interest in gossip or courtships.

Refreshments completed, my sister took me round the house and gardens. After seeing the limited space available to people in the city, the latter had impressed me. Not only was there an abundance of beautiful flowers and shrubs, but Anna had also made good use of the available space by planting a wide range of vegetables for our own consumption. The sight caused me to think that perhaps this would not be too bad a place after all, though given the choice, I would have immediately returned to our home in the village.

My sister had also been very thoughtful with my room. Everything I would need or could wish for had been supplied. A nice dressing table with mirror, an ample wardrobe, a comfortable divan bed, and best of all, a fully stocked bookcase. She knew how much I enjoyed reading. After our tour, I returned to papa in the drawing room while my sister went to see to dinner. Upon him asking, I confirmed I liked the house and having seen how Anna did not seem to mind my being there, thought it would be all right for a while. 'For a while' had been the determining factor in my mind, though I do not think papa picked up on it.

After dinner, all the events of the day and the lengthy journey caught up with me and I excused myself. No doubt you will appreciate how, by this time, I had felt emotionally, mentally and physically exhausted. So much had happened in such a short time. That morning I had been at the convent. Had then passed our home and through the village. Had subsequently journeyed through unfamiliar territories, and finally found myself in this strange city. I had struggled to draw the two ends of the day together, but had just ended up in a fog of uncertainty and anxiety. Yet again, a kaleidoscope of clashing images invaded my mind and soul. On top of my disconsolation and missing mama, I worried about what would happen to me now, what I was going to do in this place, and how long I would be staying. I had always been active and the thought of sitting idle for long spells of each day was anathema. Of course I could help round the house and in the garden, but that would not take all day. The future seemed unfathomable. All these worries prevented me from sleeping. When I would be able to return to mama and what I was going to do had been primary concerns. Unknown to me then, papa was to unexpectedly provide a solution to the latter.

5

Lust

Thankfully, papa had grown into a wise and sensible man, the irresponsibility and pleasure seeking of his youth having long passed. He obviously understood, despite my youth, it necessary to do what he could to secure my future. In those days, general acceptance had been a girl's fate would be determined by who she married. The husband would be responsible for her welfare thereafter. Papa was not so naïve as to take such an outcome for granted. He could see political and social conditions would likely change in the not so distant future. Therefore, nothing could be guaranteed. He wanted to ensure I could support myself, come what may. He must have had prophetic insight because, as you will come to see, my life ultimately necessitated me supporting two. But that is for later in my tale. Now back to where we were.

Though, as said, expectation was a girl would marry and consequently not require a trade, papa, not one to be daunted by convention, thought it wise I learn something new. When he asked what I would like to do, my immediate response had been tailoring.

How mama and other ladies in the village transformed a mix of fabrics into beautiful dresses, suits and coats had always fascinated me. Men's suits, which required so much more detailed shaping and accuracy, had especially intrigued me. Papa thought it a wise choice because even in times of austerity people still needed clothes. A couple of days later, he informed me of his success in securing an apprenticeship with a small family-owned tailors. It turned out not to be an actual apprenticeship in the traditional sense because he paid them to teach me the skills rather than them paying me a minimal wage. I did not really understand the difference then.

Regrettably, the family was to prove uncouth, hostile, brutal and mean, and by no means honest. From the very first morning they treated me as a servant, no that does not convey the true nature of it, I was more their workhorse and slave. It would be called domestic slavery now. They constantly made me clean up the terrible mess always left in the kitchen, sweep the yard, and worst of all, clean the toilet. On one occasion this had been full to the brim with excrement, the sight and smell of which almost brought me to the point of vomiting. Naturally, I objected. However, their aggressive and violent response left me with no choice. I had to plunge my arm in, right up to the shoulder, to unblock it. Mama consistently taught us to be hygienic, explaining how it helped prevent many a disease and would keep us healthy. You may therefore imagine how this incident left me feeling. But there was never any letup. Each day I asked to be taught about tailoring and each day they simply bullied me into being their lackey. You need to remember I was still very young and of small stature and consequently had not the wherewithal to resist. You may wonder why I did not tell papa. I was terrified of what he might do. As I mentioned earlier, he was a very just man and hated all aspects of injustice. Whenever he encountered such, his anger was fearful. I had seen it when the teacher had, mistakenly in my opinion, thought a school friend and I had been misbehaving and had caned us both. I had thought papa was going to kill her. How much more would his temper be aroused by my current treatment? In the end, I found my own solution. Each morning I left the house as usual, but instead of going to the tailors would spend my day in local parks and then return home at the expected time. Papa and Anna must have eventually realised something was amiss. I never brought examples of, nor demonstrated, what I was supposedly learning. I overheard papa telling my sister he thought it likely because of either my youth or inability I was not mastering the skills. That had stung. I knew I was more than capable of learning. However, I had no wish to be responsible for any hostilities or injuries, no matter how well deserved. Eventually Anna told me, realising I was not getting on at the tailors, she and father had decided I would no longer need to go. How the relief I felt did not overflow is a mystery. Possibly because it would have betrayed the truth not to control it.

So there I was again, back at my sister's with little to do other than help round the house and garden, all of which hardly filled the hours. The rest of the time I spent lost in my morose thoughts or in reading. All I wanted was to return to my home and mama. Anna had always been astute and, understanding my condition, allowed a short period for me to adjust to this new life. However, she had not been prepared for me to remain in my negativity indefinitely. She started inviting neighbours and friends in the hope of them creating new areas of interest to draw me away from my sad thoughts. But, of course, I had not been interested. I did not like being among strangers or having to adopt a polite facade that, in my case, primarily comprised remaining silent. I had no desire to get to know these people. All I wanted was to be left alone. I appreciate this may sound selfish and perhaps even silly. My heart was broken, my spirit crushed and my previous joy of and in life was gone. I was never out-and-out rude. That would have been unacceptable. However, I made no effort to engage, only speaking when a directly aimed question required a response. Then it would usually just be a yes or no. Despite my obvious disinterest, Anna and papa persevered. Neither the type to give in.

One day a family my sister and papa were particularly friendly with suggested we join them on a municipal picnic. These were the days when neighbourhoods were, just as they had been in England, communities in which everyone knew and helped each other. Municipal and community events had been a regular part of life. However, several obstacles to me joining them arose. Papa was due to attend to some business on the scheduled day and my sister would have to attend university lectures. Without another relative present, there would be no one to chaperone me. In those days expectation was for single women, especially younger ones from families like ours, to be chaperoned when out. I confess I had been glad, not really wanting to go. I was to be disappointed. The adults discussed the issue for a while until papa concluded, having known these people for sometime and consequently trusting them, it would be acceptable for the matriarch of the family to take on the role of chaperone. I leave it to you to imagine how annoyed I had been. Alone with my thoughts and memories of mama was all I wanted. I hope by now you appreciate the devastating impact her passing had on me. An impact that has continued throughout life.

On the day, the family arrived as appointed and took me off. Though I would not have acknowledged it, I will admit to you an inquisitiveness had started to arise. Except for when we had initially arrived and my short walks to the tailors and subsequently the parks, I had not ventured far from the house. The last thing I expected to see were fresh open spaces with large evergreens and robust clumpy bushes, but that is exactly what I now saw. In time, I would know there are many such areas in our metropolis. Several are in raised positions, granting panoramic views across the city. It really is beautiful, with blue sea bounding one side and mountainous backdrops enclosing it elsewhere.

The picnic spread had been very impressive. Following tradition of the time, all attending families had brought their own specialities. I cannot convey in words all the varied aromas and tastes except to say they were marvellous. It seemed, for a while at least, all the negatives in my recent life had been an illusion. If only they had been. While enjoying this repast, a son of one family offered me a small glass of something. I hesitated. He assured me it was something his relatives made and he drank himself. That led me to accept. I should mention it was common in those days for families to make their own wines and spirits, or at least those who still lived in rural locations. The straw covered bottles and containers I had seen on the train would have contained some of these. I took a sip. The next twenty plus minutes remain a blur. Apparently, I started running round like some headless chicken. Remember, I was still young and consequently not yet exposed to concentrated spirits. The drink turned out to be one of the stronger ones families made, it would be better to say distilled, from grape pressing residue. Naturally, the adults became concerned, especially when I would not heed their calls to stop and tell them what was wrong. Though our society of the time had been a relatively safe one, women could go out at night without a second thought, they were concerned because of the surrounding trees and bushes, behind which anyone could have hidden. Sexual abuse was not something we heard of, but it would be naïve to think it did not exist.

Eventually, one woman caught me and, holding me firmly, asked what was wrong. It took a moment for my brain to slow its dizzy circling and for me to focus. I felt sick and told her so. Fearing something untoward had occurred, the senior members present summoned the police. They decided to exam me for signs of any possible 'interference', taking my companions and me to the local police station to do so. Unbeknown to me then, the men present had taken hold of the boy who had given me the drink. They were determined, if there were any signs of interference and it turned out to have been by him, we would be married there and then. At gun point if necessary. Virginity was crucial for a girl. To have lost it, by whatever means, prior to marriage, meant society would consider her a 'ruined' woman, with all the subsequent consequences. Not only would this be a stigma on her but also on the family name. Something it was almost impossible to recover from. No respectable man, or parent, would consider such a woman for marriage. I appreciate this may seem odd in these days when such considerations have been effectively thrown out of the window, but then it was vital. It was a terrible ordeal having a stranger look under my skirt. I still get shivers at the remembrance. No one but mama had ever seen me unclothed. To everyone's relief, they found me to be perfectly 'intact'. After it was all over, the boy had bashfully apologised. He had only wanted to be friendly and meant no harm. Unfortunately, his parents had not seen it as so harmless and had severely scolded him. They were a wealthy, well educated, family and I think expected better from their son, though what they meant by 'better' I have little idea.

Having accepted my tailoring apprenticeship a failure, papa again became concerned about my future. It was also a worry that I had received little education. You may remember this had only been for a short period when accompanying my sisters to school. Of course, that ended with mama's passing and my subsequent sojourn in the convent. I need to mention the educating of girls was not considered an essential then. As previously said, most families expected daughters to be provided for by their husbands. This may seem an archaic notion now. Then it was a prevalent expectation throughout civilised society. However, papa was not willing to leave my future to such a chance. I am sure he realised changes were on the horizon. He had therefore concluded, along with Anna, it wise to obtain some further education for me. At least it should help open up better opportunities for me later in life. The issue then became of where. Unlike the school back home, most of those in the city were large, impersonal, academies. Neither thought, considering my continuing depressed state, I would cope well in one of them. I think they were right. In the end they decided, and agreed, to place me in the hands of aunt Frances, the wife of papa's brother. The one who had met us at the station. She was already home teaching their own son. However, this arrangement held another issue for me. Because of the distance between our homes and the undesirability of me travelling across the city each day, I was to live with aunt and uncle for most of the time. There would be the occasional weekend back with papa and Anna but other than that my life was to undergo yet another uprooting. Happy with this arrangement, I was not. However, as yet a child under the care of her father, I had no option but to obey.

Uncle Leonard had subsequently collected me and taken me to their home in a delightful, open spaced suburb. Though he was a diplomat of the highest standing and owned a lavish mansion in the most fashionable part of the city, he and aunt preferred to live in what they referred to as their 'country home'. In reality, the suburb was only a twenty-minute drive from the centre but, as said, belied the fact by being open spaced and fresh. Even the roads were just compacted earth or occasionally gravel. The house was within a large compound surround by very high walls and an equally high gate. I never asked, but suspect the reason for such high walls had been twofold, privacy and security. As I have already told you, the society of the time was fairly crime free. Nevertheless, with uncle's senior diplomatic position, it may have been circumspect to limit the family's vulnerability. Aunt and Robert, their son, were waiting at the door to great us and along with uncle made me very welcome. I had gratefully noted, as we drove into the compound, how rural it all looked. Numerous fruit trees lined the drive along with an abundance of rosebushes. Aunt had a passion for them. Further in, I had spotted a variety of other fruit bearing bushes, as well as vines and even more trees. To add to all this were a mix of chickens, geese and goats and two wonderful Alsatians all freely wondering about. I had been feeling despondent at yet a further relocation. It seemed as soon as I became accustomed to one place I would be transferred to another. However, the pleasantly rural sight of uncle's home inspired me to hope I would not find it too bad living there.

Once we entered the house, aunt, without further ado, set out the agenda my life would follow for the foreseeable future. I was not to know then how short that foreseeable future would be. The daily routine was to be breakfast, lessons, lunch, siesta, in our warm climate a necessity, more lessons, free time, dinner, reading or playing games together, bed. There would be no lessons on Sundays or Holy Days. If I was there on a Sunday, I would accompany them to church. On the days when aunt had to go out there would be no lessons. The time would be primarily free, though she expected us, Robert and I, to help round the gardens and with the livestock for part of the time. Aunt was a formidable woman who broached no argument, at least not from us younger ones or from the domestic staff. Uncle had met her when on a diplomatic mission to her country. I do not know all the details but believe they quickly found an affinity. They had mutual beliefs and interests and thankfully, considering uncle's position, held similar political outlooks. It would have been very difficult if they had not. Robert told me once how uncle had confided that in the early days he used to tell aunt 'Little one I love you very much.' That amused us no end because aunt Frances was a very substantial woman and by no stretch of the imagination could ever have been considered little. One thing I may attest from my own observations is that they truly loved each other, though that did not always prevent a little waywardness on uncle's part.

Just a little amusing aside you may enjoy. As a diplomat of the highest standing, his political position, and self respect uncle always took great care of his appearance. Also, he never knew when an urgent summons might arise. Aunt Frances secretly told us, Robert and me, that in order to keep his hair from standing on end, as it had a tendency of doing, uncle wore a hairnet at night. She swore us to secrecy. Robert and I could not help but giggle at the thought of what he must look like. We just could not imagine it because, whenever we saw him, he was always immaculately turned out.

I settled into the routine and got on as best as I could with the life designated for me, though my thoughts never strayed far from mama. I still desperately wanted her and to get back to where she should be. Robert and I shared chores and, though he was slightly older, I felt we were friends. A misnomer, as it would turn out.

I have never considered myself very beautiful, but it transpired during those early months in the city I started to transition from girlhood to womanhood. Many would subsequently comment on how they thought I had inherited some of my mother's beauty. I could not see it myself. She was incredibly beautiful. Even after all these intervening years, those who knew her, not that there are many of them left, still attest to her beauty. They all say there has been no one else like her in the district. Well, whether or not I have inherited any of it, these affirmations were going to prove problematic. After lunch one day, aunt announced she had to go out and there would be no lessons that afternoon. I decided to change and attend to the animal pens. However, before starting, it being a pleasantly warm afternoon, I indulged a few relaxing moments by the carp pool. I loved watching the brilliant gold and orange shimmering colours as the fish dashed under and between the water lilies. Leaning back, I closed my eyes and enjoyed the tingling sensation of the fish nibbling at my fingertips as I trailed them in the water. I had almost dozed off when a shadow darkening the brilliance penetrating my eyelids made me jump. I looked up to find uncle with his cousin, a senior police officer who had been visiting, and Robert staring at me in a most unsettling manner. For some reason I was unable to fathom,

I felt scared. Remembering my manners, I greeted them with a comment about how nice the afternoon was and then moved away. I simply did not feel comfortable remaining where I was. Uncle's cousin had tried to stop me, but I asserted I needed to get on with my work. His nicotine stained, saliva dripping smile had been most unsettling. He had then asked me not to go but to stay and play with them, trying to force me into compliance by grabbing my arm. I asked him to let go, but then noticed what I may now describe as licentious expressions in the eyes of all three. Of course, at the time I had no idea what licentious meant, except I did not like it. Fear had now taken a firm hold and, with the added strength that provided, I managed to pull my arm free.

Where to go, as I ran from them, had been my next dilemma. I knew the gate would probably be locked and it and the walls were too high for me to climb. How could I escape their grasp? In the end, with no other visible alternative, I had headed toward the pens at the bottom of the garden. Upon seeing me, my pets, as they had become, trotted up and affectionately snuggled into my legs, as was their way. I am not sure but think they realised something was amiss. Animals can be very sensitive. Not to be left out, the two Alsatians had also bounded up. The mix of them all huddled round my legs formed a living barrier between me and the men who had chased after me. Whether it was the sight of the animals protecting me or not is open to debate, but all three came to a standstill and stared. After what seemed an eternity but could only have been a few seconds, the three with drooped heads, slumped shoulders, and shameful looks shuffled off. I felt my chest deflate as I allowed a long held breath to escape. Hesitant relief took its place, but what was I to do now? Aunt was not home so I could not return to the house. I thanked and hugged the dears who had looked after me and spent the rest of the day with them. I subsequently debated whether to tell aunt. However, as no one had mentioned the incident, then or thereafter, decided it best to keep quiet. Besides anything else, I had not wanted papa to get wind of what had happened. He would have been furious. I was terrified if he heard, he might exercise some robust discipline that, though they deserved it, I had no wish to subject them to. The fact Robert had been with them saddened me. I had clearly been mistaken. He was no friend.

6

Occupation

Except for uncle, aunt and papa, the general unrest prevalent in 1939 had not really registered with the rest of us. They, however, had understood the implications. It was not long before my homeland became engulfed by the Second World War. Our troops fought valiantly but had been no match against the superior forces and equipment. In short time we became a subjugated, occupied nation. Many horrors and atrocities would follow. The first notable impact for me was papa suddenly disappearing. When I asked, uncle simply told me he had gone to the village to ensure the estates and business were in order. The truth would not surface until sometime after.

Our location within the suburbs initially spared us the full repercussions of occupation. Admittedly, the food shortages caused by the Nazi's habit of destroying national economies by flooding them with high levels of local currency started to bite early on. Other than that we were reasonably untouched. Those in the metropolis proper had not been so fortunate. Bread, the staple diet of the time, at a cost of several thousand a loaf, had been beyond the reach of most. The commandeering of almost all other foods had also taken a toll. To survive, people quickly learnt, us included, to boil stinging nettles for soup and tea and to stew roots of any tree or plant they could find. It amazes me how many of us survived on such meagre diets. Of course, not all did.

Despite his senior diplomatic standing, the enemy had thankfully not immediately incarcerated uncle. I am not sure what we would have done if he had been, though undoubtedly they would have also taken us with him. It transpired the German command wanted to set up a local administration, similar to a more notable one established elsewhere. They wanted uncle with his knowledge and experience of national government and foreign affairs to be part of it. They thought if he and his colleagues were involved with the administration, people would be less aggressive. Attempting to persuade him further, they clarified how they would not tolerate any disobedience or disorder. If he complied, he would spare his people and their families from the severe retaliations meted out in such circumstances. Naturally, uncle had not been overenthusiastic about the idea. He obtained agreement to be allowed twenty-four hours to contemplate the issue. During that period he discussed the matter with compatriots. They concluded it would be in the national interest to accept, though they would not play the acquiescent role of other similar administrations. The alternative would be to abandon the people to the mercy of less scrupulous men who would undoubtedly receive invitations to take up the role if they refused.

If nothing else, they could use the knowledge and information that would be accessible to them for the national good. They had therefore accepted, despite the underlying concerns for themselves and their families, should anything go wrong or if the Nazis detected their covert activities.

In this new position, uncle occasionally had to invite hierarchy Nazis, how I detest the very sound of that word, to dinner. A very nervous time for us all. One evening, just before some of these guests were due, an American civilian and a British soldier were brought to the house for safekeeping. Uncle and his compatriots, throughout the occupation, helped many servicemen and civilians who, for one reason or another, the Germans were after, as well as Jewish families, escape to neutral countries. It was terrible timing for us, however uncle could not turn them away. Together, we quickly ushered them into the secret underground room constructed beneath the house for such purposes. It was all very nerve-racking. The men were told they must remain silent and still and would have to use bamboos inserted through the ceiling to breathe. The upper, external parts of these were hidden among tall shrubs specifically planted for the purpose. We, Anna, who now visited regularly, and I were directed to our rooms with instructions to remain quiet and out of sight. Uncle and Aunt had been concerned because we were both young and considered attractive and there was no telling how the men's moods, or desires, may turn. Thankfully, the evening passed without incident and the Germans left none the wiser. Uncle had arranged for the safe removal of the escapees a few days later.

Naturally, with his position of responsibility, uncle frequently travelled into the centre where the government and municipal offices were located. We were always worried. People and vehicles were regularly stopped and searched and many had subsequently disappeared, never to be seen again. We feared the same may happen to him. However, he did his best to reassure, telling us the soldiers had orders not to stop any vehicle with diplomatic plates, which uncle's car had. Nevertheless, we were constantly on tenterhooks until he returned.

Over the years, I have consistently tried, and longed, to erase the following incident from my mind's eye, regrettably without success. It still troubles me to this very day. One day, for what reason I do not recall, it had been necessary for all of us to venture into the metropolis. Uncle normally insisted it safer for us to remain within the confines of the country house. I still smile at their continual reference to it as such, despite its suburban location. We all dutifully piled into his car and observed through the windows. Most of us had not been into the city since the occupation and consequently had no idea of what would greet us. It was horrendous. Even the very atmosphere, as we entered the city environs, became oppressive. Bombed buildings, bullet riddled facades, charred remains, dead mutilated corpses, refuse of every kind, and so much more lay all round. There had also been the constant display of Nazi flags. How I hated the sight. I now understood what it was to feel, 'sick to my stomach'. Yet, these were not to be the worst sights to greet us. To reach our destination it was necessary to cross over a bridge spanning a dry riverbed. This was quite normal in the warmer months, though the river was always in full flow during winter. As we entered onto the bridge I noted several men and boys lined along the top of the river bank. A group of women, babies, and children were gathered just below them. I wondered what was going on and why they were all there. Remember, I was still young and, so far, had no real experience of war. Suddenly, as if to answer my query, the explosive crescendo of machine gun fire accosted my eardrums. For a moment, I had been unable to believe my eyes. The men and boys were being mowed down. I sat horrified and stunned as I watched blood exploding from their torsos. So much blood. To add to my horror, there were women and children, who had obviously run to try and protect their fathers, husbands, brothers, sons, loved ones, also being shot in the back with no second thought. I could not understand why or how people would do this to others. Later, in answer to my questioning, uncle explained the Nazi's habitually rounded up men and boys who would be capable of holding a firearm in order to dispose of them. In addition, such wholesale slaughter was their means of retribution for any German killed. It took a long time for me to recover from the shock, though, as I have said, I have never been able to truly forget.

Shortly after witnessing the true savagery of war and occupation, the images of which continued to burn into all our souls, an unexpected turn of events would see me back in my home. This despite the travel restrictions our subjugated state imposed. Anna, besides her intelligence and quick wit, had also been very attractive and throughout had commanded attention from the boys. This did not decrease at university where she often, mischievously though never maliciously, teased her fellow male students. On her part it was just a bit of fun and initially not something to take seriously. However, as will happen, one came along whom she found fascinating. He was also very handsome. Christopher, six foot two, dark-haired, firm jawed, with penetrating eyes, strong athletic build, and intelligence to match, knew his own power. Thankfully, he was never arrogant, though many of the girls would do almost anything to catch his attention. Anna, on the other hand, knew how to play the game, and maintained a mischievous aloofness, though she also knew when to give the right encouraging signals. Christopher had been the first man to truly catch her eye. He eventually decided Anna was the one for him and to that purpose asked papa, before he had disappeared, for her hand in marriage. Accepted practice then, in all strata of society, was for men to ask a girl's father, or guardian in the absence of a father, permission to marry. Not to do so would have risked condemnation and ostracism. Though, in some ways not the ideal match, Christopher and papa had apparently got to know each other, leading to papa having a reasonably good opinion of him. Permission was granted.

In our society, and I am sure in many others, it was traditional for weddings to take place in the bride's hometown, village, or city. Of course, with the occupation, this posed a bit of a problem. Nevertheless, Anna was determined to show the German's we still valued and had not abandoned our national identity and traditions.

Anyway, nearly all those they wanted to celebrate with them lived in our rural home district. Uncle used his diplomatic connections to obtain travel permits without which we would not have been able to cross the various checkpoints. I cannot express how excited I became at the prospect of returning to our home, though papa, had he been about, would probably have registered some concern. However, he was not, and with the busy preparations I do not think anyone else even thought about the potential danger such a return might pose for me. In my soul I had not stopped thinking of, or longing for, mama.

During the rail journey, while the others chatted among themselves and with fellow passengers, I sat in a corner looking out of the window, though not really seeing the passing scenery racing by. Turbulent emotions possessed the whole of my being. Excitement, fear, and a muted inquisitiveness about what I would find dominated. What would it be like? Had much changed? Would people be glad to see me? Would mama be there? Naturally, in my logical mind I knew she would not be but in the non-logical side I dared to hope. Not for the first time a kaleidoscope of images invaded. Mama's dear loving face, her laying on the bed obscured by the mosquito net, our embracing each other, her last gurgling breath, black clothes, a dark pit, that awful wooden box, and so on. I had nearly screamed out but thankfully something returned me to the moment, enabling me to prevent it vocalising. I doubted the others would have taken kindly to such an interruption or emotional display. Though grateful no one had noticed my unsettled state, and still wishing to be left to myself, I had conversely also sensed the need for a warm, reassuring embrace or hug. But of course, that was not going to happen. As my contemplations continued, a violent tension took hold of my stomach and an iron band steadily tightened round my temples. It was painful, but I remained silent.

Thankfully, the journey proved uneventful, with us arriving safely on a warm, bright afternoon. It surprised us to find a large group of friends waiting along with our relatives. We all embraced affectionally. You never knew in those awful times whether you would ever see each other again making any visit special. How did I feel now we were back in the village? You may well ask. Happy? Well, no, not really. Diverse emotions invaded with fear being one of the more prevalent. Fear of what I would find. Fear that mama would not be there. Though, while in the city, I had partially adjusted and been able to understand mama was no more, this return awakened my old hopes. Perhaps mama would be at home. I know it seems illogical. However, I longed for her and, through the ethereal mists now surrounding me, was prepared to accept any possibility. Questions and inquiries as to our health, how life was in the city, whether we had suffered at the hands of the Nazis, and so on, bombarded from all directions. Thankfully, as the youngest, I was spared the need to respond.

I still recall the tightness in my chest as we steadily made our way toward home. I am sure my heart must have physically jumped when we cleared the brow of the last hill. There before us stood my beloved home. The only place I had been truly happy, the place where mama and I had spent many joyous days, the place where she should now be waiting. Instinctively, as I had each day when returning from school, I looked up to the balcony that traversed the whole top floor, anticipating mama standing there and waving. But of course, she had not been. She must be preparing a meal and some refreshments. Once through the door I automatically went in search of her, the old familiar furnishings providing a sense of belonging that had been missing for so long. After a thorough search that had included the gardens, pens, outhouses and some fields, I had no choice but to accept mama was not there. An electric shock of disappointment, no, it had been far more than that, disconsolateness, bereavement, abandonment, I really am not sure how to describe it, passed through me as I battled the tears. I knew it would not be acceptable to the others to witness such an outburst, especially as this was supposed to be a joyous occasion. Ultimately, I had no choice but to keep my thoughts and pain to myself.

Anna and Christopher had discussed at length whether they should postpone their nuptials until after the hostilities. In the end they concluded, because of the uncertainties war brings, the sooner their wedding, the better. Nonetheless, there was still one more hurdle to cross. It was traditional, especially in families like ours, for younger siblings to wait for the elder ones to marry before embarking upon their own matrimonial lives. Anna consequently felt it incumbent upon her to ask Helen, our elder sister, whether she was amenable to the marriage. I must point out, Anna did not simply ask out of duty or form. She really had been concerned not to upset or cause Helen offence and had been prepared to postpone the wedding indefinitely. Helen reassured her there was no issue. Her own serious courtship with the man who would become her lifelong partner was well on track. The only reason it had not proceeded further was father's absence. There had therefore been no opportunity to ask for her hand. A situation that would shortly be resolved.

I had been surprised not to find papa at home when we arrived, but had momentarily forgotten it in my earnest quest to find mama. It was now I would learn the truth of his disappearance. Papa had joined the resistance and had quickly become one of their important leaders. He was apparently on the Nazi's most wanted list. As a consequence, I was told he would not be joining us for the wedding celebrations. This was a real disappointment for us all, but we preferred he remained safe. Occupation had not been restricted to the towns and cities. Every village, no matter how rural or remote, had an occupying force. You may therefore imagine my ecstasy when Anna told me papa would in fact be joining us in a couple of days. However, she warned I must control my excitement and not draw attention to him. It seemed the local soldiers were not aware of who he was and we did not want to alert them. Upon first seeing him, my chest had contracted and throbbed painfully so much I was sure people could see my pounding heart as it hammered against my ribcage. It took a lot of effort not to shout out and run to him in wild abandonment. However, I had been unable to subdue my excitement completely. I bit my tongue, almost physically, and ran to him quietly. I had then leapt into his arms and embraced him.

Despite Anna's care of and kindness to me, papa's disappearance had left me feeling completely bereaved and abandoned, as if losing mama had not been enough. Papa eventually had to force my arms apart while jokingly asking I not strangle him. Thereafter, I spent as much time as I could silently standing or sitting close to him. Just his presence had been reassuring, as if it were the old times. Perhaps I had been deluding myself, imagining we were all together again despite not being able to see mama. Whatever it was, it was something I needed at the time.

Unfortunately, prior to the wedding, Anna and Christopher had a terrible experience. Because long distance communication, during the occupation, was almost nonexistent, people lost touch with each other. My sister and her fiancé therefore decided to visit the district market town to see if they could locate some friends and acquaintances. Their aim was to catch up, make appropriate introductions, and invite closer friends to the celebrations. Enjoying the brief respite from all the hustle and bustle of the preparations, they were strolling through the town when a group of young men grabbed Christopher and dragged him down a side street. They then started beating him up, mercilessly punching, kicking, and spitting. As mentioned, he was a fit man, but there were just too many for him. Anna shouted for them to stop, asking at the same time what they thought they were doing. She got hit for her trouble. Prior to disorientation taking hold she heard them shouting words like 'Traitor! Conspirator! Nazi!'. It took a couple of minutes to clear her head after which she yelled for them to hold off and she would produce someone who could vouch for Christopher. When in such a state, my sister can have the appearance of a wild tiger. Quite terrifying when it occurs, I can tell you. The men stopped. In the absence of any telephones, she had to send a runner to the village to fetch papa. His rage must have been tremendous. Anna told us he had growled at the aggressors, 'If we were not fighting the same war, I would kill you.' The men withdrew. It turned out they were members of the local resistance. Because Christopher was a stranger, walked with confidence, and was dressed in a smart city suit, he, to their minds, must be a Nazi collaborator. Tells you a lot about the insecure and untrusting days we lived in. Needless to say none of us visited the town again during our stay.

Despite Cristopher's bruised, scarred state, the wedding was a delight. It had been a long time since any of us had seen such joy and happiness. It was almost as if we had forgotten the war despite Nazi soldiers looking on. I think in some ways it was them being there that determined everyone to make the most of it and show we were not a people to be cajoled or intimidated. As the newlyweds emerged from the church, a group of local musicians had struck up. The cue for Anna and Christopher to lead the dance that, by tradition, spun its way through the village streets to the reception. With the prevalent limitations and shortages we feared the wedding breakfast would be poor, however, we need not have worried. All the village women had pooled their meagre rations, determined to make this an occasion to remember. It certainly turned out to be such. None of us had seen such a lavish spread in years. Anna and Christopher could not thank these generous people for their kindness enough.

As happy as I had been for my sister, I must acknowledge there had also been a weight upon me that, though I had said nothing, some had obviously noticed. It was suggested I rest on the divan in the corner of the room and watch the celebrations from there. It was traditional in rural homes, especially smaller ones, for at least one divan to be in the main room. These provided convenient resting places for a siesta on hot days and, in larger families, a bed for one or more of the children. My weariness had probably been due to the combination of journey, exhilaration at being home again, depressive effect of not finding mama there, initial disappointment that papa would not be joining us, then exhilaration that he would, and the excitement of the wedding. While watching from my comfortably relaxed position some of this partially lifted. Anna's radiant face framed by her billowing veil as she and her now husband spun round in the dance, delighting us all. Unfortunately, my enjoyment was to be spoilt. Why must it always be like that?

I mentioned before how, with the uncertainty of war and occupation, we could never be sure of seeing the people we knew again and how that made each visit very special. Everyone had welcomed us with open arms and, despite my troubled state, I had also been pleased to see them again. Now several stopped by my resting place to enquire after my health and how I found life in the city. Among them had been the local mayor. He had drawn a chair up to sit beside me and inquired how I was enjoying the festivities. Both of us agreed it had been a long time since we had seen such smiles and pleasure on people's faces. We had returned our gaze to the swirling couples when I felt something beneath the home spun bedspread covering me touch my thigh. I was horrified. It was the mayor's hand. I did not want to spoil the party by making a scene and had therefore quietly inched away, pressing myself as far into the wall as I could. However, his hand had continued to follow like some gigantic spider and had even tried to move higher up my leg. I had not known what to do. The last thing I wanted was to draw attention, especially as I feared what papa might do if he saw. I therefore knew I had no option but to deal with this myself. My young age did not mean I was stupid or without a sense of decorum or disgust. In the end, hoping it would be sufficient, I looked him straight in the eye in a manner I sincerely hoped conveyed my displeasure, well more anger really. I am not sure what I would have done if he had ignored my silent protestation. Mercifully, this was not put to the test. He had quickly withdrawn his hand, risen and left. I never saw him again.

The celebrations, as was traditional, had gone on for two days, after which we were to disperse to our various homes and locations. This was hard because papa would not be returning with us. He needed to get back to resistance headquarters apart from which he did not wish to endanger the rest of us by being seen in our company. He had taken every effort to disassociate himself even adopting a false name. Of course, our parting was made worse by the fact none of us had any idea when, or if, we would see each other again. For me, however, this was not the only sadness. We would be leaving my home once more and this time I knew not when I would see it again. To me it was where I really belonged, in the place mama and I had shared and been happy in. If I had known then it would be many years and a lifetime's experience before I would see it again, I may well have resisted leaving. But I did not and had obediently done as I was told.

7

Devastating

Life upon returning to the city settled back into the same routine, except I was now not permitted to visit Anna as often. In fact, almost not at all. The explanation had been that as newlyweds, Anna and Christopher needed space and time to get to know each other. This confused me because, as far as I could see, they already knew each other. Why else would they have married? Of course, I now understand, though at the time this prohibition had been an additional pain to my already troubled soul. Anna had become the only close relative I felt I could confide in. After what had occurred with uncle, his cousin, and Robert, it was impossible for me to share my concerns and worries with Aunt for fear of letting something slip.

The only positive in life became the pleasure I gained from the gardens and animals, all of who were now truly firm friends. There were also our lessons, which I found interesting. Grandmama and mama had instilled a thirst for knowledge in each of us. However, I could never truly relax when men were about. I was always on edge and forever looking over my shoulder in case someone tried to creep up on me. It may be hard for those who have not encountered such events to understand how unpleasant life is when you have to be constantly alert. Though not ideal, at least I felt some sense of continuation in the knowledge my life would have some shape to it for the foreseeable future. But, yet again, I was to be proven wrong. My life was about to horrendously and permanently change.

One afternoon aunt was to visit a friend. There would therefore be no lessons after lunch. Whenever I had free time, my automatic resolve was to do some gardening and clean out the pens. Having changed into an old dress, I had been going down the stairs when I encountered uncle. In response to his question, I informed him of my intentions for the afternoon. Having done so, I went to pass. Before I could he grabbed and flung me onto the hard, unrelenting, marble steps and then threw himself on top of me. To say it shocked me would be the understatement of the century. My consternation, as if not already at its highest level, escalated further when I felt him trying to pull my dress above my knees. I fought as best as I could, crying out for him to stop. He, however, continued, attempting to reassure me with, 'Come on dear, I am not going to hurt you. I just want to play'. As if that was supposed to ease my mind. His tone and the glint in his eyes had done anything but. While we were thus entwined, Robert suddenly appeared. My immediate reaction had been fear. There was no way I could fight them both. Beneath uncle's weight I watched expecting the worse. However, on this occasion, Robert did not join in. He stood watching for what seemed an eternity and then, first giving his father a filthy look, turned and walked away. I know I should have been relieved but, as contrary as we can sometimes be, I felt resentment. I think, secretly, I had hoped he would intervene and save me from a horrible fate. Uncle had also stopped, but now returned his attention to my prone form. Though my strength was proving unequal to the task, I had not been prepared to concede. I resorted to kicking, scratching and, as best as I could, punching the man who was supposed to be my protector. Of course, all this achieved was to make uncle angry, resulting in him hitting back. I was still a child and found horrific someone would show such violence toward me, let alone someone I was supposed to trust. I did my best to protect myself, but his blows were increasingly intense and I feared I would succumb any moment. However, with the ensuing wriggling and slithering such intimate aggression results in, I was able to slip from beneath my attacker and scramble onto my feet. This may seem odd, but initially I had merely stood and looked down upon the man. What was I thinking? Why had I not immediately made my escape? I think it was a case of not really believing what had just happened, had in fact happened. Any hope I may have entertained for him coming to his senses was soon dispelled. As soon as he regained his feet, he recommenced his aggression, throwing me back onto the steps and then proceeding to kick me down them. It continued hard to accept this was being done to me by a relative. I managed to get to my feet again, but before I could make a run for it, he threw me back down. This time my head struck the solid edge of one step. Thankfully, I did not pass out but, unable to grip onto anything, had rolled down the entire flight. I am grateful to say I ended up on top of some animal feed sacks previously stacked at the bottom. Without them, I would have hit the marble floor with some force and goodness knows what the result of that may have been. Unfortunately, before I could get up and make a run for it, uncle had leapt down and relaunched his attack. A monsoon of clenched hammer like fist punches rained down upon me. It was obvious he was now in an uncontrollable rage. My mind rebelled again. Why was he being like this? Why was he being so cruel? What was it he really wanted? Though blindly asking myself these questions, the truth was by now apparent, even to the naïve innocent me. It was devastating.

My little remaining strength began to fail. I became terrified I would no longer be able to fight him off. I knew if I was to survive, I needed to make a run for it. We were now in the entrance vestibule with the main door just feet away. I would have to get through it and find some means of escape. Drawing upon the little resource left, I dug my heels into the floor, turned, and, rising on my toes, sprinted toward the door. Uncle had momentarily continued lashing out at the empty air until he realised I was no longer in reach. It would have been amusing if it had not been so terrifying. That moment gave me the seconds I needed to get through the door. I then faced the quandary of where to go. Remember, we lived in an enclosed estate with high walls and gate. My mind had run through the possibilities of which there were few. Remaining within the grounds was not realistic, but how could I escape? As mentioned aunt had gone out for the afternoon and I knew, occasionally, though not always, she left the gate unlocked because it was so heavy and awkward to open. Heart in mouth, I ran full pelt up the treelined drive. What if it was locked? Even if not, would the small, now weakened me be able to open it? I scanned the lock and would have been overjoyed if I had not been so terrified, to see aunt had left it ready for her return. With all the strength I could muster, I heaved on the large iron grip. At first the gate resisted but, presumably because of the adrenaline now coursing through, I managed a Herculean pull. This provided a small but sufficient gap for me to squeeze through. Blindly, I ran for all my life with no thought for where I was heading. I just had to get away! And thus begins the horror and brutality of my subsequent life.

***

Despite the pulsating fear, I instinctively had the good sense not to just run along the main road. I dodged down and along many side streets and lanes, heading who knew where. The adrenaline still pounding through gave me the stamina I needed to keep going, though I lost all concept of time and distance. Eventually tiring, I slowed, and regaining some composure, began looking about me. Nothing was familiar. There were no recognisable landmarks. I was lost. It would have been foolish to continue running without first trying to determine where I was. Before making any rash decision, I ensured uncle was not behind me. I am not sure what I would have done if he had been. My exertions were telling, and I was uncertain of how much longer I could keep going. I needed to rest.

Naturally, just standing in the middle of the road while I took stock would have been unwise. Besides the possibility of uncle perhaps coming upon me, I had been aware enough to know it would not be good if a German soldier saw me. Looking round for some sort of shelter, I noticed an apparently deserted large house, as many were. Most families, at least those who had the means, had left the city before the occupying forces arrived. I took shelter behind the small wall protecting the entrance. Doing so provided me with the opportunity to have a proper look round. I recognised nothing but noted many of the buildings were quite tall, far taller than any in the suburbs I knew. The only conclusion there could be was, I had run all the way into the centre of the metropolis, an amazing feat considering the distance. What was I to do? Where could I go? The light was failing. I realised I could not stay where I was, behind the small wall, all night. Despite using my shoulder and knee, the door would not give way and I could find no other means of getting in. The thought then occurred I might find Anna's house, though I had no clue in which direction it would lie. Travel between Anna's and Uncle's had always been by car. Before venturing from my hiding place, I checked there was no one in the street. Having made my escape, I had no wish to now be seen. The drone of traffic had struck my ears as I emerged. Would it be wise to go that way? There were bound to be people about, but there was also the possibility I may recognise something. As I ventured forward, the sights greeting me confirmed what we had heard about life in this central area subsequent to the invasion. It was far worse than the other only time I had been into the city. Then I had the limited protection of being in the car. There were twisted, mutilated corpses everywhere. Some ravaged by dogs, cats, rats, and goodness knows what else. The stench had been awful. It had been all I could do not to vomit. Starvation and disease, not to mention Nazi reprisals, had taken their toll. There were few left fit enough, or brave enough to risk infection, to bury the dead. It was awful. Words can never portray the reality.

It turned out the rumbling had been coming from one of the city's principal thoroughfares. Standing on a corner, in the shadows, I saw the ruins of an ancient temple rising into the darkening sky on the opposite side. It had seemed familiar. Was it a place we passed when driving through the city? It took a few moments before I recalled seeing it when we visited my godmother. Her house had impressed me with its unique architecture and intricate wrought-iron balustrades. All I had to do was recall in which direction we had gone. Left or right? Which streets had we gone down? If only I had paid more attention. I knew it could not be more than a couple of streets away. Hope and excitement rose. Godmother would look after me. Which way should I go? Unlike many capital centres, this one did not just comprise office buildings. There were many residential properties crowded between. Godmother's home had been but one. Standing still on the corner would achieve nothing, so I eventually decided to investigate. It had to be somewhere nearby. Ensuring I remained in the shadows, I ventured down one street after another, sadly to no avail. All the houses looked the same, each displaying similar, though unique, architecture and structures. The more I searched, the more desperate and disconsolate I became. Where was it! Why could I not find it?! Within short time I realised I was unlikely to locate the house before nightfall and therefore needed to find somewhere for the night. Darkness had now been descending. Looking about I noted the bombed silhouette of what had once been a large imposing property, regrettably but one of many. Portions of the lower walls remained intact and appeared likely to provide some shelter from the now cooling night air. It had been a warm afternoon when I had to make my escape and only had my thin cotton dress on. Settling into a corner that not only provided shelter from the cool breeze but also concealed me from view, my thoughts ran over recent events. How had my life come to this? I now felt truly alone and vulnerable. If only I could find Anna or even papa, though I knew not where he was. For certain I could not return to uncle and aunt's. My unshed tears welled up as sorrow and horror combined with the pain I now felt from the bruises and cuts. I had been in such fear and running so fast I had been unaware of the physical damage I had incurred. Pressing further into the crumbling brickwork, as if it would provide further solace, I did my best to remain quiet and motionless, but any hope of sleep was soon abandoned. Adrenalin and fear still pumped through the whole of my being.

As you may imagine, dawn had been a welcome sight after the wretched night. I immediately recommenced my search for godmother's house. My thirst and hunger would have to wait. Though I had still been quite young, the resilience of my soul and spirit at the time continues to amaze me. Only shortly before, with mama's passing, I had wanted to leave this world and be with her. It would seem the instinct for survival inherent to most of us had taken control. Though in some respects, I suspect it had more to do with my unwillingness to give in, combined with an equal determination to resist the enemy. Remember, we were under occupation. How many roads and streets I went down is unknown to me but it was all to no avail. I could not find godmother's house. Much later I discovered, if I had gone in the opposite direction to the one I chose, I would have almost come straight on to it. Well, that is life, mine at least.

Late afternoon arrived. Miserable, dejected, cold, hungry and thirsty, I realised I could not go on like this. I needed to find some proper shelter and sustenance. There was also the danger of Nazi soldiers seeing me. We had heard they often grabbed people from the streets and that they were never seen again. What was I to do? Where could I find what I needed? I had no desire to spend another night like the last one. Though it would humiliate and possibly endanger me, I felt the only option was to try and find a friendly household who might be willing to help. I realised my youth, combined with my haggard, worn, dirty appearance, would raise questions, especially as to why I was out on my own. You will, I am sure, agree it would have been inappropriate to mention what had occurred the previous day. I decided to simply say I had become separated from my family and could not find them. Having made this decision, I now had to determine which type of houses to call at. From the reports we had heard, I was well aware many were struggling and on starvation level. Not only would it have been inappropriate to ask, but I also had no desire to add to other people's burdens. I may have been hungry, thirsty and desperate, but mama had brought us up to be considerate of others. Something I have never lost. After further thought, I resolved upon approaching larger houses, where there was more likelihood of them having servants, and any smaller ones that retained some semblance of prosperity about them. If a property looked rundown and unkempt it was unlikely the occupants would want another mouth to feed.

With extreme trepidation I began knocking on doors and where someone did answer, remember many had fled the city, explained I was lost, without shelter and food, and asked if they would take me in as a servant in exchange for some food, water and accommodation. As I think back I suspect, with my thin summer dress and weary, dishevelled state, I must have looked far more pathetic than I realised. Nevertheless, it seemed to make no difference. Angry men and women shooed me away and slammed doors in my face. It was quite daunting, especially for someone so young. Remember, I was still a child. Nonetheless, it would be wrong to entertain any harsh feelings toward these people. In retrospect, though it had not occurred to me at the time, with the occupation and resulting shortages, many must have been seeking help. Undoubtedly people were tired of the constant flow of begging refugees. There had also been the fact of Nazis frequently turning up at houses and forcibly removing occupants. Each knock at the door must have been frightening. I admit, even though they had been unable to accommodate me, it would have been nice to be treated with a little sympathy. Under normal circumstances such behaviour would deter me from pursuing my aims. Much to my son's, and my own I admit, annoyance, anything like this causes me to withdraw into myself and shy away. However, on this occasion, probably linked to my desperateness, I refused to allow the rejections to deter me. Eventually, after many more similar experiences, I knocked on the door of small, neat looking house.

A petite, dark-haired, pale complexioned, kindly looking lady had answered. This time, with a little more optimism because of her tender, sympathetic green eyes, I reiterated my situation and request. Having listened without interrupting, I noticed her visibly hesitate. This gave me hope because everyone else had reacted with immediate and direct rejection. Her hesitation and compassionate expression broke something inside me, which led me to plead. I reassured her I would do anything required, ate little, and would remain out of the way when there was nothing for me to do. I struggled to control the tears which must have been visible in my eyes. She quietly looked me up and down and, I could see, took note of my poor condition, especially my bare, filthy, bloody feet. My thin summer slippers had become victim to the rough streets and no longer existed. Raising her eyes back to mine, she asked if I could cook. This raised a dilemma. Due to my age I had never actually cooked a meal, though I had always watched mama prepare ours and had helped mix ingredients. I was therefore certain I could do it and responded with a definitive yes. To me it had not been a lie because I believed I would be able, after all, how difficult could it be? In response the lady had stepped back and opened the door further indicating I should enter. Up to this point she had held it only slightly ajar, just enough to view and hear me. As soon as I was through she had, with lightening speed and fear in her eyes, firmly closed and bolted it. She then led me to the pantry in the back of the house where she inquired my name and why I was on my own. I provided my predetermined responses. She may have been kind looking and apparently compassionate, but by now I had surmised it was not safe to trust without proper knowledge of the individual. To prevent any further probing, I added I was new to the city and had not yet memorised my family's address. Thankfully she had not pursued the matter further. I felt ashamed and had no wish to be forced into telling the truth. When I say ashamed, I do not mean for myself, though my condition was by far less than I would like when in public. My shame was for my reasonably highly positioned and respected family. To admit to uncle's behaviour would bring shame upon us all. In this day and age that may seem odd, but you need to remember society was very different in those days.

Introductions over, Martha pointed to a small jar of pasta. She explained, like everyone else, they had little and needed to make the most of what there was. She then asked me to prepare a meal for her, her husband, their daughter and myself and then left me to it. My relief at finally being accepted into a home, with the reassurance of shelter and food, proved overwhelming. I came near to collapse and had to seek the support of a chair as the long held tears and tension found release, causing the whole of my frame to shake. In all honesty, I had just wanted to sit and allow all the suppressed sorrow and anger to flow out, but I quickly recalled myself and the need to get on with the meal. I viewed the pasta jar with trepidation. How had mama done it? Recalling, I filled a saucepan with water, added a little salt, put the pasta in, and placed it on the stove. The next question was how long to leave it. In my mind's eye, I saw mama taking a piece out and biting into it. While waiting I gave the kitchen a good clean. If I were to be a servant, I would be a good one. Satisfied with my efforts I turned back to the task in hand and removing a small piece of the pasta bit into it. Finding it extremely chewy, I concluded it needed more time. At that very moment Martha returned. A frown crossed her features as she looked into the saucepan and she asked me to explain how I had prepared the meal. Adopting a gentle tone, she kindly explained I should have brought the water to the boil first. Of course, she now realised I had not cooked before. In response I had, rather defensively I am afraid, stated I had always watched my mama and had been sure I could do it. I went on to further explain I had been afraid she would turn me away. You may imagine my burgeoning guilt and mortification. They, together with my fear must have been obvious because she comfortingly reassured me she would teach me how to cook the little they had. Good to her word Martha thereafter taught me all she could.

Joseph, Martha's husband, a small, thin, pale complexioned man with dark hair and beard and gentle grey eyes, turned out to be as kind as his wife. Their delightful daughter, Sarah, completed the family unit. Joseph had concurred with his wife I should remain and have use of a small bedroom on the top floor. Even now, I cannot satisfactorily express the relief, gratitude and joy I had felt. Thankfully, my ability to assimilate new information quickly had me producing adequate meals within a short time. When not thus occupied, I helped round the house and with all general chores. I am grateful to report, they never treated me as a servant but more as a member of the family. I will never forget their kindness.

Though, as already shared, we had heard of, and witnessed, some of their atrocities, I had not really understood what it was like to live in constant fear of the Nazis. This would now change in more than one way. I had observed how my new friends were continually anxious and tense and seemed to be always twitching in the manner I had seen small birds do. It turned out they had good cause. One evening while we were relaxing, as much as one may when living in a war environment, a German patrol had suddenly smashed the front door in. They had not even knocked first. You may understand our consternation, especially as we were well aware of how they often dragged people from their homes for no apparent reason. Before we had a chance to get to the hall, the soldiers, waving rifles and pistols, had burst through the living room door. The sight of the blood spattered torsos I had seen on the bridge leapt to mind, sending a violent shudder through me. Joseph's request to know what they wanted received an abrupt 'Shut Up!' from the one who appeared to be in charge. His men had then started tearing pictures from walls, brushing ornaments of shelves, ripping furniture apart, and generally destroying everything in their path. While this was going on, the officer asked who we were. Having identified his wife and daughter, Joseph was about to introduce me when Martha intervened by saying I was her sister. Later she explained her concern about the lascivious looks many of the soldiers bestowed upon me and what they may do if they learnt the truth.

Despite all I have been through, I still find it hard to comprehend how wantonly cruel people can be. The soldiers evidently enjoyed the power they had and once their destructive rampage was over, it appeared just for the hell of it, beat us up. They struck Joseph in the face with rifle butts and slapped Martha so hard she fell. They punched me in the head until I also fell. Then they kicked, punched, and rifle butted us as we lay prone upon the floor. I recall how, in the midst of the pain, I had been unable to fathom it was really happening. Eventually they tired of their amusement and left the house laughing. Once sure they had indeed left, we struggled to stand using the scattered furniture for support. Though bleeding and bruised, we were grateful none of us had sustained any broken bones or other serious injury. Also, that there had been no attempt to rape any of us. Thankfully, though scared out of her wits, they had not hurt Sarah. Martha had protected her with her own body.

It eventually transpired this had been one of the regular patrols searching for Jewish people.

We helped each other clean and disinfect our wounds and then enjoyed the soothing effects of a warm drink. Martha then, with deep sadness, informed me we had to part and leave the house. I had not understood until she explained the soldiers were likely to return because she, Joseph, and Sarah were Jewish. Why they had not been immediately taken we had no idea. The thought of parting upset me greatly, but they would not hear of me remaining with them, stating it was too dangerous. It had been very hard for me to accept. To add further to my distress, they insisted I leave immediately although night was fast descending. They feared the soldiers may return any moment and were also going to leave that night. Joseph, his face etched with anxiety, Martha, with eyes full of fear, Sarah, still traumatised, and I, trying not to sob my heart out, embraced and kissed as we said our farewells. With blinding tears and clutching the food parcel Martha had quickly put together for me, I had reluctantly dragged my feet away from the house. All the joy and hope of having found such a loving family and home cascaded away. Emotionally and physically I was a mess.

Unable to think straight, I had not wandered far. Yet another bombed ruin was to provide me with minimal shelter for a cold and miserable night. I sat shivering, wondering how it could have come to this again. In the morning, still able to see the house from my hidden spot, I saw the Nazis return. Finding no one at home they ransacked the building before setting it on fire.

To this day, I do not know what became of Joseph, Martha, and Sarah. I sincerely hope they escaped and went on to live a good life. I shall never forget them or their kindness.

8

DARKNESS

I will do my best not to traumatise readers too much in this chapter. Nonetheless, to truly convey my story, it will be necessary to share some gruesome details but in as circumspect a manner as possible. I have suffered many unpleasant, to put it mildly, circumstances throughout my life. This autobiography would lack if it does not recount some, several in fact. However, in each instance, I have tried to limit the horror for readers, reducing details to those necessary for comprehension and consistency. I have omitted some altogether. I have not even shared those with my son who I trust implicitly. They will pass into oblivion along with me.

***

To continue my story. Obviously, I could not remain where I was. Besides my need for more permanent accommodation and a source of sustenance, there was the danger of discovery. I was now fully aware of what that could mean. Taking as much care as I could not to draw attention, I abandoned my night's shelter and wandered into the surrounding streets with no idea of where to go. I knocked at several doors hoping to find another family willing to take me in. Sadly, I only received the same rough and abrupt rejections as previously. You may probably comprehend how demoralised and dejected I felt. There seemed to be no break for me. I must have done something wicked in my life to be treated so badly. But what? With heavy heart and slowing steps, I blindly roamed without any sense of purpose or direction. The further I went, the more dilapidated and ruined the buildings became, not to mention the awful stench of rotting bodies of which there were more than I could count. I even saw dogs feasting on the remains. An image I have tried all my life to erase, without success. It soon became evident I had wandered further into the city centre where, besides the terrible sights, there was, unfortunately, a concentration of soldiers. Thankfully, I suppose that is the right term, the sight of them restored my wits. For the time being, at least, I avoided detection by darting down side streets and hiding behind the shattered walls of blitzed buildings. One of these was to provide me with shelter for another cold, miserable night. You will undoubtedly understand dawn brought no sense of relief or hope with it. What was I to do? Where was I to go? I now seriously doubted I would find anyone to take me in.

There was no point in remaining where I was, so I recommenced my aimless roaming. On this occasion it led me onto another of the city's principal thoroughfares. This was to prove my downfall. To my surprise, a large throng crowded the pavement. This was the largest gathering I had seen for a considerable time. Citizens were normally wary of drawing attention, especially when enemy military were about. I noticed, rather than the usual bustle of people going about their business, everyone appeared to have stopped, all looking in one direction. Curious, despite myself, again trying not to draw undue attention, I weaved my way to the front. Remember, I was still young and of small stature and could not therefore see over shoulders, or in fact, between legs. As I neared the curb a sudden burst of hoorays, 'Three Cheers' 'God Bless' and other such encouragements emitted from the crowd. Looking to see what had promoted this, I spotted a convoy of dishevelled, downcast, war-weary allied prisoners. It was a sad sight. Undoubtedly, they understood what was to become of them. As a nation, we were grateful for their endeavours to liberate us from the Nazi heel, consequently the watching crowd had abandoned our usual circumspection. Even I, and a young boy standing less than a metre from me, joined in, shouting our own encouragements. It was the least we could do. The young boy went further and threw the tray of matches and other small items he had been selling into one vehicle. We all wanted to show our love and appreciation however we could.

The contemptible convey having passed, I decided to talk to the boy. Before I got the chance, someone grabbed my shoulder. Terror immediately assailed. Fear was now a constant companion. I turned to find a German officer looking down at me. Dear God! What was I to do? A look I had never wished to see again pervaded his eyes. Just like uncle's on that awful last occasion. Instinctively, I stepped back and fixed him with what I hoped was an unrelenting stare. Unfortunately, it did not seem to deter him. He grasped and pulled me toward himself. I stiffened and held my body, as best as I could, in an unrelenting, uncompromising manner. I may have been young but I was not about to concede. Furious I dare resist, I watched as he drew his revolver from its holster. The grotesque twist of his mouth made his intent even more obvious. I kept my rigid stance, determined not to show any weakness or the fear raging within. If this was to be my end, so be it, but he would not get the better of me if I could help it. I expected a shot any moment but instead received a violent blow to the side of my head. He had hit me with the butt of the revolver. I stumbled, dazed, but retained my footing. To this day I have problems in that area of my head but doctors have not been able to find anything. It therefore remains undiagnosed. To my mind there is little doubt, the continuing problems relate to this incident. He then uttered something in his foul, guttural tongue. I may not have understood the words but there was no doubt of the insults. I shook my head clear and again adopted my uncompromising stance, hoping he would at last recognise it and leave me alone. How naïve we can be. Instead, he seized me again and pressed the revolver muzzle hard against my head. This was evidently it, the final moment of my life on this earth. The boy, who had stood watching, suddenly forced himself between my captor and me. Ripping his shirt open to expose his tiny chest, he shouted at the officer to shoot him and not me. Such bravery in one so young and small made my heart swell with pride for our nation. There was no such appreciation from our enemy. He simply kicked my little hero to one side and returned the muzzle to my head. Closing my eyes, I waited. A sudden commotion and the sound of a shot followed. It was strange, there was no pain. Was this what it was like to be shot? Not as bad as I had thought. A voice penetrated my bewildered musings. Was it an angel? No, it was too human. Was I dead or not? Though it felt far more, it must have just been seconds before I dared open my eyes. What would heaven look like? Would there be saints and angels? Would I see mama? But there was no heaven, no saints, no angels, no mama. Instead, to my further consternation, there was another officer wearing the uniform of our hated occupiers. Recovering from the shock, I noticed his firm grip on the other man's arm. I also noted the vast range of emblems adorning the new officer's uniform, making me think he must be someone important. He was shouting at his colleague in very harsh tones. While doing so, he, not releasing his grip on the man's revolver holding hand, turned toward the boy and me indicating, with a jerk of his head, we should leave immediately. Unsurprisingly, we wasted no time in obeying, quickly walking away. However, when we were only a metre or so down the road, we heard him calling after us. Naturally, as I am sure you will understand, fear re-assailed. Had he changed his mind? The boy and I exchanged worried glances before daring to turn round. This time relief, or what passed for such in our traumatised state, spread from foot to head. He was gesturing for us to get off the main thoroughfare. An instruction we readily obeyed, appreciating it made sense. So there were human beings among those detestable people, even if they were few and far between.

Eventually, reaching a side street where we felt reasonably safe, we stopped to catch our breath. We had been running full pelt, non-stop. Once sufficiently recovered enough to speak, my companion informed me he had to get back to his family. Apparently, each member ventured out every day, in different directions, to try and earn a little money with a set time for their return. If anyone failed to do so on time they naturally worried. They would probably set out to find them, placing themselves back in danger. It was usually dusk by that time, and it would press them to get back before curfew came into effect. I hid my disappointment as we bid our farewells. Not only was I losing the companionship of this brave fellow, but also my hopes of possibly returning with him. However, in the brief conversation we managed, it became clear despite them all going out daily, they struggled to feed themselves. They could do without the imposition of another hungry mouth. I may have been desperate but I am not selfish and was not about to burden others with my problems.

Left again to my own devices, as if I had any, I wandered aimlessly with bent head trying to think of some plan. Regrettably, in my distracted state, I failed to notice a group of German soldiers gathered at a street corner. Unfortunately, to put it mildly, as you will come to see, they noticed me before I had the chance to run. They seized and unceremoniously dumped me into the back of their jeep. Children, even very young ones, had no exemption from questioning. Was I frightened? Of course I was. I had heard enough of what happened in the city to know my situation was bad. By this time, I was so worn and demoralised I thought if it was my time to die, I would at least be free of the hardship, heartache, disappointment, and fear. Children in war-torn countries have to grow up fast. We now come to events I wish I could not recall. If only there was some way to block out, forever, aspects of our lives. But, sadly, there is not. I was tempted to leave the following out of this autobiography altogether, but that would not do justice to the truth, besides which some subsequent experiences would not make sense without it.

At the garrison I was handed over to interrogators who questioned me about my identity, what I was doing, and where I lived. As done at the houses I had sought shelter in, I avoided any defined explanation or answer. Despite the horror of what had occurred, I had no wish to implicate my relatives. They became increasingly irritated, obviously recognising there was more to my story than I was saying. I doubt their thoughts went anywhere near the truth. Watching their mounting aggression, I anticipated violence. However, before they resorted to such an officer, who had been strolling round the compound with colleagues, came across and gazed at me intently. It was unnerving, especially as I was sure I had not encountered him before. Summoning one of my interrogators, he stepped away, clearly not wanting me to hear. Both quizzically looked back at me when they finished. Upon rejoining us the interrogator ordered his companions to stop questioning and to take me to a cell. The officer's continuing stare troubled and, I have to admit, frightened me, though there was no way I was going to allow that to show. The cessation of questioning was a relief, but why was I being taken to a cell?

They left me in the damp and dark overnight with only my troubled thoughts. No food. No water. What would the future hold? Did I have a future? Regrettably, I could not control my imaginings. That a child should ever have to face such frightening images, with the consequent terror they evoked, is truly a very sad occurrence. In the morning a group of officers came and peered at me through the bars as if I were some caged animal. The black, silver embellished uniforms sporting red armbands adorned with a swastika were different to any others I had seen. Sad to say, I would soon learn these were the hated Gestapo. In their detestable, harsh, guttural tongue, one barked an order. A guard quickly unlocked the cell door and dragged me to a waiting van, into which he literally threw me. He then slammed and locked the doors, leaving me in the dark. There were no windows. The sudden jerk as the van moved off unbalanced me and I fell onto the hard, cold rails of the reinforced floor, scraping my knees. Weariness, fear, the lack of any nourishment, and the harsh tones and treatment now combined to make me feel sorry for myself. A child without the least idea why this was all happening. Nevertheless, I persevered in my determination to show no weakness, doing my best to push self-pity away, down into the recesses of wherever. These criminals would not get the better of me! We bounced along for a while but, obviously without the vantage of a window, I had no idea where we headed. I was aware of the van turning from time to time but, lacking any thorough knowledge of the city, had been unable to gauge direction. Within a short time the van came to a halt. We obviously had not gone far. Thankfully, I was now sitting in a corner, on the floor, thereby avoiding any further fall or injury. I heard the lock turning and in mental and emotional anguish wondered what was going to happen now.

The anticipated brightness of day and sunshine did not materialise. Instead, I found myself peering down a dark, grubby, uninviting tunnel. Noting my hesitation, a Gestapo clad soldier roughly grabbed and dragged me out. Not relaxing his painful grip, he continued to pull me along until we reached the far recesses of the dismal place where he ejected me into another cell. Throughout he had been spitting out something in German. I may not have been able to understand the actual words but there was no doubt they were anything but complimentary. I admit the disgusting smell and state of the place increased my fear tenfold. There was no doubt nothing good could come out of such a place, nor my situation. Thankfully, I know it seems odd to say that, but it was true for the moment, once the door was locked they left me on my own. It gave me time to recompose myself as best as I could, though the worry of what was going to happen did not dissipate.

Later, with the absence of any daylight, I could not judge whether it was afternoon, evening or night, they took me to a miserable, bare, concrete walled room. They made me sit on a lone wooden chair in the centre. A Gestapo officer then commenced questioning me about my father. This took me completely by surprise and discomposed me. It was the last thing I had expected. I should explain. In order to protect us all, papa had joined the resistance under an assumed name. A name he had told none of us, just in case. For added security, he and his comrades also kept moving from one undisclosed location to another. Anyway, it soon became apparent this officer knew who I was, though at that stage, I was able to truthfully deny any knowledge of the person he referred to. It eventually transpired there was a traitor among the resistance who had discovered papa's true identity and somehow that I was his daughter. My interrogator, along with similarly disposed comrades who had now joined him, maintained a vehement barrage of shouted demands. Where was he? Who were his colleagues? Did he ever visit? Among these were constant referrals to them knowing I was his daughter and refusal to accept my denials to knowing who they were talking about. If you have ever been subjected to such a continuous cacophony, you will appreciate how destabilising it can be. My ears and head hurt but I was not going to concede. I listened carefully to judge what they actually knew. It seemed the traitor had limited information for at no stage had they mentioned uncle. With his senior diplomatic status, it could, or rather would, have been serious if they had known. I have no idea what motivated the traitor's duplicity, nor did I ever learn who he was, but admit I find it difficult to forgive. As you will come to see, his treachery had horrendous results.

Despite the befuddled state of my head, a consequence of the constant aggression and pain brought on by glaring lights, I was aware enough to know it necessary to be careful what I said. I had no wish inadvertently to tell them anything they did not know, no matter how trivial. It was not easy. For an adult it must be intimidating to be surrounded by four burley, belligerent, screaming, men. You may imagine how much worse it was for a young child. I felt frightened, berated, confused, abused and just wanted to burst into tears. Nevertheless, I remained resolute. I would tell them nothing. To that end, I stubbornly refused to answer further questions and insisted upon looking them direct in the eyes, with what I hoped was a glare of defiance. Naïvely I anticipated this would hide my nervous apprehension and persuade them to abandon their inappropriate interrogation. I should have known better, perhaps if I had been older, I may have. Matters were to get worse.

My continual denials combined with my stubbornness eventually exasperated them to the point these grown men commenced beating me, a mere child. While a couple slapped and punched me round the head and chest, the others, with their heavy military boots, kicked my legs and shins. Throughout their aggressive shouted, more like screamed, questions continued to rain down. As you may imagine the pain was considerable but I would not give in. I decided I would rather die than give them anything. Of course, the truth was I knew little and certainly not anything that would be of any real interest to them. That did not matter. I was not going to concede. I would not help these brutal invaders of my country, no matter the consequences. Even now I look back and am amazed at my resilience and young determination. Or was it just plain stubbornness? I do not think so. Whatever it was, this is where my situation deteriorated to unbelievable levels.

I consider it too horrific to provide a full account of all that passed. I do not wish to traumatise anyone. There are sufficient accounts of wartime brutality from which anyone interested may gain a reasonable idea of what went on without me unnecessarily adding to them. However, I need to furnish some insights to enable your understanding of what I endured because it links to the next part of my life.

Exasperated, angry, and annoyed, my interrogators ceased their own brutality and summoned a group of soldiers from an adjoining room. These dragged me to a small, bare walled room, where they ripped my dress off and took turns to sodomise me. I can still feel the agony and hear them laughing at my pain and distress. This would have been terrible for anyone but for someone who has been brought up in a protected, virtuous environment it was, besides being extremely painful, an enormous shock to my sensibilities. It really is impossible to convey the feelings and emotions I suffered during this maltreatment. To think this constituted my first encounter with physical sex. It is perhaps an indication of how warped these men were that they left me a virgin. Not, as you will come to see, that would prove any real benefit. Unless you have endured anything similar, I doubt you will comprehend how contaminated I felt. Added to this was the horrific amount of blood. Mama taught us early on about hygiene and how to do all we could to avoid disease. I now imagined those bestial men must have infected me with something terrible. I understand women who have been subjected to sexual abuse and violence feel unclean, so try to comprehend how much worse it was for me, especially in view of my upbringing and age.

Once these soldiers, or rather should that be rapists and sadists, finished there 'fun' I was dragged from the room and along several depressing corridors. No doubt their intent was to scare me further. It was apparent, from the screaming and cries, men were being tortured in the rooms we passed, some even calling out 'Kill Me! Kill Me!'. It was terrible. These were ordinary soldiers who knew nothing of import however, that clearly did not matter. It was evident their torturers had been enjoying themselves. I find it hard to comprehend such sadism. Our journey ended in a grey, concrete walled room that had a myriad of ghastly looking equipments hanging on the walls and arranged on tables and trolleys. The sight was enough to send shivers down anyone's spine. Naturally, as I am sure you will understand, I was already in an awful state, but now the sight of those implements combined with the horror of the pathetic cries I had heard unsettled me further. Clearly nothing good was going to occur in this room. Nevertheless, I was not going to let them see.

The officers, my original interrogators, rejoined us as I was being strapped into a chair. They tightened the wrist and ankle restraints to the point of them cutting deeply into my flesh causing me further pain and discomfort. One soldier had then grasped the corners of my lips, pushing them together to force my mouth open. I tried to bite his hand but he was too strong for me. Another man, who was already in the room when we arrived, then attached electrodes to my gums, tongue, and teeth. Despite them appearing to know the names papa used, which was more than I did, they seemed to want me to admit to knowledge of him. What difference it would have made I do not know, or was it simply they enjoyed what they were doing. I suspect it was the latter. The man who had attached the electrodes threw a switch on a small box sitting on a nearby trestle. The pain was excruciating. It felt as if my entire head had caught fire and was being run through with sharp knitting sized needles. Looking back, I continue amazed that at such a young age, I had the ability to draw upon deep resources within me. I remained determined not to tell them anything. Unfortunately, if that is the right word, matters were not to end here.

From the corner of my eye, I saw one officer nod to the soldiers standing round the room, watching the events. In response, two stepped forward and began pummelling my face as if it were a punchbag. The continued to the point of breaking my nose, allowing the blood to free flow all over me. What may I say? To me it was incredulous this was happening. They occasionally held their blows while my interrogators vehemently demanded answers to the same old questions. To say I was dazed and in extreme pain would definitely be a gross understatement. I think I drifted in and out of consciousness, presumably my body's way of protecting itself. Each time I floated off, they threw cold water over me. This continued for a while, after which the electrodes were unceremoniously torn out. The electrode man, as I will call him, then produced a pair of pliers. The sight froze me to the core though, for a moment I could not fathom their purpose. Whatever it was, it would not be good for me. I did not have long to wait. You will understand my temptation to scream. However, I managed to push the impulse down. Anyway, my battered face would have limited my ability to produce any meaningful sound. People had often commented upon my flawless teeth, which were white, even, and gleamed with a perfect enamel finish. My mouth was forced open again. I then felt the pliers gripped round a tooth. I cannot describe or convey in writing the resulting pain and agony as the first tooth was wrenched out. Again, blood flowed over my chin and onto my chest. What on earth had I done to deserve this? I looked up into my torture's eyes as he leaned over my face, thinking, through the agony, he must surely feel sorry for me and consequently stop. Of course, that was a foolish thought. All I saw in those awful eyes and his contorted features was a twisted pleasure. He laughingly waved the pliers, with the tooth still gripped in them, before my eyes. Then, throwing it on the floor brought the pliers back toward my mouth. 'You can stop this.', hissed as I imagine a serpent must sound if it could talk. It only took another brief glance into those black, pinprick, eyes to see that would never happen. Whether or not I talked he was going to go on. It is really scary to look into the eyes of a demented psychopath. He smirked as he grabbed another tooth and continued to pull one after another.

Though I was young and under normal circumstances usually fit and healthy, it quickly became apparent, the lack of sustenance and proper shelter combined with the stresses and strains of all my recent experiences had taken a heavy toll. In this weakened state and with the current agony, my mind finally gave way. Images of my mama, papa, sisters, home, and young days flashed through in quick succession. I have since understood that to be a normal experience for many when near death. Total blackness followed. No hint of light, no light-at-the-end-of-the-tunnel, nothing. An extremely desolate place. Then there was oblivion.

These are just some of the abuses I was subjected to. As said, I have no wish to traumatise anyone and will therefore keep the rest to myself, taking those memories to the grave with me. No one else should be made to suffer because of these evil beings. I cannot bring myself to call them people.

9

Emergence

The grip on each arm was firm and painful. It must have been this that brought me into a measure of consciousness. Through the mist of my altered world, a sensation of being pushed and pulled in a variety of directions penetrated. All by my arms. My arm sockets screamed. Were they trying to wrench my limbs off? A vague awareness of some incredible weight pinning me to the ground also troubled me. I wanted to ask what was going on, but my vocal cords would not respond. The pulling and pushing persisted until I felt my body dragged across sharp-edged stones. Was this a further torture? This thought was quickly belied. Through the fog, a woman's voice triumphantly whispered, 'Yes, she's still breathing, though I think unconscious.' Who was she? There had been no women among my interrogators. Nor had I seen even one anywhere in that awful place. Just before the blackness I had been fighting engulfed me again, I heard a man respond, 'Give me a hand here.' Blackness then won through. No mortal being should ever experience such darkness and loneliness.

The defused misty grey of the shaft seemed endless. Then, suddenly, a hazy yet brilliant light penetrated my eyelids. Where was I? What was happening? 'She's coming round.' The same woman's voice I heard it seemed an eternity ago. 'Fetch some water.' It was not a voice I recognised. Perhaps she was another torturer. Perhaps they thought a woman's voice might make me talk. But, somehow, I did not think them likely scenarios. Her voice was too kind. Whatever the situation, I was grateful to find my body no longer pulled and pushed. The unknown pressing weight was also gone. I wanted to see, but my heavy eyelids appeared to have a mind to remain shut. I was not prepared to give in. Drawing upon what willpower I was able to muster, I forced them open, only to be greeted by blinding, hurtful needles of penetrating whiteness. I allowed them to close again. I then felt a cup put to my lips. The cool liquid alerted me to how dry my mouth was. I gulped, but someone immediately took away the cup. 'Slowly dear, or you'll make yourself sick.' She then gently pressed the cup back, and I gratefully sipped. It felt so delightful and life-giving that all my questions, concerns, and fears temporarily suspended. Someone gently lifted my head as I neared the bottom of the cup. Once finished, they carefully returned it to the wonderfully soft pillow. I had never expected to enjoy such comfort again. I wanted to open my eyes and see who this was and where I was. As before, my eyelids had a different idea, so I surrendered to the luxurious sensation of clean, fresh bedclothes. However, the questions persisted. Who was this? Where was I? It obviously could not be the Gestapo, or at least so I hoped. The voice was too gentle, too kind, too caring. Or was that simply a ploy, a trick to beguile me? There was no telling what they could get up to. I wanted answers. I wanted to know. Once more, I drew upon the minimal resources remaining and forced my reluctant eyelids. This time with better success. I looked into the brown eyes of a homely woman who I did not recognise. I tried to ask, but nothing coherent emerged. Unintelligible splutters and gurgles were all that came out. She gently placed her hand over mine. 'Don't try to speak. You are still very weak and tired. But you're safe. Go to sleep now. We'll have a chat when you wake up.' All I could do was look back into those kind eyes. The idea of sleep sounded wonderful, but I was afraid. I did not want to return to the black, lonely place or allow myself to be vulnerable again. However, her soothing voice and gentle touch were having a relaxing effect. She had also said, 'Safe'. That sounded so good.

Upon waking, I found myself still in the soft bed. The fresh linen and luxuriant pillow wonderful to the touch. It had not been an illusion. I struggled to lift my throbbing head but the agonising headache forced me to let it fall back. The questions returned. I attempted to recall, but discovered nothing more than a dark, shadowy blank. Though unable to lift my head, I was able to turn my body and, by doing so, examine the room. Wardrobe, tallboy, small dressing table, curtained windows, all neat, clean, and tidy surround me. I recognised none and wondered how I had got here. Wherever here was. Again I tried to recall, but there was just a thick fog where memories should have been. While in this state of contemplation, the door opened and the woman with the brown eyes looked round it. Seeing I was conscious, her face lit up with a broad, friendly smile. 'Ah, you've woken up. Don't be afraid, we're your friends. We won't harm you.' My mind wondered who the 'we' meant. So far I had only seen her. I smiled back, or at least thought I did, and determined to ask her my questions. I again struggled to sit up, this time with success. The women fully entered and placed some additional pillows behind my back. 'You've had an awful experience, but you're safe now.' Her tone and features were full of compassion and sympathy, which encouraged me. I opened my mouth to speak, but it felt dry and as if full of sand. Seeing my difficulty, she placed a reassuring hand on my arm and passed me a glass of water. Unless you have ever suffered such dehydration, you will not appreciate how welcome and wonderful such moisture can be. My mouth now felt free and this time recognisable words, instead of splutters and grunts, emerged. 'I cannot remember anything. I have tried but there just seems to be an empty space. Who are you? Where is this? How did I get here?'

'One thing at a time dear, it'll take a while for things to come back. First, let me introduce ourselves. I'm Maria.' I smiled in acknowledgment of her name. At last we had some sort of connection. 'In the next room are my husband John and our daughter Clara. We're your friends, so there's no need for you to be afraid anymore.' She then told me how they had found me in a ravine where the Gestapo threw the bodies of those they had tortured and killed. Apparently, she and her husband had been walking past when they heard a groan emit from beneath a pile of bodies. Now I knew what that terrible weight had been. I could hardly bring myself to believe it. It was a too horrific, too awful, contemplation. She shuddered as she explained how it had taken them a while to locate me under the distorted and twisted remains. 'John and I took an arm each and tried to pull you clear, but the weight was too much, so we had to move some of the corpses.' Now I had an explanation for what I had thought was a further torture. Mention of the bodies must have acted as a trigger. Images started flashing through. Cells, soldiers, screams, blood, pliers, teeth, electrodes. Walls and trolleys littered with all manner of ghastly looking equipment. Dank musky corridors, brutal punches and kicks. I shut my eyes, attempting to banish these vistas. I felt sick and became aware I was sobbing, deep, desperate, silently screaming sobs. Maria embraced and held me close while stroking my hair and uttering soothing words. 'There, there, try to forget for now.' But I could not. My captors had violated and abused in ways I could never have imagined. I am not someone usually given to such a public display. I suspect, after the strength I had forced in the face of brutality, now having someone loving and gentle holding me permitted my emotions to find release. Eventually, my tears subsided. I pulled back and looked into those sympathetic eyes. I wanted to continue with my questions, but felt too drained. She must have realised. 'You need to rest now. We can talk further tomorrow.' I smiled in acknowledgment and closed my eyes, though I well knew there would be little hope of sleep for the present.

Fifteen or so minutes later, Maria returned with a pretty young girl carrying a tray. In obedience to her mother's directing, Clara set the tray down, smiled, said she hoped I was feeling better, and then left. Hot nourishing food. I could not remember the last time anything had tasted so good. A warm drink completed the banquet, which at the time it was for me. When finished, I felt exhausted. My body had not received so much sustenance in one go for a very long time. My digestion system struggled to accommodate the richness. Maria removed the extra pillows and helped me lie back. My eyelids closed as soon as my head touched the remaining pillow. This time, sleep beckoned. I felt so tired. My questions could wait. I was safe. I went to sleep.

The next morning I felt much better. With the family's gentle and attentive care, I continued to improve day by day. John and Maria explained how it came they discovered me. In their search for information, retribution for the deaths of German soldiers, or just for sadistic pleasure, the Gestapo constantly tortured and killed. Some were only boys who could not possibly know anything of value. That did not stop them. When finished they simply threw the bodies out. In the beginning, John, Maria, and a few others did their best to give the deceased a decent burial. Sadly, it soon became too dangerous, besides which the number of corpses increased to such an extent they could not keep pace. Nonetheless, whenever passing one of the dumping sites, they kept an open ear. How grateful I am they did. As they explained, bits and pieces of what I had been through floated back. It was too horrible. A heavy, depressive, dark weight smothered my soul like a damp blanket. Even all these years later, no matter how hard I try, I cannot forget. The sights and sounds of those awful days still invade the night hours when I am unable to sleep. Sometimes they prevent sleep. Though the explanations depressed me, they at least provided answers to many of my questions. It still amazes me I lived through such terrible and agonising events and yet am here to tell the tale.

My recuperation was slow but steady and eventually I felt ready to get out of bed. I asked Maria for my clothes, only to be greeted with the news I had been naked. This shocked my sensitivities. It had been bad enough when the soldiers stripped and abused me. But to be left out in the open like that, for all to see, was too much. I subconsciously attempted to cover my body with my arms. I was ready to cry when she produced a dress from behind her back. It was one of Clara's. You may remember, when I made my escape from uncle's unwanted attentions, I was only wearing a thin cotton summer dress. With the subsequent rough living it had deteriorated to the point of being nothing more than a torn, dirty rag by the time the Gestapo got hold of me. The undamaged soft clean dress felt wonderful. Unfortunately, there were no shoes for me. Considerately, Maria looked out some clean rags with which to bind my feet so that at least I could walk about without incurring further undue damage. Occasionally she found parts of old jacket sleeves for the purpose, which provided better protection. I have a lot of trouble with my feet and suspect much of it originates from those days.

As someone accustomed to open air for a good part of each day, the four walls of the house soon felt claustrophobic. I longed for the open sky, to feel the warmth of the sun on my skin, and to enjoy the gentle breath of the wind. However, it would be a little while yet before I could indulge such pleasures. My condition steadily improved, sufficiently for me to help round the house. I was very conscious this generous family was sharing their meagre resources without any recompense. As soon as able, I insisted on joining them for their daily foraging. In war, especially in occupation, when most essentials are commandeered, shortages of the most basic commodities result. Searching through refuse and whatever else someone had discarded was an awful task, but the pervading stench of death made it even more so. Bodies, victims of war, starvation, and the resulting disease ravaging the city lay all around. I can still see and smell it all. In order to cover as greater an extent as possible, we went individually in different directions. It was therefore a relief upon returning home to find the others back unharmed. The Germans never hesitated to take anyone, sometimes because they suspected them of some act, others just for the hell of it.

In the unrelenting pattern of my life, the day came when I returned to find the house empty. With pounding heart and jangling nerves, I inspected each room, hoping against hope it was simply someone had not heard me return. A mixture of clothing, scattered over beds and chairs, and empty cupboards was all I found. Two large bags were also missing. The obvious conclusion, the enemy had not taken them but they had found it necessary to make a rapid escape. The Germans disliked people helping victims of their brutality or burying the dead. Presumably leaving bodies to rot in the streets was intended to be a warning or deterrent, though it simply incensed and made us more determined to resist. We were aware they knew of my friends and had been surreptitiously watching. Asking neighbours was out of the question. Fear of any knock meant few willingly answered their doors. Added to this, most had to scavenge like us. It was therefore unlikely anyone would be in. I desperately hoped my surmise was right. They had been so very kind to me. Without them, there is no question I would have died. I am eternally grateful and hope they found safety. I never heard of them again.

Here I was once more, with no one and nowhere to go. Again, an uncertain future lay before me. Would I never know peace? It was obvious remaining in the house was out of the question. Assuming a German patrol had been responsible for my friend's rapid departure, it was likely they would return, as they had with my Jewish friends.

Shelter and sustenance became my immediate needs, again. How many more times? Where would I find them? Seeking employment as a servant for accommodation and a little food had worked before. Reluctant though I was to once more go down that path, it seemed my best option. I admit the thought depressed me. I was also terrified the Gestapo might get hold of me again. My nervous tension reached such a pitch I became like those small timid birds, which constantly twitch while swivelling their heads in all directions. I tried to be unobtrusive while knocking on doors, but people were still rude and said no. The day was passing fast. I feared another cold, miserable night in some bombed out wreck without sustenance awaited me. However, finally, someone would take me in provided, besides general housework and preparation of meals, I scavenged for them. Accepting their conditions seemed preferable to the alternative. These turned out to be very unpleasant people who just wanted a skivvy. In their mind I did not matter. Whether I died or lived was immaterial. Foraging had never been easy but now was even more difficult because increasingly people had less and consequently threw very little out. There were also many more reduced to scavenging. The fact my new employers were unwilling to place themselves in danger, forcing me to go out on my own every day, did not help. They constantly berated and criticised if I brought little back. Inevitably, they never considered I had done otherwise. Sometimes these ungrateful wretches would not even allow me a morsel, despite the fact without me, they would have had nothing. It was a miserable existence. I put up with it for the shelter and what little food they occasionally permitted me. I could also forget any idea of companionship. They never allowed me to sit with them. Once the dining table was cleared, I retired to the tiny, cold room assigned me. Depressing thoughts my only company. Please remember, I was still a child. In the absence of prying eyes, I allowed my tears free-flow. It got to the point I even considered allowing myself to be shot. There was constant gunfire wherever you went in the city. As you see, I did not, probably because I suspected it would not be so easy and feared falling into the hands of the Gestapo once more. And, of course, there is that inbuilt sense of self-survival we all suffer with. It constantly surprises me how strong it can be.

It was during my residence with this family the Allies successfully entered the country, driving the Germans out before them. My people's euphoria, as you may imagine, was immense. Seeing the hated enemy defeated and ejected after all the atrocities inflicted on military and civilian personnel alike was something we had longed for. However, sorrow tempered the rejoicing. An increasing number of loved ones, who the enemy had taken, were not among the liberated prisoners. Stories of horrific torture and treatment emerged, with many no longer the same person they once had been. Physical, emotional, and mental injuries and consequent problems abounded. Nevertheless, overall we were grateful. I think some of us had doubted liberation would ever come. My employers remained morose and showed little appreciation for the Allied victory. I may only surmise they did not look forward to having to do things for themselves. Undoubtedly, with peace, society was going to change. Few would willingly enter into the servitude they demanded.

Naturally, the Allies' victory could not immediately deal with the shortages and foraging remained a necessity. When possible, I joined the ecstatic crowds cheering as Allied convoys drove past. Some had even found flags which they waved in joyful abandonment. For me, it was not just the joy of liberation. There was now the hope of reuniting with papa and Anna, as well as freedom from unscrupulous people. I was not so sure about reconnecting with uncle but for the time being put it to the back of my mind. It would have to be faced when the time came.

Our jubilation over the defeat and departure of the Germans was, shamefully, soon marred by internal political unrest. Violent clashes between the more aggressive supporters of each faction frequently broke out. As if we had not had enough. The general public, who each party claimed they wanted to help, were the ones suffering. We did not understand why the leaders refused to set aside their differences and work together to rebuild our country. They appeared completely unfeeling toward the suffering of others. This shattering of our hopes for peace left us far more despondent than before. After all the years of tyranny and subjugation, to have your own fellow citizens be so cruel was too much. How to organise and govern our revitalised nation was the principal topic of the argument. Should it follow the capitalist culture of successful and respected countries or the militaristic society of others? There were a few other suggestions, but those were the primary contested options. Leaders on both sides were known to be intelligent men, so why would they not sit down and discuss a workable compromise? But then, many conflicts have arisen from such stupidity. Unless you have lived through such an experience, it is difficult to imagine the greater sadness of having to evade your own people as opposed to a hated invader.

I later learnt, papa had tried to bring sense into the argument. He told both sides, 'Embrace and love each other and be grateful for our deliverance from the German occupation.' Indicating they should be working together to rebuild. Sadly, they ignored him.

With great disappointment and frustration, he left the resistance. I should mention, notwithstanding the Allied victory, many resistance members were still in hiding. Despite defeat, German spies and snippers still operated within our borders, seeking resistance members. This continued for quite a while. It did seem to be taking a vendetta rather far.

Our hopes for shortages ending were wrecked. If anything, it became worse because the internal conflict made it difficult and dangerous to transport goods. Some antagonists were little more than brigands. The regular flare-ups also made going out even more perilous, not that the people I was with cared. Whistling bullets skimming past my head became the norm. It appeared my own countrymen would achieve what the enemy had failed to do, my and other people's deaths. The resurgent hopes of a future I had been entertaining now dissipated, causing me to withdraw back into myself. I simply wanted to join mama and be free of this burdensome life. It is still a wonder none of those bullets hit, even though often exceedingly close. You may wonder why I did not leave the awful people I was with and seek refuge elsewhere. Do not think I did not try. With the new freedom to travel, which the Germans had prohibited, many families had left for the countryside. At the very least, they could grow vegetables there. Of course, they also wished to get away from the conflicts now ravaging the city daily. It may help for you to know my home society is primarily based upon rural communities. Most either had some land, usually with a small dwelling, to go to or relatives they could stay with. In theory I could have done the same, but remember, I was still young and did not know how to go about it. My options were therefore to stay or end up on the streets again.

Hoping to restore peace and order, the Allies decided to support the then ruling government until administrative structures could return to full operation. The government could then arrange a general election. Unfortunately, supporters of the opposition viewed this negatively. To them, our liberators now became the enemy. Regular attacks followed. The Allies' disappointment was palpable. After liberating the country and now seeking to assist with the rebuilding, it must have been hard to face such aggression from the people they came to help. It is with a sense of shame I am forced to acknowledge my countrymen's lack of intelligence, appreciation, common sense, and common decency. They behaved like stubborn, petulant children. Hard to admit, but truth is truth.

The people I was staying with concluded it in their own interest to align themselves with the Allies. They did nothing without selfish motivation. They allowed the soldiers to use the house during patrols or investigations, aware that the soldiers were always generous. A consequence of this alignment was the opposition now also saw us as an enemy. Venturing out became even more hazardous. Little did they care, they still insisted I go. I wonder what they would have done for food if I had been killed.

The soldiers were friendly and kind. Observing the bullet riddled walls, my youthfulness, and my treatment, they asked why I was there. As you have seen, for purposes of self-preservation, I had developed the habit of not imparting personal information. However, it was good to come across someone who seemed genuinely concerned. I longed for someone to talk to and relax with. Submitting to those longings, I ventured a brief resume of my wartime experiences, though still careful not to impart too much detail. When it came to my family, I simply said we had been separated and I had no idea where they were. They were surprisingly attentive, and when I finished appeared quite concerned.

When leaving for the day, they insisted I accompany them back to their base. You will appreciate, after my recent disagreeable, to put it mildly, experience of soldiers, I was reticent. After a short period of contemplation, my young mind concluded, as part of the Allied forces, these must be good soldiers and therefore unlikely to abuse me. The family took umbrage, demanding I remain. I ignored them. Within soul and spirit leapt. Would this be the change for the better I yearned for?

10

Reunited

At the base, they showed me every kindness. Tea and biscuits in a warm, comfortable room. It seemed like heaven. A few joined me and, conversationally, asked about my family and why I had been in that house. At first, my Gestapo experience made me wary of the questioning. Would it lead to unpleasantness if I did not provide adequate or expected responses? Of course, my worries were ill founded. Gentle tones and relaxed body language belied my fears. Nevertheless, I did not tell them everything, about uncle for example. One thing I failed to tell you is, there had been a photograph of my sister Anna in the pocket of my little summer dress. Why, I do not recall. Nor do I understand how, after being left for dead naked, I still had the picture. I may only assume my torturers had disposed of my body along with their general detritus among which must have been the remaining rags of my dress. The photograph must have been in what remained of the dress's pocket. Presumably it fell out nearby and my rescuers had picked it up. In those blanknesses that can follow traumatic events, it never occurred to me to ask. I was just glad to have it again. Looking at it had been my one little comfort. The soldiers asked to borrow it. I was reluctant. It was the only link I had with my family and previous life. However, they promised to take care of it and I believed them when they said it may help trace my sister.

When they put a further cup of tea, along with bread, butter and jam in front of me, my eyes nearly popped out. I had not seen such things since before the war. Trembling, I took my first bite. Oh! What taste! My thoughts and emotions were in a whirl. Kind soldiers, good food, renewed hope of finding Anna and papa. Left alone to enjoy the miracle spread before me, I have no idea how much time passed, so taken up was I. Within what seemed but a moment, one soldier returned to inform me they had located Anna and Christopher, my brother-in-law. I sat mesmerised. How had they achieved it and how so quickly? It transpired the ruling government had provided the Allies records and details of people living in the metropolis. The intent was to help restore order and a working administration. Are you able to comprehend my excited nervousness? To be reunited with Anna so soon went far beyond my wildest dreams. I just hoped there had been no mistake.

We bundled into a Land Rover and headed toward the suburb where they told me Anna, Christopher and their two children, Vince and May, lived. My backside barely remained on the seat during the journey. As we pulled into a curb, one soldier pointed. To my amazement, disbelief at the possibility of it really being true still floating about in my head, I saw Anna running down the drive.

The next moment my body had leapt from the vehicle and shot up the path. We fell into each other's arms, tears and sobs of joy pummelling both our frames. I was not sure my heart would survive the exhilaration or ecstatic relief. Within both of us, as our hugs increasingly tightened, a deep determination never to let each other go again pervaded. How long we remained in our embrace, I do not know. It seemed a wonderful eternity. The kind soldiers stood back throughout. Anna and I finally released each other, though our hands remained firmly clasped. My saviours took the opportunity to confirm a few details. It was obvious there had been no mistake, but they just needed to ensure all was in order. Once satisfied, they gave us a warm smile and returned to the Land Rover. Releasing Anna's hand for a moment, I ran to the curb. I could not just let them leave. There were no satisfactory words for what I felt. Thank you seemed too weak and insufficient. Against my normal nature, I leant in and gave each a kiss on the cheek. They grinned and affectionately ruffled my hair before driving off. I wish I knew who they were and where to find them. They were so kind. Their help had been nothing short of a lifesaver. I hope God blessed them and gave each a good life.

Christopher had remained in the doorway, watching. I worried about how he would receive me. It was apparent I would have to stay with them, at least for the immediate future. My concern eased a little when, with an embrace, he said how good it was to see me. Once inside the questions started. Delight at the possibility of finding each other had dominated my mind for so long I had given no thought to what I was going to say. Clearly any mention of uncle's behaviour was out of the question. I had no wish to be the cause of anyone doing something awful. He may have deserved some retribution, but where would it end? I shuddered at the possibilities. I therefore decided, for the time being, to fain tiredness and fatigue. Briefly mentioning the Gestapo and their torture did the trick. Shocked and horrified, they could not do enough to make me comfortable, telling me not to think about it for now. 'We can catch up on everything later.' Anna subsequently led the way to the garden where we sat with cool drinks talking about the flowers, birds, and fair weather. It was a bit bizarre considering what was going on elsewhere. Nevertheless, it was pleasant and relaxing to pretend for a while everything was normal. Just what I needed at that moment. We enjoyed an early dinner after which I went straight to bed. I had not entirely lied about being tired and fatigued. My plan was to think through what I was going to tell and, more importantly, what I would not tell. However, I must have been far more tired than I realised. Combined with that was the sense of safety and relief. Sleep enveloped me as soon as my head touched the pillow.

With the breaking light of dawn I woke. Accustomed to rising early, in order to clean kitchens and prepare breakfasts, my instant reaction was to swing legs out of bed and get dressed. However, the strange surroundings made me hesitate. The realisation of now being with family and safe slowly swept over me, leading me to return my head to the pillow. Tears assailed while I took deep breaths to calm my beating heart. Was it really true? In the unaccustomed relaxation of being half asleep and half awake, with no pressing urgency, the previous day's events slowly filtered back. Ah, yes, I must decide what information to impart, what to conceal, and to whom I would tell what. My greatest concern related to uncle. Anna broke my meandering thoughts as she entered the room. Immediately, without hesitation, she asked what was bothering me. She was very astute, which had always made it difficult to conceal anything from her. It would be no good trying to sidestep the details of uncle's behaviour. Anyway, her questions of how I came to leave the house in the first place were probing and no cock-and-bull story was going to deflect them.

Before regaling her with all the traumatising details, I demanded she promise never to share anything I asked her not to. Though reluctant, not knowing what I was going to tell her, she knew full well I could be as determined as her. She therefore begrudgingly agreed. With considerable agitation, I told her everything. Her fury was terrifying. Had I done the right thing? I had never seen her so livid. Upon my insistence, she confirmed she would keep the secret and did so to the end of her days. Even after uncle himself departed at the ripe old age of ninety-six. I am forever grateful to her. I had no desire for any further harm to come from the episode than already had.

Here I was then about to commence, or should that be recommence, what effectively became the second part of my life. The war, as well as the subsequent internal conflict, changed us all. No matter how hard we tried to retrieve what we had once known, our lives would never be the same. Like most children subjected to war, violence, and abuse, I had matured far beyond my years. All I had experienced, endured, and seen had necessitated self-reliance. This resulted in the loss to me of those sweet, innocent years, which should be the joy of all children. Well, as much as they could have been with my disconsolation at the loss of mama. My relatives recognised the fact concluding, rightly I would say, there was little for me to gain from further education. Irrespective of whether it would be with aunt or formal school. Anyway, the school system was still in chaos and naturally, Anna and I had no wish for me to return to uncle and aunt's home. I would therefore remain with Anna and Christopher. I have to admit, despite my enjoyment of learning and gaining further knowledge, I was grateful. Too much had happened for me to want another change just yet. It now became necessary to work out what I was going to do with my time. I have never believed in taking advantage of people's kindness, no matter who they are, and desperately wanted to contribute toward my keep. To begin with, we jointly agreed I would help Anna with the housework and in the garden. However, I faced hindrances. None of us, including myself, appreciated how the toll of my 'adventures' had affected me physically, mentally, and spiritually. Every action seemed to demand inordinate effort and energy. Incessant exhaustion requiring continual rest was my lot. It was frustrating and hard to accept. All my life I had been strong, fit, and active, always able to complete my tasks. Evidently, the treatment endured from Gestapo, fellow countrymen, and of course not forgetting relatives, all following on top of mama's untimely death, had changed matters. I began to despair of life again.

Thankfully, Anna was very understanding, though as frustrated as I with my inability. She generously constrained it, treating me only with kindness and patience. Had she been otherwise, a complete fall into the depths of depression would have been my lot. With her care and regular provision of healthy nourishment, I slowly, far too slowly, recovered energy and strength. Each passing week I was able to do a little more. However, presumably due to all that had passed, I again found it hard to conceive of any future. I simply passed from moment to moment in a state of robotic automation. Indeed, an automaton would probably have held a more positive outlook. It was hearing my sister and Christopher discuss their own future that eventually stirred something within, though I did not recognise it at the time.

I mentioned how concerned I had been about my brother-in-law's reception of me into their home. With the realisation my stay would now be long term, perhaps even years, my concern increased. After all, they were just starting on the path of family life and the presence of a third child, not their own, was hardly ideal. There was also the fact I did not really know Christopher or what type of person he was. However, his continual acceptance and insistence I treat their home as my own seemed to belie my worries. As I am sure you will comprehend, I was very relieved. I doubt I would have coped well with any further negativeness. Initially, we got on well with no discernible tensions, but matters were to subtly change.

Before continuing, it will probably be sensible to tell you a little more about my sister's husband. Christopher was tall, dark, and handsome. A cliché I know but in his case true. He was confident in his manhood and had always been popular with the ladies. A hard worker, he, with a friend, ran his own household goods company that provided a reasonable, though not excessive, income. His sense of humour was sometimes almost as wicked as Anna's. I think that was one reason they got on so well, few could compete with her. In Christopher, Anna had met her match. Never was there any doubt about his love for her or hers for him. It took nine years before Anna found any sort of acceptance or inner peace after his demise.

As you are aware, my sister had agreed never to tell anyone, especially aunt, papa, and Christopher, about the incident with uncle. However, contact with him could not be avoided. They were our only relatives in the city. Anna and Christopher consequently kept in touch and visited regularly. Naturally, I was reluctant to face uncle Leonard again and for a while we used my ill health and fatigue as an excuse. Of course, that could not go on forever. Trepidation is probably the best word for describing my emotions prior to the first visit. Would I be able to control myself? Would aunt, who was as astute as Anna, notice something amiss? How would uncle and Robert react? These and many other worries kept me awake. On the day, prior to setting off, I drew my sister to one side asking her to ensure they did not leave me alone with uncle at any time. My concerns about Robert were less. The glare he had given his father and his walking away provided some assurance. Anna agreed to do her best.

When first entering the house, I stuck to Anna's side as if glued, doing my best not to actually grab hold. Aunt hugged and kissed me with tears of joy, relieved I had been found. I do not know how uncle had explained my disappearance and never asked. No doubt he had felt guilty and probably still did. If only he knew what his actions had led to, but I was not about to go into that. When his turn came, he wisely restrained himself, simply placing his hands on my shoulders as a benevolent uncle would and giving me a light peck on the cheek. Robert just gave a 'Hi, good to see you'. I remained quiet while Anna and aunt chatted. We had agreed Anna would field all questions. I drifted off into my own thoughts as I took in the familiar surroundings once again. Consequently, I do not really have any clear idea of what my sister told aunt except she mentioned my Gestapo experience. This clearly had an impact. Aunt was horrified. Though he had remained as quiet as me across the other side of the room, uncle awkwardly twitched. Engrossed in their conversation, neither noticed the passing time. Lunch was due. Upon realisation, aunt asked Anna to join her in the kitchen while she oversaw the servants' preparations. She loved her food, as her less than small frame indicated. Prior to them rising, I caught my sister's eye, thereby reminding her of her promise. I offered to join them but aunt would not hear of it. I had been through enough and should take the opportunity to be at ease. If only she had known ease was the last thing I was experiencing. Uncle was still in the room and the thought of being left alone with him was more than I felt able to cope with. How she did not see the rise in my blood pressure, I have no idea. Of course, Anna understood and before passing through the kitchen door, turned to whisper, she would only be next door. She did not wish to raise aunt's suspicions of something else being amiss by insisting I join them. I understood and was in full agreement, but still harboured considerable concern. Tension would not permit me to sit. I moved to the large window overlooking the gardens. At least it was next to the kitchen. If it became necessary, a quick escape there was possible. In case you are wondering, Christopher had not been with us.

With deep breaths I endeavoured to enjoy the wonderful display beyond the window. However, I was very conscious of uncle sat behind me. My ears developed a tension all their own, listening for the minutes of sounds. A slight rustling had me immediately spinning round. Uncle was moving toward me. Terror clenched my heart. Momentarily stopping, he held a hand up to indicate I should not fear. He then continued until barely a metre from me. The strength of my anger as I looked him in the eye surprised me. I thought I had overcome it. Apparently not, as I found myself ready to scratch his eyes out. He glanced toward the kitchen door before opening his mouth. 'My dear, I am so sorry for what happened when we last saw each other. I do not know what came over me. I was out of control. I have really been worried about you. Please forgive me.' To forgive was the last thing I felt, yet the plea in his eyes and emotion in his voice were so sincere and convincing. Nonetheless, my instant thought was, if he had not behaved the way he had, I would never have gone through what I had. The marks of those traumas would remain with me forever. I struggled before recalling mama's teaching to always try to understand other people's weaknesses and to let God be their judge. In obedience to those principles, I fought my anger, ultimately reaching the point where I could tell him it was all in the past and to forget it. Of course, at the time the last thing I could do was forget. I am grateful to tell you, I have since found it in my heart to forgive. We never spoke of the appalling incident again. His subsequent attitude and behaviour were sincere and exemplary. A little of the old friendship was restored, though I could not help but always maintain a degree of reserve.

Life went on and my health, physical, mental, and emotional, steadily improved. I regained some of the lost weight and continued my journey into womanhood. Anna helped me through the fear and panic of my first periods, explaining it was normal and the lot of all women. It seemed like a terrible life sentence to me.

One day, when my sister had gone out, I decided to have a bath. Because of the shortages of all basic amenities war inevitably results in, including water, it had been a long time since I had enjoyed the pleasure of a good soak. Despite my resident apprehensions of which I was never truly free, even though supposedly safe now, the warmth of the water lulled me into an ethereal relaxation. If you have not experienced a mind that is never at rest, you will be unable to appreciate the magnificence of such a moment. Regrettably, it was soon over, the cooling water bringing me back into the here and now.

I was towelling myself when the door swung open. Fear immediately registered. As far as I was aware, there was no one else in the house. I turned to discover Christopher standing in the doorway gazing intently. The expression in his eyes alarmed me. I had seen it all too often. He remained for a very uncomfortable minute with open mouth before apologising and withdrawing, stating first he had not realised someone was in. I should mention, in those days, we did not have separate bathrooms. We utilised large, portable copper tubs in the kitchen for bathing. Allowing the tension to leave almost had me falling back into the tub. It transpired, he and his partner had completed the project they were working on ahead of time. They consequently decided upon a well deserved early finish. Though embarrassing because he had seen me naked, this incident should have meant nothing. However, I noticed thereafter he never seemed to look at me in the same way. I began to wonder, recalling my encounters with uncle, his cousin, his son, and others, if I was about to have a similar problem with my brother-in-law. I desperately hoped not. But life rarely goes the way we hope, at least not in my experience.

During the intense summer afternoons, when it was too hot to do anything else, we took siestas. One afternoon, shortly after the bathing incident, I was resting with eyes closed, unable to actually sleep, when I heard the door open. From the corner of my eye I saw it was Christopher. A start, similar to a minor electric shock, went through me. He was surreptitiously looking back into the corridor. That did not bode well. Debating whether to let him know I was awake or fain sleep, I quickly decided upon the latter. Hopefully he would just leave. But he did not. Instead, he sat on the edge of the bed and placed his hand on my upper thigh. What to do! Images of what had happened with the others flashed back. I was like a frightened rabbit caught in a spotlight. Looking back, I should have probably made him aware I was awake, but the fear of a further violent altercation inhibited. I stuck to my original decision but moved slightly as one would in sleep. He did not take the hint but remained silent and still. After a further couple of minutes, which felt more like a year, his breathing intensified until a raspy groan emitted, after which the uncomfortable silence returned. Judging his location, I carefully opened an eye. To my horror he was wiping himself off with a handkerchief. When finished, he stood, zipped his flies, and left. You may imagine my turmoil.

What was I to do? After all I had been through and survived, I could not believe this was happening again. With considerable sadness, realisation dawned. I was going to have to get away. Aunt Frances once told me the qualities and blessings God has given me will cause nothing but sorrow. She was referring to the minuscule portion of looks I inherited from mama. As previously mentioned, she had been an outstanding beauty. It took years for me to understand. Time has proven aunt so right. Dejection and desperation became my companions once more. However, by this time, the thought of a future had taken a firm hold. I was not so willing to throw my life away as I had been previously. What to do and where to go became burning issues. I could run away but with the end of the war and final cessation of civil conflict, the need for incidental servants and scavengers had mitigated. Anyway, previous experiences suggested it was more than likely I would fall into unscrupulous hands again. Naturally, seeking advice from Anna, aunt or uncle was out of the question. The necessity of insuring Christopher received no sign I knew what he had been up to made my torment worse. Whenever asked, I told my sister I was tired. As mentioned, she was very astute but somehow I managed to deflect her. I feel I should make clear, despite what had happened, there was never any doubt Christopher loved my sister deeply. It was simply a matter of lust that so many are subject to. I should also tell you that throughout, he was never less than kind and considerate toward me, though after the bath incident his demeanour altered. He became possessive and obsessive, constantly asking where I was going, who I was seeing, what was I doing. Whenever Anna enquired about his unusual interest, his convincing excuse was in the absence of papa he had responsibility for my welfare. You will appreciate it was not his true motivation. I felt a prisoner. It was suffocating and oppressive. I needed to escape, but how and where was a mystery. An unexpected and certainly never thought of resolution would present itself, though, with hindsight, whether it was truly such is debatable.

11

Resolution

Growing into womanhood fast enhanced aunt Frances's interest for my future. I think she viewed me as a surrogate daughter. Back then, the primary concern for young women was to find a suitable husband. Sounds rather mercenary now. But, it was normal behaviour in most societies of the time. England was no exception where are many examples of not only seeking a husband but also one with a good fortune or at least a reasonable income. As for me, with all I had been through and was currently experiencing, marriage was far from my mind. Anyway, I did not really see myself as a woman, more as mama's child. I longed to go back to those precious days. Aunt did not see it that way. Why would she? She knew nothing of what had, and was, going on. To her, I was of age and it was time to take action. The first step was to bring me out into society. Yet another old-fashioned convention, but one that held good for families like ours. Remember, we were an aristocratic, high-ranking family, though through the war and subsequent events, we eventually lost most of our wealth and prestige. Deprived of mama at too early an age, I missed out on the life issues teaching she would have given me. She was a wise woman and would have ensured I knew all I needed. As you have seen, subsequent to her passing there was no one who really cared. I was consequently ignorant of all the protocols I was supposed to know about. I did not fully appreciate what 'bringing out' meant. It was to show when a young woman was available for marriage. If I had understood, it would have horrified me.

Uncle, in his diplomatic capacity, was to host a reception for the Commander-in-Chief of the allied naval task force, a British admiral. His officers, officers from our own navy, local diplomats and politicians, would attend. Aunt saw this as a chance to fulfil her ambition. Normally, a separate dedicated ball would have been arranged. However, the continuing shortages and restraints put pay to such an idea. Formal diplomatic receptions were usually restricted to official guests but aunt persuaded uncle it an ideal opportunity. I have to admit, despite all the negative emotions I was enduring, the idea of such a party excited me. Up to this point, my only experience of such had been small birthday celebrations and Anna's wedding. Not that I ever felt deprived. I never did. In those wonderful first years, my sisters and I knew we were loved and had been very happy with our rural existence.

It is strange how we can react to differing situations and circumstances. In the midst of my depression, despondency, and disconsolation, what to wear became a troubling issue. A day dress for such a swish function would never do. You will appreciate, among the shortages of vital products, dress fabric was not a major concern. My agitation increased as the day drew near. I did not wish to provide an excuse for anyone to point a finger at me or my family. People sometimes lack understanding or empathy and can be rather unkind and cruel. I need not have worried. Aunt, as always, had risen to the occasion. During one visit, she guided me into a bedroom and indicated a large linen bag hanging on the door. In response to my quizzical look, she lifted its edge to reveal a beautiful white satin dress. I have always loved white. Was it real? I could hardly believe my eyes and blinked a few times to ensure. Where she got the fabulous material, I have no idea. She explained, aware I had no evening gowns and the unlikelihood of me finding any fabric, she had utilised her contacts. To the surprise of us both, the dress fitted perfectly. A slim pink trim to the bodice provided a perfect break between the white satin and my pale flesh. I was still exceedingly thin and frail. I could not help but twirl round and round in front of a full-length mirror. It amazed me to see reflected a woman I did not recognise. This was the first time my unconscious development into full-blown womanhood registered. It was quite a shock.

Aunt stood back, an admiring, affectionate smile gracing her features. With deep sincerity, she told me I was the daughter she never had. Hugging tightly, we allowed our mixed tears of happiness and gratitude free flow. Amid sadness, there can be moments of joy. So, except for my coiffure, which aunt was going to attend to on the night, I was ready for my first proper social event. This definitely marked a change. I began to feel a young lady. It was slightly bewildering, but an alteration I could now cope with. The dress remained with aunt ready for me to don on the evening. In the interval, during some of my darker moments, visualising that wonderful creation helped lift my spirits. So often it is the simpler things that bring us genuine pleasure.

On the day I was to precede the others, so aunt would have time to dress my hair and explain the protocols for such an event. This gave me the opportunity to see the house fully dressed prior to guest arrivals. Once in full swing, brief peeps between the milling throng were all I could hope for. It was breathtaking. True to his station uncle's town house, they preferred to live in their much smaller rural property most of the time, was magnificent. In fact it does no justice to call it a house. It was, in reality, an aristocratic mansion. Rich, opulent gilt embellishments adorned every corner and crevice. The enormous mirrors and splendid furniture no exception. Light from the vast array of crystal and gilt chandeliers gave it all a further luxuriant coating. The marble floors glistened as if oceans of mottled red, black, and white. It was something that really had to be seen. Words fail to convey the wonder of it all. After the deprivations of war it was almost too much. I may only compare it to giving someone who has been starving a meal of venison and wine, delightful yet painful. Christopher was unhappy about me going ahead unaccompanied by him. I feared he would prevent me from doing so. However, he knew better than to argue with uncle and aunt. Are you able to comprehend how wonderful it was, and the relief I felt, having this liberty? To enjoy a few hours of pleasant solitude with aunt with no one else to worry about.

Aunt did wonders with my hair, pinning it into an elegant coiffeur. The metamorphosis was such I barely believed it still me looking back from the dressing-table mirror. It must be someone else. Would it announce another's name just like the mirror in snow white? My hair completed, aunt carefully helped me into the glorious gown. We stood back observing the finished article in a full-length mirror. I truly felt an adult. It was concurrently a pleasure and a shock. A tinge of sadness registered with the realisation my childhood was now over. That those precious times I had known with mama were definitely at an end. Of course, I already knew that, but this seemed to be the final, painful confirmation.

Aunt thought it best the others see me dressed and prepared as a young lady prior to my public entrance. Anna looked radiant in a silver-grey evening gown. She ecstatically admired my hair and dress while Christopher stood with open mouth. A low whistle followed. Admiration, however, was far from his eyes. The betrayed instinct one to ignore this time. I would not allow him to spoil the evening. Aunt dismissed them prior to correcting a few strands of hair that had come loose when Anna and I embraced. Just as she finished uncle, the picture of a gentleman in black tie, entered. They had agreed to act as if it was their own daughter they were bringing out. 'You look wonderful dear. Are you ready?' I nodded though, since aunt explained I would be a centre of attention, apprehension of making a mistake troubled me. Aunt had obviously registered, telling me there was nothing to be afraid of and they would be with me throughout. Uncle then took my arm, and resting it on his, guided us out of the room. Aunt followed with Robert as her escort. They were true to their word about it being a family event. How wonderful it would be to have mama was with us had been my immediate thought. I put it to the back of my mind. Tears at this stage would not be appropriate or desirable.

The sea of gathered guests was overwhelming. As was the array of shimmering gold braid and sparkling medals. The dark blue barriers of naval dress uniforms were only broken by resplendent evening gowns. I had never seen such a range of hues and colours. It was marvellously uplifting after the grey depressive darkness of war. However, with my shy disposition, I found the attention difficult. All eyes were directed toward us. Uncle noticed and gave a reassuring squeeze of my hand. What struck most about the gathering were the smiles, laughter, and relaxed chatter. I had forgotten people could be like this. Everyone had been too afraid and tense beforehand. As you can tell from my, perhaps too detailed, résumé, this event left its mark on me. It was such a contrast to everything I had been through. I doubt I could have envisioned such an occurrence during those awful preceding traumas.

Uncle and aunt bestowed personal greetings on all while expertly steering us through the throng. Upon reaching the further side of the ballroom, uncle passed me to one of four chairs set facing the crowd. Aunt and Robert took their places next to me. All eyes were now turned toward us. I kept mine averted to the floor, my nerves all of a jangle. Uncle gave a brief speech of greeting and appreciation before encouraging all to enjoy the evening. As hosts, we were then obliged to circulate, testing my nerves further. During the process several young men approached requesting an introduction. I later learnt all were British naval officers. Though it was mortifying, I had no wish to be rude or ungracious. I therefore forced my nerves down and, when required or appropriate, proffered a smile or shook an extended hand. Occasionally, between the uniformed men and glamours ladies, I glimpsed Christopher and his thunderous stare. I turned away, determined he would not spoil the evening. The reception was a great success, and I was still on a high when retiring for the night. It seemed a fairytale yet hyper alert senses told me it was all true. It had happened. I had been to a real, sophisticated party.

Subsequently, uncle and aunt began inviting me to their home on my own. Up to this point, except for the two occasions mentioned, gown and early attendance for the reception, Anna and Christopher had been with me. After lunch two days later, we adjourned to the library, where uncle and aunt asked what I had thought of the party. My excited résumé cascaded like unstoppable whitewater rapids. When finished they quizzed me as to my opinion of the young men we met. My limited response was simply to say they seemed nice and pleasant. To be honest, I had not thought of them further. You may therefore understand my surprise when uncle stated many had expressed a desire to meet me again. Apparently, several indicting a more than passing interest. Aunt added how nice she thought each had been. I did not know what to think. My consternation increased when uncle said they had invited those they considered most suitable to visit. That threw me into a right old tizzy. Considering it unwise to give my address, they had organised for the men to come to their house. Though this made sense, on the surface at least, I came to appreciate there was an ulterior motivation. Undoubtedly, papa, Anna, and Christopher would not have approved. They still considered me too young and innocent to start meeting men, let alone possible suitors. In addition, there was the question of nationality. There was the expectation that girls from families like ours would marry fellow countrymen of good standing. Nor were intercultural marriages prevalent in those days. In fact they were very rare and usually hidden away. And, of course, there was Christopher's attitude. He would not like other men getting close to me. In retrospect, I suspect uncle and aunt had noticed his obsession. Anyway, now commenced a series of, what shall I call them, interviews, meetings, assignations? After each I faced a further keen quizzing to determine my opinion of each.

All were pleasant, though I found the flow of compliments and flattery embarrassing. I was far more comfortable when conversation moved to topics of family, country, and occupations. They were very agreeable, but when uncle blatantly asked if I would consider the gentleman just departed a potential husband, I could not answer. The idea of marriage was a concept I had yet to consider. The fact he insisted upon only a yes or no without further elaboration hindered any adequate response. It may have helped if the option to discuss the principle had been available. An answer may have been more readily to hand. However, it did not take long for me to realise here was a potential avenue of escape from Christopher.

Getting away from him had become a constantly troubling issue. I know this sounds mercenary, but believe me it was not, as you will come to appreciate. The potential however, had a troublesome aspect. Leaving my homeland. The thought of ever doing so had never occurred. Nor was it something I desired. But then, desperate situations often require desperate resolutions. Would this be my way out? Should it be? Above all, I believe marriage should be based upon love. I appreciate some have other reasons they consider valid, but I question if those relationships are ever truly happy or fulfilling. Thankfully, both my enthusiastic relatives confirmed any decision would be mine and they would never force me into a union I did not want. It was a shame these meetings had to be clandestine. Anna's advice would have been welcome. Besides aunt she was the only woman I really knew or trusted.

There were several assignations, none of which made any real impact upon me. As I mentioned, all were very nice and I am sure would make good husbands. I sincerely hope they found love and happiness. This continued for a while until a young naval lieutenant eventually caught my attention. He had the same pleasant qualities as his peers, but I found him easier to talk with. There was an intelligence about him and he appeared to be a kind and sincere person. I would soon learn how mistaken I was. His shy disposition matched my own, added to which I also thought him attractive. Six feet, slim but not skinny, dark-haired, brown eyed and very handsome in his navy blues. Nevertheless, I still felt unable to provide uncle with a definitive yes, and said so. He took this as a positive asking if I therefore considered the lieutenant a possible. Upon my affirmation, he immediately arranged for a further meeting. This led to Terrance and I seeing each other several more times. Each time I found him as easy to talk with as at the first. Though still not really wanting marriage, I understood it was now necessary for a decision. My existing life could not continue. I decided upon Terrance, though still inwardly questioning whether I could make a success of married life. Of course, I did not fully comprehend what married life entailed, but thought at least, after the experiences of running households during my wartime sojourns, I would be able to do that.

Uncle and aunt congratulated me upon my choice. My decision to marry rather than remain in my single dependent state clearly pleased them. Uncle insisted under no circumstances were any of us to say anything to the rest of the family. I felt awful and conscience-stricken, though understood there was no option if the marriage was to proceed. I cannot stress enough the depth of my guilt. There was also disappointment. On the rare odd occasions when thinking about it as a young girl, my anticipation had been of a wedding filled with joy and happiness. An event shared with all those I loved and cared about most. Obviously, this could not be now. My only conciliation, I liked and had feelings for Terrance, and knew my decision was for those and not for any mercenary purpose. Aunt immediately took responsibility for sorting a dress and decorations. She really loved these occasions. Uncle would undertake all other arrangements. Their position in society gave them access to many contacts, and from somewhere aunt procured several metres of gorgeous white satin. In the prevailing circumstances I had accepted it would either be a day dress or the gown from the party. Now I enjoyed the thrill of knowing there would be a proper wedding dress. Aunt decided to take Rosemary, Christopher's sister, into our confidence. She was a wonderful seamstress and a bit of a rebel, which purported the likelihood of her keeping our secret. Entranced, I watched as she turned the beautiful material into a gown that would please anyone. Ours was a reserved, modest society, so I was grateful it had a high neck and long sleeves. The bodice comprised pleated segments to the right which were then drawn across to the left, creating an unusual and effective finish. The full skirt, constructed from multiple triangular panels, flowed out from the tapered waist like a shimmering spring. It was wonderful. The white organza headdress would form a trailing train. It was to be held in place by a tiara of freshly picked white, aromatic orange blossom. I really cannot do justice to this wonderful creation. The ensemble was finished off with white satin shoes aunt had somehow obtained in my size. On the day, the bouquet would be a mix of white roses, white orange blossom, and white gardenia. Just take a deep breath and see if your sensations can comprehend the marvel of it all, especially in that difficult postwar era. No doubt every bride says it, but I felt a queen. Could there be any more exquisite outfit?

The mix of sorrow, guilt, some natural excitement, relief, and more on the day confused, troubled, and disconcerted. My thoughts and emotions were in turmoil. It was as if a hurricane and earthquake had combined. How could something conceived in deception ever prove successful? Could, would, God bless such a union? At least it was a union with someone I liked and in which I believed we would be happy. How wrong we can be. It was also my means of escape from Christopher's attentions. Aunt immediately noted my consternation and whisked me off to the bedroom where my dress waited. I poured out my heart, in particular the guilt I felt. Knowing not telling the others was the only way did not help. Aunt understood. A measure of relaxation seeped in as she ran her fingers through my tresses. Another remarkable coiffeur emerged, enabling me to give a weak appreciative smile.

To ensure the occasion would not be a barren one, uncle and aunt invited several of their friends. Terrance invited the admiral and a few of his peers. Because of our different religious backgrounds and my earnest desire for our marriage to be recognised by my church, two ceremonies were required. My fiancé could not really see the reason for it but agreed to everything I asked which, as you will come to see, was nothing short of a miracle. The first took place in the only Anglican Church in the city, ensuring our union would recognised under British law. I found the service intriguing. It was my first exposure to any other form of service. The minister was very kind and helpful and I got through with no faux pas. We then travelled to a small church near aunt and uncle's city house for a blessing. The priest then accompanied us to undertake the actual ceremony before our gathered guests. We needed this blessing to ensure my church's hierarchy would also recognise our marriage. I was truly relieved once it was all done. At least I now considered, and felt, we were truly married in the eye of God and everyone else.

Everyone was so nice and kind and joyfully congratulated us. Terrance beamed and received his fellow officers' hearty handshakes and backslaps with a pleasure I was rarely, if ever, to see in him again. I, on the other hand, was troubled and unable to fully enter into the cheerfulness, though I did my best to smile and hide the fact. My family still knew nothing of these events. I felt a fake and a hypocrite. How could I pretend all was well? Yes, we were properly married and nothing would change that. But where would it all lead if we remained in deceit? No, I had to make a clean breast of it. I must go to them and come clean. It must be now. Not wishing to unsettle our guests' enjoyment, I carried on smiling and thanking well wishers while discreetly, I hoped, manoeuvring to get uncle's attention. Once I had, he comprehended my unsettled state and surreptitiously drew Terrance and I into one of the side rooms. I described my deeply troubled thoughts and stated I could not go on without seeing Anna and papa. The residual Nazi forces seeking papa's demise had finally been rooted out. It had therefore been safe for him to rejoin the family. Aghast is the only way to depict uncle's reaction. He had thought, my previous apparent acceptance of the situation and willing participation in the marriage ceremonies meant it was a fait accompli. That it would go no further for the time being. Of course, he knew the others would have to be told sometime, but not yet. He warned it not a good idea to do anything now. However, my distresses was palpable, and he understood my demand to go straight away was serious. I knew uncle was making sense, but the fear of having doomed my marriage had taken too deep a hold. Reluctantly, he ordered the car to be brought to a rear entrance.

I still find the following very upsetting. When I walked into the house, I had intentionally remained in my gown, Anna screamed. Christopher stood rigid with daggers in his eyes. Papa was so furious, he lunged at uncle clearly intent on doing him harm. It will help your understanding to know beside his anger at my marrying without his permission, he also felt betrayed. Our national identity had always been a governing force with him and now here I was married to a foreigner. As mentioned, in families like ours, girls were expected to make good matches with respectable fellow countrymen. This was a further blow following the treatment he had received from his peers in the resistance, subsequent to the German defeat and advent of virtual civil war. It was as if his already depleted spirit could take no more. His fury was terrible. It is the only time I saw Terrance afraid. The strength of his violent reaction shocked and subdued. Naturally, I expected disappointment and some criticism, but never envisioned anything like this. I fell to my knees with tears streaming and begged forgiveness. Papa would not heed and initially turned away. A rejection it is hard to transmit in words. However, my pleading and genuine sorrow must have registered, allowing him to listen as I explained it had been my decision not to tell anyone. Regrettably, it did not change his attitude, but did appear to take some of the sting out of his feelings toward uncle and Terrance. The lack of any affection or cordiality and the brutal looks struck into my core. I could bear it no more and in tears ran from the house. After all I had been through this alienation was too much. My heart was torn, it felt physically. I was now convinced our marriage was condemned. And indeed I think it may have been. Appreciating nothing further was to be gained by remaining, we all piled back into the car.

The others did their best to pacify me as we headed back to the reception, the last place I wanted to go. I just wanted to climb into some dark remote hole and remain there forever. But, the guests were waiting and for their sake I needed to pull myself together. Upon our return, not wishing others to see my distraught state, aunt, who we had left to bat any enquires about our absence, whisked me off to one of the bedrooms. Uncle and Terrance, to avoid any further unwanted observations from aunt's and my absence, rejoined the celebrations. During the repair of my hair and face, aunt Frances soothed me until I was finally in a fit condition to see people without alarming them. I forced smiles and friendly gestures for the rest of the afternoon. The pleasant, relaxed, cheerful atmosphere helped me momentarily push recent events to the back of my mind. I cannot but say again how kind everyone was. The admiral's wife even surprised me with an unexpected gift. A diamanté broach that, within its oblong design held a swirling pattern similar to how interweaving branches look. It became a favourite that I wore constantly until stolen, along with most of my possessions, some years later. I still miss it. My wedding dress and it were the only mementos I had from that period of my life.

As with all events arranged by uncle and aunt, the reception was a complete success. Well, at least for the guests. The hour arrived for Terrance and I to depart. Rosemary, in addition to my wedding gown, had also made me a honeymoon two-piece suit. Being March and therefore still cool, she used a warm green, black and white flecked, tweed. This was finished off with a white clutch bag aunt leant me and my white wedding shoes. Shoes were very hard to come by and, with aunt's larger size, I could borrow none of hers. Much to our surprise, the admiral had a further gift, a reservation with the city's most prestigious hotel. Further, it was not just for our honeymoon night, but for six nights! Terrance was just a lieutenant and had no real personal relationship with the admiral or his wife, so their generosity was most unexpected. Whether it was they simply enjoyed seeing two people, happily they presumed, united, or whether they saw it as a symbol of our two nations' unity, I will never know. Whatever it was, it was very generous and very welcome. I had simply expected us to stay the night at uncle and aunts with no idea where we would go thereafter.

I was both excited and nervous. I had never stayed in a hotel and considered doing so to be the preserve of the rich and famous. That I should be staying in such a prestige one was almost beyond belief. The hotel had an excellent reputation then, and in large measure, still has. From accounts given by my parents of their travels before the war, as well as uncle and aunt's descriptions of overseas travel, I knew high society had expectations. Would I be equal to it or would I make some social blunder? Thankfully, the hotel staff were friendly and quickly set me at my ease. Indeed, it is a marvellous place. The reception area alone is breathtaking. Marble and gilt, embellishments, enhanced further by a plethora of beautiful statues and jardiniere, are everywhere. The suite equalled the richness and was further set off with a marvellous bouquet and basket of fruit, a real treat in those days. The admiral had indeed been generous. It was one of the best suites, with a balcony overlooking the city's principal piazza. Unlike many metropolitan piazzas, this was, and remains, very attractive. The area has an extensive variety of trees and shrubs between which several classical statues are set. A large central fountain with a well-proportioned bowl sits in the centre, providing respite for birds and stray dogs in the summer heat. Despite primary roads surrounding all sides, it provides a haven from the hustle and bustle of city life. Even today it is a pleasant place in which to take a break sitting on comfortable benches or in one of the cafes that have been there for generations. It is also a place from which to watch life. Much of the city's pedestrian traffic cuts through the square.

Notwithstanding the lovely suite and pleasant surroundings, I was not happy. I had told no one that Terrance had been hitting me long before our marriage. This usually occurred when we spent time on the roof terrace of uncle's mansion. No one had noticed because he was always careful to direct the blows to areas not visible when clothed. I realise now I should have said something. But being the innocent and naïve girl as I was, thought once married he would stop. How wrong. It actually got worse. I did occasionally ask why he was doing it, but he either ignored me all together or would say he did not know. Inwardly, I often questioned if it was my fault, if I had done something wrong.

12

Transition

Well, here we were, our life together stretching out into who knew where. Clearly, it would not be as anticipated. The fact we were both ignorant of sex did not help our situation. Neither of us knew or understood what it entailed. In those days, unlike now, sex was either the preserve of married couples within the confines of the bedroom or of the wayward. No respectable family would even hint openly about such base behaviour. Many considered sex dirty and not a fitting topic. Though I believe today's promiscuous lifestyle hurts many, I do not consider the old-fashioned silence provides the answer. At the relevant time, as judged from their individual development, young people should be informed and educated. They need to understand sex is to be respected and should be primarily part of a loving relationship. Enough of that. Back to my story. My ignorance of sex was further exacerbated by my inherent shyness. I think Terrance, though I doubt he would ever admit it, also suffered with some degree of shyness. At bedtime, I would change behind the wardrobe door. The thought of him seeing me naked was anathema. We would be married for quite a while before any such intimacy took place. Then it was not very pleasant. Yet another understatement.

We spent our honeymoon exploring the city, especially the many sites of historic interest, and eating in pleasant restaurants. Thankfully, Terrance had not started hitting me in public. That would come later. It was really nice to be able to discuss intelligently all we saw. How contrary people can be. Friendly discussion one moment, abuse at another. The weather was warm and comfortable. When relaxing over lunch, enjoying a coffee, or just sitting on a bench admiring the views, I asked him to describe his family and life in England. I wanted to learn as much as possible before meeting my new relatives and experiencing their considerably different culture. I must admit to being unsure whether British life and I would be compatible. The least I could do was be as prepared as possible and hope not to cause any offence through lack of understanding or knowledge.

Our six nights ended all too soon. I was sad to leave the hotel and our lovely suite, but it was time to re-enter reality. Terrance had to return to duty. Where would we stay now? We had no home and there had been no indication of us returning to uncle's house. I cannot express how grateful I was to find the allied administration had it all in hand. They had taken over a lesser hotel for accommodating serving officers and their families, or those soon to become such. To my delight, it was just down the road from the one we had been in. We could continue enjoying the same pleasant surroundings. It would also provide an excellent opportunity to get to know other officers' wives and learn more about British society. Gratefully, I may tell you these ladies proved very kind, tending to treat me, in a nice way, as the baby of the group. I was the youngest by far. They would take me with them when out for a stroll, a coffee, or window shopping. I learnt much about their culture. It sounded a little cold and their accepted practices and social taboos began to worry me. Would I be able to fit in? These relaxed outings also helped prepare me for the evenings. Terrance's violence was now regular. His return from duty always heralded a beating. I had given up asking why. It seemed my hopes for a happy settled life would never see the light of day. I would never experience again, the love once known, so many years before. I hoped mama could not see.

It was during this time our first sexual encounter occurred. Terrance had become aware, unless a marriage is consummated, it would not be seen as valid. I assume he had been discussing marriage with his peers. That knowledge must have frightened him, knowing I had every reason to leave him. He knew nothing of the troubling issues negating my return to either of my family's homes. He obtained a sex guide from somewhere, a fellow officer I suspect. As said, we were both ignorant of the subject. The result, one night he violently threw me on the bed, tied my wrists, and then proceeded to, what I may only call, rape me. It certainly could be called nothing else. Remember, despite the Gestapo's horrific abuse, I was still a virgin. Losing it brings no happy memories and in fact put me off intimate intercourse. This became the pattern of his so-called lovemaking. It appeared, without the violence, he was unable to perform. There is really no need for me to tell you how horrified, distressed, miserable, and dirty I felt.

The months passed. Spring gave way to summer. Summer slowly surrendered to autumn and the time for us to leave my homeland arrived. Naturally, we had expected it. However, now it was here I felt apprehensive about leaving all I knew to go to something that seemed totally alien. We ladies were relocated to a transportation hotel to await the preparation of our vessel while our men sailed ahead. I steadily became more anxious. First, everything was becoming a little bewildering and second, I worried if my new family would be kind and friendly or rough and harsh. My husband's behaviour did not bode well. The other wives and finances yet again took care of me, ensuring I understood what was going to happen. I visited my sister and her husband when the naval administrators announced the date for our departure. Anna and I had made up after the shock of my unannounced marriage. A reconciliation for which I was grateful. The prospect of leaving my family with such an unresolved situation pending between us was depressing. To be emotionally separated and in disagreement while knowing that thousands of miles would stand between us would have been unbearable. It is strange what stays in our minds. I recall, due to the cooler weather of autumn, I wore a green roll neck wool jumper. My young niece, in that innocent, heartrending way young children have, looked up and told me, 'You look so beautiful. I love you.' That was it. The tears would stay back no longer. She was such a dear then, but, as you will come to see, was certainly not the same person in adulthood. With a heavy heart I returned to the hotel. I would not see my sister or any of our family for goodness knew how long and this was to be my last night in my homeland.

Early the next morning, official transport took us to the port. When we alighted on the dockside, I was awestruck and a little overcome by the massive edifice towering above us. I had never stood so close to a liner. It felt at any moment we would be crushed beneath it. Except for my recent sojourn in the city, I had been accustomed to open fresh pastures. Now it felt as if the towering steel wall was absorbing all the air. I fought to breathe. Probably more due to my nerves than anything else. One lady, who became a firm friend during our cruise, noted my inert condition. Gently taking hold of an elbow she steered me toward the gangplank. This was it, my final step with which I would leave my homeland and enter a strange new world. Was I afraid? Yes, so much had happened in such a comparatively short period during which it had never occurred I would ever leave the land I loved so much.

The liner proved another alien world I would have to adjust to. I am grateful mama taught us to accept and respect other people, no matter their origin or customs. She had also instilled a thirst for knowledge that helped me, albeit subconsciously at times, to be open to new ideas and concepts. I believe this truly helped in those initial transitory times. Laura, the friend who had helped me onboard, proved far more kind and generous than could have been anticipated. Without her I think I would still be looking for my cabin. She also tried to explain the bewildering world of passageways, gangplanks, ladders, and deck levels. My confusion must have been obvious because she undertook to collect me when it was time for dinner and continued to do so for most of the trip. Regrettably, Laura had also suffered at the hands of the Gestapo. Her body still bore the marks. We agreed to both do our best to put these memories to the back of our minds. We would love to forget, but that is never possible after such trauma.

Why is it nasty things happen to some of the nicest people? Laura was the fiancé of a naval lieutenant. At his request, she was heading for his village in England to get married. Upon arrival, she found he was already engaged to an English girl and preparations for their wedding were well on the way. Naturally, she was upset, but not one to take such matters lying down. Laura was not a cruel or vindictive woman but thought it only right he should be held responsible for his actions. To that end she took him to court for breach of promise, a legal statute still active then. The court must have concurred with her viewpoint, because a settlement of two thousand pounds was ordered. Does not sound much these days but then was a substantial amount. Though some may have thought it, I may safely state my friend was not a fortune hunter. Her fiancé was not wealthy, nor did he have a vast income. Laura had truly fallen in love, leading her to willingly leave homeland and family in anticipation of a happy life together. I never met the man so may not proffer any opinion of him. We lost contact after Laura returned home. I hope she found happiness and someone who truly cared for her.

Back to my tale. The voyage was thankfully uneventful, and we arrived in the port of Southampton on schedule. Terrance's ship had arrived a couple of days earlier, enabling him, together with his family, to be on the dockside ready to meet me. Understandably, I was anxious whether his parents and sisters would like me. Whether they were as rough and inconsiderate and as brutal as he. I had heard accounts in my homeland of new wives who had to live in their in-laws' homes being treated no better than a servant. Sadly, my elder sister suffered similarly, but that is another story. While the ship manoeuvred into its berth I stood on the side deck observing the gathered crowds and vast array of port buildings and warehouses. I had never seen such an extensive concoction of buildings, even in my home port. It was concurrently impressive and frightening, appearing to have a life of its own like some gigantic mythological beast.

My husband's parents had decided, rather than struggle on a train with my luggage and packages, to hire a couple of cars for the occasion. Private car ownership was uncommon then. However, in the end they did not have to because grandfather, who was well off, owned a Rolls Royce. In addition, a spinster aunt, who had well-paid employment, also had her own automobile. Add to this a couple of generous neighbours and you have a small fleet of waiting cars ready and willing. A consequence, of course, was a far greater crowd than expected waiting to welcome me. It was rather overwhelming, especially as I had only expected Terrance and his parents. I did my best to keep the panic in check and to hide my apprehension. Never certain what to expect, I was relieved when Terrance gave me a kiss as I stepped from the gangplank. Once I was safely on terra firma he commenced introductions. 'Ralph, my father.', his blunt opening. Ralph was a slim, straight-backed man of five feet ten. He stuck a stiff hand out, shock mine and uttered a curt 'Welcome'. I was disappointed to note his smile revealed nicotine-stained teeth. After this rather wooden introduction and greeting, my mother-in-law, Vera, decided to take charge. She was a tall, slim lady with weary, but smiling, eyes. A warm hug and kiss on the cheek reassured me of her good nature. Turning toward her three daughters, she was about to start introductions when Joy, the eldest, unceremoniously intervened. Joy was and remains a confident, elegant woman. Then there was Doreen, a shorter, more rounded woman, who appeared to shy away from me until a stern glance from her elder sister forced her to give me a quick peck. Finally came Moira, the youngest. I noticed Joy's voice and tone soften as she took extra pains to explain in one or two-syllable words who I was. Then, putting her arm round Moira's shoulders, she gently pushed her forward for me to receive a wet, sloppy kiss straight on the mouth. I learnt later my youngest sister-in-law had contracted a serious illness when quite young that had left her with a simple disposition. Whilst talking about Terrance's family, I should mention he was a twin. However, his brother, who was born first, probably forced out prematurely by Terrance, died at birth. Introductions to the others gathered followed. It was bewildering, and I was sure I would not remember all their names. For the time being, I would concentrate on immediate relatives. I could learn the rest later. I confess I felt a bit shellshocked but was gratified to find everyone friendly. Perhaps my fears, with the exception of Terrance, would prove groundless. I hoped so.

Once through customs, we all piled into the waiting vehicles. Joy, Doreen, and Moira kept excitedly asking about my family, my home, and the liner journey. Though feeling somewhat besieged, I did my best to answer. Vera obviously noted and told the girls to quieten down, telling them I was tired from my journey and should be allowed time to rest before arriving home. She turned out to be a woman of few words, but with great understanding. I was grateful, so much had changed in my life yet again and all over a short period. Time to collect my thoughts before venturing into another strange world was what I needed. The girls' bombardment cessation enabled me to rest back and observe the passing scenery. It was so different. The first thing that struck was no arid fields. All were so lush and green. A result, I would come to learn of the substantial rainfall this country enjoyed. It was so refreshing to look at. I liked it. The crops and meadows were also unfamiliar, as were the patchwork quilt fields. I was a little disappointed to note no vines, rows of melons, nor fig, orange, lemon, peach, or apricot trees. However, the pastures of grazing sheep and cattle were a delight. In my home climate, few breed cattle and there are few sheep. Goats, being far more hardy, are a primary stock. The rolling, undulating hills and downs were also unforeseen. No forest-covered mountains and rocky outcrops. The abundance of deciduous trees also surprised. I was accustomed to pines, cypresses, olives, and evergreens. Yes, it was all very different, but I found it pleasantly refreshing. It gave me hope a calm, quiet life might be a possibility. A hope never to be realised.

We eventually entered more suburban territory, where the clean, neat roads and pavements were a further delight. Back home, especially in rural communities, the largely unmade streets and lanes are always dusty, and often rough. The rows of shops with their pleasing facades and window displays were another unexpected encounter. Our small rural shops have mostly dark interiors and very utilitarian fronts where the range of products is usually displayed in higgledy-piggledy hillocks. The one disappointment was the endless rows of all the same, depressing, dull brick and masonry terraced housing. I was used to open, airy, detached residences, all built in varying designs and at all sorts of angles. Each bright and cheery with wonderful displays of flora and happy conversing households enjoying it all. There were no such scenes here. It all seemed rather cold in comparison. Of course, I now realise the English climate rarely lends itself to such pleasantries. Nevertheless it was slightly disheartening. I worried the people would be as dull and cold as the houses appeared.

Lost in these thoughts, I have no idea how long we travelled. Eventually Vera, who was sitting in the front, turned and told me not to be surprised by the reception we would receive when arriving at their house. Apparently, a journalist had heard of my pending arrival and had written a small piece in the local newspaper. Remember, I mentioned how intercultural marriages were not the norm at the time and consequently attracted a lot of interest. As we turned into a residential street Vera let out a deep sigh and informed me we had arrived. I noted, with a thankful heart, properties on one side were not as dull as those we had been passing for what seemed hours. These were semidetached with small front gardens sporting various flowers and shrubs. In what now seemed usual to me for this country, a continuous row of small terraced houses occupied the other side. Quietly, I hoped my new home would not be one of those. I was prevented from taking anything further in because, despite my mother-in-law's warning, the waiting reception was far beyond anything either of us could have foreseen. I could see Vera was as shocked as I. A waving, cheering crowd completely blocked the road. It looked like a street party expecting a film star, or even royalty. Flags together with white, blue, and red bunting adorned the lampposts. It was overwhelming. The crowd at the port had been difficult enough, but this was beyond. Beside the neighbours, people from round the city had turned up. The newspaper article had certainly done its work. We were forced to stop and alight some distance from the house. The jovial crowd initially parted to allow us to exit the cars and then closed in again. Everyone seemed to want to shake my hand, proffering their own personal greeting. Though appreciating the kindness, I felt mortified. Such public attention is not something I have ever craved or enjoyed. My father-in-law appeared equally troubled. In time, I learnt he was a private man who disliked such attention as much as me. Of course, thunder hovered in Terrance's eyes. How could it not, with the throng surrounding me, especially so many men? I wondered what it would cost me that night. Besides the general population, journalists, radio commentators, and photographs manoeuvred to get close. The constant flashing bulbs added to my unsettlement and proved quite blinding. I did my best to answer the rapid-fire of questions, but gave up all hope of remembering any names. Though I had done my best to learn as much as possible about this country and its social observances, I remained wary. What if I made a social blunder and offended anyone? That would be terrible. We eventually managed to beat our way into the garden of my new home that, I was very pleased to see, was one of the semidetached properties. Even then people leaned over the wall in their curiosity.

Either Ralph or Terrance, I am not sure who, unlocked the door and we all, with considerable relief, piled into the narrow hallway. Do not get me wrong, we all appreciated the genuine kindness shown. Nevertheless, it had been overbearing. It was as if the claustrophobic crowd had crushed the breath out of us. We all needed time to recuperate. Vera ushered us into the front room, which I came to appreciate was indeed very special. The room was usually reserved for formal visitors, Christmas, and other special occasions. It was a mark of how my new in-laws viewed me. Shame Terrance did not see it that way. She and the girls then went off to prepare some refreshment, leaving the men quietly chatting in a corner while I occupied a comfy armchair by the window. I was grateful to have a few moments in which to clear my head. Over refreshments, with the ubiquitous cups of tea, the others gleefully recited who they had seen or recognised in the crowd. I wonder where the English would be without their tea. Revived and refreshed Vera took me on a tour of the house. It was different, but pleasant enough, especially the elongated garden at the rear. We then climbed the stairs to the third-floor rooms, which my mother-in-law informed me had been set aside for Terrance and I. How thoughtful to allow us space of our own, not something every family did. The only concession was we were to have our meals with the rest of the family. There was no room for a separate kitchen beside which these would provide opportunity for us to get to know each other better. Vera then left me to freshen up and see to the luggage a neighbour had recovered from the stranded cars. Changing into a comfortable dress and cardigan, I prayed our Lord would make this a happy and contented home for us. I was still naïve enough to think matters would be different now we were in my husband's own home. How ridiculous.

By the time I returned downstairs dinner was on the table. English food is so different and initial sight of the dark brown gravy almost had me vomiting. I had never seen the like. Already starting to feel homesick, the strange fair exacerbated my sensations of being parted from all I knew. Would I be able to cope with this new culture combined with my husband's tendencies? It is hard to believe now how the sight of the gravy affected me. I now absolutely love a well cooked English roast with all the trimmings, including the gravy. We often fail to appreciate that change is not always bad.

It is needless to say, after the wonderful greeting we had received, my beating that night was worse than usual. I suppose it confirmed my worst, though suppressed, fears of nothing changing. Whatever

I may have hoped, underneath it all and despite my inherent naïvety, I must have had some inkling Terrance would not change.

13

In-Laws

I will break my own tale for a moment to tell you a little more about my new relations.

Vera, my new mother-in-law, was, as you have already seen, a kind, thoughtful woman. I think she knew her son hit me, but she loved him. Anyway, along with sex, such things were never discussed. To even mention a taboo topic usually resulted in the offender being ostracised from decent society. Whenever she saw me homesick, dejected, sad, or depressed, Vera did her best to cheer me. I have to say, if it had not been for her continual care and support, I very much doubt I would be here to share my story with you. She saw I struggled with English food and that Terrance's behaviour affected my appetite, so she negotiated with the family. Rationing was still in force, meaning people had to make the most of what little was available. Vera was a wonder at it. Every day, three nourishing meals, together with afternoon tea, appeared. How she managed this still amazes me. She must have been observing what I could eat and what I clearly could not stomach because, though I did not learn of it until years later, she negotiated for the others to exchange some portions of their allowance for those I was unable to cope with. By so doing she ensured I received some decent nourishment. Vera was also an incredibly talented seamstress. A talent much in demand and utilised by her to bring additional income into the meagre family pot. Forever there were piles of customer's dresses and outfits laying round waiting completion or collection. Despite all the demands of the household, Vera never failed to have everything ready on time. I continue astounded at how she achieved all she did.

Ralph, my father-in-law, was a quiet man who did not believe in showing emotion. More than likely due to his education and upbringing during a period when to reveal how one felt was considered bad form. In other words, to adopt a popular idiom, not to wear your heart on your sleeve. Possibly as a consequence, or maybe by nature, I am not sure which, he was always formal and reserved with strangers. People found it difficult to converse with him, though he never portrayed aggression or rudeness toward anyone. Much to the family's astonishment, he took an almost immediate liking to me. He often asked me to sit with him to talk about the everyday matters he had been contemplating or events reported in the news. He even teased me. On one occasion, he warned me against eating too many wine gums, a sweet I enjoyed. If I did, I would get drunk. I enjoyed his company, discovering him to be an honest, truthful and genuine man. His quiet tone was also relaxing and refreshing, providing an oasis from the norm of my marital life. For his part, I suspect he viewed me as sufficiently removed from his immediate family to be comfortable discussing a whole range of topics. He also knew I was trustworthy, never repeating anything told in confidence. My one disappointment was that he smoked. A habit, or should that be addiction, shared by his son. A habit I had more than one reason for disliking.

You have already heard about some of Terrance's proclivities and will read far more in subsequent chapters. Nevertheless, I feel it is worth mentioning a couple of his peculiarities here. It will probably surprise you to learn my husband did not drink. In fact, he never, not once, set foot inside a public house, bar, club or the like. Second, despite the brutality, he never used foul language. Hard to believe I know, but all true. He did, however, smoke incessantly. At times chain-smoking, lighting the next before the existing one had extinguished. With my healthy, hygienic upbringing I found this difficult. The ash and constant smell that embedded itself into everything was horrible. As you will no doubt have already guessed, I said nothing. Thoroughly washing everything and opening the windows while he was at work was the best I could achieve.

Now to my sisters-in-law. Joy is the eldest, most balanced and organised of the three. She always knew what she wanted and would go for it, provided no one would get hurt in the process. An intelligent and practical woman who also has an artistic streak. Embroidery, home furnishings, seashell pictures, wonderfully fine porcelain figurines, are among her many achievements. Joy has always been elegant and, in her younger days, required a new outfit for each of her weekend outings. Outfits her mother, despite the ever present demanding schedule, somehow always made in time and to the latest styles. I still have a black-and-white photograph of Joy on a bicycle in a smart dress and coat.

The second eldest, Doreen, had inherited all the difficulties of a middle child. Not having received the attention a firstborn enjoys or remaining the baby of the family for very long. This was exacerbated by her younger sister's obvious need for greater care subsequent to her serious illness. A talented knitter, Doreen unexpectedly, considering her reticence when first greeting me at the port, presented me with a beautiful FairIsle twinset. I loved it and was certainly grateful for the warmth it provided in the colder climate.

I have already mentioned Moira, the youngest of the three girls. Moira was a lovely innocent. Vera had a real battle with the authorities subsequent to her daughter's devastating illness that resulted in some brain damage. In those days, accepted practice for such people was for them to be installed in an institute, usually a mental hospital. Regrettably, in many instances, if not the majority, this was quite unnecessary and very cruel. There was no way Vera was going to allow that. Though a peaceful and kind woman, when aroused my mother-in-law could prove very determined. The battle apparently ragged for sometime. It was not until those in power came to appreciate Vera's NO, meant NO! that it ended. Moira became her constant companion thereafter, helping as best she could with whatever was to hand. My advent simply expanded the group to three. At the time there was little else for me to do beside which I wanted to contribute to my and Terrance's upkeep. An endearing trait of my young sister-in-law, though I have to admit it could sometimes be a little inconvenient, was leaning close to whisper a secret. Of course, it was never anything serious, generally relating to some experience. For example, how people behaved when she was in hospital or what the doctors had done. This continued into her seventies when she sadly made her final departure, though I think it was far later than many had expected. I think it is very unkind to treat people who suffer a condition like Moira's, as if they are imbeciles. Provided we stuck to matters she had some understanding of, it was always possible to have a conversation with her. In a visit, shortly before her passing, we, my son was with me, he got on well with his aunt, mentioned going out of the country. Moira's immediate response was to tell us to not to forget our passports, and to make sure we locked the house and car up. She clearly had some comprehension of life's requirements.

A quick aside to share an amusing incident from these times when it was just the three of us in the house, Vera, Moira, and me. The rest were at work during the day. Back home in the village, when I was still a young child, there was no such thing as running water in houses. Almost every day we had to fetch what we needed from the nearest supply. In our case it was a very old, long running underground stream that flowed through a rock wall in a small valley behind our house. It still flows to this day. Thankfully, a road has been constructed now, but back then it could only be reached by means of an excessively steep, very narrow path. I remain amazed none of us incurred any injuries, except for scratches gifted by the overhanging undergrowth. Water barrels and buckets had to be taken down and then carried back up the steep, hazardous track when full. No easy task. Buckets were carried on poles placed across shoulders, barrels on backs. As with many, if not most, children, I wanted to do as the adults did. One day, despite being told it would be too heavy, I insisted I wanted to carry one of the water barrels. They kept telling me I would not be able to lift it but I stubbornly persisted. I think, appreciating my genuine desire to help, they decided to concede and let me find out for myself. Copying the adults, I sat on an outcrop so they could fit the straps over my shoulders while the barrel was standing on the same level. It almost pulled me head over heals when I tried to stand. Determined, I continued to strain and strain but it just would not move and I become cross and irritated. Mama, wisely, had not interfered and let me continue until I, with considerable frustration, admitted defeat. Sometimes we have to learn from experience, even though I should have known mama and the ladies could be trusted. Mama told me they understood I wanted to help and could do so by carrying one of the buckets. It still brings a smile to my face when I see me trying to shift that barrel.

Obviously, as you have seen, we were not able to carry large quantities of water home, so everyone took their laundry to the stream. Believe me, doing the washing, including bed linen, by hand in the stream was not easy. However, we all enjoyed the opportunity to chat and laugh while scrubbing and bashing our linen against rock indentations, which acted as scrubbing boards for us. I have to tell you it was, and remains, a beautiful spot with the steep valley sides, wild flowers, and sentinel trees. It has always been a favourite place of mine and one I insist on visiting whenever we go over.

From the above you will appreciate how exciting it was for me to find that, in my in-laws home, we could do our laundry in the comparative luxury of an indoor space. With running water! In those days washing machines were the preserve of the wealthy. The rest of us had to utilise our own limbs and strength when laundry day came round. On my first occasion, Vera showed me the large stone sinks and mangle housed in the utility room, secreted away at the rear of the building. Once sure I understood how to operate the mangle without trapping fingers or crushing buttons, she passed over the box of soap powder and left me to get on. This was the first time I had seen soap powder. Back home we used the block soap my mama made. Thinking how easy the powder would make washing, compared to the hard work of rubbing clothes with block soap against a rough surface that I had been accustomed to, I turned the tap on and poured some in. At first, watching the bubbles as they rose, with the various colours of the spectrum reflected through them, was fun. However, that ended when I realised they were not stopping. Horror struck as I watched the overflowing suds spread across the floor and then rise like some phosphorous mystical being. Not knowing how to deal with the carnage, I ran to the kitchen, grabbed Vera by the arm, and dragged her to the utility room. Anticipating a scolding, I waited. However, instead of being cross, she simply laughed and explained I had put too much powder in. Moira had fun playing with the bubbles while her mother fetched a mop and bucket, and the two of us cleaned up. I have never forgotten the episode. Subsequently, I always started with little powder until accustomed to the proper measurements.

Well, that turned out not to be such a quick aside nevertheless, I hope you found it interesting. It certainly provides insight into a completely different way of life.

Any fears I had of the girls considering my presence an intrusion were soon dispelled. All three treated me as an actual sister. This helped me feel more at home and less awkward. I was still unsure of English customs and fearful of making some horrendous blunder. They soon taught me what was, and was not, acceptable. For example, in my homeland it is standard practice when greeting someone to kiss them on both cheeks. This applies across the board, woman to woman, man to woman, woman to man, and man to man. I now had to adjust to what seemed the colder exchange of a handshake and a smile. It was certainly a huge taboo for a man to kiss another man, even if it was only on the cheek. As said, I found this reserve rather formal and cold but quickly realised it was simply a difference in culture. There was also the stiff-upper-lip syndrome to adjust to, of which my father-in-law was certainly an archetype. But, within short time it became clear the British could be just as considerate and caring as my people.

Though their mother consistently provided them with beautiful, stylish outfits, all three girls still enjoyed clothes shopping. I should mention in those days, unlike now, visiting a town centre was not a frequent daily occurrence. Such visits were special and exciting.

Winter was approaching fast, and Vera became concerned for my welfare. I was underweight and still trying to acclimatise. Deducing from her heavy workload she probably would not have time to make me an overcoat she decided we better buy one. There were also the limitations of my meagre wardrobe, primarily consisting of lightweight clothing. They were appropriate for my home climate but not for the inclemency of this country. When Vera announced the proposed outing, Joy and Doreen had virtually knocked the rest of us over in their haste to change into smart day dresses and shoes. Moira had hardly remained still while her mother tried to dress her. Their energetic glee was infectious and, though I had little idea of what to expect, it also rubbed off on me. It heightened the curiosity I was already feeling. Shops back home, especially in the rural community I initially grew up in, were little more than open fronted storage units. A multitude of products wrestled for placement within each. Clothes were not one of them. Talented mothers, grandmothers, sisters, wives, and friends made everything we needed. I remember one occasion when we were with the usual evening gathering of ladies, I mentioned these earlier, mama chose to work on a skirt I had asked for rather than the usual embroidery, crocheting, or lace making. While in Vienna she had purchased a Valencia skirt, the base material of which was a charming mid-blue. Upon this, circling the complete skirt, had been sewn wine and dark blue ribbons similar to the style you sometimes see on Spanish flamenco dresses. I thought it wonderful and asked mama to make me one the same. I had been absolutely thrilled with it and when first trying it on had rushed from room to room looking at myself in the various mirrors. Naturally, I also showed it off to my friends. Along with all other clothes mama had purchased abroad, mine was also to be kept for special occasions, such as weddings, christenings, and birthdays. It was however, considered too bright for church despite its ankle length. All our clothes had to be ankle length then, as suited the modesty and church teaching of the time.

Back to the tale in hand. One weekday, a small troupe of five women emerged from the house and headed off down the road. Like most British towns of the time, ours comprised a primary high street lined on each side by impressive, bright, clean, smart, cheery, plate-glass fronted shops. Side streets housed smaller ones which were just as presentable. I had never seen the like, even in the metropolis of my home country. Once inside, the range of goods, fabrics, designs, and colours blew my mind. Never had I faced such variety. At best I had anticipated a choice of one or two styles and perhaps a couple of fabrics. The girls sedately, not wishing to make an obvious spectacle of themselves, lifted various outfits asking each other if they thought it suited. It was clear they could spend hours thus occupied. However, being the practical woman she was, Vera insisted we first see what coats were available. Then, if time permitted, the girls could have a good look round. For my part, I was so taken aback I had simply stood and watched their pleasure.

The coat department was yet another revelation. So many styles, colours, and fabrics. I had fun trying on so many, though it felt slightly sinful to indulge in such materialism. Church doctrine infiltrated every aspect of life back home. But it could not be so wrong could it when I felt so lighthearted. A strange sensation I had forgotten existed in the midst of my husband's brutality. Ultimately, I settled on a mid-grey, herringbone weave, full length, all wool coat that felt wonderfully soft and warm. It would certainly insulate against the cold and damp. Vera approved, having first checked the stitching and strength of the fabric. She then suggested, while we were at it, I get a good pair of sturdy shoes. My own were definitely not up to the hardships of an English winter. This turned out to be another delight. So many shoes in one place and of such variety. The only issue was size. International sizes were a thing of the future. Consequently, the assistant requested I put my feet inside a large wooden box. It seemed an odd request, but as none of my in-laws flinched, I accepted it to be a normal practice. It horrified me when I looked down through an aperture in the top. Luminous green skeletal feet stared back at me. It terrified me. What had happened to my feet? Would I be able to walk again? Noting my distress, the others quickly affirmed it was nothing to worry about. It was simply a machine that used x-ray to assess foot size. I was relieved my feet were still in one piece when I took them out. The assistant brought me some shoes to try on while I calmed down. Yet again the choice was mesmerising. Prior to my trying any, Vera lent in to discuss the requirements. Just any shoe would not do. They had to be fit to counter the decidedly moist climatic conditions of this country. A closed pair with a sensible heal would be best. I could go on but I think I have bored you enough. My eventual choice was a rich deep blue pair with a lovely wine coloured trim and delicate bow. Again, having checked the stitching, soles, and heals, Vera approved. I loved the look of those shoes but, as you will see later, came to regret my choice. This had indeed been an interesting, exhilarating, and revealing day.

Just a little more, before closing this chapter, about Vera and another relative not mentioned so far. I have already outlined my mother-in-law's busy lifestyle. It was amazing how she balanced housework, cooking, sewing, and taking care of us while also pursuing other activities. Besides custom tailoring, Vera also took time to create beautifully detailed doll garments. Each perfect in every detail. Once appropriately dressed, she donated the finished dolls to charity. I do not think anyone recorded how many she made over the years, but there is no doubt the volume was considerable. Her continuous contribution was eventually noted and an award bestowed. However, Vera did not receive the tribute herself. A rather uncouth aunt took credit even to the extent of accepting the medal at the public awards ceremony. This occurred after I had left the family home. I still wonder why no one intervened, not even to set the record straight. I may only assume it was due to the nature of this aunt. She was a forceful figure who was frequently blunt, rude, and demanding of her own way in all things. Truth is she was a bit of a bully, backed by her more than ample frame. The family probably decided to follow the path of least resistance. A shame, in my opinion, Vera should have received the credit. The only thing to acknowledge is this aunt's unpleasant character probably suited her employment. She was a prison governor.

14

Surprise

From what I have shared with you so far, you will have undoubtedly comprehended we were not wealthy. In fact, it was a constant struggle to make ends meet. This troubled me because I did not feel I was really contributing. Helping round the house was something, but it quickly became apparent my daily presence was, in reality, superfluous. Vera, with Moira's help, had managed well enough before my arrival. The wheels of my mind started turning to see if there was some better way for me to help. I hated the idea of Terrance and I enjoying all the benefits without adding to the family pot.

Looking back now, I wonder at my boldness. I was still very shy and unaccustomed to being out in public on my own. I must have been determined because one day I ventured, on my own, into the town centre with the purpose of seeking employment. Of course, I had no idea of what was involved or what I could possibly do. Bewildered, I stood in the high street for a while looking about me. How did one go about finding a job? Who could help me? What could I do? The prevailing expectation of the time, even among many women, that 'a woman's place was in the home' did not help my situation. Consequently, at least in the morally acceptable employment market, the choice was very limited. Eventually, the local cinema caught my eye. Perhaps? Taking a deep breath to steady the butterflies I went and asked for, and was offered the position of usherette. I had to ask what that involved but once explained felt happy I could do it. I almost skipped my way back home, feeling very pleased with myself. Vera and Ralph were taken aback, but once they assimilated the information congratulated me. However, they wanted to check, because of my youth and different cultural background, all was in order and the employers had not taken advantage of me. Their final conclusion, all was good, contract, working conditions, and hours. Considering it only right, despite his behaviour, I be home with my husband in the evenings, I had agreed to afternoons only. Vera thought this very sensible. I further confirmed all my earnings would go into the family pot, for which they expressed sincere gratitude.

Terrance was less than enamoured when I told him that evening. 'I suppose there are men at this place.' It may sound silly, but I never really understood his jealousy. Whenever out, whether or not with him, I kept my eyes down and avoided visual contact with anyone, man, woman, or child. He could even be jealous of them. I affirmed, except for the manager, most staff were female. However, that did not satisfy because inevitably many of the patrons would be male. It was, however, too late for him to prevent me taking the job unless he wanted to countermand his parents, a thing even he was reticent to do. There was also the fact I had already volunteered my earnings to the family pot. As you have probably now come to expect, my beating that night was a severe one. I asked him once why he insisted on beating me and what it was I had done wrong. His response was to tell me I never did anything wrong and was too good and perfect. It was the others he did not trust. Make sense of that if you can.

Working at the cinema brought back early memories. As a child it bewildered me where all the animals and people on the screen came from. Our rural community, combined with the warm climate and the fact cinemas were not a thing then, meant the few screenings we were privileged to enjoy were held in open air lots. Afterward I would dive behind the free standing screens to seek out the characters I had been enjoying but of course never found any. Mama did her best to explain and patiently fielded my often repeated questions until I eventually gained some comprehension. Nonetheless, in later years it still took a while for me to understand how MetroGoldwynMayer got the lion into the circle of their logo. I admit I still take delight when I see it.

My usherette duties were not onerous and could often prove quite fun. On one occasion I recognised a famous American film star in the audience. My female colleagues were beside themselves, especially, as it seemed all such stars of the time possessed reasonable visages. I am sure some of them came close to wetting themselves. It did seem strange someone like him would attend a small, local showing. I assumed he was either on holiday and just wanted some respite or his agent had arranged it for him, even though it was not one of his films. I should mention this was when there were no such things as multiplex cinemas. There was one screen and only one film per week or fortnight. As required, I went forward to usher him to a seat, not expecting any conversation. However, he greeted me with 'Hi Doll, you like to come to the states with me?' His jovial manner had us both laughing as I left him at his seat. You will often hear me state I do not consider myself particularly attractive, though others appear to have a different opinion. I may only assume it was this that had prompted his unaccustomed greeting. I simply put it down to the fact he was probably used to people kowtowing and had developed what he considered suitable, though insincere, responses. Needless to say, we never saw each other again, though I did subsequently see him in one or two films.

Unfortunately, as seems to be my lot, the job was not without its issues. The manager developed more than a passing interest and often attempted the attainment of a kiss. Thankfully, I was aware enough to know how to sidestep his unwanted advances. However, it meant each and every week I had to face the challenge of seeing him in private. The then normal and accepted routine was for each of us to collect our weekly wage from him in his office. Sexual discrimination employment regulations did not exist. Consequently, there were no deterrents and no one to complain to. Managers were the ones in charge and therefore wielded considerable, if unwarranted, power. Although there were occasions when it got a bit close, I survived these encounters even if often left unsettled. Vera unwittingly provided the recovery period I need. Each day when returning home a pot of tea and a freshly baked cake of loaf, I love bread straight from the oven, waited. Sitting quietly together, enjoying the goodies and a chat were some of my happiest moments from my otherwise harsh existence. I think Vera also looked forward to the short break in her heavy schedule. Until now, I have never told anyone about the manager's behaviour. What Terrance would have done if he found out, and not just to me, worried me. It was therefore best, as has often been the case in my life, for me to cope alone.

In the previous chapter I mentioned how I would come to regret the purchase of my lovely shoes. Such a shame as I really did like them. Unfortunately, though they had felt comfortable in the shop, they proved wrong for my feet. They rubbed terribly and caused my feet to bleed, especially round the large toes. I was really disappointed. I had anticipated enjoying these shoes for a long time. Terrance, surprise, surprise, showed no sympathy and refused my request to go and buy another pair. I should have known better than to even ask. He went so far as to state, as they had been my choice I had to live with them and that from now on I was to wear them every time we went out. And would do so until they wore out. He seemed to take great delight in watching my agony. Why he continually wanted me to suffer was still beyond me. Sometimes he even made me wear them in the house. He really did posses a cruel streak.

He had said I would have to wear them until they wore out. I therefore did all I could to destroy those lovely shoes. I bashed them against hard rough surfaces, soaked them in water, cut them with knives and razors, but nothing made any noticeable dent. In those days, all shoes were constructed from good quality leather, even the less expensive ones. Mine were middle range. In the end, exasperated and in ever-increasing pain, and despite my desire not to bother her, I confided in my mother-in-law. Even going so far as to tell her of her son's reaction. One look at my feet and the angel had me soaking them in a warm, wonderfully relieving solution. She subsequently cleaned all the blood away and bandaged my sore extremities. I asked what I was to do. She told me not to worry, she would sort it out. When I asked how, she simply put her index finger to her lips and then summoned the girls to get ready. I do not remember why, but they were at home that day. The usual excitement arose when Vera informed them we were going to the shops. I had not expected that, but remained quiet as instructed and dutifully followed directions.

This time Vera made the choice. A lovely soft leather beige pair with an overlapping serrated tongue and low heels. They felt wonderful on my sore feet. Back home, she immediately informed Ralph, presumably to account for the extra, unexpected, expenditure from the meagre family resources. He surprised us all by not only approving, but also commenting on the shoes. He usually took no notice of outfits or accessories. When Terrance arrived home his mother told him straight he should be ashamed of himself for letting me suffer so. His response was, 'She wanted them. It was her choice.'. The glare bestowed upon me gave notice of what was to follow. At that stage he still limited his violence, physical and emotional, to when we were on our own, though that did eventually change. Did he really think he was fooling anyone? We all lived in the same house, for goodness' sake! However, he was their son and brother. I never saw my shoes again. Whether they ended up in the dustbin or Vera gave them to charity, I have no idea. I was simply glad to be rid of them, despite how much I had liked them. Regrettably, the rescue proved too late to prevent bunions on both feet, which have given me considerable pain and trouble throughout my life.

I have entitled this chapter 'Surprise'. Here is why. One day I felt rather unwell and vomited. Vera gave me the good old English standby, a cup of tea. Really, what would the British do without their tea? It helped rally me a little, though I still felt unwell. This repeated itself over subsequent days with nothing, tea, broth, or rest seeming to help. I felt completely washed out and increasingly anxious. It also bothered Vera leading her to eventually, with the mutual agreement of Terrance and Ralph, taking me to the family doctor. I still remember him with great affection. He was a very kind and gentle man. You will probably have already gathered it was unusual for my father-in-law to involve himself in such goings on. He normally left it to the women. I suspect, beside the fact he was probably genuinely concerned, his wife had pushed him. I may only surmise she wanted to have some moral support should her son get out of hand. As if to prove the point, while the doctor was examining me behind a screen, Terrance presented himself. Undoubtedly, not trusting the man to be alone with me, especially in such circumstances. This clearly irritated the doctor, who, a little caustically, told my husband, 'Can you not see there is a screen there? Please go.'

Terrance was visibly taken aback and I was afraid he would become violent. The air hung heavy for a solitary moment before he turned and left. I think his respect for the man, who he had known since childhood, overruled his other emotions. The doctor, turning his attention back to me, gently prodded about until, with a look of satisfaction, he stated I was fine and had a beautiful little lump. He then jokingly chided me for throwing away the food that had been brought across the oceans. The country was still recovering from the effects of war with consequent shortages, which could only be made up by imports. My manifest confusion made obvious I did not understand, prompting Vera to lean over and tell me I was going to have a little baby. I sat stunned. Could it be true? Had I really, despite the traumas of Terrance's rapes, fallen pregnant? Wonders never cease. The tidings finally sinking in, happiness and excitement replaced the confusion. Besides the expectation in my home culture of married couples always having children, I from my own early childhood had always wanted a family. My early life had been happy and I longed to recreate a similar safe, loving, and happy home for my own children.

Vera, Ralph, and later the girls were also overjoyed. This would be their first grandchild and niece or nephew, respectively. I anticipated Terrance also being happy with the prospective advent of his first child. Wrong! By this time I had developed into full adulthood and had been blessed, or some may say cursed, with a perfect physique. To me this was just a partial inheritance from my mama, who had been strikingly beautiful. Add to this people often, and unfortunately, commenting on my looks. Looking back, I wonder if some of my husband's behaviour was due to insecurity. Perhaps in part, but that does not justify all he did to me. His response to the news of our baby was simply to say in a rough and aggressive tone he was glad because it should ruin my physical appearance. My joy was momentarily marred as dark despondency sought to gain control. I had hoped the news of a child would give him a sense of fulfilment and maybe even contentment and even perhaps cause him to treat me a little more humanly. I was clearly very mistaken.

Though my husband's attitude astonished and disappointed and continually lurked at the back of my mind, I quickly regained my spirits. How could it be otherwise with such wonderful news? Together with the rest of the family, I joyfully prepared for the miraculous event. Vera knitted endlessly, and the girls bought lovely little gifts. Terrance's maternal grandfather also shared our happiness. You may remember he was one of the people to meet me upon my arrival in the country. He was a lovely man, kind and generous to a fault. You will hear more of him later. Regrettably, his wife was of a different ilk. A prime example is her daughter, Vera's, twenty-first birthday. As the one and only present, her mother sent half-a-dozen eggs from their farm. Ralph had been so incensed he immediately jumped on his bicycle and when returning the eggs told her, if that was all she thought of her daughter, she could keep them. It amazes me such a kind gentleman could have such a cold spouse, but I suppose that is life. Look at my own. I never met or learnt anything about Terrance's paternal grandparents. I have no idea why not.

Conveying how thrilled I was with the prospect of my first child is difficult. Throughout, I sang and talked to the darling within, looking forward to the time when we would play and chatter together. Unhappily, this display of affection for someone other than himself infuriated Terrance. His jealousy knew no bounds whether it was of strangers who showed an interest or, as you will come to see, of anything I cared for. Almost immediately, he took to putting me up against a wall and, while pinning my arms above my head so I could not protect myself, kicking and kneeing me in the abdomen. I was past caring about myself but cried for him to be careful of the baby, not understanding he actually wanted to kill our child. Just shows how insane his jealousy was. My child was already the love of my life and I was terrified he would cause serious harm. Of course, he ignored my entreaties. I did not know what to do or where to turn. His family loved him and were forever reluctant to say anything.

One day he even kicked me down the stairs. Remember, we lived at the top of the house, on the third floor. Tumbling all the way to the ground floor, I ended in an immobile heap where Moira found me. In her childish manner she started jumping up and down shouting, 'Terrance has killed her! Terrance has killed her!' It emerged, anticipating us coming down, she had been waiting in the hall when she saw Terrance attack me. Hearing the commotion and thudding and her daughter's cries, Vera ran from the kitchen to discover me dazed and bruised but not unconscious. She quickly checked my breathing and then sought to quieten Moira, telling her everything was okay, not to worry, and to calm down. Having succeeded, she returned her attention to me and lifted me from the floor. She then guided me to the prestigious front room, where she settled me on the sofa. She told me not to be afraid and to rest and she would return shortly. 'Not to be afraid'. How could I be otherwise? My mind was in turmoil, hardly believing what had just happened. Resting back upon the elevated cushions, I prodded round my abdomen, endeavouring to determine whether my baby was hurt. Rather silly really, as I had no experience or knowledge of pregnancy.

True to her word, my mother-in-law returned within ten minutes with the inevitable pot of tea. I know I keep saying it, but really, what would the British do without it? However, my only concern was for my baby and I pleaded Vera check if he was okay. Obligingly she placed her hand upon my stomach and felt round my ribcage, back, and neck. Once completed she assured me she thought the baby was fine and I had suffered no breakages. Relief swept over me. The fact I suffered no serious injury seemed a miracle and astonished us both. I trusted her opinion and did not feel the need for further medical consideration. These were the days when most married women were stay at home housewives living within established interactive communities. They were proper communities then, with most willingly helping their neighbours. The elder, more experienced ones would teach the younger how to deal with all sorts of things, including childbirth.

A self imposed, unspoken rule my mother-in-law adhered to, was not to usually say anything on these brutal occasions. Whether this was because Terrance was her son, who she loved, or out of a desire not to make matters worse, I am not entirely clear. Perhaps it was both. However, this must have been one episode too far. There and then she told him he should treat me more gently, otherwise I was likely to die on his hands. He was furious. He grabbed my arm and while dragging me toward the front door shouted, 'We are leaving this house!'. When his mother realised what he was about, she placed herself in the way, begging him not to go or take me away. But he would not heed and continued dragging me onwards. By now Vera had got into such a state she collapsed on the doorstep. I do not think I need to explain the turmoil within me. Nor the pain originating from my bruised and battered body. Terrance, instead of stopping to check his mother, as anyone would expect, simply stepped over her comatose body, hauling me after him. Up to this point I had been trying to get my arm free from his vice like grip, but this latest outrage shook me to the core. I had never seen him treat his mother so cruelly. I had thought he loved her, if not me. Subconsciously, I ceased struggling. Uncontrollable hysterics then engulfed. The command to stop my wailing got me dutifully biting my lip. I did not want him to start hitting me or, more importantly, our child. Showing no concern for what people might think, he dragged me down the street to a bus stop on the adjoining thoroughfare. When it arrived he shoved me onto the bus headed for a nearby town. Where was he taking me? Where were we to stay? What was he going to do? Questions dominating my thoughts, but ones I dare not ask.

At the other end my husband yet again gripped my arm and dragged me to a house I had never seen. It turned out to be the home of a friend of his who, as you would expect, was more than a little surprised to see us on the doorstep. However, the enquiry in his eyes went unanswered until we crossed the threshold. Once inside, without even bothering to introduce me first, Terrance drew his friend aside. Out of earshot I do not know what he said, but the outcome was this kind gentleman offering the use of a room in his home. The arrangement allowed the use of the room only. He did not want his family inconvenienced. At least we had some shelter, though no money. Terrance had used the few pennies he found in his pocket for the bus fare.

After a couple of days without food, we were, unsurprisingly, hungry. Do not forget I was pregnant. Terrance therefore sold his de-mob coat that he happened to be wearing when he kicked me down the stairs. He must have been on his way out. You may recall this was shortly after the end of World War Two, when many ex-servicemen struggled to find employment and an income. It was quite normal for them to sell or pawn some of their military regalia. Eight shillings may not sound much these days, but at the time it was enough to prevent starvation, at least for a while. I do not think Terrance had explained to his friend how desperate we were. They probably thought we were eating out during the day. The loaf of bread and piccalilli we got is still a meal I remember. Even now it seems it was one of the best I have ever had. Such a shame piccalilli no longer tastes the same.

In our constrained circumstances I thought my husband would want us to work together to find a resolution. But no, I was proven wrong again. The beatings continued, and whenever he went out, which he did most days, he locked me in the room. In effective solitary confinement my mind continually turned to despairing questions. Would I ever win through? Would he never cease his violence? Would he ever show any care, let alone love, for me or our child? Would my life be forever like this? Looking back, I believe the combination of our desperate circumstances, my pregnancy, and the non-stop beatings affected my sanity. One day a bee got into the locked room and started flying in front of my face. Through the defused daydream mist, I recall thinking it must believe I am a flower. I may have even started to accept it as a fact. When under such severe stress, our minds seek ways of escape. As you know, this was not the first time my mind and sanity had to face such challenges, nor was it to be the last. As you see, I survived almost intact, I think, but then we never really completely know ourselves.

Just a few days into our stay, my husband's friend accosted him to say he should stop hitting me and that he was having difficulty preventing his wife from coming up to throttle him. Evidently, the noise had carried through the walls and floorboards. My unspoken fears were then realised. He would not allow his family to either witness or be traumatised by such behaviour. We must leave. Though I had never been permitted contact with the family, I had deduced these were kind and generous people. I suspect it was not just his wife who had to hold back from exercising some violence upon my husband. The friendship ended with our departure. I never saw or heard of the family again. It appears to be my destiny to lose contact with every nice, decent, kind person I ever meet. Does feel rather like a curse. What have I ever done to merit it?

Here we were again, homeless and penniless. I was afraid. Visions of us living on the streets, me in my expectant state, flashed through. Terrance was also at a loss and, though not giving one iota for my comfort, evidently did not relish the idea of a night in the open. Concluding no other option existed, he went cap-in-hand to his grandfather. I mentioned how kind and generous a man he was, but not that he was also fairly well-to-do. It is more than probable he had heard of our distressing departure from the family home. However, being the considerate soul he was, he withheld from berating or criticising my husband. He told us to make ourselves comfortable while he went out for a short period. He returned within the hour to inform us he had found a house for us to rent. Joy and gratitude swept over me. This was beyond my wildest dreams and hopes. I wanted to express my heartfelt appreciation, but Terrance would not allow me to speak to him. It seems shameful and pathetic now, but I had learnt to sit or stand meekly whenever he was in conversation. This was irrespective of whether any connection existed between the other person and me.

The house was very pleasant and again far more than I expected. Grandfather introduced the lady sitting tenant, who turned out to be a dear. She had the sole use of one ground floor room and shared the kitchen and bathroom with us. In case you do not know, a sitting tenant is someone with the right to remain in a property no matter who rents or purchases it. It is usually under contract with, in most instances, a lifetime right. It was a fairly common practice in days gone by. To have somewhere to live was great, but my relief was mitigated by concern for how we were going to pay the rent, let alone afford food. Terrance was unemployed and I, due to the precious bundle who insisted upon lying on a nerve for the whole nine months, was unable to work. He would never discuss such matters with me, believing, strange as it may seem, considering his usual demeanour, it the man's place to provide. Even if the woman did work, she was not deemed worthy of inclusion in financial decisions. Younger readers may find that difficult to accept, but it used to be the norm. My anxiety provided sufficient courage, or perhaps desperation, for me to murmur my concern. Of course, I did not expect any response from Terrance, nor, in fact, received any. However, my worries were immediately alleviated when grandfather, without any preceding comment, paid the rent and discreetly gave his grandson money for food. He was truly a caring and unpretentious man.

The lack of funds, and perhaps also his grandfather's quiet generosity, appeared to bring Terrance to his senses. He became more energetic and proactive, and within short time secured a position with a removals firm. Thankfully, the salary proved sufficient for us to pay our own way. Grandfather had been so good to look out for us, but I at least felt rather guilty about continuing to impose upon him. He had made clear he would go on paying until we were in a position to do so ourselves. Terrance, on the other hand, did not seem to care and appeared to take it for granted, almost as if it was his right. I was therefore very thankful he had gone to the effort of getting a job.

Needless to say, the beatings continued and, in fact, got worse. I was hard pushed to understand why. I hardly went out, so these could not be the consequence of someone having shown an interest. Upon further consideration, noting how he continued to aim for my abdomen, I realised he was still trying to kill our child. His jealousy knew no bounds and made him blind to all natural or proper considerations. One day the sitting tenant asked why I put up with it and why I did not leave. I had not appreciated she could hear all that was going on. My honest answer was I had no one and nowhere to go. Unfortunately, neither of us noticed my husband standing nearby, within earshot. You may imagine his fury. In a most aggressive manner he told the lady to mind her own business or else. The next morning, we discovered she had packed and left during the night. Her fear must have been considerable, especially as she was on her own. I never saw her again, which is a shame, as I did rather like her. Telling my husband what I thought and how cross I was that he should have threatened and intimidated such a vulnerable lady was out of the question. To be honest, and I know some of you may find this strange, I do not believe, in the depths of his soul, Terrance was really evil. Probably, much of what he did came out of insecurity rather than anything else. That, however, did not justify or excuse his brutality. It was wrong and nothing could say otherwise.

In addition to his general jealousy of anyone indicating the slightest interest in me, my troubled husband was insanely resentful of any affection I showed. You have seen how, as a child, I loved animals and had many pets. I still miss them. Vera was fully aware of this and on one of the rare visits her son permitted, had given me a kitten. My natural inclination is to always expend unbounded affection on animals, especially the younger ones. I just cannot help it. I should have realised this would lead to no good. One day Terrance snatched the kitten from my arms and stormed out of the house. Upon his return, he gleefully informed me he had killed it. Presumably he drowned the poor creature. Unspeakable horror engulfed me. Despite everything, I still had not comprehended how far his jealous cruelty could extend or to what depths it could lead. Needless to say, my distress incurred further punishments.

Another innocent pleasure was reading, with me often getting lost in the stories. From our earliest years my sisters and I were intrigued by and interested in foreign places, cultures, and societies. Probably inspired by the tales our parents and grandparents shared of their overseas travels. Books opened a window through which we could peep. Of course, there were also enchanting worlds and romantic tales of heroines and princesses with who I frequently identified. A carry over from those innocent days with my sisters, which is perhaps a reminder I was still comparatively young, although now a wife and mother. Yet again Terrance saw this as the expending of affection on something other than himself. He beat me and destroyed all my books, telling me I was never to read again. Unable to face the likelihood of additional violence on top of what I was already enduring, I submitted to his unreasonable demand.

My low, depressed spirit undermined any initiative I may have had to rebel. Reading has been a struggle ever since. I hate giving in to these psychological and emotional limitations, but no matter how much I try still find them difficult to overcome. I do now read to some extent, but it is slow and in short bursts. Somewhere in the depths, the dark fear of retribution continues to linger, even though, mentally, I know the threat no longer exists and the fear is foolish.

A further, perhaps surprising to you, enjoyment, was watching football when, subconsciously, I often kicked out in empathy with the players. Upon seeing this Terrance would kick me very hard in the shins. The pain was excruciating. I still suffer with leg pain, suspecting some of it originates from those occasions when he wore his steel capped demob boots. It may have simply been the fact I was enjoying something he was not involved with. It may also have been that he thought I was showing an interest in the male players, though I gave him no reason to think so. I do not know. In retrospect, he probably considered it a display of affection for something other than him. I have never really enjoyed watching football since, though I do like to know if my chosen team wins a game and still feel disappointment on the rare occasions they do not.

No doubt you will have gathered I value family. However, at the time, this was virtually denied me. Despite grandfather's house being nearby and the family home but a twenty-minute walk, I was never allowed to visit on my own. Perhaps he was worried I may let slip the full extent of his brutality. Did he not realise the family knew? Though his presence on such occasions created limitations, it was always good to see Vera and the girls. They were effectively the only real family I had in the country. My homesickness remained intense. I missed my family terribly. These rare visits helped in measure, especially with the girls treating me as an equal, making them valuable substitutes for my own siblings.

One evening, yet again for no apparent reason, Terrance beat me up and threw me out of the house. Bear in mind, I am pregnant. No amount of pleading induced him to let me back in. Not knowing what else to do, I spent the night under a bush in the front garden. With the light of dawn I decided to seek help from grandmother, thinking a woman may understand my situation better. Thinking back, it would probably have been wiser to ask grandfather. Why on earth I had not thought of going the night before, I have no idea. Bewildered and fearful for my baby's safety my mind could not have been working properly. Brushing myself down, I started out, but Terrance must have seen me pass the front window. Shooting through the door as if a bolt of lightening he simply, as if nothing had happened, greeted me with a hello and a question of where I was going. Needless to say, he did not permit me to proceed. Once back in, he beat me again. For what reason I do not know. As always, I had no idea what had brought on the original beating and throwing out. He did not usually resort to that. After some consideration, I concluded he must have thought a night in the cold would cause me to lose the baby. How a father can hate his own child so much still bewilders me. There is the remote, very remote, possibility it was some kind of cry for help that assumed I would go to his parents or grandparents and ask them to intervene and stop his violence. I have heard of such things. However, I think this is perhaps being unrealistically kind. Terrance was simply jealous of our child and wanted him out of the way. I say him though, in those days, there was no way of actually knowing the gender until birth.

More than likely because of the beatings, my baby turned. Just as well because it is reasonably certain if he had not, his head would have been crushed when his father struck, kneed, and kicked me in the stomach. Consequently, he was in breach position. This would explain his weight laying upon a back nerve throughout the nine months. To say it was agony would be an understatement. This on top of all the other pain. The doctors, who at least I was still permitted to see, expressed serious concern. My baby was large and I petite at only four and a half stone. I should mention, never allowed to attend consultations alone and because he had to work, my husband agreed to his mother accompanying me. It must have been very hard on her with all the other work and duties she had to attend to. But she never complained and always tried to make each visit as lighthearted as possible. The doctors prodded mercilessly and even took to turning the examination couch on end, effectively hanging me upside down. Whatever they tried, the baby would not turn. Throughout, Terrance never ceased beating, kicking, and attempting to throttle me. He seemed hellbent on destroying his own flesh and blood. Whenever asked about a bruise, I would just say I had fallen, missed my step, or walked into a door, using my pregnant state as an excuse. This was sufficient for those who did not really know me, but I doubt it fooled anyone else.

15

Advent

Anticipating complications, the doctors insisted upon my admission to hospital some while before the advent was due. Their concern was such, they allocated five surgeons, three of them Queen's surgeons, to oversee the birth. Everyone did their best to reassure me, but I could not help the nervous fear. Everything indicated a dangerous, difficult, and painful time ahead, with no guarantee of a successful outcome. After lengthy discussion, the general agreement was to try for a natural birth. More than anything I wished for that, though the intimation was it more than likely a caesarean would be required. In preparation, my husband had to sign an authorisation. He was probably only too glad to give his consent, hoping it may result in loss of the baby or at the very least a destruction of my physique.

When the time came, they informed me no anaesthetic would be given due to the baby's breech position. They had continued trying to turn my little darling right up to the end, but without success. In case you do not know, the danger with a breach is if I stopped pushing at the wrong moment, my child could be strangled by the umbilical cord. The labour went agonisingly on and on to the point I wondered if it would ever happen. Oranges are not a particular favourite, but just before the actual birth I asked for one. I think all the prodding, manipulation, and turning upside down had left me dry. My baby was eventually delivered. Upon all the surgeons declaring I had a lovely son, I immediately insisted on seeing him. With all the violence, I feared he may be badly damaged, missing a limb, or seriously disfigured. After checking everything and assuring myself he was complete, I passed out. I think it was my body's means of protecting me. I was utterly exhausted, not to mention badly torn inside and out and all without anaesthetic.

The damage to my person in extracting my son was so extensive that we had to remain in hospital for six months. With me sitting upon an inflated rubber ring for most of the time. It was far too painful to sit normally. Those months gave my physical body the chance to recover and me the opportunity to have some rest and regain my strength. Six months without one beating was worth all the pain. And now I had the joy of my beautiful son. The surgeons commended my bravery and congratulated me on the birth of a healthy child, for which they were clearly relieved. Everyone was kind and thoughtful, except for Terrance, of course. On one of his first visits he complained I still looked the same. Throughout, he had not hidden his hope the pregnancy would change my looks and make me less attractive. By nature I am a sensitive soul and naturally was even more so in my current condition. The additional emotional stress caused by his words resulted in my breast milk hardening. Unless you have had the experience, you will not be able to comprehend how painful this is. Sadly, this meant I could not breastfeed my darling. In my opinion, and that of many others, breastfeeding is the best way to develop a healthy child. But there, it was not to be for me. Thankfully, my son has grown into a healthy man, though as you will come to see, there were many challenges in his early life.

My baby was truly beautiful. I know all loving mothers say the same, but my bias was supported by others. You may remember I mentioned how nice the family doctor was. Whenever we went to see him in his surgery, on the ground floor of his home, my son would immediately disappear. Upon hearing of our arrival his family would rush down, grab my baby and handing him from one to the other, squeal what a lovely child he was. Normally, I would be beside myself if anyone touched him. Naturally, I was always anxious he should suffer no violence but in addition had the concern of possible infections and parasites. Remember, hygiene is a real issue with me. However, the family was just as nice and kind as their father and, compared to others, generally hygienic. I knew he would be safe in their hands. Virtually the same thing happened when I first went to visit my own relatives back home. Again they would grab him and give gentle little bites to his legs. Sounds awful I know, but back then it was their way of showing affection. Bite is perhaps too strong a word, it was more little, gentle, nibbles. So there you are. I may be biassed, but evidently my child was considered adorable. He always was and remains so to me.

Regrettably, the time for my son and I to leave the hospital came round all too quickly. Never mind, I thought, perhaps the presence of our son would make my husband more amenable. How wrong could I be? Will I never learn? In truth, despite my hopes, in the depths of my heart I think I knew. It was therefore with some trepidation I returned to our house. It would have been nice to say home, but I could never feel like that about it. Never certain what Terrance would do next, I never relaxed, fear being my constant companion.

Though the nurses had been very kind and considerate, they had unfortunately not taken sufficient care when changing nappies. Consequently, my baby had rather bad nappy rash. I should mention disposable nappies were a thing of the distant future. Ours were made of cotton terylene which have to be washed throughly after each use, usually by hand. Naturally, though normally a placid child, the discomfort made my son a little grizzly. It worried me. With his temper and impatience, Terrance was unlikely to tolerate a crying child. As any reasonable person would expect, to deal with the issue I had to change my son's nappy regularly and apply cream to the nasty sores. However, not being one of those people, his father grew increasingly annoyed. He often shouted at me to 'Leave him! He'll get over it!'. I attempted to explain about the rash and the fact, like all babies, himself included, our son could not do things for himself yet and needed me to take care of him. But, of course, it fell on deaf ears. In my inherent naïvety, I had still thought the fact of our son now actually being with us, rather than an enigmatic embryo, would bring his father's parental instincts to the fore. Need I say more as to my foolishness? If anything, he became even more jealous with all the consequences that entailed. I still find it hard to accept a father could be so displeased with the presence of his own flesh and blood.

Terrance was particularly nasty if woken from his sleep. It therefore became quite an issue ensuring our son remained quiet at night. To this end, each and every night, I held my baby in my arms, allowing his little head and body to rest against my chest. Relaxation and sleep were out of the question for me. What if my son cried and woke his father? Most nights were fine however, on the odd occasion when the discomfort caused my son to whimper, I would take him downstairs. I had learnt how to move silently so as not to disturb my husband, even to the extent of learning where each squeaking floorboard was located. The constant lack of sleep combined with my ever present fear did fatigue me and obviously impacted my daily life. The blessing of motherhood helped keep me buoyed but it was terrible, when there should have been widespread joy, to have to live with such tension and fear. However, though I did not know at the time, it was nothing compared to what was to follow.

Naming our son proved difficult. As you already know, my husband was insanely jealous of anyone, male or female, particularly male, who showed any sort of interest in me. It did eventually dawn upon me besides his need for my sole attention, he was fearful someone would take me away. Goodness knows I had every reason to go. However, despite my constant emphatic remonstrations of not being interested in anyone else, his jealous insecurity made him deaf to the truth. Consequently, and despite my vehement denials, whenever I suggested a name, he accused me of being in love with someone of that name. It got to the stage of me, rather out of character then, pointing out he never came up with an alternative. I began to wonder if our son was to remain nameless. After further meditation, it crossed my mind that naming him after someone famous, or at least a public figure, who it would have been impossible for me to have met, may get somewhere. Naturally, I also had to ensure there was no one in our circle with the same name. He did eventually agree, having first determined it could not be someone I knew or loved.

The next hurdle, or so I thought, was the matter of christening our son. Knowing how important this was to me, it was more than likely he would be difficult about it. Much to my surprise, and probably the only time I have been proven wrong about him, he proved amenable. I did wonder if there was some evil intent behind this, but decided to risk it and take full advantage of the unexpected goodwill. When we married, I had given an undertaking to christen all our children into my homeland's branch of the christian faith. Terrance had agreed to this at the time though, as evidenced by many subsequent events, there was no saying he would not change his mind, if only to be belligerent. Again he astonished me by confirming his willingness. Why could he not be like this all the time? Risking the likelihood of a beating, I pushed the advantage by asking how soon the christening would take place. It progressed surprisingly fast, especially considering the additional organisation required to get a member from the hierarchy of my church's representation in England to come to officiate. My gratitude to my husband for sorting it all out, particularly in view of his usual behaviour is hard to express. It is of great importance in my culture to ensure babies are properly welcomed into our faith.

Some forty years later, I learnt my gratitude had been misplaced. Terrance had allowed me to think he had undertaken all the preparations. It transpired it had actually been lovely, kindhearted, generous, grandfather. Not only had he made all the arrangements, but also paid for everything. Including the costs for the minister's three-day visit together with hotel and aide. I feel terrible never to have had the opportunity to thank him.

Christenings of this nature were a rarity then, especially where we lived. Its uniqueness caught the attention of the local press, resulting in a full-page article. I still have a copy of the newspaper together with original photographs the publishers were kind enough to give me. These have since proven even more valuable because they are the only ones with the three of us together. At least my son has something to remind him of his father, even if the memories are not pleasant. The event proved a complete success. My baby behaved and whereas most cry when made wet, he did not. In fact he gurgled with quiet laughter. In truth, despite the difficult circumstances of our life, he was mostly a happy, contented child.

Terrance, with any stretch of the mind, could never be called an adventurous eater. His staple diet comprised fried egg and chips, followed by a bowl of cornflakes. The only break to this was on Fridays, when he was happy to follow his mother's tradition of having fried fish in place of eggs. It was tedious having to fry every day. Concerned for his health, I occasionally suggested he try something different. As no doubt you anticipated, I received an abrupt refusal. However, I pushed my luck one day by preparing a salad made in the style of my homeland's cuisine. There is no way I would ever describe what passed for a salad in the England of the time, one or two lettuce leafs and half a tomato lying forlorn at the edge of a plate, as such. Having endangered myself for another beating, I was taken aback when he conceded to try it and then his affirmation that he liked it. Of course, this did not change his overall demand for his usual fare alongside, but at least he was occasionally having something healthy.

The other irritating and sometimes difficult issue with his eating was, he demanded the meal be ready on the table as he entered through the front door. On one occasion our son had been poorly, and it had taken a while to settle him, causing me to be behind with the cooking. The meal was half prepared when the sound of the door opening and closing reached my ear. Our son's excited greeting of 'Daddy, daddy' followed. He was still very young and had not yet understood, despite the violence, his father's lack of interest. There was then an unusually loud noise in the hall. Ever fearful of what Terrance may do when alone with his son, I with palpating heart, ran. It remains incomprehensible to me that my son's father was so jealous and seemed determined to destroy his own flesh and blood.

The sight of my darling boy being kicked round the floor as if he were a football greeted me. Instinctively screaming at him to stop, I threw myself on top of our crying son. It made no difference. Instead of stopping, Terrance simply altered to kicking me. When in a rage I was sure, despite his professed love for me, he was quite prepared to kill me. I managed to keep my baby shielded with my body. At the same time, in an attempt to also protect myself, I tucked my head as far as possible beneath my shoulders. Eventually, whether due to his temper having run its course or fatigue, I have no idea, our attacker ceased and disappeared into the living room. It is amazing my son was not suffocated. I had held him so tightly. Having calmed him and ensured no serious physical damage had been done, I returned to the kitchen with my boy in his pram. Then, without a word being uttered by either of us, I gave my husband his evening meal. I had no desire to provoke him again.

Terrance's habit, when attacking his son, was to aim for his small, delicate head. Without fear of exaggeration, I may confirm one blow from his clenched fist would have crushed the fragile skull. When not punching, his other preferred method of destruction was smothering him with a cushion or pillow. Unsurprisingly, I was constantly on tenterhooks. The slightest change in household sounds or an unexpected silence had me running. Unfortunately, it was not always practicable or possible to have my son by my side. If he were home, Terrance would inevitably attempt some mischief. Recent media revelations have shown my husband was not alone, though I may be grateful he never attempted to sexually abuse our son. That was left for me.

There was an occasion when I left my baby in his pram by the front room bay window. It was a sunny day and with the open window thought the fresh air would be good for him. I went to attend to something in another part of the house when a commotion had me running back. It appeared, while happily kicking out, my son's foot became entangled in one of the curtains. The rail hung down and one curtain had come off and lay across the pram. Fine in itself, you may say, but standing over the pram, ready to strike, was his father. With a speed that must have appeared as lightning, I crossed the room and threw myself across the pram. From somewhere, probably my sewing basket, Terrance had got hold of a robust wooden coat hanger. He applied such force it broke across my back. Again, once whatever it was in him had run its course, he simply left. The pain was extreme, but at least I had saved my son. As I regained my feet, of all times for it to happen, I felt my period commence. Oh well, just something else to deal with. With my baby in my arms I went upstairs to clean and change. The blood was unusually thick and uncomfortable but it was not until the opportunity to talk with Vera arose, did I understand it had been a miscarriage. The first of many to follow. It turned out I was especially fertile, notwithstanding the brutality and rapes. My son is the only one to have survived. The others either miscarried or departed shortly after birth. Undoubtedly, the result of being punched, kicked and kneed in the stomach while being held against a wall. Unless you have undergone such an experience, it is impossible to convey the impact such behaviour has. How it affects emotions and mentality, except to say it destroys any sense of a viable life or any hope for a worthwhile future. If it had not been for my son, I suspect I would have withdrawn into myself and pined away.

This latest incident, possibly due to its combination with the miscarriage that had affected me deeply, proved a breaking point. It truly felt as if something had broken within me, even to the point of having jagged edges. I did not feel I could take anymore. It had to end. Desperation took control. The next day, after Terrance left for work, with my son in my arms, I settled down by the oven and turned the gas on. Gas was still poisons then. You may think me very selfish to want to take my son with me into the hereafter. But what choice did I have? What would happen to him without me? A far worse death at the hands of his father, I am sure. It is strange how our minds work at such times. Obviously, there must be diminished responsibility. My son started crying, whether from his sensing something seriously wrong or because of the pungent smell of the gas, I do not know. The thought then struck of what I would do if he died before me. I could not bear that. There was no way I wished to see him die. In my crazy reasoning, or should that be unreasoning, mind of the moment, I took him to the bedroom, made him comfortable and after kissing him, returned to the kitchen intent upon finishing what I had started. Terrible confused mentality. However, my mind would not rest. Again the idea of what would happen to my baby without me to protect him struck. I turned off the oven, retrieved my son, and cradling him close enough to feel his little beating heart, sat and cried. How long we remained like that I have no idea. Thereafter, in a psychological haze, I continued with the housework. What else could I do?

All the violence, miscarriages, fear, and never ending worry for my baby, combined to detrimentally effect. I remember one day when on a bus, having what I assume was a hallucination. In it, Terrance was from a wealthy family who did not know he had married. The illusion told me they were nice people who would come and rescue me from their son's cruel grip. What tricks our psyche can play when we are desperate. In my case, not for the first time, I was longing for an avenue of escape. There is absolutely no doubt my mind was unbalanced. The negatives having combined to drive all reasoning from me, as you will see from what follows.

16

Desperation

That night, as usual, I sat in bed with my son in my arms. Terrance was fast asleep. An idea switched on within me. I quietly rose, and avoiding squeaky floorboards, left the room. I then navigated the four flights of stairs to the small cellar, where my husband kept his tools. An ethereal mist appeared to surround, providing the impression of moving through an illusory world and yet, somehow, I knew it was all real. Every fibre within trembled, and my body did not feel my own. However, my mind was surprisingly clear. Crystal clear with the predetermined plan. I say predetermined, but that is only so far as it occurred while watching my husband's rhythmic breathing, terrified our baby may make some sound and wake him.

I am not really able to describe any feelings. There did not appear to be any. Perhaps I had psychologically divorced myself from what I was about to do. Almost straight away I found what I was looking for and was halfway up the cellar stairs when I heard a voice. Had he woken? But no, it was not his voice. It sounded like Elvis Presley's.

I had only heard him on the radio, but always thought how nice he sounded. Later, upon seeing films and documentaries, I considered my opinion confirmed. The voice boomed, or so it seemed to me, 'Do not do that. There is a better way. Go back and stay quiet.' You may imagine how overwhelmed I was, but at least it brought me back to my senses. Looking down, it slightly shocked me to see I was holding a hammer, even though it had been the instrument I had gone to collect. My insane plan had been to return to the bedroom and smash Terrance's head. Had I really become so desperate? It sends cold shivers down my back now to even think of it. I have always believed in God and, in retrospect, am fairly sure this was Him preventing me from what would have been a disastrous action. The mist and haze having now cleared, I quietly returned the hammer to its exact position. Terrance was always particular about his tools. Without interrupting my husband's sleep, we returned to bed. Throughout, my son had been in my arms. I kept the incident to myself until recently, when I finally told my son. Terrance's family never knew. As far as I am concerned, they never will. What good would it do now? Neither did I ever tell them about his constant attempts to kill our child. Why upset them? There was nothing they could really do.

In the morning, once left to myself, I contemplated the night's incident. Allowing what I could remember to play like some horror film. Just imagine if things had transpired as predetermined. How would I have felt to have done something so sinful, so brutal? What would my son's life have been like if he had a murderess for a mother?

To be responsible for that is too horrific a thought. There is also the fact, the intervention saved me from the gallows. The death penalty was still in force then.

Unhappily, there was no respite from the daily struggle to protect my son and myself. I frequently prayed Terrance would find another woman and leave us alone, though, as strange as it may sound, I still loved him. Who is able to fathom the human psyche or heart? A subsequent attempt at destroying his son and my consequent beating when trying to protect him proved too much. I just could not take more. Grabbing my baby in my arms, I ran from the house. My intent, to go to my mother-in-law, spill the beans and ask for help and shelter. There was nowhere else I could think of. And, I now knew, when pushed, she was prepared to stand up to her son. I believed Ralph and the girls would also once they knew of the truth. Sorry to say, Terrance saw me leave and chased after me. With sufficient a head start I was able to stay in front for a while but I was weak, barely four and a half stone, and could not keep the pace up. He caught up with us at a railway level-crossing where he punched me full in the face. My nose broke and blood poured everywhere. It must have looked like some horror movie. The blow left me dizzy and disorientated. Nonetheless, I managed to focus upon some passers-by as they shouted for him to stop. His simple retort was we were his wife and son and he could do what he liked with us. This evidently shocked them however, one had the good sense to summon the police.

The police had no need to inquire what was going on. I am not sure if I was relieved or scared at their arrival. Relieved someone in authority had arrived to intervene or scared of what my husband may do. When in a rage he had little control and could be even more excessively violent than normal. Though he lashed out at anyone who came near, the officers managed to separate us without injury. The ambulance crew, who the officers had summoned, expressed concern regarding the damage done to me. Thankfully, they quickly determined my son was unhurt. It was just all the blood over him that had caused their initial worry. Headaches have never been a problem for me, but on this occasion I had a real beauty. Presuming it the result of all the stress, fear, and blows to my face, I was not unduly concerned. However, it transpired I should have been. In order to administer medical attention, the paramedics, as they would be called now, asked me to pass over my baby. There was no way I was going to do that. I am sure you will understand after all we had been through, to even let go of him for a moment was not going to happen. My refusal irritated them, but the police, noting my distress, intervened and instructed them to let me keep hold of my son. They went further and robustly told the crew they would ensure we reached our destination safely. I think this was something virtually unheard of, to refuse to let the ambulance take us. I may only surmise why they did this. Instead of the main hospital we arrived at one of the smaller cottage ones, which existed in most areas at the time. These were far more personal and attentive and certainly had a lot going for them. Of course, I understand the health service has to consider costs, but I do wonder if we would not be better off if some of them still existed. I suspect they did this to diminish the possibility of Terrance tracing us. Everything occurring so quickly left me slightly phased and dizzy. However, I felt safe. In those days there was never any question about the reliability of those in authority.

The examining doctor informed me I was truly fortunate. The blow, that should be blows, to my nose had forced the nasal bone up and into my skull. Apparently it had only fractionally missed penetrating my brain. This was the cause of my terrible headache. It would be necessary to stabilise the bone straight away to ensure there was no further danger of it moving. If it did, it would unquestionably pierce my brain. The concept was very frightening. Having stabilised the bone, the doctor considered it would be wise for me to remain under observation for a while. Again I insisted my son remain with me and if he did not, I would walk out there and then. How long we were there I am unable to recall except to say it was a lengthy stay. All the watching, dodging, and fear of Terrance had left me exhausted. I cannot express the relief of having a period when I could forget, at least for a while. In many ways it was quite surreal. Nevertheless, I enjoyed the rest and peaceful time with my baby. Eventually, the doctors became satisfied the bone had settled, and there was no further risk of it moving in the wrong direction. I am pleased to say they did such a good job that there is no visible distortion to my nose, as is often the case with such breakages. You just need to look at some long-term boxers to see what I mean. I do occasionally have slight problems, but that is a small price for having survived what could have otherwise been a life ending incident.

I now faced an uncertain future. What was I going to do and where would I go? The thought of returning to Terrance was anathema. But did I really have any other choice? Without an income, food, or shelter, I was stuck. I could hardly believe I was back in this situation. My wartime years had been hard enough, but to face a similar prospect now, in peacetime, was beyond belief. Gathering up the little we had, I, with baby in arms, dutifully headed toward an unknown future. You may therefore understand my relief, and surprise, to find the police officers waiting for us. In those days it was unusual, and I believe prohibited, for them to become embroiled in domestic disputes. Neither were they supposed to move a woman without the husband's knowledge. I never asked, but suspect they used the fact the incident had taken place on a public highway to navigate round the rules.

Though uncertain of what they proposed, I knew they could be trusted and happily went with them. Well, happy is probably not the correct word. Happiness was far beyond me at the time. The next thing I knew, we were being greeted by a kind family who provided refuge for women in my position. I had no idea such places existed. They were certainly not as commonplace as they are today. There was only room for one woman and child at a time for which I confess I was grateful. I needed space to reorientate and contemplate possibilities and parameters for the days to come. I recall how cold the upstairs room they had given us was, but said nothing. To have a haven where, at least for a short while, I could let my guard down was enough. It was also good to have quality time with my son without the constant fear of him being beaten or worse.

Although the accommodation was provided free of charge, I was determined to contribute in any way I could and not take the family for granted. It transpired the lady of the house had a heart condition, so without it being asked or expected, I set about helping with the general household chores. Unfortunately, the peaceful state of affairs was not to last long. Somehow, Terrance discovered where we were and started skulking round the property. He never knocked on the door or anything like that, but we all knew he was there, creeping about and hiding in bushes. Naturally, it was unsettling for us all. Eventually, the lady had to tell me how frightened she felt and with her heart condition did not feel she could cope. She was very apologetic, but I understood and the last thing I wanted was to be the cause of any trouble for her. If the rest of the family had been round during the day, it would probably have been different, but they all worked. Consequently, she had to bear the prime responsibility for their 'guests'. I packed our few possessions while she contacted the police. Again, to my surprise and gratitude, they came immediately. I truly had not expected that this time.

We made our found farewells after which the kind policemen whisked us off to a large mansion where a household servant greeted us. I never met the owners. It was an upstairs-downstairs household in which only senior members of staff had any contact with the family. To this day I do not know where it is because whilst there we dare not go out. The house and walled garden were our confines. A large, comfortable, and warm room would be our home, where we were left to get on with our lives. Nevertheless, as is my usual predisposition, I did not want to impose on such generous liberality. This time I helped in the kitchen that, being below stairs, avoided any possible awkwardness of me bumping into the owners. Once again I hoped my son and I would be able to enjoy some tranquillity and freedom from the fears that had dominated our lives. However, as I suspect many of you know, life can be unfair. Yet again Terrance discovered us. How? I have no idea.

My son and I were in the garden enjoying the fresh air when Terrance suddenly jumped in front of us. He had been hiding behind one of the large laurels dotted round the garden. Before I had a chance to react, he grabbed my arm and dragged us out through a side entrance. My darling boy was in my arms. Naturally, I screamed. I honestly thought this time he really would kill us. Some staff came running and attempted to prevent him from pulling us into his car. In response, he shouted, we were his wife and child and he had the right to take us away. The staff did not know what to do. In those days a husband was considered to have full rights over his family, irrespective of whether he was a just or reasonable person. An archaic concept compared to modern day attitudes but regrettably a prevalent one of the time.

Once in the car, he begged me to forgive him, stating he would never be violent again and, to prove it, had a surprise waiting for me at home. Yea! Yea! You are no doubt thinking. It has all been heard before. And, of course, you are right. However, I was tired of running and simply wanted what I had always wanted, a quiet, happy family home. Perhaps he would be different this time. When so repentant he could be most convincing, especially as I knew he believed what he was saying himself. Though my heart doubted enough was enough, I did not want to go on running and hiding. I decided to take the chance. The surprise was a wonderful radiogram, a real luxury in those days. I still have some of the heavy duty 78rpm records. We settled back into our way of life, unfortunately in every sense. I cannot claim to have been surprised, but it was sad to be confirmed right again. How I would have loved to be proven wrong. His violence was if anything worse and I had to keep a constant guard. It was very wearing.

My narrative has shown Terrance, as with any troubled person, I suppose, had inconsistent and contradictory traits. You have seen, almost from the start of our relationship, his constant violence. And the inconsistency of him asking forgiveness at most unexpected times. As I have mentioned before, further contradictions in his character were, he never used bad language, nor did he drink. Neither at home nor in pubs as his peers. In those days, and for all I know it may still be, most men accepted regularly meeting up in public houses to be part of their masculinity. However, Terrance never paid heed to this. Perhaps it was a family thing, for the same was true of Ralph, my friendly father-in-law. From what I have witnessed and heard over the years, many will consider I should have been grateful for this abstinence but, quite honestly, I do not see it. How could his violence have been worse even if he had been drunk? Would he have tried to kill us less? Unfortunately, he smoked a lot. In fact he chain-smoked most of the time. One of his delights was to burn me with the glowing ends. I usually managed to keep the burn marks covered, but it was far more difficult with the bruises and welts. He had ceased confining his punches and kicks to areas my clothing would cover. He no longer appeared to care what people thought. If asked I would say I had fallen or walked into something, though it was blatantly obvious not all my injuries could be attributed to such an occurrence.

One day a knock at the door took me by surprise. Terrance's jealousy, suspicion, and frequent rudeness, limited visitations. Cautiously, I opened the door a crack to find, much to my surprise, a gentleman I recognised standing on the doorstep. The corner of one main shopping street was occupied by a secondhand shop in which I liked to browse from time to time. Besides finding English knickknacks interesting, I also thought to learn more about the society I now lived in. It was a virtual Aladdin's cave to me. Over time, I got to know the friendly owner and his wife a little. It was the owner who was standing on my doorstep. Once over my initial surprise, I greeted him with a hello and a nice to see you. However, the lingering question was obvious. He smiled and asked if he could come in. What should I do? Terrance was not at home, besides which we rarely allowed anyone we did not know intimately in. In response to my manifest hesitation, he informed me the police had sent him. As you may imagine, I was quite taken-aback. Why would the police do that? Though my encounters with him at the shop had been brief, they had been sufficient for me to gage he and his wife were decent people. There was also the added incentive of my curiosity and concern. I let him in.

It transpired he worked for the National Society for Prevention of Cruelty to Children, more commonly known as the NSPCC. Apparently the shop's income supported its work. He proceeded to tell me the police had been informed, by whom he did not say, of my return and that they were concerned for my child's safety. I assured him all was fine. Nevertheless, he requested to see for himself. Reluctantly, with my hygiene paranoia I did not like other people touching my child, I permitted him to examine my baby. Thankfully, up to this point, I had been successful in protecting him, meaning there were no bruises or injuries. Of course, I did not mention my husband beat me regularly, though I am sure he must have guessed. Having assured himself my child was unharmed, he went on to say he was obliged to keep a regular eye on my son's welfare. He would therefore call at frequent intervals. I immediately expressed concern for what my husband's reaction would be when he found out. He instantly assured me Terrance would never be told and visits would be when he was out of the house. The man proved good to his word. My husband never found out, and my continuing protection ensured my child remained unharmed. During this period I was even more on tenterhooks. Can you imagine what my husband's violence would have been like if he discovered? Death would have been a welcome relief.

In retrospect, it is hard for me to accept we lived in this state not for weeks or even months, but for years. How I managed to stick with it, I really do not know. Determined willpower, I guess. So much I wanted to succeed in creating a happy family home. As if that was ever going to be possible, but at the time I still hoped. After a couple of years Terrance decided to go into business for himself. He had always been interested in electricity and had been an electrical officer in the navy. He would therefore establish himself as an odd-job electrician. However, appreciating that would not provide a sufficient income on its own, at least not until he had an established reputation, he also decided upon a taxi service. The latter had the advantage of being an all-hours business that could be run outside normal working times. He used the little money we had to advertise both ventures and to purchase a car. Obviously, it would take time to establish both, which meant we would not have a regular income. There would therefore be no money for the rent that he had paid since entering full-time employment. As you know, prior to that, generous grandfather had helped. To give Terrance his due, and much to my surprise, he decided on this occasion it inappropriate to ask grandfather for further help. Especially as it would more than likely be long term. My surprise was because, beforehand, he had appeared to take grandfather's assistance for granted. With nowhere else to go, he approached his parents, requesting if it was possible for us to return while he established himself. They readily agreed and gladly gave us our old rooms. I am unable to truly express how delighted I was to be back with Vera and the girls. Once again I would have daily contact with them. Terrance could hardly forbid it whilst we lived in the same house. There was also the added delight of being able to enjoy Vera's wonderful baked goodies again.

Needless to say, nothing really changed except our location. The violence and daily attempts to despatch our son continued. As before, the family did their best to ignore what was going on. Should I be bitter about that? No. As mentioned previously, husbands were seen as having full rights over their spouses and offspring. Besides which, they loved their son and probably did not know how to deal with the issue. No doubt they were also fearful of inciting a possible escalation.

The fear, stress, and tension continued to affect my health, resulting in the loss of even more weight. I became increasingly concerned I would not be able to continue protecting my son. It would take one lapse only for my husband to achieve his goal. I still find it hard to accept a father could desire the destruction of his offspring.

Eventually, after a further two to three years of living in this state, I realised I could take no more. It was inevitable, especially with my deteriorating health, I would fail at some stage. My decision to leave was a very bold one, not just for me but also socially. Single parenthood was not really seen as acceptable, except perhaps where someone had been widowed.

17

Flight

I dare not tell anyone my intention. There was the danger of them accidentally saying something within Terrance's hearing. I tried to intimate to Vera my feeling of it being impossible to go on any longer and that something had to change. Though she nodded in vague agreement, I do not think she really comprehended what I was trying to say. The thought of leaving her, Ralph, and the girls upset me but, if we were to survive, it had to be done.

I prearranged as much as possible without my purpose becoming obvious. My family back home had, over time, included small financial gifts with their letters. Had Terrance known he would have taken it from me. However, though on the first couple of occasions I nearly told him, I quickly realised it would be unwise. Had I a premonition of what was to come? Possibly, after all he had been confusingly violent from the beginning. Though it was not much, the money would be sufficient to finance the initial commencement of a new life. Knowing everyone, except Moira, would be out on a particular afternoon, I surreptitiously prepared by packing all my son's clothes and a few of my own. Once certain all the others had left, I ordered a taxi telling Moira I was just going to collect my son from school, which I did. However, we did not return.

You may recall, when we first left his parent's home, Terrance got a job with a removals firm in a nearby town. It turned out the owner's wife was from my homeland and, though not usually allowed by my husband, she and I had struck up a sort of friendship. It had been good timing for me because I had been feeling particularly homesick. The family had a large house on a very pleasant avenue. The business occupied the ground floor. In my desperation to get away, I had not really thought through my escape plan. Where to go? What to do? It then crossed my mind my friend Kate may have room for us while I sorted something more permanent. I gave the taxi driver their address.

Apprehension took charge when we pulled up. Though I considered Kate a friend, we did not really know each other, and here I was about to ask a substantial favour. Admittedly I only intended it to be short term, nevertheless, it would be a favour of consequence. I feared she may consider it rather presumptuous. Kate was naturally surprised to see me but greeted us warmly. I quickly explained my situation, that I had left and was looking for somewhere temporary to stay while I sorted myself out. With constant interjected apologies for troubling her and asking such a favour together with beetroot coloured blushes, I asked if she would be able to help. Could she accommodate us, short-term, I emphasised, while I found somewhere more permanent? While reassuring me it would have been no bother, Kate explained her own current family circumstances prevented her from being able to help. Apparently several family members were staying. I hid my disappointment as best I could, but did now feel scared about what I was going to do. Kate thought for a moment and then told me about a friend, a married woman, who was having an affair. It seemed rather bizarre she should mention this now. She explained this woman and her lover rented a room for their assignations. Why tell me? Then it struck. Surely she could not be thinking? Anyway, what type of person rented out rooms for such purposes? It would not be somewhere I would want to be. Out of politeness, I did not express my thoughts. People have to live their lives the way they want, but it struck me as very unpleasant. I could see Kate was utterly serious about the possibility. I was not persuaded. Nevertheless, in my now desperate circumstances, I decided to wait and see. She telephoned and asked her friend to come over.

The likelihood of my liking someone who was so blatantly having an extramarital affair was remote. Even more so when Kate informed me the woman's husband was a decent man. Some people do not know when they are well off. How much would I have appreciated a considerate, nonviolent spouse. However, when introduced, I was surprised to find us taking an instant liking to each other. She was not the emptied headed, silly person I had expected. It also transpired, though the fact had no bearing upon my liking her, she was a fellow countrywoman. Kate explained my dilemma. That someone else should be told of my circumstances was embarrassing. To my surprise, Kate's friend instantly said of course we could have the room, provided the landlady agreed. I thanked her, though inwardly feared she and her lover may still want use of the room. She must have perceived because, without me having to ask, she told me they no longer required the room. Whether the affair, or marriage, was over or they had somewhere else to go, I have no idea and never asked. Without further ado, appreciating the urgency of us needing somewhere for that very night, she took us in her car to the house. The Northern Irish landlady manifested the harshness so many from that region epitomise. However, like so many, she also turned out to have a good, though unsentimental, heart. It cannot have been easy living in a society where hatred and violence are an everyday norm. The Irish troubles were in full swing at the time.

You may imagine my disconcertion when she informed us she rarely accepted people with children. You may also imagine my relief when she went on to say, because she had known my new friend for a while, she was prepared to rent the room to me. I was so grateful. What if this had failed? Just imagine a young, attractive woman with a young child left on the streets at night. We agreed a rent which I paid in advance. I think that helped set things on the right footing immediately. Conveniently, there was a school further down the road that was suitable for my son. Thankfully, they accepted him without question.

Having now sorted somewhere to stay the next hurdle was finding employment. Prior to leaving, I had confidentially spoken to the manager of the cinema I worked in, explaining as much of my situation as I thought necessary. It really is horrible having to tell people of your failures and especially of the brutal circumstances that led to them. I knew I was taking a risk telling him. You may remember how I had to resist his advances, but I needed to be practical. Thankfully, he proved understanding and told me he would ensure there was a job waiting for me in one of the two cinemas serving my destination. When the chips are down, it is surprising how some people can prove far more than expected. He was good to his word. A position was waiting for me.

So far, except for the odd comment, I have left it to your imagination to consider how I was feeling. Nervous, anxious, fearful, go some way, but here I was a lone woman with a young child in a large, unfamiliar town. Besides Kate and her husband, I knew no one. I felt vulnerable, very alone, and conspicuous. On the other hand, matters had worked out better than anticipated. Within hours I had secured accommodation, employment, and schooling. It had been a bit of a whirlwind and it was not until later I was able to take it all in.

When settling my new employment, I ensured the hours would permit me to escort my son to and from school. However, I did also, as a precautionary measure, instruct the school no one else was to be permitted to collect him. In the unlikelihood of me not being able to make it, which would only be if I was seriously ill, the person coming for him would have some form of identification from me. I was terrified Terrance might discover our whereabouts and attempt to snatch our son. He was more than capable of doing so. Either to kill him or to hold him as ransom for my return. I appreciate that sounds extreme, but the truth is the truth. He never seemed to get past the hatred, or jealousy, he had for his own son.

From the start I realised the salary from the cinema would be insufficient. I now had rent to pay, food to provide, and clothing to purchase, starting with a new school uniform. A second job had to be obtained. I perused the postcards on Post Office boards and in shop windows advertising vacancies. You do not see it very much these days, but back then it was a normal means by which small businesses found employees. The local press was my other avenue. It was there I came across an advert for night orderlies in one of the large local hospitals. You may recall how shy I am by nature and the thought of approaching strangers being traumatic for me. However, desperate circumstances require desperate measures. Add to this my determination to ensure I could pay my way, to never to go into debt, and not to seek financial help from anyone. All combined to overrule the hesitations. I applied and went for an interview on my own, albeit with a volcanic eruption in my belly. The duties would require me to assist with non-medical matters, which I felt confident I could do. They offered, and I gratefully accepted the position, agreeing to start straight away.

You are probably wondering, in the back of your mind, about my son. How was I going to work nights and still look after him? I had confirmed with my landlady that she would be willing to take care of my son overnight if I got the job. It went against the grain to leave him in the care of someone else, but I had to be practical. I needed the extra income. Upon returning from the successful interview, we put the matter on a formal footing with me agreeing to pay her an extra two pounds per week. That may not sound a lot now, but back then it was a vast amount, and it was on top of the two pound ten shilling rent. My combined salaries only amounted to six pounds. It may not appear, with what was left over, the second employment was worthwhile. However, to put it into context, a week's groceries could be secured for two shillings and sixpence, twenty-five pence in modern coinage. The surplus, though small, would enable me to pay my way, to handle any unexpected demands, and hopefully to put a little aside for the future. I had no idea where life would take us. I have to admit, after all we had been through, and though I thought the landlady could be trusted, my concern for my son never ceased. I just did not think anyone could protect him the way I could and would if the need arose.

My first entrance onto a male ward, in a nice new pink uniform, is one I will always remember. The chorus of cheers and yelps was loud and most unexpected. You may recall many considered me attractive. I apologise for mentioning this more than once, but that mindset had already caused me problems and would often result, as you will come to see, in the most unfortunate incidents and malicious treatments. Thankfully, on this occasion, it was all quite innocent and lighthearted. Over time several patients would occasionally pretend they had a secret to tell me and when I bent closer attempt to kiss me. Others insisted upon telling me, repeatedly, what I believe was a true account of a woman who had hung herself in the bathroom. These were mischievous men who knowing the story scared me a little, used that as an excuse to try and 'comfort' me. We all laughed when I told them what naughty boys they were. There really was no maliciousness in them. No doubt many would now jump up and scream sexual harassment, but it was simply good natured fun. In truth it was therapeutic for them and for me. It was nice to be able to laugh again, especially as nothing inappropriate ever occurred.

Naturally, the job was not without its challenges. On one occasion I was asked to work on a TB (Tuberculosis) ward. It was then a very dangerous and infectious disease. My refusal took everyone by surprise. This was definitely not the done thing. Everyone was expected to follow orders without question. We lived in a far more disciplined world then. The management could have summerly dismissed me but thankfully they had the sense to ask why. I told them I had a young child and was not prepared to risk his life. Normally some sort of disciplinary reprisal would follow such a refusal but I heard nothing further. I suspect they appreciated my action was not self motivated but born out of a genuine desire to protect my son. You may understand my gratitude. I needed the income and it would have been hard to find another job with suitable hours.

One drawback to my constant working was, when not at school or with my landlady, my son had to be with me. Thankfully, the supervisors at both the cinema and hospital, proved very understanding and permitted him to stay in private, non-public rooms while I worked. I did not consider the situation fair on him, but I was not in a position to do otherwise. I am proud and pleased to tell you he was always well behaved and did not appear to mind. From an early age he loved reading, so we always ensured he had a book with him as well as his drawing block. Later in life he did take up water and oil painting, many of which adorn the walls of my home. He was also a patient child and due to his good manners and politeness popular with other members of staff. On the rare occasions when my landlady was away for a day or two, he was allowed to sleep on a makeshift camp bed. I am not sure what I would have done if my supervisors had not been so obliging. I would probably have had to resign and face an unchartered and difficult future. Thankfully it never came to that.

It did not take long for me to recognise, a little wistfully, that my landlady came from a close knit family. The long distances that separated many of them made no difference. This observance impacted me rather hard. Not only was I missing my family back home, but I was now also separated from Vera, Ralph, and the girls, my English family. I longed for the intimate comfort and reassurance of a warm, loving, non-threatening hug. That, though I did not know it at the time, was something I would never experience again. As I write this, I can feel the tears in my heart. After the tender love of my early years, when I knew nothing else, it remains hard to accept my lot changed so dramatically. Never to know such tenderness again. Why?

A relative of my landlady, a nephew, cousin, or something similar, managed his own band and whenever they had a gig nearby would pop in. It was heartening to see the warmth and affection with which they always greeted each other. No, I was not jealous or envious.

It was simply good to see there were still people who shared such a relationship, even if it was never to be for me again. Naturally, I suppose, he asked who I was and what I was doing there. Once in possession of the details he took quite an interest in my son and I, and made a point of chatting with me whenever he visited.

Over time, we came to know each other moderately well. I am truly grateful to report there was never any intimation of romantic or sexual over or undertones. His whole demeanour was that of a friendly acquaintance, for which I was thankful. Subsequent to my flight from violence all I really wanted was a friend. Someone I could relax with and, hopefully, trust to some degree, though I have always remained wary. Unfortunately, it would not just be my ex-husband who let me down, but more of that as we continue. During one visit he told me how sorry he felt for us. After all we had been through, we could probably do with a break. I had not mentioned to anyone how tired and downcast I felt but it must have been showing. The combination of my night work, day job, rushing to take and collect my son from school, and striving to feed us both and clothe him left little time for rest. Disappointment at my failed marriage and anxiety for the future also added to my psychological, emotional, and physical struggles. The upshot of this kind man's observation was, much to my surprise and slight consternation, he offered to organise and pay for us to have a few days away at the next place his band was booked for. My consternation was due to a number of factors. Throughout my life I have made a point of never being indebted, especially financially, to anyone. In addition, it is important never to give anyone the idea of something more to a relationship than there is. In reality, we were simply acquaintances, not even friends in the true sense. So far all had been fine. I did not wish to risk that changing. There was also the concern of us being on our own in a strange place and country. The gig was in Europe. However, he proved intuitive and considerate because, without me saying a word, he immediately reassured me as to all matters. I still hesitated. As you will come to see, I normally refuse such offers outright. However, he had addressed my concerns, and I appreciated the offer was genuinely meant. Accepting was also made easier by the fact I believed there were no hidden agendas.

We found ourselves in a most delightful spot with fine weather, truly welcome after the British climate. Swimming and strolls through the lovely surroundings occupied our days while each evening was spent in the locations my friend's band played. Thankfully, the European society permitted children, meaning my son could be with me all the time. After all we had been through with his father and the upheaval of running away and establishing ourselves in a strange town among people we did not know, it was so good to have continuous non-violent and non-threatening time together. It was nice and truly therapeutic to forget, at least for a short while, all our troubles. Though I had sorted a home, work, and school, life was still not easy. Not that it ever really would be again. I almost felt guilty indulging in such cheerfulness and innocent fun. For example, despite my son's young years, and much to the delight of other patrons, I tried to teach him the foxtrot. We really did have so much lighthearted fun.

The place we were in appeared to have a reputation for comprising a relaxed, fun-filled, ritzy environment. Consequently, though it attracted all strata of society, it was principally the preserve of the highly placed and wealthy. One evening a royal head of state, from a non-European domain, along with his entourage, made a grand entrance. He was apparently visiting the area on his yacht. Really, how could you possibly refer to those immense structures as a yacht? It was more akin to an ocean-going liner. I recognised him because he was a distinctive figure who had featured in the national press and newsreels of the time. My son and I were sat at a table enjoying a cool evening drink, not really taking much notice, when one of the royal aides came over and told me his master would like to dance with me. Naturally, I was flattered but knew his reputation as a philanderer besides which I did not consider him attractive either in person or personality and therefore declined. There was also the fact I had no desire to be involved with such a high-profile public figure. As you will also come to see, the thought of such exposure is anathema to me. An anathema that has cost. That was an end to the matter as far as I was concerned. However, the next thing I knew was the man himself firmly taking my hand and determinedly pulling me out of my seat. You can guess how this behaviour made me feel. Under normal circumstances I would have immediately withdrawn my hand with a sharp word of reprimand. Subsequent to escaping my husband's brutality, I had learnt to stand up for myself. However, on this occasion, not only was I conscious of the surrounding, well-healed, patrons, but also of my young son's presence. Making a scene in such a place would not be good and remember there were also the man's security staff to consider. I was not so naïve as not to appreciate they were more than likely to step in if they thought something untoward was taking place. I have to say, despite his substantial size, besides his philandering, he loved his food and drink, he was a remarkably good, agile, dancer. My son, not accustomed to being left on his own in such places, within moments had come onto the dance floor and inserted himself between us, or rather our legs. The sight of the three of us dancing together delighted everyone including my dance partner. The light from flashing camera bulbs, mobile phones were not even on the horizon then, and laughter bounced from the walls. We had an enjoyable evening, which ended with my flat refusal of his majesty's invitation to attend a party upon his yacht. I had a good idea of what would more than likely be attempted if I went. We parted on good terms and he sailed off the next day.

A theme that would arise from time to time throughout my life now rose its head for the first time. In addition to his band, my friend had a side line working as a freelance photographer for model agencies. At his request, I permitted him to take some respectable photographs. He told me how much the camera loved me, how beautiful I was, and I should really go to an agency. He was certain they would want to contract me and offered to contact some agencies he knew on my behalf. I declined. Not only was I too shy for such a life, but was also concerned about the effect such an occupation, should I get a contract, would have upon my son. Neither was I very sure of how I would cope myself. Public exposure of any sort has never appealed. I am not one to seek the fifteen minutes of fame so many look for.

Thankfully, my friend respected the decision not pushing the point further. The only thing he did say was what a shame people should miss out on such beauty. All very flattering but also frightening, for me at least. Although nothing was ever said and there was never any attempt at intimacy, I suspect, deep down, he would have liked us to marry. I am grateful to him for never bringing such a suggestion up and for always respecting me.

Those few days away had been thoroughly enjoyable. We returned from our break fresh and revived.

Beside the failure of our marriage, I was very sad our escape from Terrance would result in loss of contact with all my in-laws. My English family. It would be forty years before I saw any of them again. I had been extremely nervous but need not have been. Joy, who I made the first contact with, had welcomed me warmly, as had also the others when I saw them. Joy, my son and I have since enjoyed some catching up. We also had the pleasure of seeing Vera shortly before she passed away. She had done so much for me. I am certain without her care I would not be here to share with you.

18

Arterial

Once again, and yet again I did not know how, Terrance discovered where we were living. He began turning up at the house shouting abuse and threats. As I have mentioned before, it is really strange how even on these occasions he never swore or used bad language. Up to this point I had done my best to forget our past, or at least to put it to the back of my mind. I do not think you may ever truly forget such treatment and events like those we had endured. I preferred to concentrate upon creating, as best as I could, a new life for my son and I. I also saw no point in unnecessarily telling people all the details. The horror of it all was bad enough. But there was also the shame I felt in acknowledging my husband's violence and abuse and the consequent failure of our marriage. Unfortunately, there was now no avoiding the telling of all to my landlady. His behaviour could not be ignored and had to be explained. She listened with sympathy as I related the extent of his brutality and, though said nothing, was evidently shocked. I left nothing out, including his constant attempts to kill his son. Combining this information with his current aggression, she became alarmed at what he may attempt. That led her, without a by your leave, to contact the local police. Once in possession of all the details, they communicated with the police force who had been involved in rescuing us from Terrance in the past. I admit by this time I had grown afraid, especially for my son. Based upon what I told them and the information gained from the other police force, they decided it appropriate to allocate police protection.

Protection amounted to the constant presence of a police officer outside the house when we were in and then at my son's school when he was there and I at work. They had accepted my reasoning that he was more likely to go after our son as a means of getting at me, as opposed to directly attacking me. I have to acknowledge I was not entirely sure of this premise myself. However, as the protection had to be limited to one officer, I considered it preferable to protect my child. If he went for me, I would have to deal with it. To some this may sound an adventure and romantic. Be assured it was anything but. It was very frightening as well as frustrating. You can never relax, be yourself, or go about as you would like. In addition, the idea of needing what amounted to a bodyguard horrified me. Surely this was the life of the influential and wealthy, not of poor ordinary souls like us.

The police also obtained a restraining order. Unfortunately, this could not entirely extend to preventing access to his son. They had to grant him supervised contact. This meant, once a week, I had to leave my son with a policewoman at the local station. The law did not permit me to be present or even nearby during these visits. To say I was apprehensive during those hour long separations goes nowhere near defining my emotions. The entire hour was torture. Until I returned to collect my baby, I was constantly terrified something may go wrong. Not once did Terrance ever turn up. He always phoned with some excuse. The car had broken down. He was not well. He had been in an accident, and so on. I kept reiterating to the officers he was not interested in the boy but just wanted to get at me. Eventually, they reached the same conclusion and applied for the supervised contact order to be withdrawn.

One afternoon when I went to collect my son from school, I was horrified to see his father holding his hand and leading him away. My worst nightmare had been realised. I leapt across the intervening space. Amazing how the adrenalin of fear can propel us. Grabbing my husband's arm, I screamed at him to let our son go. Despite the adrenalin, shock must have impacted for a few seconds because during that minuscule moment he had dragged our son into his car, a Mark 10 Jaguar. Thankfully, not sure that is the right word, I recovered sufficiently to allow me to jump into the car before he pulled away. There was absolutely now way I was going to let go of my son. Whatever the cost, then and now, I will always protect him. He is my life. All I have done is to try and provide him with the best life I could.

Some of you may be wondering what had become of the policeman who was supposed to be guarding my child. He must have been dozing because it was not until he saw me grab and shout at my ex-husband he came to life and, too late, started running about. At a later time, after the event, I asked what he had been thinking. His reply astounded me. Seeing it was the boy's father he had thought it okay for him to take him. What on earth did he think he was protecting my son from? He simply held his head down sheepishly and, other than a mumbled 'sorry', made no further response. A lot of good that was. I could not help my anger, but managed to restrain myself from saying anything further.

Terrance immediately put his foot down and sped away from the school, with me pleading for him to let us out. He headed for one of the primary roads leading out of town and into the surrounding countryside. Throughout he was shouting unless I agreed to go back to him he would crash the car and kill us all. I knew he was more than capable of doing so. Despite my fear and very real terror, I could not assent. I had tried too many times with nothing ever changing, except the brutality usually got worse. It never occurred to me to lie simply to get him to stop. Naïve or what? Instead I continued to plead for him to let us out. He took no heed and while fiercely glaring at me put his foot further down, reaching one hundred miles an hour in no time. This although we were now in narrow country lanes with tight sharp bends. I should point out, in those days only high-class cars could reach such speeds while the rest of us mortals were accustomed to a more sedate pace of travel. Widespread, individual ownership of cars was something for the future. Foot power and public transport were then the norm for most. Consequently, a hundred miles an hour was truly frightening.

High hedgerows bordered the lanes, so it was impossible to see if anything was coming from the other direction. As we skidded round blind corners I screamed for him to stop. He would not listen. At one point, in my terror, I nearly grabbed his arm to make him stop, but thankfully thought better of it. If I had followed my instinct he would have lost control and we would have undoubtedly crashed. At such a speed the outcome would have been a foregone conclusion. All this time, my protective instincts had me tightly clenching my son in my arms. I remain amazed I did not crush the life out of him.

Besides his natural upset at what was passing between his father and me, my son had never been a particularly good traveller. The constant twisting and turning, not to mention speed, all became too much. He cried out to his daddy he was going to be sick. Instead of giving a sympathetic or compassionate reply, his father simply, with anger, told him to be sick then. He was. It was now I became certain my husband intended to kill us all. In desperation, I decided, with my son still in my arms, to jump out of the moving vehicle. In retrospect, I appreciate had I done so, my child and I would no longer be here. When my husband realised what I was about to attempt he shouted not to, that we would be killed. In his bizarre way he still cared, about me at least. It was increasingly evident, he would be glad to be free of his son. I still do not understand how a father can be like that.

Perhaps my attempt to jump out had some sort of impact, or maybe it simply brought him to his senses. Whatever it was, my husband slowed the car, eventually drawing into a wooded lay-by where he turned the transmission off. We sat for a few seconds. He appeared to be dazed or in another world, while I struggled to regain breath and equilibrium. It must have only been minuscule seconds before he twisted in his seat to face me, and said he could not live without me. Receiving no immediate response, he went further. Saying he would prove his love he produced a razor from somewhere. Before comprehension hit, he had sliced both his wrists. It is impossible to truly explain the erupting emotions that engulfed me. Horror, incredulity, after all it was us he always harmed never himself, protective instinct, for my son, denial, I could not be seeing what I was, and so on. The question then arose of whether I should just get out of the car and leave him there. I could not. It goes against my nature to let anyone suffer, even him. Thankfully, self control quickly overcame my shocked inertia. I tore strips of fabric from the hem of my dress and bound his wrists as best as I could. Once the flow of blood stemmed, I got out and ran back to the road waving for someone to stop. But no one would. It was then I realised my son and I were covered in blood. Unless you have witnessed such an event it is hard to believe the volume that emerges in an arterial fountain, let alone two. We must have looked like something out of a horror film. Left with no other choice, I stepped into the road holding my son to one side at arm's length. There was no way I was going to let go of him, even for a moment. The bumper of the next car made contact with my legs before coming to a halt. As you may appreciate, both the driver and I were shaken. I also worried he may just pull back and drive off. I waited until sure the vehicle was fully stopped before running to the driver's side. Goodness knows what was going through the poor man's mind as he looked me up and down, perceptibly noting the vast amounts of blood. Bending to speak through the crack at the top of his window, I spoke, or rather shouted, a plea for him to please call an ambulance and that someone was bleeding to death, pointing in the direction of where my husband sat in his car. I assured him I wanted nothing else. He may have been concerned there was more to it. I shouted, as he drove away, for him to please not forget. You need to bear in mind this was long before mobile phones and it would be necessary for him to find a petrol station or one of the iconic British red telephone boxes. Service areas as we know them now did not exist then. I had no idea where we were but am forever grateful to this unknown samaritan because he obviously knew and had done as I asked. It was not long before an ambulance arrived with a police escort.

Upon seeing the blood and his bandaged wrists, the police asked what had happened. My husband tried to tell them he had cut his wrists on a broken window, which was rather foolish as they could see there were no damaged windows. They took us to hospital where the doctors checked and dressed his wounds properly. To my surprise they discharged him there and then. I had anticipated them keeping him in for observation, at least for a few hours, if not overnight. I may only surmise but suspect, observing how clean and straight the cuts were, they comprehended what had happened. They must have also realised he was not a genuine suicide risk. Throughout I had remained as silent as possible, not wishing to exacerbate matters. Anyway, I was far more concerned for my son and ensuring he was okay. The police kindly drove my husband to his home and us to ours. Presumably his car had been taken to the local compound for later collection. I should mention, those attending to the injuries complemented me upon the dressings. Apparently, if they had not been so well done my husband would have probably bled to death. Still gives me the shivers to think of the possibility.

Though I should have realised otherwise, I had hoped this would be an end to my husband's persecution. Naïve me. He continued hanging around and constantly tried to engage me in conversation. Thankfully, he attempted no physical contact. Nevertheless, the whole situation was stressful, and I remained constantly anxious for my son's safety when he was away from me. The failure of that policeman at the school had undermined any confidence I may have had in the security his presence was supposed to have provided. I really did not know what to do. Everyone who knew us and what was happening said I should get a divorce. Such an idea was abhorrent. To me, marriage was, is, for life. I appreciate this may appear odd for many in these days of easy divorce. Most societies and cultures in those days, especially in my own, considered divorce shameful. I suppose, deep down, I did not want to admit failure, which it would be to me, even though I was not the instigator of our troubles.

My landlady and her friends were fond of us and became increasingly incensed with my husband's behaviour. I think they soon recognised how naïve and innocent I was in the ways of the world. Looking back I have to say, despite all I had been subjected to, I think they were correct. In the end some of their, how shall I put it, boisterous, tough, unsentimental, navvy friends, decided he needed to be taught a lesson. They arranged to get together at a specified time to beat him up. Now, to show you the naïve, soppy person I can be. The idea terrified me, so I told my husband, who, just like the coward he was, ran faster than a startled rabbit. Before he disappeared from sight I made him promise to telephone me once home, so I would know he was safe. I cannot stand to see violence done to anyone or anything. I may suffer such myself but never want others to be subjected to such treatment even though, sometimes, I think they may deserve it. There was also the fact I still cared. In retrospect, it may have done him some good to have the beating, though, with such a heavy-handed lot, the outcome may have been far worse than intended. I could never have lived with that on my conscious. As you would expect, they were very annoyed and frustrated by what they perceived to have been their bad luck. Of course, I never let on what I had done. They would not have understood and may have even turned their aggression toward me. It frightened me for a while they might find out, but thankfully they never did.

All these latest incidents with my husband and his continuing harassment left me very downhearted. I had thought it all in the past. Instead, I now fretted endlessly about what I could do. I even considered another disappearing act. However, to date, these had spectacularly failed. Ultimately, after many sleepless nights and tortured days, I reluctantly concluded my friends were right. There was no option but to apply for a divorce. I certainly had sufficient grounds. It is hard to put into words how this made me feel and you may consider me foolish, but I continued reticent. After all, it went against my cultural and religious sensibilities. It was concern for my son and the wish to be free from fear that finally overcame those sensibilities and my deeply felt emotions. From the point of instructing a solicitor, and throughout the intervening period, I remained in turmoil. I felt guilty at breaking what I believed to be one of the strict religious codes of my church. The sensation of having failed to do my duty and keep my marriage together burrowed deeply. I worried about what my family would say. The fact my son would have no father in his life also saddened me. And the fear I was doing the wrong thing pervaded my thoughts. Nevertheless, there was relief at having started what I hoped would lead to the conclusion of my troubles. Such a mixture of thoughts and emotions was draining, causing what little sleep I managed to be fitful. All I truly wanted was to disappear, to be left in peace, to be allowed to rest and sleep. That was not about to happen. If for no other reason than my son, I did my utmost to keep my strength and morale. However, the truth is I felt low, weak, tired, and always, always fearful.

One day, while heading for home with my son, I felt weaker than usual and had difficulty holding any thought or directing my footsteps. Without warning, not even the sensation of one, I collapsed. Some passers-by must have called an ambulance for the next thing I knew I was being taken to hospital. After a full examination, a series of questions, and much debate, the doctors concluded the constant haranguing, combined with my fears and previous experiences, had resulted in a nervous breakdown. I do remember my hair went peculiar, just as if it had been singed and even fell out from some areas.

Though I had been able to answer questions and provide limited detail of what life with my husband had been like, I, as you would expect, was in a confused state. Collapse, blackout, strangers, foreign environment, unsettling medical equipment, and rushing staff combined to bewilder. However, and very thankfully, there were sufficient of my wits left for me to become concerned about my son. I feared he would be forgotten, or even become lost, in the hospital melee. Nor did I want him unduly frightened by all the emergency room goings on. The doctors and nursing staff were obviously preoccupied. After all I was not the only emergency they were dealing with. It therefore took a while but eventually they comprehended my concern and willingly called my landlady. I initially felt I could trust her because she had been looking after my son when I worked night shifts. Even so I could not relax. Fear of what might happen to him without me dominated. There was also the troubling thought of my husband using the excuse of my hospitalisation to claim custody. What would have happened to my boy then? Consequently, against medical advice, I discharged myself.

Upon my return home my landlady reluctantly felt obliged to tell me she was anxious. Her elderly and infirm mother also lived in the house. With my husband's aggressive behaviour and tendency to violence there was no telling what he may try. He may even try to gain access into the property. Therefore, with real regret, she felt there seemed little choice but to ask me to find somewhere else to live. Naturally, this upset me and I feared she was actually asking me to leave there and then. Noting the fact, she quickly assured me we could stay until I secured new accommodation. I was truly grateful for such thoughtfulness. We had got on well with a degree of friendship having developed. We were both sad about the need to part but accepted it the sensible, and only, solution. Priority for her own family had to take precedence, as it did for me. In addition, as she pointed out, there was the possibility of avoiding my husband's detection in a new location. If only that could be. In view of the kindness, despite her anxiety, I felt it was only right I start searching immediately. I would have preferred a period in which to rest and recuperate, but that would not have been fair.

The search was to prove a difficult task. In those days, unlike now, a lone woman with a child was unusual. People, more often than not, attributed immoral circumstances, never thinking, or so it appeared, to enquire. Therefore finding any decent accommodation became a challenge. There were landlords of properties in extremely rough and dangerous districts who would consider the like of us, but they were usually unscrupulous and mercenary. Besides the undesirability of these places, I was not prepared to place my son, or myself when it came down to it, in a worse situation than those we had already experienced. I scoured the local press and mentioned to a few friends my predicament. Two of them told me about a house on their street in which rooms were rented. Apparently the lady owner worked on a short-haul cruise ship and due to her frequent absences rented most of the rooms, partly for security and partly to earn additional income. Though the property was not in the best of areas, it was near the town centre, meaning I would be able to walk to my places of employment, my son's school, and the shops. The consequent saving on travelling expenses would be welcome. My friends arranged an interview for when the woman was on shore leave that culminated with her accepting me. It turned out she also took social security lodgers, which was to be a new encounter and an eye opener. The room was adequate, though it only contained one single bed that I made comfortable for my son. I slept across two chairs, utilising blankets and cushions to soften the hard surfaces. While talking about sleep you may wonder what happened with my son at night now I no longer had my landlady to care for him. Explaining my predicament the hospital supervisors kindly agreed a change from night to morning duty. My reputation as a hard worker had clearly helped, though I think they would have been willing to accommodate me regardless. There was a reduction in salary due to losing the night allowance that I tried to make up for by extending my usherette job into the afternoons. My friend Kate agreed, for a small fee, to look after my son along with her daughter when he was not at school and I was working. I still took him to and collected him from school and provided his meals. This arrangement had two advantages. First, I could still earn a reasonable income. Second, I had the evening and nights with my son. With my previous night orderly work we had not really seen much of each other. I had missed him very much.

19

Divorce

My divorce case was to be heard in the courts of my husband's hometown. It will not surprise you to hear on the day I felt a nervous wreck. Nevertheless, I was not prepared to give in to the emotion. I was determined to present myself in a fit light, especially as my son's custody also formed part of the hearing. I therefore reached deep to summon all the strength I could. Remember, besides the normal trauma of a divorce, I was also battling the fact all this went against my beliefs and the religious and social acceptances of my home culture and society. What would my family think? Would those who knew us back home reject and ostracise us? Would my home church excommunicate me once they knew? Add to all this my overwhelming sense of failure and you may have some concept of the state I was in.

Above all else, the potential for possibly losing my son drove me crazy. It was all I could do to stay focused and on my feet. Can you imagine what would have been my son's fate if his father got custody? Despite all her goodness and willingness, I knew Vera, my then mother-in-law, was unlikely to succeed in protecting her grandson. Such thoughts and considerations exacerbated my fears and apprehensions. These threatened to overrun my determination and the little strength I had mustered. My head felt light, my heart palpitated, my breathing grew shallow and rapid, my stomach somersaulted, and my muscles ached with the tension.

With my shy disposition, entering the court with the thought that everyone would be looking was daunting and traumatic. Once in, the number of people present staggered me. Many were those I had come to know when living in the town. This surprised me very much because I had told no one about the case or court appearance. In fact I had not had contact with any of them since leaving. Clearly, somehow, news of the hearing had got round. I later learnt these kind souls had decided, upon their own volition, to attend and bear witness. You will see in a moment, I had a lot to be grateful to them for, no matter what the eventual outcome.

As you would expect, my solicitor had summoned the police to present the record of their involvements in our domestic affairs. Unexpectedly, for me at least, the family doctor was also present. I assume he heard about the hearing in his capacity as a police doctor. He kindly informed the court, affectionally referring to me as the poor child, I could make anybody happy and asked what more would anyone want. My friend from the National Society for the Prevention of Cruelty to Children, in his role as one of their inspectors, had also turned up. He generously informed the court he could vouch for me and I had kept my home so clean it would have been possible to eat from the floor.

Beside the official witnesses, several of my previous neighbours had asked to give testimony. They told how my husband would never grant them admittance and had rather made a point of scaring them away. Among these had been a woman who I had got to know through her fascination with my washing. She wanted to know how I got it so white. She also testified to my cleanliness. Throughout each person told the judge how I loved and cared for my son above all else. All of this was so unexpected and kind, but did little to alleviate the fears and apprehensions. I simply gritted my teeth, white-knuckle gripped the rail before me, and did my best to give a little smile to the person complementing me. Internally it was as if there was liquid jelly sitting on top of a volcano.

Eventually the judge came to his summoning up. I am afraid I rather desperately interrupted before he had really commenced, telling him if he took my son away from me I would surely die. Having got it out I could no longer suppress my nerves and emotions. I collapsed. Despite what I have already shared, you may wonder why my state of tension had reached such a high pitch. My concerns were exacerbated by the fact, in those days, it was far more normal for custody to granted to the father because they were usually the one with an income. Most wives did not work. Being a housewife was the norm, and society widely expected them to be such. Consequently, they had no independent means of support. I dreaded the judge would follow the precedent. Proceedings were halted while a couple of court ushers lifted me into a chair and brought a glass of water. The judge patiently waited until I was sufficiently recovered to comprehend. I felt rather embarrassed and foolish, but he kindly reassured me and said to take my time.

Once he saw I had recovered, he, without the slightest hesitation, God bless him, gave me custody. I nearly collapsed again, this time with relief. A dam within appeared to have burst as all the tensions, fears, emotions, and anxieties flowed. It would be some time before I would be able to fully believe, but for now that release was more than sufficient, though it did leave me feeling weak. He went on to say my husband deserved to have a wife who treated him the way he had treated me. Prophetic words, as you will see. He then leant across his bench and, peering over the top of his half-moon spectacles, wished my son and I all the luck in the world. He added he was sure he would never see me in a court again. I almost ran across to kiss him but was able to exercise self control and limit myself to truly heartfelt, very sincere, thank you's. Subsequently, he proceeded to discuss the matter of maintenance with the barristers, but I interjected to state I did not want any. I did not want further involvement with my husband. I just wanted to be free from him. Anyway, I knew he would never have paid. After some discussion the judge and his colleagues allocated one shilling a week for our son's maintenance, equivalent to ten new pence. He had accepted my request in part by not allocating anything for me. I was told later he did this so there would be some means of comeback for the future if the need arose. Of course, my husband never paid and I never pursued the matter.

I cannot convey how I felt upon leaving the court. Suffice it to say, I was overjoyed. I may have near suffocated my son as I clutched him to myself in sheer happiness. I was ecstatic. Friends and neighbours congratulated me as I profusely thanked them for so unexpectedly turning up and giving such favourable testimony. Despite all the cruelness in the world, there are moments of genuine kindness, care, and appreciation. These may be rare but are all the more surprising, gratifying, and precious for it.

After all the years of oppression and brutal violence it took a while to believe we were free. In my mind I kept questioning. Were we truly free? Was this really the end of my husband's tyranny? Was my son truly safe? Was I really not going to get any more beatings? It was so bewildering. Some time passed before I felt it possible to accept we could now live our lives without constant fear. That we really could do what we wanted, when we wanted, and all without threat.

The proceedings, especially with the accompanying qualms in respect to my son's custody, not forgetting the inevitable fears and tensions, left me drained. Naturally, I was happy to be free, but where to go from this point challenged me. I could simply return to working and doing my best to provide for my son. However, this new turn and final conclusion to my previous life somehow unsettled me. I needed time to reorientate. We may have escaped my husband and be able to lead our own lives, but the fear of him turning up and the probable violence that would ensue never departed. There was no question we could do with a recuperative break. Eventually I decided a visit to my family was in order. I had not seen them since relocating to England and I missed my sisters terribly. It was also time the whole family met their nephew and cousin. Children are an important component in our culture and not to have met my son was out of order. Though my decision made sense and would be the ideal solution, I remained hesitant because ensuring a regular income was a constant paramount. It was my sole responsibility to provide for my son and myself. Nevertheless, though my income had not been great, I had saved a little. I judged it should prove enough to finance such a trip, provided we found economic travel facilities. Also, rather than stay at some unknown, barren hotel or resort, I intended staying with my sister. Being with loved ones would be far more relaxing and therapeutic and would save the additional costs which inevitably arise when at a hotel or similar. Naturally, I would contribute toward food and such, but that would be comparatively less. I do not believe in using people, no matter who they are or how willing they may be. I can hear the cogs in a few of your minds. No, I was not about to impose myself upon my sister without warning. In letters she had always made clear, if, when, I was able to return we were to stay with her and I knew she meant it. Doing so would also enable us to catch up properly. After so many years apart there was little doubt, with all the differences and challenges in our respective lives, each of us would have changed. We had been but girls when last we saw each other.

Decision made, the thought of seeing them all again excited me but I knew I had to keep my feet firmly on the ground. We were not leaving forever. I therefore needed to ensure we had somewhere to come back to. My landlady agreed, for a fee, to keep our belongings until we returned, fully aware we would be away for a lengthy period. A further advantage of staying with my sister. A hotel or resort would have restricted us to a week or two. Sadly, as you will come to see, all my plans and arrangements in this regard went pear-shaped. I could barely believe it, but I am jumping ahead.

Ecstatic at the thought of finally going home again is hardly a sufficient description of my emotions. I could not help but constantly talk about it with those I knew, never having really got over my homesickness. I not only longed to see my sisters but also my father and the rest of our relatives. It was not until we returned to England I discovered my ex-husband had heard of our plans. Presumably, someone had mentioned them to an acquaintance or friend who had then, directly or indirectly, informed him. One thing I was sure of is it could not have been any of my friends who knew our history. Pathetically, and despite the fact we were now divorced, and I had custody of our son, he posted our photographs at ports and airports with instructions that we should not be allowed to leave the country. Whether he had authority to do this with regard to his son, although I had custody he was still his father, I do not know. He certainly did not have the right with respect to me. Thankfully, I knew nothing of this at the time. I was anxious enough about undertaking such a long journey on our own and it would have worried me further. That would not have been good in my already weakened state. As mentioned, I needed to find economic transport, which turned out to be rail. Cheap package tours, holidays, and charter flights were yet in the distant future and unheard of at the time. My ex-husband had apparently failed to consider the option.

The journey time was considerable and I must admit it did become tiring and uncomfortable. This was exacerbated by the fact, to keep within my financial limitations, I had only booked seats without sleeping berths. Our discomfort was alleviated to some degree by the fact our fellow travellers were pleasant and nice. Just imagine if they had been mean and grumbly. In those days it was primarily educated and civilised people who travelled. I appreciate that may sound snobbish but it is not intended to be. I am merely trying to paint a picture of the times for you. In more recent years, probably due to the advent of cheap travel, I have had the misfortune to travel with some very rude, uneducated, and selfish people. I initially thought that was being harsh but have found many other travellers making the same observations. Why do people have to be so inconsiderate of others? Whatever happened to respect? Gratefully, I may tell you this journey was made the more pleasant and enjoyable by the fact people travelling to the same destination gathered together. Usually from the same cultural background, they would share traditional foods and drinks, play national music, dance and laugh together. It was all good, innocent, fun and made the journey time pass quicker. Just imagine having to sit for days and nights on end watching out of the windows for the entire trip. Notwithstanding the varied and lovely scenery, it would have been truly tedious.

Anna, my sister and Christopher, her husband, met us with a very warm welcome. I had been concerned about my brother-in-law.

You may recall the difficulties that had arisen prior to my leaving. Anyway, he was fine. Matters seemed to have calmed in the intervening years. As excited and pleased as we were to see them, it was not possible to hide how tired, dirty, and hungry we were. Though we had food on the journey it had not been much, or that substantial. My sister, who was an excellent cook, provided us with a wonderful meal enhanced by the general catching up chitchat. After, rather than sit together as we would have liked, my son and I bathed and went to bed. I think we slept for twelve or more hours straight through. Sympathetically, notwithstanding their eagerness for news of all that had occurred with me since leaving, they held back their questions for the next day.

I have already indicated how extremely ashamed I was of my failed marriage. Undoubtedly, many of you find that difficult to comprehend, but in my society wives were expected to hold families together, no matter the circumstances. Something I clearly failed to do. My sense of failure continued for many years. Throughout the journey, in the time before falling asleep, and in my initial waking hours, I had contemplated what to tell my family, and perhaps more importantly, what not to reveal. Final determination was not to tell everything, especially nothing about the unrelenting beatings and how my son's life was under constant threat. There would have been no point, besides upsetting them there was nothing they could do. I did however, ensure they understood how considerate and kind my in-laws had been. Divorce was almost unheard of in our culture therefore, naturally, it intrigued them to hear all about it. When asked why it had come about, I simply sidestepped the issue by saying it was just things had not worked out. Hardly a satisfactory response, but having stated it with the pathos I truly felt, they did not press further. In later years my sister told me she had realised there was more to it and that I was not happy but decided not to ask. She could see it would only cause me further upset. To partially satisfy their curiosity, I depicted the court scene and action, providing what information I considered necessary without accidentally giving any of the horrible brutal facts away.

In the same way as we are interested in different cultures and lifestyles, they wanted to know about England and its ways. Describing the British style of housing they, like I had been, were less than impressed, especially of the endless identical terraces. Unless you have lived in a country with a milder climate like my homeland that has very individual constructions, it is hard to understand this dislike. As best as I could, I went on to convey English culture. Compared to our warm, open society, it appeared chilled and cold to them. I explained it had to me until I came to understand what lay behind some of the social acceptances and behaviours. Stiff upper lip and all that. In an attempt to satisfy their curiosity further, I also described the variety of shops, my places of employment, public transport, and so on. It really was a different world, far more so than now, though marked differences remain.

20

JURISDICTION

Since my leaving, Anna and Christopher had moved into their own home within what was then a developing suburb. However, at the time it looked little like it. Like many others, Christopher had secretly built the house at night on what was in effect waste land. Through a loophole in the law, a person had the right to claim a property as their own if they built it undetected. The law has since dealt with the loophole, which is probably good but definitely not so much fun. On that visit, because all building had to be done in secret, the area had a sparse population, though you would not believe it now. The district has grown into a fully developed, overcrowded, thriving, self-contained suburb. Everything residents could require is available from the vast mix of shops and services. Then, it was still quite barren. I particularly remember the bakery at the top of a nearby mound that had more the appearance of a waste dump than anything else. It was the only building on it. It may help to know bakeries were and remain an essential cultural component. Bread has always been a staple of our diet and is bought fresh every day. The wonderful, mouthwatering aromas penetrate the entire surrounding district during the mornings. I freely admit to loving freshly baked bread. My son, accompanied by one of his cousins, enjoyed collecting our daily supply and the sense of responsibility it gave him. On one occasion, the baker warned the bread had only just been taken out the oven. Still a young child, he always had to carry the four long loaves across his arms. Due to the heat he was shirtless and returned with burnt chest and abdomen, but proud he had not dropped any of the loaves. Thankfully there was no lasting damage. He was more careful thereafter. You may wonder why his cousin had not helped. They were not allowed. My son has always had an independent streak that has since benefited him.

Considering the stealth with which it had to be built, I am glad to say my brother-in-law had not skimped. It was a nice, well proportioned, even if not overly large, house surrounded with garden. As was traditional, it had a flat terraced roof that commanded impressive views across the city. My son and I enjoyed going up there. In the day, to benefit from the brilliant and warm sun and at night, to take in the breathtaking views of the illuminated city, especially its ancient ruins. My sister had stocked the garden with aromatic blossoms and a variety of vegetables. Most people had little and therefore relied heavily upon self-grown products. A substantial side terrace provided the primary focal area for the family and for when there were visitors. Because of the warm climate much of life is lived in the open. Laughter often echoed, and it is where we had great fun.

I still have a couple of photographs of laughing faces and youngsters hanging off the metal poles and trellises supporting taller plants.

Despite my concern for a regular income and consequently the need to get back, I had not thought about how long we would stay. It was simply good to have got away with the knowledge of our freedom the court ruling had enabled. I think I was still in a bit of a fog, subconsciously sensing my need for rest and recuperation. It was therefore with gratitude I accepted Anna and Christopher's reassurance we could stay for as long as we wanted. I suspect they understood my need for time to readjust. There was now opportunity for me to contemplate our future. I do not think I had truly understood how different our lives were going to be.

I failed to mention my son's problem with blisters. They covered him. Apparently, it was something to do with his father's blood. In my opinion, it probably had more to do with the man's unhealthy diet. Egg and chips, and on Friday's fish and chips, constituting his normal intake. Vegetables and fruit were anathema until I eventually got him to try a salad made in my homeland's style. To be honest I could understand his dislike of what passed for salad in England then. It had been with trepidation I suggested the idea, anticipating another beating for having been so bold. This was to be one of those extremely rare occasions when he listened and, having deigned to try it, admitted his liking. I still had to produce the usual egg or fish and chips but was permitted to insert the occasional salad. The doctors, we had seen more than one, told me nothing could be done and the condition would probably continue until my son was eighteen or more. Naturally, this was very upsetting, especially as my boy did suffer. However, the unadulterated air, brilliant sunshine, and clean sea, we went swimming regularly, combined with the truly fresh greens and fruit of my homeland, had good effect. Within a very short period the blisters started clearing and were completely gone by the time we returned to England. They have never risen their horrible heads again.

As our stay lengthened, several thought it would be wise for my son to attend school. The idea posed problems. He was young and still in the process of learning our language and consequently unable to communicate clearly. A prime example is, before knowing where it was, he was desperate for the toilet. I suspect his aunt understood what he wanted but, determined he speak the language fluently, pretended not to. My arrival into the kitchen discovered him literally hanging from Anna's arm in sheer desperation. Realising his distressed need, we made a point of clearly pronouncing the word. He never forgot it. At the time our language was rich and elegant. Unfortunately, the advent of modern day budget flights and holidays with the resulting increase in international travel for the masses, not to mention television, has diluted it. The inevitably reduced world culture and social expanse has resulted in English words, British and American, being widely adopted. This is especially true for general amenities. Regrettably, this has been to the detriment of ethnic languages and cultures. For example, toilet is now the standard word for that amenity.

Having considered the suggestion for a couple of days, we decided my son should accompany his cousins to their classes. Normally he would not have been admitted at their older level however, all recognised he could not attend without someone to help him with the language. I suspect the teacher regretted the decision because it transpired they hardly taught any of the set curriculum. All the pupils wanted to know about English schools and life. The teacher was also interested and therefore allowed the distraction to go on. It certainly sounded as if everyone had fun on the days when he was in class. We did not think it fair and therefore did not permit him to go every day. He learned nothing new, but being ensconced within the school hub helped develop his knowledge and ability with the language. Quite honestly, I do not think he really understood the pupils or the different education structure. Compared to British institutions, the discipline was weak and the children generally unruly.

Anna and Christopher were very good to us but, though they never indicated anything, I had no wish to sponge. I undertook such tasks as I could round the house, but it was hardly enough to repay their kindness. I was at a loss as to what else I could do. Unexpectedly, my dilemma was resolved when my brother-in-law introduced me to one of his more prosperous clients. You may recall Christopher with a friend had established a successful household goods business. Andrew, the wealthy client, owned a factory and would regularly call in at the house to place, confirm, or adjust an order. I think he preferred the informality of a home. Anna, with my assistance, would serve refreshments in the drawing room. We consequently, all got to know each other reasonably well. He was a very pleasant, well-educated man. Having heard a little of my circumstances and apparently observing me moving round the house, he deduced I was at a loose end, so to speak. He suggested I may like to work for him in the factory, making clear, if I accepted, it would be at a full salary. I was quite taken with the idea. I saw two benefits. First, it would provide me with an income. Concern over my diminishing funds was a constant at the back of my mind. Second, it would also enable me to contribute more substantially to the housekeeping. Andrew and I looked to Christopher who, despite my now more mature years, still saw himself as my guardian. Knowing his friend well and holding him in considerable respect, my brother-in-law raised no objection or obstacle. I would oversee quality control of items produced in Andrew's factory. A position I felt more than capable of fulfilling. Later I learnt the post had not existed beforehand but had been created especially for me. This knowledge still brings a slight blush to my cheeks.

We, Andrew and I, got on well and sometimes he would take me for lunch or afternoon tea to his beautiful home, where I met his delightful mother. With each passing week he became more affectionate and did eventually propose. As is normal with such wealthy, highly placed families, a prospective bride is an important decision. It is one in which the elder members consider it their duty to participate. In truth, many demand the final decision regarding whether the marriage will proceed be theirs. Andrew's father having passed, his mother was now the respected head of the family. We had taken an instant liking to each other and having met me a few times, she unequivocally approved. She was even so kind as to say she thought it a good match, which slightly surprised me considering my financial standing. She must have appreciated I was no fortune hunter. And may I say, I never have been.

Naturally, I was flattered such a family would consider allowing me into their circle. However, though I did like Andrew, I was still tender from all that had preceded. I was also fearful of another relationship. In addition, I really wanted my son and I to enjoy our newfound freedom without any ties or complications. Added to this, Andrew's wealth and the attentions it naturally attracts frightened me. You will come to see this was a continuing theme. Having considered all these aspects, I ultimately declined. Like any man who has opened himself to make such a proposal, he found my decision difficult. He however, though noticeably upset, graciously accepted. He understood the basis of my refusal and in particular that it was not personal. I am glad to say we remained friends and continued to enjoy times together. Thankfully, neither did his mother take umbrage. Anna and Christopher, on the other hand, were anything but happy. To them it would have been an excellent marriage, I suspect primarily because of his wealth, though they also liked him.

When accepting the employment, I ensured regular days off were a component. With my previous, almost round the clock, working routine, my son and I had missed out on meaningful time together. This visit was an opportunity to make up for that. The new income also helped me relieve some of the extra costs our visit put on the family. Anna and Christopher never said anything, but I was more than aware. I was also aware our constant presence deprived the family of their own quality time together. It would have been a shame not to take advantage of the excellent climate of my homeland, so I made a point of taking my son to the seaside as often as possible. The sun and sea, as mentioned, were also good for his health. This also meant my sister and family could enjoy their own meaningful family time while my son and I enjoyed ours. Besides the swimming and sunbathing we also visited places of historic interest. I wanted my son to learn as much as possible about our history and culture, ancient and modern. This may sound like boasting, but as acknowledged by his regular teachers, my son was mentally far in advance of his physical years. He has always taken a keen interest in all sorts of things and loves to investigate. A trait that still marks him now, sometimes to my distraction, because he constantly wants to be both physically and mentally active. One project at a time is too little for him. He must have at least two, three, and often more on the go, and usually in different disciplines.

Meals at home were the cultural norm. However, like many others, Anna and the family enjoyed the occasional outing. Unlike Britain, such outings were primarily family affairs, which definitely included the children. My son was excited about the event on two counts. First, that we were going out at all. As said, social culture of the time expected the majority of meals to be at home with excellent home cooking. Indeed we loved those, but it was nice to have the rare change that also provided a break for my sister. Second, we were not going until ten o'clock. Social life then did not really begin before, probably a consequence of the warm climate. I recall my son's initial reaction when we pulled into a muddy courtyard and the headlights illuminated what may only be described as a large corrugated iron shed. He said nothing, but his demeanour indicated how unimpressed he was. Matters changed markedly once we entered, when his little eyes brightened. The place was cheerfully lit and packed with patrons, laughing, singing, eating, and drinking. Wonderful traditional foods and carafes of local wine filled several trestle tables that ran the entire length of the building. The musicians and dancers dotted round the room, all in bright national costume, added to the infectious atmosphere of fun, happiness, and joy. Gratifyingly, because as a rule our people never drink without eating, drunkenness is virtually unknown. They simply go out to enjoy themselves with friends and relatives and to meet others similarly disposed. As mentioned elsewhere, ours is, or at least was, a warm, uninhibited society in which perfect strangers were happy to interact. None of the hiding head in a book or newspaper or, in these days, a phone or tablet. Lifelong friendships were frequently established at these events. We found seats at a table that was thankfully against a wall. One in the middle of the crowded room would have proven difficult as we comprised a party from two, filled to capacity, cars. It proved a wonderful evening. Regrettably, these establishments no longer exist. The club culture that has grown up since does not compare. I do miss those innocent, fun days.

Not long after, another of Christopher's clients called at the house to discuss an order for supplying his fleet. It transpired he was a very wealthy shipping magnate. To cut a long story short, he also became more than a little interested and also, ultimately, proposed. I was flattered, especially as he seemed a nice person and was very good looking. Nevertheless, those attributes could not negate the experiences with my ex-husband which, as you are now aware, had made me wary. Add to that my determination not to have my son exposed to the possibility of further trouble. How naïve we can be. Admittedly, many would have considered it a good marriage, but I had additional concerns. His vibe gave the impression he could become jealous, especially of anyone paying attention, and that he would want me all to himself. I had certainly had enough of that though, regrettably, it became a recurring theme in my life. Again, to Anna and Christopher's consternation, I declined. It was more than likely his wealth they were thinking of. Other than employment, I have never believed in letting financial considerations dictate life decisions. Of course, it is nice to have sufficient, but there is far more to life and money should never be the controlling factor.

We were having such a pleasant time my troubles started to seem a distant dream. Unhappily it was not to last. A letter from the British embassy quickly shattered our relaxed enjoyment. I had no idea they even knew we were in the country. Presumably, they got the information from immigration control from when we entered. It could also have been from the details I gave when attending a function for British citizens held at the embassy. The letter stated, because our stay had almost reached the year mark, if I did not leave immediately, my son, as a British National, would be taken from me and returned to the United Kingdom. Shock, horror, fear, and terror are hardly adequate words. My emotions went everywhere, nowhere good for sure. My son is my life and the thought of having him taken was just too appalling. I had not understood at the time, but apparently, as part of the divorce proceedings, something like a residency order had been issued with regard to my son. I am not sure, but it seems the authorities viewed staying somewhere for a year as being resident in that place as opposed to simply visiting on holiday. Matters were made worse by the letter only having arrived within one day of the year. Needless to say, I was terrified and could not prevent myself from bursting into tears, not knowing what I was going to do.

Thankfully, Christopher kept his head and took control, immediately investigating available transport. Remember, this was before the advent of easy to get, inexpensive flights. Andrew happened to call in, he rarely made prior appointments, and kindly also contacted his business associates. Eventually, after what I may only describe as a nail-bitting period, not that I have ever bitten my nails, they discovered a ship leaving for England that afternoon. My elder sister also happened to be making one of her rare visits to the city and joined in the mad melee of us all running round packing up as much of our belongings as we could. I suspect it would have amused us all if it had not been for the situation. We must have looked like participants in a slapstick comedy. However, it was anything but amusing. It was chaotic and frightening. When as much as possible had been crushed into our cases, Andrew took my son and I together with our luggage in his large car while the others followed in Christopher's.

It may seem strange to some of you, depending upon your own culture and background, but at the time we did not have the advantage of proper civilian liner ports. Ships simply utilised beach heads where the sea had sufficient depth to accommodate them. In rather sweaty, dishevelled, and trembling condition we arrived to find the liner had already set sail. I nearly screamed the tension I felt, but was able to swallow it. What were we going to do? What would happen now? Would they really take my son? My tears and terror were tangible.

In case any problems arose, the police always attended landings and sailings. Upon hearing my predicament, they instructed us to get into their launch. They would pursue the ship, which was still visible, heading for the horizon. We hardly had time to say our farewells. In all the excitement, my elder sister, who was small of stature, lost her balance and fell into the sea. She had been carrying our heavy winter coats, which we would need for the English climate. My immediate concern was for her safety, forgetting for a moment my own predicament. When hauled out, the poor dear was shaken but otherwise unharmed. We all breathed a sigh of relief and then refocused upon the matter in hand. Our rescued, dripping coats were unceremoniously dumped on us and we were virtually pushed into the launch.

We waved and blew our kisses as the launch pulled out. Again, the sensation of a torn heart engulfed. It had been so long since we had seen each other. How long would it be before we did so again? Or would we ever see each other again? Would this be the end of the happy times I had enjoyed with them? Would my son be deprived of family? I could feel the tears returning. Without warning, the police, appreciating the need for speed if we were to catch up with the ship, accelerated. It was so sudden I nearly fell overboard. Only the timely grab of a side rail saved me. As we neared the vessel both policemen tried to make the crew understand we wanted them to stop, but to no avail. One of them then had the idea of seizing their megaphone and shouting 'Captain's wife! Captain's wife!'. I was shocked, but it had the desired effect. The ship slowed, permitting us to draw alongside. However, the launch was too low for us to reach the ship's ladder, posing yet another problem. In the end there was no option but for the officers to lift my son and I enabling us so to reach the baggage hold entrance. We were just able to crawl into it. They then pushed our luggage after us. Not a graceful entrance, but at least we were on the ship, headed in the right direction, and away from the clutches of officialdom. To say I was grateful to the police officers would be the grossest of understatements. I was even more so because it was very unusual for our police to be so helpful. Regrettably, I could not properly express my sincere appreciation. I had to do with shouting it from the deck. I hope they comprehended the true strength of it.

Because the officer had shouted 'Captain's wife!', the captain himself came to see what was going on. I was concerned he may feel offended and angry and was also scared of what he may do as a consequence. He had every right to put us off whenever and wherever he may wish. However, he proved warm and welcoming and ordered his purser to sort a cabin for us. I think he found the whole incident amusing. He then insisted, once settled, we join him for dinner. Considering the means of our arrival and not having a reservation, I anticipated being squeezed into some tiny out-of-way cabin, but to my surprise the purser ushered us into a very comfortable one. Perhaps a consequence of his captain having given the order. In case you are wondering, Christopher had the foresight to give me extra money to defray our travelling costs. We were in a bit of a mess after having crawled through the baggage chute, so took a little time to sort and clean ourselves. After, we sought out the restaurant where one of the waiters kindly guided us to the captain's table. Undoubtedly, most of you will understand, even in these less formal days, how people consider dining with the captain a true privilege. It certainly brought a lot of looks in our direction, people clearly wondering who we were to be granted such a prerogative. I admit I felt rather embarrassed by the attention. Upon reaching the table, the captain immediately put me at ease with his warm smile and even warmer welcome.

In my homeland, it is, or at least was then, normal for a large bowl of salad to be placed in the centre of the table, enabling all guests to serve themselves as they wished. My son has always loved salad and before I realised what he was about, had dragged the bowl in front of himself. Then, without ceremony or further ado, he started digging in. I was mortified and told him to put it back. His simple response, in his childish, endearing voice, was to tell me it was his. He was accustomed to having his own bowl. I continued to tell him quietly to put it back until the captain intervened. As a fellow countryman he was delighted my son had such a healthy appetite for our traditional foods. He told me to let my son be and ordered another bowl for the rest of the guests. At the end of the meal, and further to my embarrassment and I suspect the grudging of other guests, he insisted we dine at his table every day of the lengthy trip. A very unusual and marked privilege. At first I became anxious about his friendliness, fearful I was going to have trouble with unwanted attentions. Thankfully, I had no need to fear. He was genuine and courteous throughout and made what could have been a very awkward situation, as unbooked passengers, a pleasant one.

Until a storm broke, we had been enjoying a relaxed cruise, assisted further by the knowledge I was no longer in danger of having my son taken from me. It was indeed a great storm, the like of which I had not experienced before. The wind lashed, the sea heaved, and the waves became colossal. This was when we discovered neither my son nor I were good sailors. We often had to lean out of the porthole for obvious purposes. Occasionally, clutching tightly to ladder railings and anything else that came to hand, we ventured onto sheltered decks. Fresh air seemed to help a little. I also insisted at least once a day we stagger our way to the restaurant, concerned without some food in our stomachs the linings would become torn. One evening, after dinner, we were returning to our cabin when the waves became larger than ever. A ship's officer broadcast an over the tannoy warning for passengers to move away from the side decks. Clutching my son's hand I dragged him to safety just as an enormous wave literally formed an arch over the deck. It was an incredible sight, reminding me of the massive naves we see in ancient cathedrals. Unfortunately, in the process of being dragged, my son had dropped his favourite toy of the time. A motorised motorcycle Christopher had given him. It is a shame we no longer see such engaging toys despite modern technology. He kept asking me to let him get it but I was not about to risk him being swept overboard. He kept pleading and I felt terrible, but the risk was too great. A fellow passenger, noting the situation, kindly strolled out and retrieved the toy. Much to everyone's amazement he returned completely dry, not even the hint of dampness. As said, the wave had formed a complete arch over the ship. He was very nice and we got to know each other a little during the remainder of the journey. Ships can be such friendly places. I suppose it is because everyone is encased together for protracted periods. The remainder of the trip was uneventful, and we arrived on schedule. Clearing customs without incident, we headed for our lodgings.

21

BULLIES

Due to our long absence, I did not feel it appropriate to just walk in. To me it would have been very bad mannered. Consequently, I rang the doorbell and waited. It took a couple further rings before the landlady opened the door, but only slightly. I had not been sure she would be there because of her short-haul cruise ship employment that took her away for a few days at a time. Before continuing I should mention, since it bears upon her behaviour toward me, during our prior residency I came to note her to be a harsh, uncaring woman. An example is the occasion I saw her aggressively grab her daughter's hair and then bash the poor girl's head back and forth against each of the hall walls. I assumed there had been some sort of disagreement, but who knows because I also felt sorry for her son, who she likewise roughly abused and put upon. Sad, but back to my own tale. In hindsight, I suspect she may have seen us approaching through the window. Just as she opened the door, and before I had the chance to say anything, she rather sharply told me there was nothing there for me. Taken aback by this unexpected outburst, it took me a few seconds to recover sufficiently to ask about our room and belongings. Her blunt response was to say the dustmen had accidentally taken all my trunks and possessions, with no mention to the room. My further question of how such a thing could happen simply brought the reply she was not there at the time but understood they had all been stacked in a communal area. The assumption being the dustmen must have thought they had been put out for them. I found this rather odd because of my having given her sufficient rent and more, as agreed with her, to retain our room and belongings. Quickly assimilating the information, I surmised she must have been letting the room again. No doubt without declaring the additional income. It was the only explanation I could think of for my trunks and possessions being, to quote, stacked up in a communal area. To say I was shocked would be an understatement. It was hard to believe what I was being told.

Not prepared to be dismissed so easily, I insisted upon going to our room. She just stood in the doorway, preventing us from entering. Evidently, she no longer considered the room mine, despite having taken a substantial amount of money to keep it for me. Thinking there may be a better side to her, as well as unwilling to concede so easily, I asked where we were supposed to stay. A shrug of the shoulders said enough. Then, suddenly pointing without allowing us through the door, she told me the dustmen had not taken my brown metal trunk, that incidentally I still have. The entire account sounded so bizarre it crossed my mind she may have stolen my things. This thought was further enforced by the fact this trunk had been the only one to be locked. As you may imagine, my anger was gathering force though, gratifyingly, I was able to hold back the rising tears. I told her it was not right and I had given her the room rent together with what she had asked to look after our belongings. The hard-nosed woman just stood unblinking, looking me straight in the eyes. I still do not really understand how people can be so callous. It was clear she was not going to relent. Before turning away, I told her I would return shortly for my trunk.

The town's central police station was not far, so I went and explained, asking if there was anything I could do. The officers I spoke with told me they knew the woman was a thief, but had never obtained any concrete proof. As to my situation, because I had been away for so long there was absolutely no question she would have disposed of everything. Without hard evidence or eyewitness testimony, there was nothing to be done. I could lodge a formal complaint, but it would probably not avail much. Disappointed to receive such a negative summary I was left with little option but to accept the situation as it stood. I hailed a taxi and went back to the house to collect my remaining trunk. What no one knew is I had secreted several five-pound notes in the trunk. That was one reason for it being locked. Five pounds in those days was a lot of money. Experience had taught me I could never know when I would need ready cash. I confess sometimes I still think about the lovely things stolen and even miss them despite the intervening years. Most were mementoes from when rebuilding my life and creating a future for my son. Included were also some precious items, well precious to me, from earlier life. You may recall my mention of a little icon from the convent I had been taken to when my darling mama passed and a diamanté broach wedding present. In addition, there were vast arrays of personal effects, coats, dresses, suites, etcetera, both mine and my sons's. There were also forty pairs of new, unworn shoes. At the time I had a passion for shoes, perhaps stimulated by the remembrance of when I had none and had to walk barefoot. I will never forget the pain of torn, battered, bleeding flesh upon which I had to walk each and every day. I attribute some of the foot difficulties now prevalent to those times. Others must be the result of my ex-husband's kicking my shines while wearing heavy duty boots. It was not until sometime later, how I do not recall, I discovered the cruel, evil woman had a shop in another town where she undoubtedly disposed of stolen goods. It turned out, until I informed them, the police were unaware of it. Of course, this knowledge came too late for me. Anything I might have recognised would be long gone.

Now I had my trunk the next question was where we were going to go. Not able to think of anywhere, I decided to approach Kate and see if she could help again. You may recall she helped find somewhere after I escaped my husband. We had not spoken for a long time, so it surprised her to see us standing on the doorstep. Yet again, I had to detail our unexpected circumstances. She, like me, wondered if my son and I would ever be out of trouble. If only! You may remember on the last occasion, due to visiting family, she had been unable to accommodate us herself. Thankfully, this time there was a free room that she very kindly and willingly offered. I have no idea how I held back my tears of relief and gratitude, though I think I went a bit overboard with my profuse thanking. It was a very nice, large room that my son and I would share. Once left alone, I collapsed on the bed in floods of tears emanating from anger and disbelief, at the treatment we had been subjected to, relief, at having found somewhere and not being left on the streets, and true deep felt gratitude. I must record that Kate and her husband were exceedingly good to us throughout our stay. I can never thank them enough.

Now we had somewhere to stay, albeit temporarily, I needed to re-establish some source of income. The manager of the cinema where I had worked before proved glad to see me and, without hesitation, offered me my old job. The hospital managers were also pleased to take me back as a night orderly. Kate kindly agreed to take care of my son at night. Thankfully, he was never any trouble, always behaved, and was a good sleeper. Matters were working out better and quicker than I had hoped. My son's previous school also accepted him back, giving me confidence he would continue to receive a thorough and good standard of education. The masters assured me they would do all they could to ensure he did not lose out because of the unduly long absence. We agreed the fact he was intellectually ahead of his years should enable him to catch up. I am proud to say he did.

Finding accommodation, work, and schooling so quickly was a relief. However, the amalgamation of experiences in attaining lodgings made me think hard and long about the future. We could not just go on basically begging for somewhere to live. Having mentioned this in passing to some friends they asked why I did not put my name down for a council place. This may seem a bit naïve, but the truth is, up to this point, I had no idea such a facility existed. I had not really thought about how people got to live in local authority properties. Still, I was reluctant because of the reports I had heard of council estates, which were anything but positive. Though they appreciated my sentiments, my friends pointed out it would at least provide us with somewhere private, with our own amenities. It would also remove us from the mercy of landlords and ladies. I considered the positives and negatives, ultimately deciding to ask for my name to be added to the waiting list. I concluded it would, as my friends suggested, provide us with an independent home where we could arrange matters to our liking. Without interference from others. Once aware of my circumstances, the council confirmed I met the criteria for acceptance. However, they informed me the waiting list was very large and it would probably be some time before they could offer me anything. A more immediate problem therefore arose. Though Kate and her husband continued to be very good to us I did not think it right to impose upon them long-term. I had also indicated our stay was only to be brief while I sorted matters. Therefore, as the council could not help straight away, I started looking for more permanent accommodation.

Between the time of escaping my husband and visiting my family, I got to know a few people. One, who came from a country near my homeland, had mentioned she let out rooms. I decide to visit and ask if she had a vacancy. I was overjoyed when she told me a room that was large enough to accommodate both of us was available. She also thought staying with her would be good for my son because she had four boys he could play with. Regrettably, as you will come to see, I would repent having made such a move. Unfortunately, the woman proved neither clean nor hygienic however, as the saying goes, 'beggars cannot be choosers'. I ensured our room was always clean and tidy and did my best to avoid contamination when using shared utilities. My mama's teaching of hygiene and how to avoid disease combined with my war experiences have, as previously mentioned, left me hypochondriac about cleanliness. I must always wash and disinfect everything we use. If I do not my nerves are constantly on edge. Yes, this often makes life difficult, but I simply cannot relax if anything, in my opinion, is unclean. Despite this mentality and the corresponding actions, I must make clear I thankfully do not suffer from obsessive-compulsive disorder. I understand it can be very debilitating. My hypochondria does not prevent me from leading a normal life. It simply adds to my workload.

My landlady's boys turned out to be boisterous and rough. The kindest way I can put it. I did not really like them playing with my son for fear of some harm befalling him because of their brusque ways. However, I could not always prevent the play. Neither did I want to be rude to my hostess or cause a problem between us. Sadly, my fears were to be realised. A friend who worked long-haul ships used to give me lovely large boxes of chocolates he got in the

United States. These were not available in the United Kingdom. My son and I loved them. From the start I had taught him we should never be mean to others and, wherever possible and appropriate, share what we have. As a consequence, he automatically gave the boys some chocolates. Rather than showing gratitude, the greedy boys wanted to take the whole box. My son refused. He understood the gift was primarily intended for us, though we shared some. The bullies responded by hitting him round the head. It needs to be born in mind my son was much younger than them. I regret to say all four were very much of a bullying disposition.

During that night my poor boy constantly tossed, turned, and groaned. I was concerned but unsure if he was simply having bad dreams and therefore waited the night out. In the morning it was clear something was wrong. I telephoned the surgery and requested a home visit. The doctor told me not to worry, it was a simply an earache, and prescribed aspirin. That night and during the following day he was still markedly unwell, so I called the surgery again. A different doctor came and again told me it was nothing serious and not to be anxious. In the end, four different doctors gave similar responses. Notwithstanding these assessments, it was obvious to me this was not just a young child's illness. The night following the fourth doctor's visit my son was distinctly worse and asked me to hold his head saying he could not stand the pain anymore. Something had to be done. Wrapped in a blanket, that is him not me, I carried him to a hospital. No simple task as he had grown exponentially and was far heavier than most children of his age and the hospital was some distance.

The accident and emergency doctor and nurse, once aware of the continuing symptoms, immediately insisted upon taking my son from my arms. I cannot really describe my emotions. After all we had been through the last thing I wanted was to let him out of my sight. Trust that others, unknown to me, would look after him and not abuse my darling had been eroded. However, I knew I had to let them do their job without hindrance. Needless to say, I was terrified and could not sit still. I am surprised they did not charge me for the holes I must have worn in the waiting room carpet. Within short time the doctor returned and suddenly embracing me cried 'Mother oh mother, you have saved your boy's life'. In confused fear and terror, I looked in his eyes for an explanation. My son had meningitis and had been in the last throws. If I had been one hour later he would no longer be with us. He was in isolation and with the correct medication would make a full recovery, though there might be some side effects. They would not know until after his recuperation. I nearly fainted, whether from fear and stress or from relief, or a combination, I am unable to say. Dressed in protective clothing, I was permitted to see my boy for a few minutes. I managed to hold back the tears, not wanting to frighten or upset him further. There was noticeable improvement the next day, the consultant confirming all was going well. My son would have to remain in hospital for a while and I should go home and get some rest. I did not want to leave, but they insisted. It was hard for me to do so. After everything I was constantly fearful when he was not close by. To monitor his condition and ensure a full recovery, his stay extended into several weeks. It was a difficult time for both of us. We had never really been separated before. A new and unwelcome experience.

Visiting became a serious problem. He never wanted me to leave and would incessantly howl when I did. To avoid any possibility of contagion for other patients, the doctors had put him in a separate room rather than on a general ward. Unfortunately, his window faced the main hospital path, meaning he could see me. Unluckily, there was no alternative route. He would bawl and screech ever louder. It broke my heart. There was one nurse who could calm him, but if she was not on duty, there was little hope. No one else had the knack. Following a couple of these outbursts, the doctors told me his getting into such a state was neither good for him or other patients. They considered it detrimental to his recovery and requested I no longer visit. I was only to return when he was to be discharged. The thought of such a separation tore at my heart. Not a single day had passed in his short life without us seeing each other. Appreciating they were talking sense I reluctantly agreed. I am not sure what they would have done if I had not. Have me arrested or obtain a restraining order? However, my constant fear for his welfare drove me to breech my promise, in part. I had to at least get a glimpse to assure myself he was well and safe. Creeping into the hospital grounds, I would peep, from a distance, through his window. Unfortunately, he spotted me one day and nearly brought the hospital down with his screams and cries. You may consider my son's reactions to be indicative of a spoilt, selfish, and naughty child, but he never was. It was simply that he was not used to being away from me. Subsequently I had no option but to stay away altogether. The only alternative left was for me to telephone twice a day. The nurses were very kind, understanding, and patient. Thankfully, it was not long after I received the summons to come and take him home. You may consider my actions over the top but please remember, in my son's brief life, his father had tried to kill him at least two or three times each and every day and others, such as the four boys, had proven cruel and unkind. Everlasting fear of what might befall my child, if I were not around to protect him, was my incessant companion.

Meningitis, as you may or may not know, usually leaves some defect. Despite no obvious problem presenting, my son had to be examined by a psychiatrist to ensure there had been no brain damage. I was not permitted to go into the appointments. Presumably to make sure all responses were his own and not influenced by me or my presence. My son told me about the tests, one of which I would like to share with you. The psychiatrist showed him a series of pencil line drawings and asked if there was anything wrong with each picture. One showed a man standing on a horizon with the rising sun behind him and his shadow lying to the rear. When asked if anything was wrong, he immediately thought how silly the psychiatrist was. Thankfully, he did not say it out loud. Recalling the incident still makes me laugh. Of course, the shadow should have been in front of the figure. My child was passed as having no defect or damage, apparently a very unusual outcome. Tears of joy flowed down my cheeks. My son on the other hand was simply glad to have finished with the tests which he had found tedious and boring. Remember, he was considered intelligent and intellectually ahead of his tender years. I know it sounds like constant boasting, but it is remarkable considering what could have been his condition after all he had been subjected to. His formative years had been brutal and it would have been easy for him to be a completely different person to the one he is.

The combination of filth, total lack of hygiene, boisterous bullies, serious illness, and so on confirmed it was time to find somewhere else to live. I no longer wanted, not that I ever had, my young child exposed further to four ruffians. I also wanted to get away from the filth. Shortly after my son's hospitalisation, I was talking with my landlady-come-friend in the kitchen. I did not consider the inciting incident could be ignored and therefore, careful not to adopt either a harsh or abrupt tone or stance, stated her children had no right to hit my son. Regrettably, rather than listen and appreciate the validity of my comment, she became violently angry. Undoubtedly, part of this was the common reaction of any mother whose children are being criticised. However, the strength of her viciousness took me by surprise, frightening me to the point that, in my weakened state, I fainted. The episodes of leaving my homeland under threat, our stolen possessions, finding somewhere to live, and fear and worry for my son had taken their toll. When I came round I found the woman had left me where I had fallen, under the kitchen sink. So much for having thought her a friend. This was the final confirmation, as if I needed it, of my need to move. I was disappointed to find yet again, what should have been a settled and pleasant existence had been wreaked by inconsiderate and selfish behaviour.

Above all other considerations was concern for my son to have a full recuperative period. I also still felt really drained from all we had been through. Though we had only visited recently, and returned under worrying circumstances, I thought a return to my family for a short break would be good. I would certainly take care not to overstay this time. The period between the two visits was sufficient for the authorities to appreciate England was intended to be my son's permanent place of residence. As before, I searched for the least expensive mode of travel, rail proving to still be the affordable option. Again, I only booked seats without sleeping berths. It would be tiring and a little uncomfortable, but we could catch up with sleep and bathing at Anna's. Gratefully, the journey proved uneventful. I really did not need any further upsets or difficulties. The look in their eyes, as they greeted us at the station, indicated how glad the whole family was to have us with them again. I had feared it may have felt an imposition to return so soon. As ever, their home was filled with laughter and joy, making it a true pleasure to be there. Quite honestly we did not need to go out to feel more relaxed and stress free. However, as before, to ensure they had their own uninterrupted family times, we did.

Our lovely, carefree holiday was interrupted once again, but this time not by the authorities. My son got sunstroke. Christopher, my brother-in-law, had taken his nephew out on the back of his motorbike. They were going to fish at a small cove where the fish came in close to shore. My son had taken his shirt off resulting in the nape of his neck being exposed for the complete trip. Remember, my homeland has a hot climate with intense sunshine, especially in summer. The sun had been above their heads beating down with all its inherent strength. No wonder Icarus's wings melted. By the time they returned my boy was quite unwell. The family doctor administered what treatment he could and instructed us to keep my son in bed on a light diet, especially local natural yogurt. Unfortunately, though you would never believe it now, at the time he was not very partial to the strong flavoured product. Therefore, to make it more palatable, we added honey. He never ate it all, insisting we only give him the portions with honey in them. He was not being difficult, it is simply at the time, yogurt made him nauseas. Possibly an inheritance from me. Neither my sisters nor I like milk. Thankfully, despite this apparent fastidiousness, he recovered fairly quickly. We were then able to continue with our nice relaxing holiday.

The worry for my son, for a second time in a relatively short period, did tell on me. However, my sister was as good as gold and, with her cheeky character, soon lifted my spirits. The warm climate and great food also helped sustain my, and my sons's, physical being. Sorry to say the time for us to depart came round all too quickly. Nevertheless, I was determined not to repeat the previous experience of outstaying our welcome.

Upon arrival at the rail terminus, we discovered there were two trains for our destination. Each followed a different route. I determined which I thought the correct one for us and bade our farewells as we boarded. To part from my loved ones again tore my heart. If it had not been for my son I may have returned forever. I never really got over missing my family. However, I believed my son, as a British citizen, should have the benefit of an English education and life. It was his birthright. And, of course, there was the existing residency order.

Some fellow countrymen and women, sitting by an open window on the other train, shouted across that the train they were on was the one we required. They had overheard our discussion about which was the correct train. I was fairly certain I had not made a mistake and said so. They however, became insistent to the point of making me doubt myself. We alighted with our luggage and made our way across the platform. With little room over or between the seats on this other train, I was told to utilise the baggage racks at the end of the carriage. I was not very pleased. After all my unhappy experiences I usually like to have my possessions where I can see them. Those who had called us across, particularly the women, were very friendly and insisted we sit together. I thought how good it was to meet such nice people and from then on considered them new found friends. Wrong yet again! The journey began pleasantly enough with us chatting and laughing together. All changed when the guard arrived and told me we had the wrong tickets. Mine were for the other route. I had been correct. He informed me I needed to purchase new tickets to reach the destination where we would be able to board the correct train. I pointed out, as we already had tickets for that portion of the journey, both trains followed similar routes in places, it was unnecessary. Nonetheless, he insisted and in the end I had no option but to concede. If I did not he would put us off at the next remote stop. Needless to say, I was upset. I had been correct in my original determination and now this unexpected expenditure had taken all my remaining money. My new friends attempted to console, but I was a little cross with them for having insisted upon us changing trains. I was also worried by the fact I now had no money. What if we met with some further obstacle?

Upon arrival at the designated station I decided it unwise, this time, to take matters at face value. Attracting the attention of a rail member of staff, I double confirmed the accuracy of what I had been told. We arrived at the baggage racks to discover all our luggage had gone, nowhere to be seen. A search of the surrounding vicinity threw up nothing. The guard, once I located him, went to search the other carriages and luggage carts. I agreed we remain where we were so he could find us again but, with the passing time, became concerned about missing the correct train. The thought of being stranded in a strange place, with a young son and no money, frightened me. The guard could not locate our luggage and had no option but to conclude someone had taken them. He then abruptly left without making any offer of assistance. It then crossed my mind my new friends might be able to help. However, they were nowhere to be seen, which seemed strange because they were supposed to be travelling to the end of the line. Then it struck. They must be the culprits! Despite never having much money and consequently always careful, I was fully aware cheap products rarely lasted. I therefore made a point of always buying the best I could. They must have thought, due to the quality of the luggage, there would be valuable contents. They were in for a big disappointment. After the previous theft we had little. I doubt our meagre clothes would fetch much.

Time was running out, our train was about to depart. It was obvious there was now little chance of retrieving our belongings. Also, if we remained, we would probably be in a worse dilemma. Getting on the train was really our only option. We crossed the platform to find it already packed. We could not even get through the desperate scrum surrounding the door. Need I say my level of concern shot skywards. It looked like, we were going to be stranded, in this unfamiliar place. Unexpectedly, some police officers came to the rescue. It transpired their senior officer, seeing our plight had sent them over. They commanded the people to stand aside, which they did without question. This was a country where, though generally detested, authorities are never disobeyed, not in their presence at least. Nevertheless, this sort of intervention was unusual, leading the other passengers to assume we were people of import. This was a nation where people appreciate and respect their celebrities. The crowd spontaneously cheered and voiced sweet greetings. All rather embarrassing, even more so considering our actual state of affairs. Thankfully, our original, correct tickets included seat reservations. We found them, settled, and despite our impoverished condition and upset managed some measure of relaxation. At least we were on our way and not marooned. Anger with myself, for my gullibility quietly fermented. Would I never learn?

We arrived in London on schedule. Before continuing, you need to be aware, the theft had left my son and I with nothing but the clothes on our backs. Summer clothes not fit or suitable for the English climate. Once through the barrier and out of the station, I stood with no idea of what to do. Remember, we had left our accommodation. I had planned on finding something temporary. An inexpensive hotel or bed-and-breakfast while searching for new living quarters. That was now out of the question. My darling boy attempted to comfort me with news of him having some pocket money left. He promptly produced a few pennies. For his sake I did my best not to cry, smiling, thanking, and hugging him, but it all proved too much. Destitute again, as if my wartime encounter with it had not been enough. How cruel life can be.

I was wandering round in a bit of a daze, trying to fathom some solution when a young man asked if I was okay. He introduced himself with a surname I recognised from my homeland. In response to my question he confirmed he was from there and explained he was a travel journalist. He had been hoping to gather passenger comments about the journey for a weekend article. As you will probably have gathered, under normal circumstances I am a private person who does not discuss personal or family matters. These were not normal circumstances. Still suffering elements of shock and disorientation, I blurted out our story. He was kindness itself. Notwithstanding all the horrors in life, mine at least, there are moments when it is possible to believe in guardian angels. He told me not to worry, he would sort something for us. I think he realised I was rather naïve and inexperienced in such matters. The upshot? He secured a place for my son and I in a Greater London Council hostel to which he also kindly took us.

22

Discovered

At first I found the hostel environment intimidating. It was completely different from anything I had encountered before. I worried we would not fit in and may consequently encounter problems. Thankfully, once the journalist explained my situation, the staff proved kind and understanding. In answer to my question about paying for the large comfortable room we were to occupy, I was told not to worry. They would help sort that out. Relief began to infuse me, as the fear of having to roam the streets for the night had been nullified. My new friend and champion, if I may call him that, had stood quietly to one side while matters were settled. Now they had been he informed me of his need to get back to meet a deadline. Clasping both his hands within mine, I tried to thank him for his help, but could not sufficiently do so. He had achieved so much for us within such a short time. It was disappointing to think we would probably never meet again. I owed him so much and had hoped for an opportunity to show my gratitude at some later date. I am glad to say my assumption of not meeting again proved incorrect. Very kindly he continued to take an interest in our welfare and regularly called in. It was nice but also presented challenges. With each visit he was evidently becoming increasingly attached. I could have said something but felt it unkind to do so and therefore aimed to maintain us in a friendship. However, my hope of averting desire for a deeper rapport did not work. He eventually proposed. To support his case, he told me besides his own happiness there would be two other positives to us marrying. First, it would provide a stable home life for my son and me. Second, our marriage would probably persuade my ex-husband our union was truly over. Something I doubted. I did like him, but frankly remained afraid of getting into another relationship. Added to this was the fact, despite his genuine caring, I did not think him the right person for us. Naturally, he was upset, but I am pleased to say we remained friends. He continued to visit, even a couple of times after we finally departed London. As seems inevitable with the nice people I meet, we eventually lost contact. I have no idea where he is or what he is doing now. He had been such a genuine friend without who goodness knows what would have become of us. It still sends a shiver down my spine to think of the possibilities.

In line with normal procedure for any new resident, I had an interview with the hostel supervisor the following morning. I explained as much as I thought necessary, making clear I had neither ready money, job, nor income. He instructed me to return to his office an hour later, saying as I left not to concern myself about any of those issues. Upon my return, he greeted me with the news that they had found a school place for my son and a job for me. I would be working as a machinist in a factory on the South Bank. At the time I did not know where that was. He went on to say, my hours had been arranged to enable me to take my son to, and collect him from, his classes. This was far in excess of anything I could have hoped for. I am not sure what I had expected. Nothing in all likelihood after all my previous experiences. I could not stop thanking him, truly grateful my son's needs had also been considered. So often you hear of children just being put into care with little thought of what that would mean for them. I appreciate those involved aim to help, but so many horrific tales abound.

Up to this point I had never really utilised public transport. Now, suddenly, I had to learn and master the London system. It was a terrifying prospect, but I was determined to succeed. First was getting to school and from there the South Bank. How on earth I managed to navigate the London busses and never get lost beats me. I would never dream of trying now. A little incident to tell you. One day when on a crowded bus with my son in my arms we had to stand at the rear. Inquisitive as ever, my boy discovered the request bell and pushed it. The conductor, we still had them then, stormed up, shouted and threatened to hit him, even lifting his hand. My much heightened protective instincts immediately came into play, causing me to give him a hard, and I suspect ferocious, stare. Through gritted teeth, I breathed a 'You dare!'. My tone and glare must have done the trick. Clearly shocked someone would stand up to him, he backed away, stiffly turned and slunk off with his tail between his legs, to coin a phrase. Fellow passengers smiled approvingly. No one likes petty dictators. To this day I still have little idea how I negotiated London. Now, on the rare occasions I go there, I depend upon my son to get us round safely. He is confident with the underground system and always gets us to our destination without mishap.

My new employer's premises were near the OXO tower, which my son and I visited recently. What a change! I think the redevelopment of both the tower buildings and the South Bank has been a great success. It is now a pleasure to stroll along there. So different from the dirty, unkempt streets of my time. Colleagues and management were very sweet. They constantly ensured I understood the working routines and requirements and all was okay. At the end of the first week I gratefully received my salary. In those days, weekly wages, in cash, were the normal payment method. I immediately went to a clothing store and bought my son warm trousers, shirt, and pullover. Remember, we were still wearing the summer clothes we had left my homeland in. In my son's case this comprised a summer weight, short trouser, sailor suit, totally inadequate for the British climate. I was concerned for his ongoing health. A light summer dress was all I had. When we returned to the hostel a member of staff immediately asked for my wage packet. A request that took me aback, especially as they made it in an aggressive manner. Asked why it was open, I explained my son's clothes had been inadequate and he had been freezing. I had therefore purchased some warmer clothing for him. They summoned the supervisor and made me aware I was in trouble. In my defence I must make clear, no one had told me they expected me to take my unopened wage packets back to the hostel. My explanation was not considered acceptable until a member of staff pointed out my son clearly needed warmer clothes and I had not bought anything for myself, nor anything luxurious. I was told, rather ordered, in very plain terms with an unspoken but implied threat, from now on to take my unopened wage packet to the supervisor or nominated official every week. No further action would be taken with regard to the present offence. To say I felt relief would be the greatest of understatements. During the processes of this confrontation, the possibility of my son going into care and I to prison were more than intimated. I am not entirely sure, but think the situation, had it progressed, would be treated as fraud. Eventually I came to appreciate, because of how many of the residents behaved, why management had to take such a firm stance. Now the requirements had been outlined no further problem arose with me.

I continued to work hard, saving what I could after paying the rent or rather having it removed from my wage packet. I did eventually purchase warmer clothes for myself. Thankfully, neither of us fell ill through being underdressed for the British climate. A fashion incident you may like to hear about. My son's sailor suit had been made to my design. I always liked to dress him smartly. One day while walking along, a couple stopped us. The woman exuberant about how delightful it was to see a boy so nicely dressed. Boys traditionally wore drab, dull clothing. I think most considered it masculine, any other format resulting in questionable, ostracising suggestions. In these days, when fashionable clothes are universally available and acceptable for children, some younger readers may think the concept ridiculous. However, that is how it was. They were very different times.

At weekends all the other female residents, most with children, made themselves up and ventured out for a night on the town. They did not appear to consider it wasteful to spend on makeup and cigarettes. This is probably the reason for management insisting upon unopened wage packets. While they prepared for their night out, I was usually on the floor of our room playing with my son. I loved these times with him. Each week, without fail, one or more would put their head round the door and ask if I was going to join them. They never understood my lack of interest, nor that all I really desired was a quiet, happy home life. Drinking and clubbing was for them the way life should be led. They laughed when I said I was going to remain with my son, obviously considering me crazy. They attempted further persuasion by telling me how beautiful they thought I was and that they could get men to buy them drinks if I was in their group. I suppose this was the lifestyle that had led to them having children they did not really want and ending up in the hostel. This was also a time when unmarried motherhood was frowned upon. Matters are very different now. Local authorities will do all they can to accommodate women who find themselves in this predicament.

Though most of the women were, in their own way, friendly, I had no actual friends. At times I felt very alone despite my darling boy. After all, he was still a child. One day I decided to spend a few of my precious pennies to send Vera, my ex-mother-in-law, a postcard. Looking back, I suspect it was simply the fact of making contact with someone that inspired it. However, I would regret this careless moment. Late one afternoon, a few days after sending the card, a fellow resident came to announce there was someone downstairs to see me. Automatically, I asked how it could be. I had told no one where we were. With a shrug of her shoulders, she simply reiterated there was someone to see me and went off. Nerves attacked as I speculated who it could be, quietly hoping there had been a mistake and it was someone else the person wanted. With trepidation, I descended the stairs. You may imagine my astonishment when I discovered Terrance standing in the vestibule. Yes, I felt a little fearful but at the same time, despite all our history, it was good to see a familiar face. I must have been more lonely than I realised. He had traced me by the postcard's postmark. I had not included our location. It must have taken him a while but shows how obsessed he was. His response to my question regarding what he wanted was to ask what I was doing in such a place. Then, without waiting for a reply, he told me he still loved me and wanted me back. I pointed out we were now divorced, and I did not, could not, trust him. I will not bore you with details of yet another of his begging and pleading sessions. The upshot was I agreed to return with him. You may consider me foolish, naïve, stupid even, but I had to get away from that place. Though the hostel had provided shelter and a job with a small income, I had no wish to stay longer than I had to. Anyway, after rent deduction and purchase of necessities, there was little left to save. I had visions of us stuck there for years before I could afford to move. I detested London life and sorely wished for us to breathe again the relatively fresh air of a parochial locality.

The thought of seeing Vera and the girls had also inspired me. However, I had wrongly assumed Terrance still lived with them. It turned out he had left the family home and now rented rooms in a nearby town. The accommodation was comfortable and in a nice area, but I was very disappointed not to return to Vera and the others. But, at least we had escaped London and the despondency that had descended upon me.

As usual, Terrance had promised all would be different. What do you think? Yes, you are correct, nothing changed. Almost immediately he started beating me and still seemed determined to kill our son. I still do not understand. My champion, the journalist, had kept in touch, which was very nice as he knew we would never be more than friends. One day he turned up on the doorstep of my new home. Unfortunately, Terrance returned early for some reason and there was the most awful scene. If my friend had not been agile, I think it quite possible my ex-husband would have killed him or at the very least given him a severe pounding. Regrettably, the violence involved in this altercation seriously frightened the two spinster sister landladies. The shock to their sensibilities resulted in both being unwell. The result, they asked us to leave. Besides anything else, they found such behaviour intolerable. That they had been put thorough such an ordeal saddened me. Their request, however, did not unduly upset me. My thoughts had been revolving round the fact, though I still cared for him, I was not stupid. There was absolutely no way I was going to remain. What a fool I had been. It was idiotic to think Terrance would ever change.

In those days a lone woman with a child was unusual, in public at least, and people frequently automatically attributed immoral reasons for it. Consequently, as you have seen, it was difficult for them to find decent accommodation. It took endless searching, but eventually I found a room in a very nice large house in a respectable area. The spinster owner however, informed me she was not keen on having a child in the house. Before she had the chance to dismiss me out of hand, I asked her to at least meet my son. I explained he was in no manner mischievous, was a quiet child, and would always be with me. I thought all lost when she drew breath in. However, having obviously used those seconds for contemplation, she agreed to meet him. She was a shrewd woman, and I think detected my desperation and honesty. I had not hid the truth from her. I immediately fetched my boy. After spending a little time talking with him, she agreed he was not like other children and did not appear to have a disruptive disposition. To my relief, how often in life I have had to hold my breath, she decided me a suitable tenant. From my meagre store, the little I managed to save while at the hostel, I gave her the first week's rent in advance. Rents were far more realistic and reasonable then. I mentioned my aim to find employment but she need not worry because when not at school my son would be with me. To counteract the cloud passing over her features, I explained how previous employers had permitted him to stay in private rooms or quiet corners. She must have been mulling this over while we talked, because she suddenly came out with the suggestion of sending my son to boarding school. The idea shocked me. I had never dreamt of letting him away from me. Who would protect him if I was not there? She pointed out he would receive an excellent education and would not have to be dragged round with me. I admit, it was not ideal for him to spend so much time in my places of employment, which were not a natural environment for a child. But then, our lives were hardly conventional. This also made obvious, though she had taken a liking to my boy, she did not really want him round all the time.

Over the following days I considered the matter. Eventually I came to the realisation her advice was not solely based upon selfish consideration but also out of a sincere concern for our welfare. The more I thought, the more I concluded the idea made sense, though I did not really want us to be apart. The outcome, once settled in our new accommodation, I went to the local authority offices and got a list of boarding schools within the county. My primary requirement, besides it being a good quality, reliable institution, was for such a school to be within a day's travel. My new landlady kindly offered to go through the possibilities with me, confirming the final decision would be mine and mine alone. She was an educated woman who I felt I could trust to guide me to suitable choices. The name of one private college particularly caught my attention. Not the best basis for such an important decision, but as it so happened, a good one. The headmaster-owner and his wife were lovely people, both of whom immediately took an interest in my boy. An interest that continued throughout his residency. I will explain shortly how I managed to finance this choice. This was one of the hardest things I have ever done. After all we had been through, with the constant need for me to be on guard, parting was truly difficult. I was continually worried, especially about who would protect him if the need arose. The headmaster assured me he would keep a firm eye on my son and look out for his welfare. Though he was a man I considered trustworthy, I could not help my anxiety. After all, I am a loving mother.

Our new accommodation comprised a pleasant fourth floor attic room that was larger than it sounds. It was one of three rooms on that level. The other two were rented by two elderly spinster sisters with who we shared a small kitchen. That worked out well due to us having different routines. Thankfully, my son and I have always got on well with older people and they seemed to enjoy the innocence of a young child.

Bounding one side of the respectable district in which we now found ourselves was a broad tree-lined avenue. A primary access road for the town. In the process of daily life it was frequently necessary for me to cross this busy thoroughfare. Quite a few children had to negotiate it every day. In view of the obvious danger to life and limb, a policeman usually attended the crossing. This was before the days of lollipop women and men. Police had to cover a number of varied duties and responsibilities then. Our regular crossing policeman was a nice, friendly, and fun-loving person. Often upon seeing us approach, normally when taking my son to school, he would call out 'Bella Donna' or some other admiring remark. He would immediately stop the traffic, whereas his normal routine had been to wait for a suitable gap in the flow prior to moving into the road. Pedestrians and drivers would look to see who was so important for him to make such remarks and to take such immediate action. I must reiterate, these were the days when clean, genuine, and innocent fun were the norm. People simply enjoyed themselves. There was none of the moroseness often evident in these so-called modern enlightened days. I think he may have fallen a little in love with me, but again, it was all innocent and certainly not in the least bit threatening.

Regrettably, my ex-husband somehow discovered where we lived. I have absolutely no idea how he kept doing this. He however, did not know which apartment was ours and therefore made no attempt to access the property. Instead he parked in the road, even sleeping in the car, and tried to speak to me whenever I left or returned. I grew very weary with the constant harassment, continuously having to tell him to go away and reiterating that, with our divorce, he no longer had a claim upon me. My landlady observed what was happening and suggested I should have a proper talk with him to try and straighten matters. She kindly offered one of the sitting rooms for the purpose. I had little hope of achieving anything, but thought I might as well try. He told me again how much he loved me and could not live without me. How he was a changed man and things would be better. Would I marry him again? I still cared for him and nearly accepted his proposal. Thankfully, after a few moments' hesitation, common sense stepped in. I recalled how many times he had said similar things and how nothing had ever changed. Stating my inability to trust him again, I refused. He became furious, lurched forward, and grabbing my throat, tried to throttle me. The violence had me staggering back. His continuing momentum then had me crashing through the window. Thankfully, the room was on the ground floor and, though badly shaken, I was not unduly injured. With the combined assistance of other residents, he was evicted from the house. Sadly it did not stop him from continuing to hassle me, which left little choice but to obtain another restraining order. As before, he ignored it. That is until I summoned the police. They must have given him a serious warning because he subsequently stayed away. It was some time before I saw him again. Naturally, this ended any idea of re-marriage. I still cannot quite believe I ever seriously considered the option.

23

INCOME

Having registered my son as a boarder with the private grammar college, it was time to consider how I was going to pay the fees. As mentioned earlier, the headmaster-owner had taken an interest in my boy and, realising, unlike most of his students, he was not from a wealthy family, kindly offered slightly reduced fees. Nevertheless, they still had to be paid. Even before he started, I had to buy blazers, gold thread badges, trousers, shirts, college ties, college scarves, college caps, shoes, and satchel. I use the plural because he had to have at least two of most. These were on top of the usual pyjamas, underwear, socks, handkerchiefs, towels and wash bag items. Everything also had to have an embroidered name label stitched in. The college was not a cheap option. However, by him going there the problem of finding decent accommodation was dealt with. In addition, it met my desire to provide him with the best education possible in a safe environment.

At the time, I regularly met with some friends. We used to congregate in a small cafe conveniently located for everyone. Some stopped off on their way to work, others after finishing their day jobs. As you would expect from what I have already shared, they all knew how attached I was to my son. They also knew how hard the decision to send him to boarding school had been. When talking about it, my need for employment with a suitable salary to meet my new commitments came up. One suggested getting a selection of newspapers and looking through the vacancies. Someone, I do not recall who, spotted a public house advert for a barmaid and asked if I would consider such a job. I had no idea what would be required, so they explained a little. Serve drinks, take money, smile and look beautiful, was their résumé. My lack of knowledge may appear strange to some, but visiting pubs and clubs was not part of an ordinary person's general life when I arrived in the country. Their description made me unsure if it was a job for me. I remained shy and doubted I could deal with people across a bar. Nevertheless, I needed to consider all options and took a few moments, hoping someone would spot something more to my liking. My friends jointly asked why I did not at least enquire. I said I was too shy. They were having none of that. Two took an arm each and marched me out the cafe door and down to the close by public house. Without the slightest hesitation, they marched through the door, virtually carrying me. I do not think my feet had hardly touched the ground on the way. Remember, I am small of stature. They were not. As desperate as I was for a decent income, I was also terrified. I may have enjoyed momentary bravado when finally leaving Terrance, but the idea of asking strangers for employment still frightened me. My friends asked for the manager and, when he arrived, told him if he wanted to employ me he should do so immediately because if he did not he would not see me again. I was too shy to come back on my own. To understand the reasoning for this direct approach, you need to bear in mind I had now reached full womanhood. Many considered me a beauty. An attribute hospitality managers valued for their barmaids then. My friends then dropped me. My feet had still been midair. In his turn, the manager confirmed his desire to have me join the staff. Would I like to start straight away? I did. This would be a change to my working life that had a long-lasting impact.

Regrettably, though I had been looking for a salary to satisfy all my needs, it was evident this one would not be sufficient on its own. A concentrated search by my friends and I had not produced a single job with a suitable salary. I needed additional employments. This culminated with me working two further jobs. One in an electronics factory during the day, more about that later, the other a small cleaning job for the hours between leaving the factory and starting at the public house.

Prior to leaving, my friends ensured the manager understood not only had I never done bar work, but I also had little clue what was involved. I was therefore very surprised not to receive any actual training. The manager simply told me which drinks were which, the measures, and the prices. He then left me to work things out for myself. To add to the confusion, you should be aware I was not an alcohol drinker. You may therefore imagine what an alien world this was for me. Thankfully, I have a quick mind that enables me to assimilate new information fairly rapidly. At least I felt, even with the all too brief introduction, I had the rudimentary knowledge with which to begin this new venture. However, there was an element I had not allowed for. As I am sure you have become aware, I am generally a shy person. I certainly was then. When the doors opened for the evening crowd, the number of people poring through took me aback. Instinctively, I hid behind the curtain separating private areas from the bar. I truly had not thought about the volume of people I would have to deal with. Mrs Waite, the manager's wife, noticing my reaction drew alongside and with a gentle, reassuring smile, told me not to be afraid. The patrons would not bite. Taking my elbow, she guided me back to the bar and introduced some of the regulars, who kindly made me feel very welcome. A friendly acquaintanceship soon developed with many, which enabled me to relax and enjoy a laugh with them. Nonetheless, in tandem, I ensured a professional status was also maintained. It was essential they knew who had the authority, especially when the drinks had been flowing liberally.

Though I managed to pick up an understanding for most of the regular drinks, there were occasions when confusion reined. This was particularly so with cocktails. In those early days it was not unusual for me to have to ask the customer what constituted the drink. Gratefully, most did not take offence or become agitated. Rather, they found it amusing and patiently explained. A sign of how a friendly atmosphere developed between the clientele and me. Following my mother's example and teaching, I have always treated people as individuals and with respect. Irrespective of their actual or perceived social status or circumstances. It does no good to anyone to apply one broad brushstroke across any sector or group. This approach helped the cross section of customers we served feel at ease with me. I soon discovered it also enabled me to introduce, and get people talking to, complete strangers. This certainly helped in a place where single, lonely people often congregated. There were a few drinks I knew nothing about. For example, one evening a customer asked for Bacardi. I had become accustomed to being asked if so and so was in and, assuming this such a request, asked who he was referring to. A moment passed during which he fixed me with a quizzical stare before pointing to one of the hanging optics. Mortified with a sense of stupidity best describes how I felt. Thankfully, he saw the funny side and started laughing. At first it felt intimidating, but then I realised he was not being unkind and was laughing more with me than at me. Needless to say, I have never forgotten Bacardi and, over the years, have enjoyed one or two myself.

The patrons were very kind, with many frequently referring to me as goddess. I found it rather embarrassing, but over time became accustomed to it. In all honesty, I have to admit it was rather flattering, and we did have a lot of fun. This pleasantness, combined with my increasing knowledge, led to me feeling at home and enjoying my work despite being regularly tired. Three jobs did take a toll. Many amusing incidents occurred during my time there. Here is one. One evening, a large bunch of men entered in boisterous good humour. 'Where is she?', their instant combined cry. Other customers appeared to understand and simply turned to look in my direction. As one, they rushed to the bar and greeted me with friendly, jovial banter and exclamations of appreciation. This group turned out to be the town's professional football team. They became regulars who were always in good humour and out for fun. It was a delight to serve them. Another evening I remember well. Each member of the team took turns to come up to the bar while their comrades sat around tables. This should have alerted me because their usual custom had been for all to congregate at the bar, but there, my inherent naïvety yet again. One ordered several bottles of beer, which were stocked on a bottom shelf below the bar. He directed me to bring them up one at a time. Gullible fool I am, I did as asked. It took a few bottles before I realised he was trying to see down my cleavage. It still brings a flush to my cheeks. Once the bottles were lined up on the bar, he indicated for me to come closer, as if he wanted to impart some confidence. I thought nothing of this because I had become accustomed to people confiding matters they would not speak to others about. This was probably for a couple of reasons. It is often easier to talk to a relative stranger about such things. I was also known for my discretion, never repeating anything told, even if there had been no such request. Accordingly, I lent over the bar. Before registering what he was about, he had grabbed the handkerchief I wore in the top of my dress. My shyness and embarrassment when anyone tried to look down my cleavage had led to me adopting this habit. Waving it above his head, he repeatedly shouted to his friends, 'Got it!' 'Got it!', which was greeted with raucous cheers. It turned out they had a bet as to who would be able to get it. Though I appreciated the fun, I was now exposed. Instantly running into the back, I delved into my handbag and fetched a replacement, firmly forcing it into my now exposed cleavage. Though embarrassed, I was not angry or unduly offended by the playfulness and simply shook my finger, telling him he was a naughty boy. We all had a good laugh and they treated me to several drinks in appreciation of me being such a good sport. I understand some of you may think the above is narcissistic. Please be assured it is not intended to be so. It is simply, as I reiterate from time to time, that others considered me good looking, though I have never thought of myself as anything special. Many incidents in my life have this opinion underlying them and it is only right I make you aware of it.

As mentioned, I am generally not an alcohol drinker and therefore, during the first days, declined offers of drinks. Quickly coming to the realisation some considered my refusal offensive, I compromised by asking for a soft drink. Attitudes and acceptances for the most are different these days. However, at the time many men felt it an insult to their manhood for someone to refuse their offer or request a soft option. Only alcohol would do. Not an attitude I ever really understood. Bearing in mind one of my duties was to create an accommodating atmosphere, I felt I had no choice but to accept an appropriately acceptable drink. I put most on a back shelf for disposal later. Mr Waite, the manager, noted and drew me to one side. Addressing me as Titch, his affectionate nickname because I am short of stature, he suggested I accept all drinks. I had still tried to refuse some. He went on to say we would put the untouched ones back in the bottle and he would give me half the value. He made the condition that none of the other staff were to know. Most consumed their drinks and I doubt would have been willing to give them up. I, on the other hand, was more than happy to comply. It was a way to not upset customers and for me to earn a little extra. Obviously he was doing well by the arrangement since I was really entitled to the full value. By reselling the drinks he was gaining twice the revenue. Nonetheless, I was not about to complain. There was also the truth, having so many drinks given, there was no way I could have consumed them all, even if I had been a drinker. I doubt, even if I had been, I would have coped. Whether a full-fledged alcoholic would have, I am not sure. I must point out only the untouched drinks and those not exposed to any adverse element were ever returned to the bottle.

Our customers came from a variety of backgrounds, which added to the interest. Each had their own experiences and anecdotes to relate. I made many good friends and acquaintances during my time at the pub. Among them were several local television presenters, with a few of who I enjoyed the rare beauty of a genuine friendship. A friendship that continued after I moved to my next employment, where they became regulars. More of that later. Though the local docks were not too far down the road, they were far enough to avoid troublesome elements. Those seamen and dockers who preferred more civilised surroundings would make the extra effort to come to us. When in port, many of the sailors, officers and rank and file, generously brought me presents. Dolls, which I collected, some up to four feet tall. Exotic boxes of chocolates purchased in their travels. Wonderful bouquets from which I still have many of the wicker baskets and vases. Such nice and relatively peaceful memories compared with most of those I have.

Mr and Mrs Waite's marriage could never be described as ideal or happy. They were always fighting without care for where they were or who was listening. Often within sight and hearing of customers. As managers, let alone supposedly mature adults, they should have known better. During one of these public skirmishes, Mr Waite had shouted at his wife how he had got her from France when she had no knickers. Besides the fact I find all fights and disagreements upsetting, their behaviour was also bad for business. In the absence of anyone else having the wherewithal, or guts, to say anything, it was left for me to deal with the situation. Drawing them aside, no simple task in their heightened agitated state, I informed them they were exposing themselves to customer laughter and ridicule. If they wanted to fight, they should go to their upstairs apartment. This appeared to bring them to their senses. Both acknowledged I was making sense and clearly had brains. Then, finally taking the time to look at each other properly, both expressed remorse for what they had been doing. I still find it hard to understand how people of their age and experience behave in such immature ways. Regrettably, my life experiences have shown it is all too often a frequent pattern of behaviour. They never stopped fighting, but at least these were now conducted out of sight and mostly out of the hearing of clientele.

A few months after starting at the pub head office telephoned to ask Mr Waite what he had done. The takings had shot up. I do not know for sure, but got the impression prior to my arrival the business had been struggling and was in danger of being closed. He said it must be the new barmaid, going on to tell them a little about me. Subsequently, head office management informed him I was no longer his responsibility but theirs. 'She goes with the fittings' was their term and, without further ado, increased my salary. Naturally, I was grateful, though not sure I liked to be considered part of the furniture.

The charm and fun were not restricted to the pub. Local residents often flirted and laughed with me as I made way to work. A small yet amusing and indicative event occurred one evening while walking along the high street. A young man ran in front of me, fell to his knees, and, in his words, started to worship me. The consequence of my goddess nickname. It was all good natured fun and in no way meant to be irreverent. Nor was it in the least threatening. We had a hearty laugh. This took place many years ago when it was safe for a woman to walk out on her own, no matter the time, day or night. We never thought twice about doing so. It is sad to see how society has changed. Despite all I have been through, I still do not comprehend why some people find violence appropriate or necessary. I suspect much of the increase in violent behaviour is because of children no longer being taught their own value and that of others. Consequently, there is a serious lack of respect, self respect included. I am not so naïve these days and understand the pressures modern society imposes. However, I do not believe that is a valid excuse for violence toward others. Better get off my hobbyhorse, though the absence of respect continues to upset me.

It was well known among staff, at the end of business my till was always accurate to the farthing. Younger readers may not have heard of such coinage, but at the time it was a valid component of everyday expenditure. A farthing equates to a quarter of a penny and was in wide usage then. All the other tills were regularly out. A result of carelessness and, in some instances, theft. I am certain, along with myself, Mr and Mrs Waite were aware some helped themselves to what they liked to refer to as petty case for their shopping or socialising. Having detected this behaviour at an early stage, I insisted upon my own till to which no one else was to be allowed access. I was therefore shocked and angry on the evening my till was found to be under the recorded takings, certain I had not made a mistake. I never had. It appears I have a natural ability for mental arithmetic. I suspected and confronted Mrs Waite. She did not even try to deny her involvement, just asking how I knew. I simply told her I knew. She then admitted to making the till wrong because she thought her husband might be having an affair with me. She should have known better. Everyone knew I would never do such a thing. I felt insulted and not a little angry. Mr Waite had made evident his interest in me, but I had put him right, making clear I would never consider such a thing. She really should have known. I told her how insulting and upsetting I found such an accusation and was halfway to leaving. She immediately apologised. I went on to say if she had a problem with me, she should talk to me, check her facts, and not try to undermine me. In view of her manifest remorse, I decided to stay feeling fairly certain there would be no repeat. From then on, she treated me like a best friend. I think the incident caused her to appreciate I was no danger to her with respect to her husband.

My health was generally good, but naturally, there were occasions when it was not quite so robust, especially with my round the clock working. Even on those occasions, I endeavoured to attend my places of employment. I have never believed in taking time off for the slightest reason. There was, however, one instance when I knew it was hopeless to go to the pub. The job required I be alert, friendly, and on my feet all night. It was clear I would not be able to manage this time. I therefore made the very rare telephone call to say I would not be in. Two days later Mrs Waite turned up on my doorstep. Apparently, customers kept asking for me and were not satisfied with the simple replay of me being unwell. Mrs Waite asked, or I should say demanded, we, my son was home for school holidays, stay in the family apartment above the bar. She considered patrons would be happier if told I was upstairs. By request of my loyal clientele, she brought their best wishes for a speedy recovery and the lovely bouquets and boxes of chocolates they had given for me. I do not like being away from home, but acquiesced, primarily to ensure job security. It was clear she and her husband were nervous about losing custom if I was not around. Remember, the business had been in trouble before my arrival. The consequence for me if they had to close was obvious.

The Waites had a daughter who was a few years older than my son and rather forward for her age. One afternoon, feeling a little better, I had gone down to the bar but returned for some reason I do not recall, probably to collect a handkerchief. Entering the living room I discovered the girl attempting to get my son to expose himself. It was evident this was with the intention of going further. Horrified and incensed, I told her to get out. No one messes with my son, no matter their age. I immediately gathered our belongings and told Mrs Waite we were returning home. To alleviate any genuine concern, I confirmed I was feeling much better and could look after us both without assistance.

Earlier I promised more detail regarding my electronics factory employment. As you know, I needed to find sufficient income to pay college fees and meet my day-to-day commitments. It was obvious the pub salary would not be enough. The advert for the factory position implied a reasonable salary. Therefore, though I had no experience of such work, I decided it would do no harm to at least try. To my surprise and delight, the recruitment board looked upon me favourably. They also guaranteed full on-the-job training. I honestly had not expected such understanding. They gave me the position of quality checking some of the minute commodities the factory produced. Until recent years, when age and health have exercised their influence, my eyesight had been excellent. A bonus for me was that those of us employed in such work received an extra allowance. The job required me to check nine different aspects simultaneously. This necessitated, with the exception of the one leg I stood on, the use of all my other body parts. The floor managers did jokingly say they really should find something for that idle leg to do. As if!

It turned out we were on piecework, though I had no understanding or concept of what that meant at the time. I have never believed in sculling round or avoiding work and only ever took short lunch breaks and the occasional toilet break. Usually just two a day, I have a very strong bladder. I learnt later my output was consequently far in excess of most and the highest for the entire section. You probably know piecework requires timesheets and such to be completed. I found them confusing and honestly did not understand how to fill them in. Appreciating my predicament, the other girls kindly undertook the task for me. It would be very much later before I realised, because of my high output, the others were being shown up. Regrettably, many did their best to avoid doing more than was absolutely necessary. Presumably theirs were second incomes, and they did not have the needs and pressures I did. It transpired, during the process of completing the forms for me, the girls were taking much of my excess and sharing it among themselves. Discovery of this was disappointing. They were always good to me and, in a nice way, treated me as the baby of the section. I admit I still possessed my inherent innocence and naïvety. Nevertheless, this was very naughty and dishonest and deprived me of goodness knows how much additional income. Income I really needed. I suppose I could have pursued the matter. If I had, they would more than likely have been convicted of fraud. But I did not have the heart to do so.

These same girls also had a few laughs at my expense. I never understood the following until, many years later, when my friend Hanna explained. I usually had a sandwich with me for lunch, but occasionally bought something in the staff canteen. On one of those occasions, some of my colleagues pointed to another queue in which there was a woman we knew. They told me to attract her attention by calling 'You in the far queue'. Due to my accent and mispronunciation of some English words, this apparently sounded like 'F.... you', much to the merriment of other staff. On another occasion, they told me to ask one of the girls, who had a cough, if she would like a 'Sweet for cough'. This was apparently interpreted, again to everyone's amusement, as 'Sweetie f.... Off'. Even now I blush at the thought of having had my words so misinterpreted, but as said, at the time, I had no idea. Just as well as I am sure my blood vessels would have been in danger of exploding.

The work was demanding and tiring, but I was young and full of energy. It wears me out now just to think of it. On top were my multiple work routines. From the factory I went directly to my cleaning job. There is nothing really to tell you about that. One cleaning job is much like any other. It was only for the couple of hours between leaving the day job and arriving at the pub. Since I went from one job to the other without going home or having any opportunity to change, I wore three layers of clothing. Dress for the evening over which I wore my cleaners overall and over it all the factory uniform. This saved a lot of time and energy, enabling me to strip each layer away when it was no longer required. The bus journeys provided for catnaps, which were essentially my primary sleeping periods.

I mentioned earlier I had been unwell, but the truth is my almost twenty-four-hour regime was taking its toll. Regrettably, my recovery from the earlier episode was to be short-lived. One morning, while in the ladies, I suddenly felt unwell, found it difficult to breathe, and experienced tight tension in my chest. I had been talking with one of the girls at the time and, sensing I was about to go down, grabbed her. Unfortunately, I tore her clothing as I collapsed with what turned out to be heart failure.

The consultant did say he had seen people who were burning the candle at both ends, but I had surpassed them all by also trying to burn the middle. The attack obviously left me in a weakened state. I was unable to return to work for a while. This did not help with my recovery because I was constantly worried about money. I only received statutory sick pay for the factory job, which would not cover all outgoings. I needed the income from all three jobs. Thankfully, I had saved a few pounds, which helped through this period. It hurt to see my hard-earned savings so rapidly diminish.

Recovery from heart failure is typically a slow business, but, due I think to my overall general fitness, it was not long before I was able to resume some employment. Obviously, I could not immediately return to all three. Especially not the factory with its requirement for me to be constantly on my feet. Or should that be foot? Not to mention having to utilise all other limbs. The tiredness and weakness irritated me, but I was determined to overcome them. Initially, I returned to the pub. The Waites were kind and caring, had their apartment upstairs where I could rest when necessary, and there was the supply of food, if needed. It also helped I was now confident with the work and customers were sufficiently good natured not to make it a burdensome task. My son was also at college, so I had no concerns for his welfare or vulnerability to Missy Waite.

Though on good terms with most customers, I made a general point of not socialising with them outside the pub. However, believing myself to be a reasonably accurate judge of character, I indulged occasional, I stress occasional, exceptions to my rule. Remember, most of the time I was on my own with little interaction outside of work. In addition, my three job routine was tiring and sometimes I just needed a break to revitalise the engine. After all, I am only human. Yes, of course, sleep was a priority, but sometimes we need a complete break.

A rather nice man, who had become a regular patron, professed himself deeply in love with me. Not the first or last to do so. He would like to take me out for an evening. Considering him a pleasant, no-nonsense person, I accepted. However, prior to doing so I made clear, as I always did with the very few I went out with, there would be no messing about, including kissing, unless I said otherwise. Beside my inherent worries about opposite sex encounters, I do not believe in being intimate with someone I barely know. Nor do I consider it fair or right to allow for any possible misunderstanding or perceived deception. Younger readers may see this as very old-fashioned, but that is who I am, and who I am happy to be. Indicating his understanding and agreement, he told me we would be going to an exclusive country pub. His description made it sound very nice and a place to look forward to visiting. It was in one of the attractive villages dotted round the forest locality he was talking about. Many millionaires lived in the district and, though people referred to it as a pub, the venue was really more of an exclusive club.

While driving toward our outing, he, for no apparent reason, pulled off into the forest edge. Immediately, my fingers clenched and my breathing became laboured. The taut band round my chest hurt. Before I could get a word out to ask why we had stopped, he had leant over and tried to kiss me. Seriously upset, especially as he had confirmed he understood, I forced him off, telling him straight there would be none of that. Belligerently, rather than drawing back and apologising, he, with piercing darkened eyes, told me to get out! Though fear had now entered, I had learnt a lot since my husband and was not willing to concede. Refusing, I told him he had to take me back, all thoughts of an outing abandoned. Regrettably, he became alarmingly aggressive. Fearful of repeating experiences with my ex-husband, I reluctantly exited the vehicle. He barely gave me a chance to get my legs clear before driving off at speed. I did not know where I was and wandered round in tears. Why did things always end up like this for me? I could not fathom it, but I must have done something wrong in my life to constantly deserve such treatment. It is only in recent years I have come to realise it is mostly to do with my worldly innocence and naïvety, which, to my son's exasperation, still inhabit me. I really do want to believe in people's sincerity and goodness. Perhaps I would be different if my upbringing had been harsh and uncaring, but I am very glad it was not. Those early years may be the only truly happy ones I enjoyed, but at least I had them and continue to enjoy the memories.

With no signposts or buildings about, I had no clue in which direction to head. Eerie dusk was also descending. Lightheaded in the midst of a whirling brain fog, it is evident, in retrospect, despondency and anxiety had befuddled my mind. Hesitatingly, almost as if they had a mind of their own, my feet shifted one way, then another. What if I went the wrong way? I could end up in an even more remote spot. The mist in my head continued to swirl and disorientate until the sound of a car engine recalled me to the moment. Looking round, I saw it was him. My legs froze, my stomach somersaulted, and my chest became restricted again. I could not help biting my lip or gritting my teeth, knowing it was unlikely I would be able to fight him off for long. I was defenceless against a man of his strength. Running was an option, but where would I go? Anyway, my feet felt as if set in concrete. Even if I had been able to get them moving, my ability to outrun him was seriously doubtful. While in this undecided state, he drew alongside. Was this it then? However, instead of leaping out and attacking, he appeared to have come to his senses. Apologising, he said he would take me home, promising no further inappropriate behaviour. Reluctant but with little choice, I got back into the car. Good to his word he took me straight home without further incident. I never saw him again. This is just one example of how what should have been a lighthearted, relaxed evening turned into anything but. Unfortunately, this was to prove a pattern.

Another I broke my rule for was Richard. On a day out with some of his friends, he kept insisting I imbibe the multiple drinks he pushed my way. This despite me having told him I did not want so many and could not cope with so much alcohol. However, he would not listen. I suppose this may have been because he was a well off, car sales owner and gentleman farmer, clearly not accustomed to people refusing him. Nevertheless, I was not going to allow him to force me into something I did not want and walked out. He chased me and grabbing my petite frame, lifted me off the ground. Through gritted teeth, he informed me no one walks out on him. Was I now in real trouble? He was a tall, broadly built, powerful man who I could not fight. One quick squeeze of his hand would have done for me. Moments hung in the air. Thankfully, he had true affection for me and willingly forgave what he saw as my indiscretion. Once we got matters clear and he understood why I had walked out, I continued to see him for a while.

Intentionally, I had not told Richard very much about my life with Terrance. I preferred to try and forget, not that I ever really have, and not talk about those times. I had said enough for him to know it had not been a happy marriage. As far as I was concerned that was sufficient and thought no more on the matter. However, it transpired he had gained further knowledge from some of my work colleagues, with who I had shared a little more. It would seem they had also informed him Terrance still bothered me from time to time. In his own way, Richard was protective. He was also a proud man leading to him feeling affronted that anyone should interfere with someone he cared about. Consequently, he decided to gather some of his friends and acquaintances with the unified aim of teaching my ex-husband a lesson. I have since learnt car sales people of the time had a tendency to associate with undesirables. He certainly appeared to be involved with some of society's less savoury elements. Their intent was not conveyed to me. However, I got to hear about it. Terrance certainly deserved a good lesson. Nevertheless, I became concerned so many violent people with one combined purpose would go too far. There was no doubt they could kill with little thought. There is also the fact I hate violence and certainly did not want such a thing upon my conscious. Besides all that, I have experienced and witnessed too much of it and do not want any imposed upon others. I find it hard to understand why people who have been subjected to such treatment would condone anything similar being meted out to others. Of course, I am aware of the concept of revenge, but does it really achieve anything? Surely it is better to encourage positiveness in society. Not wanting Terrance to get hurt, I telephoned to warn him, for which he was grateful. I subsequently stopped seeing Richard. This incident showed me he was evidently not the sort of person I wanted to be associated with. In view of the earlier incident, his probable reaction when informing him of my decision worried me. Thankfully, his affection for me, which was genuine, won through. He also respected me and for that reason reluctantly accepted the situation.

24

NIGHTCLUB

I had been at the pub for a few years when the owner of a newly established nightclub offered a substantially better salary. I was initially unsure and asked for time to consider the proposition. You will appreciate a nightclub is a very different prospect to a pub. I mentioned his offer to some friends and was delighted to hear that those who had been there thought it a very nice place. They assured it was in no way sleazy, as many in the town had the tendency to be. The man returned a few days later, repeated his offer, and took me to look over the premises. The congenial atmosphere and tempting increase in income were having a positive impact. There was also the fact, once he explained what would be required, I did not consider the work would present any difficulties. This positive combination resulted in my acceptance. As so often with life moves, I was sorry to be leaving the pub. My employers, in their own way, had been good to me through the years. I also felt a little guilty after the kindness they had shown during my illness. Nevertheless, I did not think I should let that prevent me from improving my position. In addition, my outgoings were increasing exponentially. My son was growing fast and the cost of living was starting to go up. The move would clearly be the right course.

Besides the standard nightclub facilities of bar, band, restaurant and dance floor, it also incorporated a gambling establishment. I say gambling, though in reality, for most punters, it was more of a social pastime than hardened gambling. It certainly added to the overall ambience with roulette, several blackjack tables, and a variety of other games. I am not a gambler and had no interest in getting to know more than necessary to fulfil my role. We initially agreed I would run the main bar. However, within short time, the manager decided he wanted me to croupier one of the blackjack tables. I suspect this was more than likely due to me being considered good looking. I did not wish to undertake the task, nor have any dealings with that side of the business, but he was fairly insistent. My need for the job and the possibility of losing it if I refused, his increasing determination implying it a likely outcome, resulted in my reluctant agreement.

The work was not arduous and thankfully, most players were pleasant. As mentioned earlier, the gambling for most was social however, there were a few who took it further. One evening, a young man lost a considerable amount and became desperate and suicidal. He told me, and anyone who would listen, he was going outside to kill himself and we would all be sorry when his body was found. Unless you have experienced anything similar, it will be hard for you to comprehend the impact of such a circumstance. The emotional drain is considerable. Anyone who has been involved with someone in such a state will understand. Even though events like this rarely occurred, I knew I could not deal with more of the same. I said as much to the manager, making clear either he returned me to the bar or accept my resignation. I may have wanted the job, but this incident had been a step too far. Thankfully, he heard. I went back to the bar.

I have always looked for the best in people, believing there is good and honesty in all of us. Sadly and with surprising consistency, in my experience at least, people frequently let themselves down. As briefly mentioned earlier, in previous employment I had seen staff help themselves to cash from tills and consume drinks they had not paid for. Both of which troubled and appalled me. Now, while running the blackjack table, I witnessed croupiers pocket money losing punters had laid down. I find such dishonesty and downright theft incomprehensible. There is no need for it and it simply impacts society for the worse, for all of us. Sad to say, it appears not only is such behaviour on the increase but has also become an acceptable trait.

The hours were very different to any I had encountered before. Work commenced later and did not end until the early hours. It was frequently dawn before I left. Evidently this was going to impact my other responsibilities. Despite the substantial increase in salary, additional income would still be required if I was to pay the college fees. In view of the hours I was now working the factory and cleaning jobs were no longer realistic options. The question of what alternative to look for was troubling me when a solution presented itself through someone I had met during my time at the pub. Public house landlords were in the habit of visiting each other socially. Most appeared to be on good terms, though they obviously also saw these visits as opportunities to observe competitors' offerings. One owned a restaurant-pub, which was not as commonplace as they are today. He had previously asked me to work for him, but with my three jobs it was not possible, especially as the salary was far less than my existing incomes. My club salary had now increased sufficiently for me to re-consider the offer. The principal attraction being the hours. He required someone for the ten to three shift, to cover lunchtime, and five to eleven in the evenings. Obviously, the evening shift was out of the question, but the earlier one would enable me to have some sleep, do my housework, and remain at the club. He was delighted when I asked if he still had a vacancy. Whether he had or not, I never knew. It became evident, whatever the situation, he was going to make room for me. He pressed the point of me also undertaking evening shifts, but I unequivocally informed him it was not an option. He accepted, grateful to at least have me present for the midday period. I subsequently resigned from both the factory and cleaning firm. Another advantage of this new position was the broadening of my work experience. I now had to take and serve food orders as well as drinks. Thankfully, as previously mentioned, I am blessed with a quick mind and the ability to assimilate new information readily. The cuisine was to a very good standard and reasonably priced, though a little above those of a good quality cafe of which there were many in those days. Cafes used to serve full meals rather than just sandwiches and snacks. The owner enjoyed his food and ensured he only employed top quality chefs. The clientele were also generally pleasant.

As occurred in many of the places I worked, I met some very nice people here. Harold was one. He was one of those people round whom there is a calm and quiet aura. Though not classically handsome, he embodied a masculine attraction. He was also quite shy. I liked Harold and enjoyed his conversation and company. Eventually he asked me to dinner, an invitation I was more than happy to accept. He took me to a lovely riverside restaurant where we enjoyed our meal at a window table overlooking the river. We watched as sailboats and river punters worked their way up and down. He always took me to good quality restaurants in which menus allowed as to have whatever we desired. It took a while, but eventually he overcame his shyness and started talking freely. Among other things he mentioned, he piloted his own light aircraft. With his reserved sense of dress and shyness, few would have known he was a millionaire. This was when a million was worth a million. The revelation took me aback. I honestly had no idea. It amused him and I think he was grateful. It did away with the possibility of me having gone out with him because of his wealth. As you have seen and will again, such wealth actually frightens me and I prefer to avoid it. Throughout, he was a perfect gentleman. A real treat. For example, he always took us in his elegant custom made sports car that boasted a striking walnut dash. I am not good with car models so cannot tell you what it was except it was exquisite. He always insisted I wait for him to open my door before alighting or boarding. Sadly, some people today consider such behaviour boring, unmasculine, or sexist. All I may say is, on the contrary, such behaviour is wonderful and a sign of genuine character, consideration, and intelligence, rarely seen these days. Regrettably, respect for self and others appears to be considered an archaic concept. If only today's generation realised what they are missing. Deep down everyone wishes to be respected, but respect has to be earned by showing good character, appreciation, and respect for others. Sorry, got on my soapbox for a moment, but the lack of these attributes in modern society saddens and irritates me no end. He was also a generous man, always insisting upon paying when we were out and at Christmas presenting me with bouquets of beautiful white lilac. I have no idea where he got them, but they must have cost because they were definitely not in bloom within the United Kingdom at that time of year.

Working at the nightclub, despite the late hours, was pleasant. The customers were cheerful and the management fair and friendly. The owner was a New Zealander and, like so many of the people I have met from there, a calm and affable person. He was also a responsible employer. He looked after his staff and ensured sufficient security personnel were always on duty, though rarely required. Clientele tended to be primarily good-natured people with decent incomes. Any troublemaker was soon dealt with and barred for life. As usual, customers and I got to know each other and we were quickly on good terms. Even wives, who at first were wary because of my looks, soon became grateful for my presence. They soon came to realise their husbands would get nowhere with me, though they did try it on. As you have seen, I very occasionally went out with someone for a meal or drink, but in truth, really had no time for personal associations. Even if I had, I would never have considered seeing anyone who was married or in a relationship. That is anathema to me. Wives, girlfriends, and lovers soon understood and consequently trusted me.

One day some of my colleagues together a few clientele suggested we go out for a night in London. These were the days when parochial towns still had limited stylish venues. Things have changed since. They claimed to know nice places and it would not take too long to drive there. Distances are relative to what one is used to. For me, who rarely ventured from town, it was a long way. Nevertheless, the return journey would be achievable within one night and still allow plenty of time to enjoy ourselves. I would normally have turned down such an invitation, but I felt worked out and in need of a therapeutic, relaxing break. I also considered the proposed company trustworthy. Therefore, one of my rare nights off saw us heading out of town in the large, comfortable car one of our customer friends had provided. Chatting and laughing on the way proved restorative in itself. They had not lied when saying they knew some nice establishments. We enjoyed a lovely dinner, followed by drinks in a couple of different places. Unfortunately, the others, including the driver, were not as moderate in their drinking as I. Later, in their inebriated state, they said we should find a hotel for the night. There was absolutely no way I was going to agree. First, it was more than obvious where this was going to end. A few in the group were not particularly moral or virtuous. Second, I had my day job and was not prepared to let my employer down. My refusal did present a problem because none of the others were fit to drive. In the end I said I would, though it had been years since I had done so and then only under a provisional licence. Surely it could not be that hard to recall. If the car owner sat next to me and told me what to do, we should be okay. If I am honest, I have to admit to being very nervous, but it would be better than staying in London overnight. It is a city I have never liked or felt safe in. You may recall I am small in stature. Consequently, the first matter to deal with was how I was going to reach the pedals and yet simultaneously see through the windscreen. Naturally, my stilettos, which added to my height when standing, had to be abandoned. They adjusted the seat to its maximum, enabling me to just about reach. I managed to manoeuvre into the traffic that, thankfully for London, was quiet. Beginner's luck dealt with my concerns of not being able to stop the car when necessary. All the traffic lights were green. I still wonder what would have been the result if any had not been. While the others slept, I kept the owner awake by constantly talking, mostly asking what to do next. He told me when to turn, when to go straight on, which roundabout exit to take, and so on. Since this event occurred prior to the advent of power steering, making turns could have proven problematic, but thankfully I was strong and did not find it hard to control the weight. However, I was not confident enough to undertake any degree of manoeuvring and therefore restricted myself to inside lanes. There was no motorway in those days, so I did not have to face the challenges of multiple lanes and fast driving. How I managed I am still uncertain, but we arrived safely in one piece. It was as well it was very late, or early, whichever way you prefer to look at it, and that I kept to a reasonable speed. If the police had stopped us, I would have been in serious trouble. I had no licence or insurance, though the fact did not cross my mind at the time. I just wanted to get home.

After this I attempted to relearn driving skills but never had the time to undertake a complete course. Then, having noted whenever someone I knew was involved in an accident it was usually due to some crazy act by another driver, I chose not to pursue the matter in later life. I would always be watching other drivers, which would not be good for my own concentration. I remain nervous of getting into a car with anyone other than my son, who, though he drives a little faster than I would like at times, is observant and careful.

Between finishing my day job and commencing at the club, I occasionally meet up with old friends. This was usually at the small cafe we had frequented for many years. Some of these were the ones who carried me to the pub and suggested the manager employ me there and then. You will understand from what I have shared, my time was very limited nevertheless, I did not want to lose touch with most of them. Beside Hanna, who was not part of this group as her life revolved within different social circles, these were really the only friends I ever had. I will tell you more about Hanna in a moment. Unfortunately, there was one who was rather a bitch. Excuse the expression. Thankfully, she infrequently joined us. I was not concerned about losing contact with her. Lamentably, she maintained contact with me.

The woman was certainly not grateful for what she had. I met her rather nice husband and children on the couple of occasions she invited me to her home. She had no appreciation and after seeing how she treated them thought she should have had my husband. She made sure to keep her figure by only eating prime steak or fish while serving spaghetti or some other pasta to her family. Her retort when the children dared say anything was they could eat what they wanted when they earned for themselves. She always took her husband's salary off him at the end of the week, never acknowledging him to be the primary earner, without whom they would have struggled. Eventually, she wore him down completely. Breaking his spirit to the point of him signing the house that had been his for years, long before they met, over to her. Two hundred and fifty pounds, a ridiculous sum even in those days for a three bedroom, detached bungalow with fair sized gardens all round, was all he got. I am surprised he got that much out of her. She was truly a mean woman. Shortly after he became a Buddhist. I suspect it was the peaceful teachings which attracted him. His life had been anything but peaceful during the years of his marriage.

Back to my friends. Those of us who were particularly close agreed, should we eventually lose touch as was more than likely in the way of life, to meet back in the cafe in fourteen years. Why fourteen I do not recall, but with all that occurred in my subsequent life, I never made it. Shame, it would have been nice to see my friends again. The cafe has now gone and everyone we knew has moved, just like me. Over the years I was only able to maintain contact with Hanna, who as said was not part of the cafe group.

Hanna was the one and only person I ever considered a best friend. We met while I was working in the pub, hitting it off almost immediately. She certainly was a fun character. We enjoyed many a laugh together. One example is the evening we arranged to go to a country pub with some acquaintances. They took their own car while we followed in Hanna's. It was old and typically decided to break down in the middle of a dark wooded area. In full length evening gowns and high heels, we were hardly dressed for the event. But what choice did we have? Discarding our shoes, we exited the car and applying all our strength attempted to push start the reluctant vehicle. It stubbornly clung to the muddy surface of the lane we were in. We stood back to gain breath and regain strength and then reapplied ourselves. The initial resistance suddenly evaporated and the car moved at greater speed than expected. We fell full body length. Eventually, we managed to get up, dresses, hair, and faces, all covered in mud. It was one of those silly occasions when, rather than get upset, we burst out laughing. We could not stop for a while. Not unusual when in Hanna's company. I still smirk when recalling the incident. Someone should have had a camera, it would have made a fun picture. Nothing really seemed to bother us when together.

Sadly, even that contact ended when she no longer got in touch or replied to my cards and letters. Many years later, my son managed to find her overseas phone number. We spoke but once, though she seemed annoyed. I am not sure, but it may have been she also had to pay for incoming calls as you do in some countries. I have since heard from someone who knew her ex-husband of her passing. Life, as I well know, carries many disappointments. I no longer have any friends and if it was not for my son would be totally alone in this world.

One other event that occurred while working at the club, and one that left its mark, I would like to tell you about. A merchant navy officer who frequented the club when in harbour, invited me to a dinner dance on his ship. With my inherent reserve I was unsure. In the end, some of his fellow officers persuaded me, telling me these were always good fun and nicely organised. I had often heard how elegant and exceptional naval dinner-dances were. They encouraged me to accept with each assuring to make certain no one imposed themselves upon me against my wishes. These intelligent men had witnessed how I frequently had to deal with unwanted attentions. On the evening the weather was unusually fine. Organisers decided to take advantage by setting dinner tables, band stand, dance floor, bar, and so on, on the poop deck. To make it even more attractive, they decorated it with chandeliers and silk curtains. It was a truly enchanting spectacle, with the crystal prisms of light bouncing off the silver service and brilliantly polished plates. The conversation was lively, the dinner superb, and the wine excellent. Unsurprisingly, with the before, during, and after drinks, the point came when I needed to 'powder my nose'. Holding the event on the poop meant the facilities were at the further end of the gangway, traversing the starboard side. I was about to unfasten the hatch when two women jumped upon me, one grabbing at my breasts while her companion attempted to kiss me. Momentarily stunned and off balance, I struggled to regain equilibrium. Thankfully, I managed to do so fairly quickly. I pushed them off, but they kept coming. I began to fear I would be incapable of dealing with both, at the same time wondering what on earth had caused the unwarranted attack. My apprehension was increasing exponentially when some officers appeared on the scene and intervened. The commotion had attracted their attention.

Why had these women attacked me? I had never seen them before and as far as I was aware, had done nothing to offend. In response to my bewildered questioning, the officers informed me they were lesbians who had taken more than a passing fancy. I still do not understand why, at the very least, they had not struck up a casual conversation or sought an introduction. Apparently, so I have subsequently been informed, some prefer this sort of aggressive approach. That opens up all sorts of thoughts and possibilities for psychological analysis, but that is not a task for me. The confrontation had simply been very frightening. My naval companions determined not to permit the occurrence to spoil the whole evening. They ordered more of the excellent wine and a sumptuous dessert, and chatted and danced with me for the rest of the evening.

I felt at home working in the club, if you follow my meaning. It was a nice, good quality, and friendly venue. I looked forward to working there for a few years. However, as usual, my hopes and aspirations were to be ruined. One of the male customers became very possessive and started stalking me. A very frightening experience. He would not listen to reason and constantly tuned up wherever I was and tail me. Thankfully, I became aware of it before he had the chance to follow me home. It may sound strange, but it never occurred to me to involve the police or attempt to obtain a restraining order. Not that I consider they are worth the paper they are written on. Eventually, it got to the point where I no longer felt I could cope. I think only those who have been through such an experience may appreciate how draining and stressful it can be. The strain ascended to such a point that one evening I vomited while at work. It did not help that I also had a cold. The owner did his best to help me, but in the end I had to tell him I could not go on. I did not want to give up my job, but felt I had no choice. As I previously mentioned, my boss was a nice person and clearly understood. He regretted I would be leaving, but remained determined to help as best he could. He instructed his staff to tell my stalker, when he asked, as he inevitably would, that I had left and returned to my home country. Everyone knew I was not English by birth. And so, a very pleasant job ended.

The loss of my job was a great disappointment, but I could not afford to wallow in self-pity or be without the income for long. Needing to find reasonably paid employment quickly, I went to work in a small nightclub. It was one of those nice, more intimate places to which some friends had previously taken me. The owner had made clear he would be interested in employing me if I was available. As a smaller establishment the workload was not excessive and, yet again, I met people I knew from other places. It was common for clientele to rotate round different venues, though most had one or two they favoured. Regrettably, this job was also not to last long.

It quickly became evident the owner's wife and daughter were very jealous of me. Why, I have no clue. Their snide comments and constant attempts to undermine made work very unpleasant. After a few days, less than a week, I think, but do not really remember, I left without giving notice. I just did not turn up nor return to collect my earnings. I had never done such a thing. To let people, in this case the owner, down in such a manner went against all my inbred instincts. It was simply I could not face having to explain about his wife and daughter. It would have been unfair to him. Jealous women can be some of the nastiest people, and to this day, I do not know what troubled them. I was only ever on professional terms with my boss without any flirtatious behaviour or intimations of anything improper. I am guessing it was something of that nature that had got into their heads. If only they had been intelligent enough to observe. There would have been no question. The only other possibility I can see is the good looks I was purported to encompass. Perhaps it was both. But really, they had nothing to fear from me.

25

CATWALK

So, yet again, my need to secure another job and that at very short notice, presented itself. I have often recounted I could not be without a full income, even for a day or two. I was determined not to fail in meeting my obligations and would go without food to do so. The owner of another, less salubrious club had, for considerable time, tried to get me to accept his employment offer. I did not want to work there. Nor did I like the idea of having to walk through the rough district even in daylight, let alone when dark. But I needed the income, and he was willing to pay a reasonable salary. I therefore accepted. Desperate times often lead to desperate decisions.

Understandably, considering the location, the clientele were less refined than the ones I was accustomed to. Nevertheless, as has always been my practice, I treated each and every one as someone deserving respect. We are all unique in one way or another and deserve to be treated with regard. Sophistication was out of the question. However, addressing them as individuals in their own right and making clear I was listening made a positive impact. This was especially important because most were accustomed to being ignored or spoken to in a rough and dismissive manner. In return, they learned to treat me with deference and not as one of the hussies they usually encountered. I am not being judgemental or inappropriately critical. I am simply representing the facts and terminology as they were at the time.

As you have probably gathered from the above, I never liked being there. The only saving grace, if it may be called that, was the owner's desire, having got me to work for him, for the arrangement to continue. He ensured I was looked after. As it was such an unsafe area, particularly once daylight had departed, he arranged for a taxi, at his own expense, or a trusted employee, to take me home each night.

One evening, a man aggressively demanded to see the proprietor. I felt my abdomen instinctively tighten. When informed the owner was away, he became even more confrontational and demanded money from the till to play the one-armed bandit machines. Naturally, under normal circumstances, such a demand would be refused. However, in view of his belligerence and evident likelihood of resorting to physical violence, I gave him a pound's worth of sixpences. Some of you may have no knowledge of such coinage. This was prior to decimalisation. Remember my previous observation of how most gambling was a fun and innocent pastime? Sixpence, five British pence in today's money, was a normal outlay then. Of course, from television reports and documentaries, I am now aware such recreation was, for many, the first step to developing a serious problem.

We did not realise it then. As he headed toward the machines, he turned and snarled menacingly his determination to wait. From the back office, I telephoned my boss's home to warn him. The man had refused to give his name, so I could not tell my employer who it was. He said he would be right over.

As soon as he entered, the unpleasant man pulled a gun from under his jacket and started chasing my boss. The sight of the weapon startled all of us, staff and clientele. It may have been a rough place, but this behaviour was extreme even for here. Alarmed and fearful, I really just wanted to get out. However, recognising my employer needed assistance, I did what I could to intervene and prevent the menace from catching his prey. It did not bear thinking what the likely outcome would be. Hoping to slow him or perhaps stop him altogether, I slid stools in his way and attempted to distract him by shouting questions. Finally, my boss escaped through one of the service doors and with surprising alacrity, was lost to sight. Furious, the man started waving his gun toward me, asking what I thought I was doing. Foolishly perhaps, I said he had not told me who he was and what he wanted and this was no place to carry out a vendetta. I went on to point out it no longer mattered as his target had got away. His hard stare resulted in a tingle of fear travelling down my spine. I had visions of him using the gun on me. A lifetime later, or so it felt, in a grating tone he confirmed he would get him!, meaning my boss.

Some hours later, my employer telephoned. I confirmed the man had gone and within a short time he turned up, unable to thank me enough. That was it, nothing further was ever said. To me, it appeared he had somehow got himself involved with criminal elements. Not an inappropriate conclusion considering the clientele spectrum. I am sure I do not really have to tell you I resigned. Putting up with rough, uneducated customers was one thing. This was completely another.

No income again! Would it ever be otherwise? It was now up to me to determine who I might approach. In the midst of my debating the issue, I received an unexpected invitation. It was to work at a very nice, out-of-town venue in a small village that sprawled along the banks of a lovely river. Apparently, my reputation for being a good, reliable worker and person had circulated. I had in fact also met the owners and manager at previous employments. It was an all-inclusive venue. In addition to the usual bar, lounge, and dance floor, there was a casino, and a good quality restaurant. There was no need for patrons to venture elsewhere for a night out. It was also an appealing daytime destination. The village green, which the building faced, was impeccably maintained, making it a pleasure to look upon. Other affable pubs, down country lanes, and along the river bank, also populated the neighbourhood. A variety of entertainment was to be had, with each venue having its own style and atmosphere. Many prosperous patrons frequently enjoyed complete afternoons wandering through the vicinity. The lovely location, as well as the river that was broad and deep enough to accommodate the yachting fraternity, brought many additional visitors in spring and summer. This was far more a place and clientele

I had become accustomed to. I enjoyed going to work and looked forward to working there for a while. As mentioned, this was an out-of-town venue, but thankfully the bus service was good. The bus route passing near my home helped. After work, always late night, a taxi was provided and if it failed to turn up, there were many willing, and trustworthy, lift offers. We were continually busy, very busy, however the agreeable customers and peaceful atmosphere of the district negated any sense of stress. I believe nice surroundings make a significant difference to a working environment, as also do the people.

As you may imagine, persistently changing and having to find employment was stressful. Thankfully, throughout the upheaval, I still had my ten-to-three restaurant-pub job. I was especially grateful for it because, as you have seen, I lost out on salary while transferring from one employment to another. I needed to keep up all payments and was determined never to get into debt. Even if I had been willing to try, it was almost impossible, in those days, for a lone woman to secure a bank loan.

Though I was enjoying my new position in the village club and my other employments, I realised there was a limit to how long I could maintain the three job routine. I had obtained another cleaning position for the hours between the restaurant-pub and club. It therefore seemed practical for me to continue scouring vacancy adverts for better paid positions. Despite the combined incomes, my finances remained under constant strain. Besides paying the college fees, and for uniforms, books, and so on, I also had to fulfil my rent and utility commitments. In order to achieve this, I mostly lived on one roll a day or occasionally a fried egg and chips. Just to provide you with an idea of how constrained my situation was, I will relate one event. An occasion arose, thankfully the only one, when my son was unwell while at college. Over a protracted period he daily, round the same time each morning, became weak and faint. Initially, masters, together with the resident boys' nurse, wondered if he was putting it on due to it being exam period. Considering their long-term acquaintance with my son, they should have known better. He would never do such a thing. Of course, along with most, there were the usual exam nerves, but throughout his entire school career, he never attempted to avoid them. The college doctor attended daily, examining and quizzing my son about what he was feeling. Eventually, he determined, my boy was not getting enough nourishment to keep up with his growth, despite the good quality college meals. He was growing fast, very fast for his age. He therefore directed my son to be sent home with a message for me to give him every good thing I could. Naturally, out of maternal love and concern, I would have done that anyway. However, I could not afford for both of us to have substantial meals. I therefore resorted, while ensuring my son had the best of everything, to chewing the pips and cores of the apples I gave him. I was not prepared to get into debt for any reason. Thankfully, despite all the stress, worry, wear and tare, I suffered no long term ill effects, though regularly tired. I had a robust underlying constitution.

Besides ensuring I met all my commitments, I also desperately wanted to save. My eventual aim to buy a home of our own. The existing income made it difficult. A disheartening situation, as you may imagine. Alongside this was the constant fear of falling ill or being unable to work for any reason. My salaries were hourly without benefits. If I did not work, I did not get paid. Employment regulations were very different in those days. You will therefore understand my interest when a position in a holiday camp was advertised in the local newspaper. Not only was the pay better, but accommodation and food were included. At least that should reduce my daily expenditure and enable me to put a little aside. That said, even if my application proved successful, I intended to retain my existing accommodation. As you have seen, my experiences had proven how employments could easily end with little notice. I knew it unwise to assume permanence in anything and therefore wanted to ensure my son and I had somewhere. Of course, that meant I still had the rent to consider. I did not leap to the decision and pondered the idea for a few days, eventually concluding it a viable option.

The interviewer's reaction as I entered the room made it obvious I already had the job. Was that wishful thinking? No, as I have mentioned before, many considered me very attractive. Something I had to get used to though it embarrassed me and I could never quite make out why they thought me so. Looking back, I must be appreciative. This opinion opened employment possibilities which may otherwise have remained closed to me. I had anticipated the usual barrage of delving questions, but they could hardly bring themselves to ask any. Nevertheless, we did go through my work experience as protocol demanded. My bar work certainly reigned favourably because it enabled them to perceive how I was accustomed to dealing with a vast variety of characters. They offered, and I accepted the job there and then.

They wanted me to start straightaway. However, I was unequivocal about my determination to work off the periods of notice my existing employments required. This, except for the one incident I told you about earlier, has always been my ethos. I do not believe in failing employers or leaving them high and dry. Neither will I let others down if I have given any sort of undertaking. It saddens me so many do not seem to care. If something else catches their interest, or they simply feel lazy, they will fail others without a thought. I think my display of commitment impressed the interviewers, though that had not been my motivation for stating my resolution.

Upon informing them of my decision, my existing employers did all they could to get me to change my mind. However, l had to explain I really needed the increased salary the new job offered. A salary they could not afford to match. It was a sad time for us all. We had worked well together. Each reluctantly confirmed they understood, knowing I was determined to provide the best I could for my son. They wished me success but in no uncertain terms made clear if I ever needed a job back in the area I was to contact them. They would always be pleased to reemploy me. Very nice and flattering, and I assured them I would bear their invitation in mind should the need arise.

Having fulfilled my resignation obligations, I headed for the holiday camp where I was given responsibility for running the main campsite bar. This meant I was employed as a senior member of staff and consequently had my own chalet. With my hygiene hypochondria, this was a Godsend. I would have found it almost impossible to share a small chalet and bathroom. The camp was located near the edge of high seashore cliffs, meaning the geographical terrain was fairly exposed. When the inevitable adverse elements struck, the entire area was whipped about, resulting in my little exposed chalet being rather cold. I found it hard to keep warm. I was still considered medically underweight. Thankfully, the campers' facilities were always kept warm, so all was fine when I was working. I am not sure I would have survived otherwise.

When off duty most of the staff left the camp. It was impossible to get any proper rest while on site because campers had no concept of us being off duty. They always wanted something. It was on one of these outings I was first introduced to the famous fresh cream teas of England. What a delight, I have loved them since, though my now ageing system does not cope so well with the richness. Nonetheless, I occasionally indulge and accept I have to pay the due price. Our rural outpost was really beautiful, but it meant there was little else in the immediate area. However, some of my colleagues had discovered a very nice, reasonably priced, restaurant not many miles away. Though our contracts included meals, the camp food was not the most appetising. Therefore, occasionally, on my part at least, we indulged in a meal out. It was at one of these I encountered horse meat, not that I knew at the time. I would have vomited on the spot if I had. To me horses are pets and not meant for eating. It still makes me queasy to think of it. Reluctantly, I must admit to how nice it tasted. I have since understood horse is probably the cleanest meat there is. Needless to say, I have never eaten horse flesh again.

Now, this may not come as a surprise to some of you, though it was certainly something I had hoped to avoid. One of the male staff became rather taken with me. His character and personality were that of a likeable English rogue with all the charm such people can display. Characteristics everyone enjoyed. However, he was very transparent about his wish to visit me in my chalet. Something I would never entertain, no matter who the person.

One day, soon after my arrival, I fainted. Something I am not accustomed to doing. Clearly, though I had not realised to what extent, my previous round the clock working had run me down. The English rogue was very good to me while hospitalised, doing his best to help and cheer me up with his jokes and anecdotes. I quickly saw the situation needed to be controlled. When recovered sufficiently to handle the moment, I sat him down and explained as much as I felt necessary of my circumstances. I emphasised my need for a friend I could trust not to abuse the relationship and not for a boyfriend. Not something many men like to hear. However, to give him his due, he confirmed his understanding of my need and agreed to such a friendship. As with most likeable rogues, at least those I have come across, he was a sincere person and, within limits, could be trusted. Temptation is sometimes too strong for some. We became good friends and good to his word, he left me alone in the romantic sense.

As you would expect, a variety of entertainments were provided for the holidaymakers. A body beautiful contest was one. Along with some colleagues, while enjoying a brief break from our duties, I was watching from the sidelines as entrants paraded down the catwalk. Suddenly, with no hint of a warning, I found myself pushed out onto it. I froze, horrified to find myself before a full audience. Remember, I am essentially shy and consequently found this public exposure mortifying. I am not sure how long I stood there like some frightened rabbit caught in the glare of car headlights. I suppose it must have been seconds, though it felt much longer. Penetrating through the tumultuous hurricane raging within my responsibilities as a member of staff finally exerted itself. I was here to ensure customers had a good, enjoyable and safe time. Therefore, despite the inward trembling, I forced a smile and proceeded along the catwalk. In truth, all I wanted was to run. I managed to control the urge, and following the preceding contestants' example, walked slowly. The watching crowd cheered, obviously delighted to see a member of the camp staff participating. If only they had known the true state of affairs. Again, following the real contestants' example, I paused before the judge's table before almost running off. Wishing to put the whole matter behind me, I was about to direct my footsteps back to the bar when I heard, over the tannoy system, my name announced as the contest winner. Consternation is hardly an adequate word, my intent to get away from there as fast as possible had been forestalled. Of course, I could have ignored the announcement, but that would be failing in my duties. I had no option but to return to the stage to collect the award. Admittedly it was very flattering, but as an essentially private person, I could have done without it. I certainly have no wish to repeat the experience, ever.

Unfortunately, the salary for running the bar proved less than I had been led to expect. There were all sorts of clauses and conditions in the contract I had not understood or really been made aware of. The job was not going to meet my needs. I informed the management, telling them if they wanted me to stay, I would require an increased income. We eventually agreed, as a second job outside bar hours, I could clean chalets. So I ended up again working most hours of the day and night. It is hard to put into words my disappointment. This job had appeared to offer an opportunity for a more relaxed and normal life, not to mention the ability to save a little more. Working all those hours was tiring, but I persevered. I had to ensure I could still pay the college fees and rent for my retained accommodation. In the end, I only remained for a few months. The job had not been what I expected and in view of the hours I felt I may as well return to working as I had before. At least I would be in my home and could eat the food I preferred. I left without regret. The work had been different, but had added nothing to either my life or work experience.

26

николай NIGHTINGALES

Just as I was leaving the holiday camp, my sister, Anna, let me know our father was terminally ill with cancer. Sadly, I had not seen or spoken with him since leaving my homeland. Not that there was any estrangement. It was simply distance and a lack of easy access communication facilities. These were the days when few homes had a telephone and mobiles were yet to be thought of. Yes, for younger readers, there was such a time, no smartphones, no tablets, no home computers, no internet. Can I hear the drawing in of breath in horror?

Back to my tale. One thing never in doubt was my papa's love for his country and its citizens. He was bitterly disappointed when, subsequent to the war, people started not only arguing but also fighting among themselves. His good advice to shake hands and work together for the good of the nation had been rejected. He had been a primary, respected resistance leader, but now found himself ostracised. I do not think he ever overcame the bitter disappointment. Thereafter, he led a quiet, reclusive life, seeing few people.

The timing was problematic. My son's summer vacation was about to commence. I wanted to see papa before he passed but did not wish to desert my boy. I did not consider what would be a sad and difficult occasion suitable for a young child. What to do? In the end I contacted the college and explained my predicament, hoping they may be able to provide a solution. The headmaster informed me of the two nurses they employed, the one who cared for the boys would be staying on for a while. This was a mixed gender college. She would use the time to catch up on paperwork and to ensure all necessary equipment was available or had been ordered ready for the new term. My son could remain as there would be someone to look after him. Though glad to have this resolution, I must admit I felt rather guilty. Not only would it be as if I had abandoned him, but he would also be on his own in the mansion house that formed the primary college building. Beside the nurse, the only others around would be ground staff. My only consolation had been his ability to enjoy his own company and to entertain himself. Besides reading and studying, he has always loved to learn. He also delighted in the substantial grounds, woods, and country lanes surrounding the college through which he liked to walk. Even now he prefers to walk whenever possible rather than drive.

Regrettably, papa passed before I arrived. Anna told me how he had lain his head on her lap and quietly left. Quietly, despite the considerable pain due to the cancer having spread throughout his body. He had always been a strong man and character. I was heartbroken. This had been my last chance to reconnect with the man I knew loved me unconditionally.

My instinct was to return home, but having managed to get a reasonably priced holiday package, decided to remain rather than waste it. The hotel was pleasantly situated, with just a road between it and the seashore. I have not mentioned how even prior to receiving the sad news, I had become depressed. Perhaps the cumulative result of the hardships and disappointments. I am not entirely sure why, but, whatever the cause, I concluded it time to end it all. However, the thought of a lot of blood revolted me. As always, even in this, I wanted everything to be clean. Cutting wrists or anything similar was out of the question. Did I really think about such things? I must have. Strange as it seems, despite having made the decision, I decided to first continue with my holiday. Who understands the mentality of someone in this state? I loved sunbathing and swimming in the sea, I do not like swimming pools, and carried on going to the beach each day. Even now I fail to understand this strange behaviour, but that is as it was.

The path leading from the hotel to the beach passed some very imposing properties. While on my way one morning, a gentleman standing by the gate of one of the more superior houses greeted me. I did not know who he was, but was attracted by his friendly, unthreatening politeness. In spite of his evident ill health, he subsequently made a point of greeting me each morning. It could have been a bit creepy, but his genuineness and obvious education negated any such feelings. Occasionally, when the temperature and weather were suitable, he would walk with me. It was a delight to chat with him and we came to know each other quite well. Eventually, he told me he would like us to marry but dared not. Apparently, though it could not be legally proven, his son had been assassinated by business rivals. They had made it to look like an accident, but he assured me there was no doubt about the truth. Therefore, if he adopted my son, as he would if we married, it was more than likely the same fate would await him. It was not until my return to England I saw some news footage in which my friend featured. It turned out he was an extremely wealthy and powerful international business man. To find I had been associating with such apparently dangerous, though sophisticated, society staggered me. I have known many wealthy people but have always noted their inability to relax and constant awareness of possible dangers to themselves, their families, their staff, and their friends. I prefer a quiet, ordinary life rather than constantly having to look over my shoulder or round the next corner. It may mean a less prosperous existence, but to me it is preferable.

Obviously, I did not go through with my suicide plan. I am not sure why, but think the kind man had restored some trust and confidence in people and life. There was also the probability, in talking to him about my son, my responsibility for him had reinserted itself. What had I been thinking? He would have been all alone without me. Not only that, but the authorities would have more than likely returned him to his father. I had little doubt, if that happened, he would finally fulfil his intent to kill his son. I keep saying it, but I really do not understand such mentality. To want to murder your own offspring is beyond me. But with my return, this would not happen. Sometimes we simply need to stand back and embrace an objective and realistic view of our lives and circumstances. Matters are often not as bad or insurmountable as they appear.

You will recall I had resigned from the holiday camp prior to my trip consequently, upon my return I was in desperate need of new employment. My meagre savings had provided the funds for the journey and continuing commitments of fees, rent, and so on. These were now so depleted I was in danger of not being able to meet those responsibilities. My family had given me a little money that represented a small inheritance from papa, but it was not much and would not last long. Full-time day employment combined with an evening job would probably be best. Compared to the hourly salaries I had been accustomed to, I was sure the salary for a full-time position would be more substantial. An evening job would supplement this and hopefully enable me to save more realistic amounts rather than the petty cash I had been managing so far.

This time I went to the employment agency. I am not sure if these still exist, but at the time most cities and towns had at least one. My reasoning, or should that be assumption, had been they would have checked credentials and therefore should have details of reliable and responsible firms. I was very fortunate to find myself in the hands of a willing and helpful assistant. So many seem to begrudge working themselves, let alone helping someone else find a position. Having explained what I was looking for, he searched through the agency's records for vacancies, which appeared to meet my criteria. A situation in a local factory looked like it might meet the bill. I consented to him forwarding my details.

Upon seeing in the list of my previous employments, barmaid, those assessing applications immediately rejected mine. They would not consider people of that ilk. I doubt they would get away with that these days. Unbeknown to me at the time, the agency gentleman went back and told them I was different and not a stereotype barmaid. That sounds awful now, but it was an understood descriptive term then. He went further and told them they really should meet me before deciding. I am eternally grateful to him. They must have trusted his opinion because I was called for interview.

To my surprise, there was no intimidating long table of interviewers. Instead, it was a nice, reassuring sole lady who greeted me. We discussed my capabilities and reasons for wanting the job, which ended with an invitation to accept a position in their laboratory. Another surprise because the advertised vacancy had been for the main factory floor. The lady had assessed it unlikely I would survive among the hardened female staff who worked there. Again, that sounds awful but subsequently meeting some of them I suspect she had been correct. Do not get me wrong, they were generally good-hearted but tended to be rough in speech and habit. Though, as you know, I have survived endless hardships, I still had a sensitive nature and took things to heart in the absence of gentleness. No doubt some of you will think me a bit of a sissy, but I had been brought up and taught, at least in my first few years, the value of polite, considerate behaviour. Something, though tested to the full, I refuse to abandon. A little kindness goes a long way and to my mind should be reciprocal. Just a quick aside, during the interview the lady noted I wore no facial makeup. The truth is, I only occasionally, and that only for a short while, employed a little lipstick and light mascara. This was really just to help conceal the excessive tiredness. I have never used makeup of any other sort.

From the beginning, the kind lady took an interest in my welfare. She ensured I understood all the contractual conditions and how factory life operated. I was responsible for collecting samples and quality testing them. It was fairly straightforward work and consequently did not take long to learn. Regrettably, my line managers, all middle-aged women, made life a little difficult. The cause appeared to be jealousy because of my perceived good looks. The situation was not helped when the local football team undertook a goodwill visit. Unfortunately, they zoomed in upon me, taking little notice of anyone else. If dagger looks had any substance, I would not be here to share tales with you. My work was reasonably self contained, meaning there was little requirement for regular contact with the ladies. This allowed me not to permit their resentment to bother me unduly. Though if we had been in frequent proximity, I would have done my best to ignore the issue and concentrate upon whatever it was we had to discuss. It helped that other staff did not appear to be envious or have any problem with me. It is sad so many are discontented and do not appreciate their individuality. Age and ill health have changed me and I admit it is not always nice to see it in the mirror. Nevertheless, I know who I am and have an appreciation for the qualities I am privileged to have inhabit me. I am certainly not envious of the good-looking women I see, though it occasionally makes me a little wistful.

As expected, though good, the salary alone would not enable me to fulfil all my wishes and dreams. An additional, by default evening, job would be required. I called upon the owners of a restaurant come club who had asked me to work for them in times gone by. Despite the open invitations, I had decided not to return to previous places of employment. I think I just felt in need of a fresh start. Well, as fresh as I could make it. With this job there was the added attraction that as the work would be twofold, waitress and bar management, the salary should be higher.

On the evening I went to ask I was surprised, despite it being opening hours, to find the place virtually empty. It gave the appearance of a business on its way down the tubes, to coin a phrase. It made me wonder if I should be applying for work nevertheless, there was nothing to lose by asking. Mrs Badger, joint manager with her husband, knew me. As I have mentioned before, owners and managers of pubs, restaurants, and clubs often called in on each other. Greeting me warmly, she asked how I was and where I had been. Apparently my absence had been noted. After a brief résumé of my movements, I explained the reason for having called in. Her hesitation confirmed my original thought. She did not try to hide the fact business was slow, but went on to say, if I was serious, she would be delighted to have me. However, in view of the present circumstances, they would not be in a position to offer a substantial salary. I inwardly debated for a moment but it was well known many customers liked me and would make a point of frequenting the establishments I worked in. Regrettably, it was often to the detriment of places I had left. We agreed I would work there for a while and see what happened. If trade increased all well and good, if not, that was left hanging in the air. Our discourse gave the impression this would probably be the last chance for the business. I asked whether Mr Badger would be in agreement, bearing in mind it was with him the holding company usually dealt. She told me not to worry. He would do what he was told. She was right.

When finalising my responsibilities I insisted upon my own till, that no one else would touch. I made clear this was an intractable requirement and if anyone else used it I would leave. You may consider I was making this demand from a powerful position, knowing she really wanted me, but that was not the case. My tills have always been accurate, but I was fully aware some people cheated. I was not prepared to subject myself to any possibility of my till failing to balance at the end of the night.

Due to the reduced custom, my work load initially proved light. There were a handful of diehard regulars, some of who knew me. They evidently told a few friends I was back because within a matter of days trade increased markedly. Many told me how nice it was to see me again and how they had missed my presence. This was gratifying because I always considered it part of my job to make people feel welcome. Mr and Mrs Badger were thrilled. They had not been this busy for a very long time. Thoughts of having to close the venture evaporated in the midst of the hubbub. I was also grateful because my salary increased along with the takings. Mind, bar staff pay was notoriously low at the time and I never really received appropriate recompense. At least it supplemented my day income and enabled me to save a little more than I had been able to previously. Generous gratuities also helped. In principle, tips had to be shared with all the staff. However, customers who were aware of this would give me something for the pot and then quietly pass a further amount that was strictly for me. At first I felt awkward. However, I eventually came to appreciate my clientele's desire to reward me personally for my service to them, and it was not as if the others were missing out.

The increase in trade did have a downside. Customers liked to stay late, often very late, consequently my going home time also became later. My hours were not set but extended or retracted as appropriate. I do not recall them ever being retracted. Obviously, this impacted my sleep and rest and time for housework and other requirements. Bear in mind, I also had my full-time day job. As you have seen, in previous times, especially when working three jobs, I coped with little sleep, though I had hoped those days were behind me. But, as the saying goes, 'beggars cannot be choosers'. My system simply readjusted back to the inward mechanisms that had enabled me to manage in such times. My son, who has also had to cope with little sleep at times, tells me it is adrenaline that takes over. He said he was okay provided he did not stop. Presumably, now and previously

I was surviving with adrenaline rushes, though in those days it was simply described as 'living on your nerves'.

Most of my customers were amiable and when time permitted, we enjoyed agreeable general conversation. I say general because, for my part at least, I prefer to keep away from personal topics. It was in these casual conversations I mentioned, when young, my sisters and I had often been referred to as the singing nightingales. We used to love to sit on the branches of our large cherry trees and sing together. We never realised people were listening. I thought nothing more of this until a woman I did not know asked if I would audition for a television talent show. At the time it struck me as a bizarre request. Who on earth would want to hear me sing? I suppose it was flattering, but appreciating how public such an event would be unhesitatingly declined. I told her I was too shy to participate in such public activities. Obviously not accustomed to being refused, she was not prepared to take no for an answer. Annoyingly, despite my constant firmness, she kept coming back. As patiently as possible, I continued to decline until she eventually, though ungraciously, accepted my decision. She did attempt what may only be described as emotional blackmail by telling me I was robbing people of a real treat, not only with my singing, but also with my beauty. Nevertheless, my shy disposition prevailed. The thought of such exposure was, and remains, anathema to me.

27

SOCIETY

I frequently mention how I met some very nice people through work, which made it more enjoyable. You may recall Harold, who I met in a previous employment. Having left that place and working away from the district, we lost contact. However, he heard I was back and showed up one evening. It was a genuine pleasure to see him again. He wanted to know where I had been and what I had been up to, and listened attentively to my résumé. He started to come in regularly, eventually asking why I exhausted myself working the various jobs when I could marry someone like him and have an easier life. He was comfortably off financially.

My experiences with Terrance, my ex-husband, had made me afraid of getting involved again. The very idea of another marriage left me fearful. Of course, I did not tell him that, but simply responded by telling him I must be stupid. There was nothing else to say without going into unwelcome and unnecessary detail. Few knew what I had been through, and I wanted to keep it that way. It would have been nice to think I could eventually forget, but it is impossible to forget such trauma. He continued to come in clear hope of me having a change of mind. Once he realised it unlikely, his appearances steadily declined until they ceased altogether. It was sad. I liked him. He was genuine and I would have liked him as a friend. In retrospect, I think he would have been kind and loving to both my son and I, but I was too afraid to consider an intimate relationship. Well, as the saying goes, that is further 'water under the bridge'. At least I still have pleasant memories of those times, which sometimes help offset my more horrific moments.

Around this time a member of the aristocracy started to frequent the club. For the purposes of anonymity and security, I will not mention his title or status but to say he was highly placed. Mr Badger, too happy to have someone of his stature frequenting his establishment, agreed to all his requests. Among these were the sole use of a corner table and that I always serve him. Naturally, this resulted in us getting to know each other quite well. He was sophisticated in a manner that exemplified his class, good looking, intelligent, and a gentleman in every sense. Over time he asked many questions and among other things I told him of my son. I still shied away from private personal matters, but was always happy to talk about my boy. I do not recall what prompted it, but in one casual conversation I happened to assert whoever purported to love me would have to love my son as much or more. Goodness knows what I was thinking. It was however, a principle I would mention whenever someone proposed a closer connection. You will understand, after all we have been through, I am very protective of my child. Even now, though he is a full grown man, I consider it my responsibility to look out for him. Responsibility is perhaps the wrong word. Perhaps 'my life's purpose' is more appropriate.

You are aware, in general, I declined social invitations, though there were the occasional rare exemptions. This gentleman would be one of those. Not because he was an aristocrat or wealthy, but because he was a genuine, likeable person. There did not seem to be any deceit or arrogance in him, despite his highly placed position. On the agreed evening, a rare one off for me, he took me to a very exclusive country club. Aperitifs were followed with an exceptional dinner. While enjoying after-dinner drinks, he said he would like to marry me and to provide for my son. He would pay college fees, organise a subsequent university education, and ensure he was okay thereafter. I would not have to worry about my son's future. I had not expected this yet, though it was apparent it would occur sometime. His thought through considerations regarding my son however, were a complete surprise but did trouble me. At the time, I did not understand how matters operated within his society. He seemed to be implying, should I agree to marriage, a desire not to have my boy with us in daily life. All his suggestions would lead to him continuing as a boarder throughout his education, boarder at college and resident at university. This upset me because it appeared to be going against all my expressed wishes, especially that of having my son close by. I now understand, years too late, this was not the case. It was simply how he understood the best could be provided. It was the path he and all his peers had followed. My refusal upset him terribly. I only saw him a couple of times thereafter. He knew I was not going to change my mind. Again, this was such a shame. He really was a nice person and I believe would have been a good husband. Had I made a mistake? I think not. Looking back, I am not sure I would have enjoyed the publicity or responsibilities of such a high profile aristocratic marriage.

I think it appropriate at this point to handle any possible miscomprehension that may have arisen. From what I have shared so far, in this and previous chapters, it may appear I was constantly involved with someone. That is not the case. In sharing my story, to avoid it becoming laborious, tedious, and boring for you the reader, I strive to limit details to high and low points and avoid the nitty-gritty of my on the whole humdrum days. My narrative therefore moves from one interesting episode or encounter straight to another, sidestepping the mundane as much as possible. In many cases there were years between each event.

Another matter I must make clear. I come from a strict and refined background and was taught self respect. Something I still value. I never slept with any of the men I went out with. Sex, for me, is a sacred part of marriage and is not designed for casual, passing pleasure. In addition, even if I had been inclined to think otherwise, my ex-husband's actions had destroyed any concept of it being pleasurable. My rectitude, defined as morally correct behaviour in the dictionary, may seem odd to many modern day readers, but it is part of my upbringing. I remain happy for the principle to be my ethos throughout life. Yes, of course, there have been those who wanted intimacy, but no matter how genuine, nice, or handsome I never accommodated them. I was never rude and in most cases was able to continue on friendly terms. I think they understood it was my choice and not a reflection upon them.

One year an American friend arranged a surprise birthday celebration for which he had hired a suite of fashionable function rooms. Goodness knows how much it cost. The venue was very popular and always in demand, attracting premium fees. I was thoroughly spoilt by one and all. Many presented me with incredible bouquets, among which were numerous arrangements of orchids, which I love. These were not the limp orchids of today but the glorious, full-bodied, proud, waxy blooms. They would probably be called old-fashioned now. Orchids of today are still nice but really do not compare. A couple were in deep coloured glass vases, but most were presented in ornate whicker baskets. I still have some of the baskets and vases. Fond memories. Not only had my friend invited many of the people I knew, but had also engaged a good quality band who entertained us with excellent music. There was also an abundance of food and drink. I could not fathom how he had organised it all without me hearing. Someone usually lets the cat out of the bag, so to speak. Horrible thought to think of a cat trapped in a bag, but not on this occasion. You may imagine my immense gratitude and my immense embarrassment due to my rudimentary shyness. It did not help that everyone wanted to wish me a happy birthday and dance with me. Nevertheless, if I am to be honest, despite my embarrassment, I was quite thrilled by the whole event.

Sadly, as it always seems to be for me, there was one slight upset. Well, a bit more than slight. One guest was a lesbian who evidently found me attractive. She would not stop following me round. After my previous experience I was naturally wary. Thankfully, probably due to the fact I was never on my own, she did not attempt to make direct contact. Nevertheless, it was an issue, and I did not want the celebrations marred for anyone. I racked my brain for ways to prevent any repeat of the previous occasion, the one where two ladies actually leapt upon me. Ultimately, I decided it best to keep dancing for the whole evening and avoid 'powdering my nose'. Thankfully, I have a strong constitution. With the mixture of slower, among the more agile, dances dancing all evening presented no real difficulty. I may have been generally underweight, but I was nonetheless fit. I also enjoyed the varied company of my dance partners.

At the end of the evening I wanted to express my enormous gratitude to my friend by giving him a kiss. It was well known I rarely kissed anyone consequently, such an event would be recognised as a very special thank you. The task was however, not as easy as it sounds. He was very tall and I of short stature. In the end, I had to get on a stool. Those still round smiled, and some even clapped. It really was a rarity to see me do such a thing. I was kindly given a lift home which dealt with the two issues of avoiding any possible accosting by the woman and of how to transport all those marvellous bouquets.

On busier evenings Mrs Badger employed a couple of extra personnel. To one I have much to be grateful for. Janet, who worked as a waitress on these evenings, was South European and could be quite fiery. However, we got on well. There are two incidents I want to share with you when Janet came to my aid.

The first occurred one evening when a group of five male customers asked Janet which was my drink. I am not a great alcohol drinker, but, as mentioned before, some customers got upset if we did not accept their offer of one. We therefore had the habit of keeping a drink handy and taking an occasional sip. Janet could be a little innocent and credulous and did not always comprehend English humour. She naively pointed out my glass.

Within a millisecond of my next sip I felt unwell and violently vomited. Thankfully, Janet saw and came to my aid. Supporting my limp form on her arm, she manoeuvred us toward the kitchen. Mrs Badger, who had been working in the office, saw and following us in asked what had happened, realising all was not as it should be. I was in no state to answer, so Janet explained, mentioning how the men had asked about my drink. Her subconscious must have started putting two and two together. No fool, astute, and very experienced in the business, my employer must have twigged exactly what was going on. Some sort of drug had been put in my glass. It was worse for me than most because I never took medication, not even aspirin, meaning my system was chemical free. Any drug introduced would therefor have a field day. In later life, when illness required medication, I had considerable trouble. Doctors frequently had to cease the treatment. It is interesting to note my son also reacts badly to medical drugs with doctors having to find some alternative or just simply leaving him without. While my boss and Janet were engaged in this conversation, the group of men appeared, saying they had noticed I was unwell and offered to take me home. Mrs Badger eyed them ferociously. She was not a woman to cross. They had the good sense to leave and never return. She later took me home herself. I dread to think what would have happened had those uncouth people got their hands on me, especially in my debilitated state. I can never sufficiently thank Janet or Mrs Badger. The possibilities had they not intervened still send a shiver through me.

The second incident could have seen me disabled for life, perhaps worse. Because I was considered attractive, men often gave more attention than they should, especially the married ones. One, who from time to time frequented the club with his wife, was always particularly friendly and sociable. Too much so for his wife it turned out. So one of them could enjoy a few drinks without compromise they took turns to drive. On the evening in question, they were preparing to move on to another venue when his wife could not get their car started. It will help if you remember this occurred many years ago, prior to the advent of electronic automobile systems and controls. It was normal for vehicles to need a push to jumpstart them. I have no idea what it is like these days, but then management, staff, and regular clientele tended to be like one large extended family who willingly assisted each other whenever the need arose. Along with the others, I helped push their car. To the surprise of all, the engine sprang into life within seconds. In the same instant I heard Janet screaming at me to look out. It transpired the woman had put the gear into reverse with the clear intent of crushing me against the wall. At the very minimum, both my legs would have been broken, though I suspect the damage would have been far more extensive. Janet's timely warning enabled me to jump out of the way. It had been a close call. It is staggering how dense these women can be. Although her husband was always charming with me, it was obvious to all there was nothing more in it. Jealousy is a horrible and ugly characteristic, as I regrettably have good reason to know. Shocked and angry, I could not help but confront the woman demanding to know what was wrong with her. I do not recall if I shouted or managed to keep my tone under control. I then asked if she did not realise I had been trying to help their marriage, not destroy it. Their marriage had been in trouble for sometime and out of a genuine desire to help I had been attempting to reconcile them. At this point Janet could no longer control herself calling the woman a horrible bitch. It was her way of expressing concern for my welfare. We were all astounded and shaken.

Some while after those appalling incidents I became friendly with an American merchant navy officer. He was of mixed parentage with his father American born and his mother from my homeland. He never missed the opportunity to call in whenever his ship berthed at a nearby port. Visits were usually of short duration and for that reason our friendship developed slowly. I call it a friendship, though it was obvious he was emotionally and physically attracted to me. He did however, balance it by saying how pleased he was to meet someone he considered agreeable who also shared his mother's ethnicity. On my part, I have to acknowledge he was very handsome. He did become quite attached and in token of his affection gave me his ring. One I had never seen him without. It was unusual in that the large deep coloured amethyst, set in a smart, sturdy gold setting, was diamond cut underneath, leaving a broad smooth surface on top. Beams refract through it wonderfully whenever held up to the light. I was reluctant to accept, but he insisted and would have clearly been offended if I had not. I always valued the ring and have since given it to my son, who, though not a jewellery man, expressed how much he liked it. He has continually worn it as its discreet sophistication suits him. I know he will always look after it.

Time passed until one day he told me he would not remain in the navy much longer. Though he enjoyed seeing the world, it was time for him to settle and become a family man. In my culture family is considered paramount. Not having children tends to be frowned upon. Even the poorest, with little materially, value the passing of an inheritance, even if just the family name. In preparing for this change he had set up his own jewellery business within the United States. How would I like to manage a shop while he and his business partner did the buying and developed custom? He extended the offer by also including an option for Christopher, my sister Anna's husband, to join us in America to set up his own enterprise. He would assist with contacts, formalities, and in establishing the business. I had mentioned in conversation how my brother-in-law's business back home had become a little haphazard. Both sounded attractive and exciting propositions, especially as it had been a dream of mine to go to the United States. Nonetheless, I had to consider all possible scenarios. Life has shown me you cannot take anything for granted or at face value. I also needed to think about the impact such a move would have on my son. This despite the fact, America was then presented as, and I believed it to be, the land of opportunity. I believed we could do well there. The possibilities were exciting, but, as tempted as I was, I would not allow my enthusiasm to overrule common sense. There was also the issue of his very apparent desire for us to marry if I accepted the venture.

He still had some time to serve, and the short irregular visits provided opportunity for me to think. I must give him his due in that he did not try to press me into an immediate decision but waited patiently, although the question constantly hovered whenever we saw each other. In a rare telephone conversation, I informed Christopher of the offer, but, as I had anticipated, he rejected it outright. He was very patriotic and would not hear of leaving the country he loved. In addition, the children were in the midst of their long-term education. His refusal did not really influence my decision. Admittedly, if I had gone, it would have been nice to know family were nearby. No, my final decision was ultimately determined by my friend's character. My observations led to a belief that he was likely to be an extremely jealous man. I was not prepared to chance it or the probable consequences. One such relationship had been quite enough. I was determined never to have a repeat, no matter the cost. One example will help you see why and how I reached my conclusion. Ugly jealousy had manifested on an occasion when he chased a taxi in which he thought I and another man were passengers. The first I knew of it was when he burst into the club shouting 'Jezebel!'. It took a few moments to get him to tell me what was wrong. I assured him it had not been me in the taxi. He would not listen and continued calling me Jezebel. It was not until one of my colleagues explained it had been her with a boyfriend and they had thought it was her husband chasing them he believed. It was far too late for me, 'once bitten forever shy'. Understandably, fear of how another relationship may turn out reasserted itself. He had been very generous, and I liked him very much, but was not prepared to take the chance. I declined his offer of a life in America. Yet again, it had been necessary to upset someone who, on the whole, had been very kind. I heard later, out of spite it seems, he took two other families over with him. Both wives originated in his mother's homeland. Apparently, they all found success with substantial resulting wealth.

Despite the besetting hardship, violence, and unpleasantness my life was subject to, I enjoyed occasional fun moments. Before I forget, I would like to share one with you. I had become friendly with the son of a wealthy family who owned a successful ferry company. He was a bit of a character who, although owning a very nice car, preferred to show off on his top of the range motorbike. One day, unexpectedly, he turned up on it to take me out. We had been out socially a couple of times. As this had not been prearranged I was not dressed for a motorbike ride. My normal attire comprised figure hugging dresses that reached to just above my knees. On this occasion I happened to be wearing a leopard print design. My first inclination had been to turn down his offer but then thought why not, it would be fun. Not my usual attitude, but sometimes, especially when life has been difficult, we need to let our hair down. However, there was no way I was even going to try and straddle the monster bike. I rode sidesaddle. It is hard to convey the lighthearted fun this generated. Drivers blew their horns and passersby waved and cheered. As I keep saying, those were innocent, fun loving days when most people simply enjoyed the moment without any malicious undertones. My friend throughly enjoyed the attention and for me it was a moment of clean lighthearted fun. I had few of those. Thankfully, he was an experienced motorbike rider, so we came to no harm despite all the distraction.

Warren, a very different gentleman, came into my life a little before my American friend's departure. He was Southern Irish, with all the charm and gentleness generally associated with that nation. Becoming a frequent patron at the club, he soon observed I worked hard, had more than one job, and supported my son without the help of a husband. Over time we got to know each other quite well, eventually leading to him saying he would like to adopt me. He was old enough to have been my father. Well, at least that was different. I could not help but laugh, not unkindly. It just made it sound as if I was still a girl without responsibilities rather than a grown woman with a child. He explained he simply wanted to provide for me. Such genuine concern harbouring no hidden agenda made a pleasant change. Though, of course, I could not agree to the idea. Warren remained sincere in his desire to help and kept spoiling me with many generous gifts. Normally I would have found it embarrassing and inappropriate to accept them, however, there was no arguing his sincerity. Anyway, he would often just leave the gift and disappear. One day he asked if I would join him in a visit to his Southern Irish family. Certainly a different proposal to those I normally received. Cautious as ever, my initial instinct had been to decline. However, having got to know each other over a very long period, I knew full well there was no harm in him. His unmistakable genuineness assured me there would be no attempted funny business. He truly simply wanted the best for me and my welfare. Nevertheless, I still hesitated. To accept would go against the overriding principle I had lived by for so many years. Many had told me how beautiful Southern Ireland was and I had often thought how nice it would be to see for myself. I was also ready for a break. Tiredness from my round-the-clock routine was starting to tell again. After further contemplation of all relevant points and possible outcomes and concluding it would be safe, I accepted his generous offer.

On the flight out, the stewardess kept bringing drinks even though I told her I had not asked for them. Nevertheless, she insisted they were for me but would not say who was sending them. It was obvious someone was. Looking round, I finally spotted a group of seamen I knew from the club. They were crew from one of the major liners. Naturally I thanked them and they in turn told me not to forget to wave the Union Jack, the British flag for those who do not know, when alighting. To appreciate the joke, you need to be aware those were the days when the IRA, Irish Republican Army, was particularly active. Thankfully, I was not so naïve as to comply. Just imagine if I had!

Warren's family were all very sweet, welcoming me with open hearts and arms. Anyone watching would have thought I was a long-lost member of the family who had returned after many years' absence. Their warmth was overwhelming and, just like my new-found friend, genuine. They could not do enough for me. It really was a treat. During my stay Warren and the family made a point of showing me all the sites and places of historic interest. When we went to see the Blarney Stone they insisted I kissed it, for good luck. It was something all visitors were expected to do. The fact, because of the way it is supported, you have to kiss the underside posed a bit of a problem. There is no option but to get right under the stone. As you will have gathered, my dresses, made to my own style by an excellent seamstress, were figure hugging and stopped just above my knees. In addition, I always wore high heels. It was simply the fact I was used to them and rather foolishly, as later life has shown, never thought to wear any other style of shoe. I suppose it was that I needed them for my evening work and they therefore became my norm. Getting beneath the stone therefore became an event. One that attracted considerable attention. I have no idea how many got a good view of my backside or how many photographs were taken. I fulfilled my responsibility as a tourist and kissed the stone, not that it made any difference to my life or subsequent experiences. It seemed I was to be denied the supposed good luck.

My friend's generosity had always been excessive and now I found the family to be equally big-hearted. A simple small suitcase had accompanied me, but I returned with two new large ones filled to capacity as well as packages. Among these were two very large paintings. I had merely mentioned how nice they were. There were also several pieces of Waterford crystal, which the nation is justly proud of. They also gave me some lovely icons. The family was Roman Catholic. Warren had also bought me a beautiful coat because it had been rather cold and I did not have one with me. I was thoroughly spoilt by one and all. Southern Ireland had certainly lived up to everything I had been told.

A Black American, I think I am allowed to say that or should it be African American, basketball team were waiting for their flight when we arrived in the airport. Naturally, they were all very tall but, unusually, they were also all good looking. Probably due to the warm send off we were receiving, they noticed us when we entered the booking-in hall. One came over and greeted me with a 'Hi sis'. To understand his greeting you need to know, as a young woman, I loved sunbathing and had a very deep tan, which had prompted his joke.

Warren retired to his homeland shortly after this holiday and we sadly lost touch. It is a shame by one means or another I always lost my decent friends. I have the lovely memories but it would also be nice to still have the opportunity of enjoying their company and friendship. I hope he and my other friends went on to have happy, peaceful, and fulfilled lives.

28

Misstep

Kate, the removal firm owner's wife, and I had kept in touch. She was one of only a few people who knew where my son and I lived. You will understand, after all we had been through with our various moves attempting to avoid Terrance's detection, I was very particular about who I told. One day she called to tell me some people from the local authority had been asking for me. They would not tell her what they wanted but asked for me to contact them direct myself. Previous experiences with Terrance and our son's custody caused me to be rather apprehensive, to say the least. What could it be about? To my relief, it turned out my name had risen to the top of the local authority's housing list. It had been so long since my request for accommodation had been accepted, I had forgotten. The occurrence proved timely. Despite how much I liked the people and accommodation, I came to appreciate our attic room could not be long term. We needed a more permanent, self-contained home. My son would not be at college forever.

They invited me to view an apartment within an estate five miles from town. Not the most convenient place to get to work from. However, the need for our own home was pressing me, so I agreed to see it. The nearest bus stop was on the main road running along the estate perimeter, meaning I had to walk part way. Sadly, the loitering populous did not impress. The looks, unpleasant manner, and rather startling language, and that was only the words I understood, were unsettling. I was tempted to turn back, but commitment to my word whenever I give it thwarted the idea. Passing some obviously private residences gathered in a small corner, I soon entered the grey dismal estate. The flat itself had a reasonable layout. Two bedrooms, a sitting room with balcony, an adequately sized kitchen, and separate bathroom and toilet. It would have fulfilled the purpose, but my experience of the residents, as related, put me off. Not only had I felt uncomfortable, but there was also the issue of my son living there during his long vacations and subsequent to completing his education. I declined.

A little while later an invitation to view another property arrived. It turned out to be the same one. The only conclusion I could reach was this would be the only choice they were going to offer. This was supported by the tone and wording of the invites. Intending the move to only be a temporary measure, hopefully I would be able to afford something in the private sector or perhaps even purchase my own soon, I decided to accept this time. Just as well, it seems. Some told me how they had similar experiences. One having been sent to the same property five times! Believing I would now be able to save a little more, I expected our stay to be short-lived. Regrettably, it was not to be so. Due to a number of circumstances which will reveal themselves as we continue, my 'temporary' stay lasted nine years!

To give you some idea of how inconvenient the location was. There was a very heavy snowfall one spring day that brought the town to a standstill. For some reason I needed to get home in the period between finishing at the factory and beginning my evening job. I do not recall the reason, but it must have been important for me to undertake the following. With the thick snow and consequent public transport chaos, a colleague kindly offered several of the staff a lift home. A short distance out he realised there was too much snow, so took us to his more centrally located house. He offered drinks all round, but I declined, still needing to get home. The rest happily accepted and appeared to settle down for what would become a drunken orgy perhaps, more than likely, more. I decided to walk the five miles. They must have been watching me through the window because I could hear them laughing as I struggled in the deep snow. Undoubtedly, they were expecting me to turn back. Anyone observing must have thought I was crazy. The snow was so deep in places I sunk up to my waist. I did not think about it at the time, but in retrospect realise what a bizarre sight I must have been, dressed as I was in my simple figure hugging dress and high heels. I reached home safely, though wet through and slightly exhausted. Having dealt with whatever had driven me home, I, with my usual resolve not to let my employers down, repeated the excursion in reverse. No doubt people at the time thought, and perhaps even you think I was mad. On my part, I was gratified to have achieved both aims. Getting home in the first place and then back in time for the club opening. As far as I am concerned, other than death or a debilitating illness, there is never any excuse for not going to work.

The various places I had rented had always been furnished consequently, I only had two pieces of furniture. A small yacht table that was ideal for the kitchen, and an upright chair, both of which I had purchased from friends when they refurbished their yacht. The only reason for purchasing these had been that not all accommodations had dining areas. Besides the fact I dislike eating off my lap, I wished my son to maintain his good habit of eating correctly. I transported these and our few possessions in the limited hours I had between jobs. Beds, seating, full sized dinning, and so on had to be purchased and delivered within the same hours, though on different days. Of course, this activity limited, in fact negated, rest intervals nevertheless, though tiring the joy of having a place of our own kept me buoyant. The decoration was dowdy and miserable which, I subsequently understood, was typical for these types of apartments. Purchasing paint and equipment on my way to and from work, I utilised the same hours to clean and redecorate. I have to say I was quite pleased with the outcome, especially so because to complete it as quickly as possible, I had painted in frantic manner.

Though there were, thankfully, only six apartments in our block, my privacy personality and working hours were not conducive to me getting to know my neighbours. In many ways it was a solitary life but it suited me. However, one couple made a point of catching me in. It turned out they were the leaders of a local political party. Both were middle-aged and thankfully not over aggressive with their political activities. Their duties appeared to consist primarily of leafleting, meetings, and letter writing. Despite my interest in current affairs, I am not, overall, a political creature. Throughout our stay, they were always kind to me and took a liking to my son, who they met when he was home on vacation. We never embraced their ideals or attended their gatherings, though it was clear they would have liked us to. Gratefully, they never spoilt things by attempting to push their philosophy upon us. Later I will tell you of another family who befriended us, particularly in a time of need.

Somehow, and yet again, I never discovered how, Terrance, my ex-husband, heard of my move into the flat. He turned up on the doorstep, but to my considerable surprise was entirely friendly. My stomach had turned at the sight of him, but his quiet demeanour persuaded me to let him in. We chatted about ordinary matters such as how we were and what we were doing. Still wary, I did not give details of where I worked or the location of our son's college. While talking I was thinking how nice and different it was for us to be having such a normal time. All I had wanted was a quiet, happy family life. Unfortunately, he ruined the moment by saying he thought we should get back together. Such a shame, as we had been getting on so well. You will comprehend I told him that was no longer a possibility. The friendly disposition vanished, and I saw the all too familiar glaze in his eyes and the warning agitation. The clench in my stomach and tension round my chest nearly had me doubling over.

I resisted it as best as I could, determined not to concede as I had in the past. Within minutes it reached the point where he was chasing me round the dining table. Whether he intended to hit or kiss me, I was unsure, more than likely the former. The sudden change had thrown me off balance, but within a minute or so it dawned upon me how stupid this was. I stopped, stood my ground, and stared him in the eyes, allowing all my anger to be in plain evidence. This resulted in him also stopping. I assume he now realised he could no longer manipulate me because without a further word he left. My son, who was home on vacation, was understandably upset. He had shouted at his father to stop and I fear may have tried to intervene if I had not brought the matter to an end. I have no doubt Terrance would have hit him.

I will break for a moment to share something a bit lighter. You may recall, from my earlier recollections, I love animals. I would have liked a pet, but obviously a dog or cat would have been impracticable. A creature that could be cared for sufficiently in the limited time I had would be ideal, but what? In general conversation with some of my customers, my love of nature and desire for a pet came up. One told me of a friend who bred experimental breeds of budgerigars. Thankfully, experimental simply meant he crossbred different strains. That would certainly fit the bill since I could provide food and water in their cage. I could let it out and clean the cage within the short periods I had at home. Decision made I went to the friend's premises. It did not take long to choose a beautiful white boy. Though white, he was not albino, having normal eyes and feathers of a light blue hue on his chest. The gentleman kindly advised about cage types, toys, bath, and food. It is hard to convey how thrilled I had been, especially as my new companion had his own personality and immediately appeared to take to me. I believe strongly an animal's instinct can be trusted. If they cower or are aggressive, it usually turns out the recipient is not of nice character. I am not being judgmental. It is simply my lifelong observation. We were happy together and in the rare times when I could relax at home, he would sit just beneath my chin and chirp contentedly. He even learnt some words which was enchanting. I had never tried for this. I simply talked to him as I would a child, making his mimicking of me even more delightful. My son made some recordings within which, except for the occasional chirp, it was impossible to tell who was speaking, me or my delightful budgerigar.

Now we come to the topic after which this chapter is named. As my son grew the lack of a father figure troubled me. At the very least I thought he should have some male influence. It is not good for any child, male or female, not to have the stimulus of both parents, especially in the younger years. What to do? I was afraid of entering into another relationship, especially marriage. My early life experiences, particularly those with Terrance, remained traumatic memories. You have seen how I had plenty of opportunities, but feared the possible development of jealousy with all the likely outcomes. I also feared the proposer may consider my son an unwanted irritation. There were also my concerns related to wealth. As you have seen, many who proposed were well off, with some also occupying elevated social positions. Many I have met and heard of apparently long for a famous life in which they are constantly targeted by the media. The very idea is an absolute horror to me. Anathema is the word. I prefer to remain incognito and live in a quiet, peaceful manner.

Despite the troubling fears, concern for my son persisted. Consequently, the prospect of another marriage loomed. I was tormented. What to do for the best? We had managed so far with no indications in my son's behaviour or demeanour of anything lacking. That should have been sufficient reassurance, but I had got it into my head he needed male influence. How bizarre and contrary our minds can be at times. The result, I was on the verge of making another disastrous decision.

A widower, who appeared to have a pleasant personality, had started visiting the club regularly. In my usual attempt to make clientele feel at home, I had chatted with him when custom allowed. We did go for a couple of meals and he introduced me to his adult daughters. In due course he proposed. To be honest, I would never have considered him if it had not been for those concerns outlined above. My son's wellbeing has always been paramount to me. I still had my usual reservations and continued unsure. Eventually, after further inner debating, I decided to outline what I was looking for. First, I made clear my overriding priority was my son's welfare. Then went on to say, before I could consider marriage, he would have to agree to keep college fees paid so my son could complete his education there. That I was looking for someone to help my son understand the masculine world. That I required a companion and did not want a sexual relationship. You may feel I was being rather hard in expecting my husband to do without conjugal rights. As I relate throughout this autobiography, Gestapo, relatives, and first husband had destroyed any desire for such intimacy. In fact, my stomach turns at the very idea. Such is the result of abuse, for me at least. In response, he told me at his age he did not want sex. At the time I thought him an angel, but later learnt my appreciation was misplaced. He eventually admitted to being impotent. As to the other points, he said he understood and agreed to everything. I thought at last here was someone I could trust. How wrong!

His daughters considered the proposed marriage a good idea. Mostly because their father was lonely and our union would provide him a companion. They also thought it would be beneficial for me. I was still not persuaded. It was someone I got to know at one of my factory jobs who provided the final impetus. She had previously asked I be God Mother and my son God Father to her daughter's twins and had observed much of what I had been through over the years. In her opinion, the prospect of a companion was a good one. She also confirmed the idea of it being helpful for my son. To her, a widower seemed the ideal choice. If only she had known!

While we waited for a registry office opening, I decided it would be useful to refresh my driving skills. Except for the incident when I drove from London, I had not driven since my original lessons, many years previous. With my busy working life there had never been time to undertake a full course, nor could I really afford it. This decision was made despite my original resolution not to drive. I was, still am, nervous of other drivers. Nevertheless, it seemed sensible to have sufficient knowledge and some degree of confidence should the need to drive arise again. My fiancée worked with cars so we agreed he would help. It proved a mistake. Due to my fear of other drivers' and pedestrians' unpredictable antics, I insisted upon first learning how to conduct an emergency stop. We went to a disused airfield in a small van. To my son's discomfort, I quickly learnt the stop. He was seated by the van's backdoors when I halted without warning. My poor boy ended up hanging over the front seat backs. He immediately insisted on getting out and waiting for us in a safe zone. Thankfully, it had been a reasonably nice day, mind I think he would have got out even if it had been pouring. On another occasion, I was attempting an uphill manoeuvre when my to be husband gave a wrong instruction. We ended up sliding back while drivers behind strived to get their vehicles and themselves out of the line of fire. Luckily we hit no one. I was cross and frustrated, and he was anything but calm. That was the last time I attempted to drive. Perhaps this should have raised some warning. Subsequently, I heard many say it is not a good idea to have a relative or friend teach driving skills. It was known to bring the worst out in both leading to disagreement and argument.

 We agreed our wedding would be a simple affair with just his daughters and a handful of friends. My son would stand in place of a father for me. However, and unbeknown to us, my friend from the factory had other ideas. She turned up with a crowd of work colleagues. It was nice and made the occasion far more of an event. I wore a mid-grey two-piece suit with beautifully embroidered lapels. My bouquet comprised white carnations, white roses, and white freesias. A tiara and bracelet consisting of the same mixture complemented the ensemble. The ceremony went well and I felt at last I had made a good decision.

My new husband's home was attached to a car repair garage with all the resulting noise and mess. It was also in a part of town I did not like and still do not. We, he had been in complete agreement, decided to live at my flat. Neither of us had much furniture. Besides the few pieces purchased when first moving in, I only had a small two ring stove obtained from the same friends as the small table and chair previously mentioned. Except for the cooker, the little my new husband possessed were seriously antiquated, worn, and unsuitable for our needs. We therefore decided to invest in a three-piece suite and nice new bedroom fittings. He continued working as a car mechanic and, although he had said he did not want me to work, I remained at the laboratory and club. With just the two of us there was no need for me to be home all day. I did give up the cleaning job I had been doing in the hours between finishing at the factory and starting at the club. Each day he would collect me from the factory and drive us home. We would enjoy an evening meal before going to the club. He spent his evenings there, meaning I did not have to wait round for a lift home.

Not that it had any influence, nor should it ever, I think it appropriate to mention a couple of points regarding my new husband, especially in view of those who usually proposed. He was much older than me and could in no way be considered handsome or the least bit good looking. I am not being unkind, it is just how it was. He had his peculiarities, I suppose most of us do. Most days he would refuse or be difficult about any request. However, on Sundays he would give anything asked for. His daughters had told me about this quirk, but I had not believed it until we lived together. Another issue arose with respect to his father. My new father-in-law had also been a widower and was notorious for not getting on with anyone. To everyone's surprise he was different with me, friendly and considerate. He owned an off-licence and, in addition to his general pleasantness, regularly gave me unusual miniatures, which I collected. I was astonished to find my husband resented his father's friendship with me. This proved an indicator of things to come. One I should have seen.

Unexpectedly, on my part at least, I regret to inform you as soon as we were married my husband went back upon all he had agreed and consented to. Refusing to continue college fees, moaning about my ongoing concerns for my son, demanding his own way in everything rather than being a companion, constantly arguing about anything and everything no matter how minor or unimportant, never attempting to offer any advice or guidance to my son, displaying signs of jealousy. The latter especially directed toward my association with male customers despite me having explained the obvious, that it was part of my work to be friendly and courteous with clientele. I was appalled and could not believe I had apparently made another ghastly mistake. It was depressing. As you would anticipate, I tackled him regarding his demeanour and attitude. He would not listen to reason even after reminding him about all we had discussed and his agreement to all. The pleasantness I had previously seen was gone, replaced by a most disagreeable and dreadful person. How people can change from one moment to the next still amazes me.

One night he was very obviously upset. When asked, he told me I made too much fuss over my son, who was home on vacation from college. This took me aback. I explained he was still a child and naturally needed to be taken care of. Had I not been here before when Terrance had raised a similar objection? Rather than having the calming affect expected, my response seemed to incense him further and, to my incredulity, he rose evidently ready to strike. My son saw and placing himself between us and, in a remarkably controlled voice, told him if he touched me he would kill him. What an awful thing for a child to have to say. Up to now I had tried to make the best of things but, to my great sadness and disappointment, it was now evident the marriage was breaking down.

Another time he asked who the man who had been following me was. I was confused and asked what he meant. Apparently he had seen someone who, by staying on opposite pavements to the ones I was on, had followed me round town. The idea shocked me. I had certainly not been aware of such an event and told him so. In answer to a further question, I said I had been going to pay the rent. This odd interrogation got me thinking until it dawned how he knew about the man. It turned out he had been stalking me himself. The revelation upset and dismayed. I had obviously made a terrible error of judgment with regard to the man who I had thought kind and understanding. By the way, I never did see or discover who it was he said had been following me.

Then came something I never expected, nor suspected. My new stepdaughters, I suppose I should call them that, though there was never any such relationship between us, and I occasionally went out together. It was during one of the excursions they informed me their mother, my husband's first wife, had committed suicide. Nothing further was said, but they transparently considered their father had driven her to it. I never told my husband I knew. He never said much about his previous wife and made clear he had no wish to discuss her or their marriage. The information raised further concerns about what I should expect and may have to deal with, especially in view of the deteriorating relationship. Why does my life always have to take such a turn?

The untoward behaviour, together with the resulting stress, led to me being quite unwell. Finally, the man, I will not call him my husband, had the sense to accept our marriage was at an end and moved out. He was so small-minded as to insist on taking the three-piece suite together with half the bedroom furniture. He also stated he would no longer pay the instalments for the cooker. This was unexpected news. I thought he had bought it outright. Hire purchase is not something I ever use. If I cannot pay for something, I prefer to wait until I have saved enough. As you know, other than mortgage, I have never owed anyone anything. The bigoted man even attempted to remove the free standing radiators, our only source of heating. This readiness to leave my son and I without heating infuriated me. With hammer in hand I told him if he touched them I would smash each and every one. He was wise enough to realise I was serious. It still amazes me we can know so little of someone, even when living together. The unexpected pettiness took me aback and left me feeling painfully upset. Naturally, people were sent to repossess the cooker. The men were very nice and clearly did not wish to leave me without any cooking facility. However, despite their kindly attempts at persuasion, I refused to continue the payments. Very reluctantly, they carried the stove away.

I was left with no option but to formalise our separation. Once made aware of all the facts, my lawyer advised I apply for an annulment. I had never heard of such a thing before, but it was apparently relevant because the marriage had not been consummated. I will not bore you with all the details but to say an annulment was eventually granted. I declined the court's offer to allocate maintenance. I just wanted to be free of the man. We never saw each other again. I began to wonder if my life was always to be subject to such historic repeats. A depressing thought. His daughters had the grace to notify me of his death some years later. They apparently held no bitterness knowing how difficult their father could be. If anything, they appeared to have expected the separation earlier than it actually occurred.

After all my carefulness it was hard to accept this attempt at another relationship had proven a further mistake, a big one. Neither had the man been any help to my son. You will recall that had been a driving force for me to even consider marriage. Not one piece of advice or direction had been offered. Just as well, I now think. Imagine where it may have led. Regrettably, the annulment and my consequent freedom brought no joy or sense of relief. All it did was reinforce my comprehension that nothing truly good would ever happen for me. I had chosen with care, so I thought, but now it appeared I was incapable of picking a decent, honest, or reliable character. The small-mindedness had, for some reason, got under my skin, leaving me depressed. I was also troubled about my financial position. The income from the two employments I still undertook was insufficient to meet college fees and all the other usual outgoings. Minimum wage legislation did not exist then. His refusal to continue with the college fees, despite having given an undertaking to do so, had resulted in me drawing heavily upon my meagre savings.

A thought just crossed my mind. In view of the annulment and therefore in theory no marriage, should I be referring to him as my ex-husband? I think not.

29

Crushed

In the end, I could not help but question the point of going on, feeling I would never achieve anything. In truth, I felt exhausted and drained. All I wanted was to sleep and sleep. How wonderful it would be to let go and allow my whole being to slip into eternal rest. In retrospect, I am astounded to see how low I had got. I took an overdose, lay on my bed, and waited for the end. I must have drifted off into unconsciousness. It was so good to let go of the tension and simply allow my whole being to relax. I was enjoying laying back upon some ethereal cloud with closed eyes when I suddenly became aware of a blinding light. Very disappointedly I discovered myself not to be in heaven. I had a vague recollection of having reached the golden gates, only to find them locked against me. I had violently shaken them and screamed to be let in but somehow, I do not recall how, it had been made clear this was not my time. I drifted off again. Upon my next return to consciousness it became clear, though confusion still rained, I was on a hospital ward. Thankfully, the nurses were very gentle and kind and slowly explained where I was and why.

To my astonishment, the next thing I remember is my ex-husband (*the real ex, my son's father*) standing by my bed. The last person I had thought about or wished to see. It seems because I had not arrived for my evening work, my employers had gone to my home to see if I was okay. As I have previously mentioned, I was always reliable and never let any employer down. They had therefore been apprehensive at my non-arrival. Though they received no answer, they somehow felt sure someone was in. After endlessly ringing the doorbell, knocking loudly and shouting through the letterbox without response, they called the police who forced the door. Details are still fuzzy, but I think the news reached someone who knew me and whose neighbour knew my ex-husband.

My son was away at college so my ex-husband, agreeing with the consultant it unwise for me to be on my own, insisted upon taking me to his home. So far I have not mentioned he had remarried and there were three children. Some may consider me biased, I will therefore relate other people's opinions of his new wife. Hard-nosed, selfish, self-interested not that they used those words, most of theirs began with the letter B or F. No one believed any of the children to be her husbands and went so far as to indicate each child had a different father. She was also a filthy woman. The house, which being rather closed in tended to be dark at the best of times, was even more depressing with the dirt and grime. You will appreciate from those accounts, she was not of a pleasant or friendly disposition. I do not think she was jealous. She simply did not care about anyone, including husband and children. In fact, she treated my ex-husband rather harshly. Something, you may recall, the divorce judge prophesied. To my further surprise he was kindness itself during my stay. He frequently took me to a nice park. A pleasant and quiet spot, which was just what I needed. He also gave me lovely boxes of chocolates, which we enjoyed picking through while at the park. Such a shame you can no longer get these, the pathetic modern alternatives cannot compare. He also took some cine-film of me as a memento. Of itself a novelty, as these were early days prior to such things as personal cameras. I assume he had got his through a business contact, remember he was in the electronics business. Despite his kindness, I did not remain in their home for very long. His wife's surliness, filth and the general unfriendliness of both her and her children proved too much. I have been given to understand the children have never been convivial people. To give him his due, I think my ex-husband realised and, without argument or attempt to dissuade me, took me home. Upon arrival he had a further surprise in the boot of his car. A television! As with cameras, these were early days and only the well-off had such things in their homes. Apparently he had been asked to repair it, he was excellent with the valve technology of the time, but in the meantime the owner had purchased a newer model and told him not to take it back. This was so thoughtful of him. Why could he have not been so considerate when we were married? By the way, he never gave me the cine-film. Presumably his wife had kept it or more than likely sold it. She was capable of anything.

The television was by no means the last of his surprises. The village he lived in was not far from our son's college. As a consequence of either advertising or word-of-mouth, he obtained a contract to set up a loudspeaker system for the college summer fate. As you know, prior to this latest event, I had avoided contact with him. Even during my stay, I side-stepped unnecessary personal details. Past experience had shown how suddenly he could change. Somehow he discovered my son was a resident student. Perhaps he saw him while working in the grounds. He apparently told the owner-headmaster he was his father. To what end, I have no idea. However, before leaving me at my home he gave me an envelope containing a cheque and note saying it was a contribution toward college fees. Everything he had done this time was so out of character and to give me money was even more so. I may only guess at the motivation. Maybe with the ill treatment at home he had finally realised what he had lost. Alternatively, he may have simply been impressed by my having got our son into college. Whatever the reason, the money was very welcome.

The breakdown and annulment of my marriage meant I was again reliant upon my own income. Therefore, once sufficiently recovered, I returned to round the clock working. I continued at the laboratory and club and obtained another cleaning job for the intervening period. Mrs Badger kindly expressed how pleased she was to have me back after my 'illness'. Also, having originally wished me all the best for my marriage in hope of it being better than hers, she conveyed condolences for its failure. Sleep was snatched on the bus while travelling from one employment to the next, and I survived on one salad roll a day.

The stress of all that had gone before and the wear and tear demanded by round the clock working took a toll and I became unwell again. Realisation dawned, I could not continue this regime indefinitely. Despite the fact my sister still enclosed a little money within her occasional letters, I must make clear I never asked for this, my savings were gone. Having to draw upon them for the college fees during the failed marriage and my subsequent inability to work had proven disastrous. I now had no option but, very reluctantly, to acknowledge I could no longer pay for the college. The headmaster was so nice and did his best to help, offering to reduce the fees further. He was even prepared to postpone them until I got back on my feet. So kind, nevertheless, I knew it was pointless beside which, as you know, I was not prepared to get into debt. Therefore, at the age of fourteen my son left. I did not have the means to send him to another public or private school, even as a day pupil. Consequently, he attended the local Secondary Modern serving the numerous council estates surrounding it. This was a difficult move for him. His college peers had been from refined, wealthy backgrounds. However, he made no fuss and in his usual quiet demeanour got on with his education.

This time I felt I really had failed and would never be able to make a success of anything. The fact my son was now also suffering made me very disconsolate. Depression descended again. It felt as if the skies themselves were crushing me beneath their weight. In truth, I do not think I had really recovered from the previous bout. Somehow I had kept going but upon reflection think it must have been automatic pilot rather than actual living.

My own experience leads me to believe it is true to say, when someone attempts suicide, they are temporarily insane. All my life my priority and major concern have been my son's welfare and now, without a thought of the impact it would have upon him, decided to end it all, again. I waited for him to go to school before taking a load of pills and arranging myself with head on oven door. It opened horizontally. My old cooker had been reconnected after the newer one had been removed. To understand my reasoning, you need to know domestic gas in those days was still deadly poisonous. It also smelt awful. I turned the oven on without lighting it and waited for my life to end. As you see, it did not. The reason for him doing so I do not know, but my son returned to discover me unconscious. How horrible and devastating it would have been for him had my attempt succeeded, had not penetrated my clouded mind. His shock must have been great but sensible boy he was, he rose above and got on with turning the gas off and moving me. Placing a cushion under my head and checking my breathing, he concluded it right to summon an ambulance. The nearest public telephones were some distance away. This was before the general ownership of household telephones. He ran with all his might only to find all three booths occupied. In one he recognised the sons of a family who had befriended us. Besides the couple above us, they were the only ones to have done so. Boldly for him, he opened the door and asked them to hurry up. They told us later he was white as a sheet and shaking from head to toe. Realising something seriously amiss, they promptly ended their call to a girlfriend, and ran home. When my son got back he found their father waiting on the doorstep. He was able to lift me and place me on the front room sofa. He kindly waited with us for the ambulance. Once the paramedics were satisfied it safe to move me, I was whisked off to hospital.

I interrupt this tale to tell you a little about the family who had helped. You may recall how unimpressed I had been with the flat's location and how the few I had passed indicated the general populace were not the sort of people I was accustomed to. Reading back that sounds awful. It is not meant to be. I simply want to be honest in my sharing with you and indicate how matters appeared to me. It would also seem, from the lack of any advances, most of the other estate residents did not consider us their type. Anyway, it was rather academic because my working routine allowed little time for chatting. However, there was this family whose sons had befriended mine. We subsequently heard them to be considered one of the most rogue families on the estate, of which there were more than a few. The father was a dockyard worker and every day would come home with some item he had acquired, by devious means, concealed beneath the bonnet of his car. Side of pork, sausages, large catering packs of bacon, and goodness knows what else. As you will appreciate, they were not the most sophisticated of people and, for reasons I never discovered, had been ostracised by most residents. As is our habit, my son and I had simply treated them as individuals, without judgment. Something I think they appreciated. As with many such families they were fiercely loyal to their own and their friends. Kindly they looked out for us, realising I suspect we were rather naïve and innocent when it came to the society surrounding us. It was they who stopped some children from playing ball against our wall. The thud of it hitting the side of the building echoed throughout and disturbed us terribly. At the relevant point, I will tell you about how their mother helped me with another situation. They had truly been kind to us, but once we moved we lost contact.

Back to the tale in hand. At the hospital I was, as you would expect, put into a high-risk ward. My bed was at the far end, next to a wall to which I turned. I remained facing that wall, not responding to anyone nor taking any food or drink. Who understands the mental logic of someone in my state? Truth is, I felt ashamed to have survived. My son told me recently, he had visited every evening but I would not turn even when the nurse told me he was there. I feel terrible he had to go through such an awful experience. Besides the stress and upset, he had to undertake difficult return journeys because the hospital was on the opposite side of town to where we lived. Much of it had been in the dark of night using bus stops in some rather desolate spots. How he managed, neither of us is sure. But he did. As he puts it, when you have to do something, you just get on with it. He was a sensible boy for his age.

Apparently, a psychiatrist tried to talk to me each day, without success. I just was not ready to interact with anyone. The matron, how they are missed from modern hospitals, kindly kept watch over me. One occasion I heard a nurse say, 'What on earth is she still doing here. She should have been moved to a neurological ward ages ago.' Matron scolded her, telling her to have more consideration and compassion, especially as she had no idea of what had been going on in my mind or life. I was there for some considerable time, six to eight weeks I think. Then, one day for no apparent reason, I turned slightly and saw the food trolly. There was something rolled up on a plate and I asked the sister checking me at the time what it was. 'An omelette', she replied. I asked if I could have some. Doing her best to hide the excitement my request caused, she took the plate from the trolly. It was a very nice omelette, though I could only manage a couple of mouthfuls, if you could call them that. She then suggested a cup of tea. I am not fond of tea but said some coffee would be nice. I managed two cups. That was the start of my recovery, though I still have no idea what provoked it.

Up to this point my mind had been clouded in darkness. Now, as clarity started to return, I suddenly remembered my son. 'Where is my son?' A woman from the welfare department happened to be on the ward and went into an immediate panic. This happened during the day shift, therefore no night staff, who had seen my son when he visited, were there. The questions flowed. How old was he? Where was he? Was anyone looking after him? They were relieved when I told them he was not a toddler. My son told me what happened after. The welfare department found which school he attended and contacted the headmaster. He immediately sent for my boy and explained he knew I was in hospital. This took my son by surprise because he had told no one. The headmaster quizzed him, stating by rights he should place him in care. However, it was now six weeks since my admittance, during which period my son had attended school every day. He was clean, smartly dressed, obviously eating, and in good health. The headmaster therefore said he would take the risk of letting him remain at home but would be watching. My son was a mature boy, learning early on how to take care of himself. He did not have to be interviewed again. I am so grateful to the headmaster for his common sense and astute judgment. 'Care' would have been cruel for my son and horrifying for me.

Eventually recovering some of my strength, the psychiatrist, to who I was now speaking, considered me fit enough to return home. They kindly arranged it for a Saturday so my son would be home for a couple of days before being left on my own. My boy, Bless him, had a meal ready cooked along with freshly baked bread, which he knew I loved straight from the oven. It is impossible to convey how good it was to be back with him and my budgerigar, who immediately flew to me and made such a fuss. It was unmistakable he had also missed me.

The challenges of trying to get back into life quickly followed.

30

NIECE

I had been off work for some weeks and being still quite weak and disconsolate, not yet up to returning to the working environment. I therefore had no option but to apply for social security, as it was called then. This was to my great regret. I have always believed we should support ourselves and not be a burden on society or family. But I desperately needed some sort of income and there was little else I could do. The mother of the family who had befriended us on the estate kindly helped me with the forms, which I simply did not understand.

To my consternation, my application was refused. It was especially upsetting because this was the one and only time I requested assistance. The refusal letter did not help as it was blunt and bordered on being very rude. Again, the kind mother came to the rescue. I did not feel confident with my written English, so she wrote a letter on my behalf. She included the question 'How do you expect me to get better if you behave like this?' We also carefully restated all the facts. The next we knew were several members of the department coming to my home to apologise for their attitude. An unusual course of action, I understand. Social security was, thankfully, subsequently granted. With hardly any money left I am not sure what would have become of my son and I without this lifeline.

Though the social security payments helped, it was not sufficient. The usual need for an adequate income to meet my various commitments was pressing. My savings had gone. Thankfully, I was generally physically fit, so my recovery proceeded at a good pace. Slowly, I was able to return to all my jobs. Naturally, I told no one what had really happened, simply stating I had become rundown and consequently anaemic. My doctor had warned of more serious consequences if I did not take time to rest.

Mrs Badger, during my absence, had taken the lead role in running the business. Her husband, who had always been inclined to drink, now drank far more. That was not all. Knowing I could be trusted not to repeat a confidence and probably needing to talk, she informed me he now also took drugs. He was out of control for most of the time. She struggled to balance the books as he would help himself to one, two, three, or more bottles a day. He also took money from the tills to finance his drug addiction. Thankfully, even in his inebriated and 'high' states, he knew better than to touch me. I truly felt sorry for her. Controlling him, let alone the business, was a full-time occupation. I did my best to help by steering him away from bottles and tills and taking advantage of his liking for me by calmly suggesting he have something to eat. He had got into the habit of not eating, primarily surviving on drink and drugs, not forgetting cigarettes. I understood he was always a little better, and more with it, after food. But I could not always be there.

To add to her load, Mrs Badger told me her daughter, who was unmarried, was pregnant. Putting the best turn on it I could, I said how nice it would be for her to be a grandmother. Instead of laughing or agreeing, she burst into tears and, leaning upon my arm, wept bitterly. Between sobs, she told me the child was her husband's, her daughter's father! I hid my shock. It would not have helped her. Apparently, in one of his drink-drug episodes, he had forced himself upon the poor girl. This is the first time I have mentioned the incident, but know it is safe to do so, as I have retained anonymity for everyone mentioned or referred to in this book. We managed the situation between us and a healthy granddaughter was the eventual outcome. Her daughter seemed to cope reasonably well, though I think she, unsurprisingly, hardened herself to life thereafter. You never really know what you are going to face in life. Nor, what other people are coping with. Something we should remember when someone acts out of character or we meet 'zany' people.

Another new experience occurred for me during this period. Four men, who appeared to be good friends, started frequenting the club. They were smart, nice looking, and always cheerful. One was a television presenter I recognised. Again I was to learn something new, they were gay. Bear in mind, I am relating incidents and experiences from several years ago. A time when it was still unacceptable to be openly homosexual. They were really brave allowing people to know, but had the sense not to flaunt the fact in people's faces. This was my first encounter with men of their persuasion, but as I have told you, I was brought up to accept people for who they are and not to be judgmental. The five of us became quite good friends, and they became very protective of me whenever anyone gave me a difficult time. They could be overzealous and I had to make clear when I was okay and did not need their intervention. Nevertheless, it was nice to meet men who wanted to be friends and safeguard me rather than trying to take advantage of, or abuse, me. It really was a refreshing change. Whenever they were about, the atmosphere was full of fun. Besides their fun-loving disposition, and perhaps more importantly, all were intelligent. It was possible to have a proper discussion with them about almost anything, without unwanted over or undertones. Eventually, though not before they attempted to help me with another issue, as you will see shortly, we lost contact. Our lives went in different directions. Inevitable, considering our disparate employments. The once high-profile television presenter appeared less and less. I think his homosexuality had caused a problem. He became persona non grata with the television channel. It was a shame. He had been an intellectual and fun presenter. I saw him in an interview a few years later and was glad to see he looked well. Why do I always lose my good friendships?

Though as you see, I had got on with life, more from necessity than anything else, my inner being continued depressed and despondent. Another failed marriage, two suicide attempts, and having to take my son out of college played incessantly on my mind. Failure, failure, and more failure was the constant tune. I felt exhausted and tired and just wanted to sleep and sleep. The combined emotional drain, I assume. Since returning to work I had been able to put away a tiny amount each week, though there was still precious little in my savings. However, I thought it may be sufficient for me to contemplate visiting my family. My recent experiences made me realise I was unlikely to survive without a break. Another suicide attempt would probably succeed. Having come to my senses with regard to my son, I had no wish to impose such a horror or burden upon him. My employers granted me a few weeks off upon the understanding I would return to work as soon as I was back in the country.

Since I would not be earning while away, I had to look again for economic travel options. As before, I found flying was still the privilege of the well off. It was certainly out of my reach. Younger readers may find this hard to comprehend in these days of low-cost flights, but that is how it was. Sea travel was also still expensive. My research guided me back to rail travel. Though the journey still took considerable time, it, without the luxury of sleeping berths, remained the most reasonable and affordable option. Though my son had grown considerably since our last trip, I was sure he would be able to sleep in our seats with his feet on my lap. I was used to doing without, so it would not prove problematic for me.

This time the train took a different route from the one used on our last journey, travelling in part through Germany. Our section of the train was rather full, so I looked for a less crowded carriage further back. At each border, the journey took us across several countries, relevant customs officials checked passengers alighting within the jurisdiction. This was before the European Union came into being. The train guard would accompany them to identify those who were going on to other destinations. When they came to our carriage, he rather brusquely demanded our passports and tickets. I had not realised the compartment was for first-class passengers. Explains why it was less crowded. Rather than politely explaining my mistake, he aggressively yelled his demand for us to move. He even laid his hands on us and physically pushed. This was too much. It brought back my Gestapo experiences. I could not prevent myself from shouting the single word 'Gestapo!'. Though the man did not speak English, he clearly understood my meaning. I feared I had really done it now. He visibly checked himself and, as we were complying with his demand, simply satisfied his ego by following us along the corridor. My blood pressure still rises when I see historic wartime newsreels or war films involving the Nazis. I can never forget or forgive what they did to me and others. Thankfully, this was the only unpleasant incident, though, as always, we arrived tired, dirty, and hungry.

It was so good to see Anna and Christopher again, as well as their children, Vince and May, who were quite grown now. Over the following days, while we recovered from our journey, I noted the whole family treated May unkindly. A leg problem for most of her life had required several very painful operations. Without a real National Health system in my homeland, medical treatment has to be paid for. I think this may have caused some resentment. Vince called her horrible names and sometimes actually hit her. Anna's attitude also troubled me. She told me not to be taken in by her daughter. She was a little cat sneaking round trying to cause trouble and twist matters to her own advantage. I thought this was just part of the resentment and untrue. In later years, I came to realise the statement was not totally incorrect. My niece did show signs of such behaviour, a most unpleasant trait. But that was later. At the time, I commiserated and wished to remove her from the mistreatment. My own abuse has made me very sensitive to other people's troubles. Wherever possible, I like to try and help. I was not initially sure how to go about rectifying the situation. After a few weeks, I carefully suggested to her parents May accompany us when we returned to England. She was more likely to find a good career job, especially as she was a clever girl. She had learnt all aspects of English to a high standard without leaving home. Even obtaining Cambridge university certificates in English. They hesitated at first, but eventually agreed. I think the combination of my reasoning and desire to get her out of their hair convinced them.

Now eighteen, there was no requirement for May to attend school. Also, her overseas education effectively barred her from attending an English university, except at considerable cost. I introduced her to English society by taking her with me wherever I went outside of work. My places of employment, where she would have had to wait in some backroom for me to finish, did not seem desirable. She would be far more comfortable at home. I also did my best to explain the cultural differences. From the start she wanted to earn. We looked for suitable jobs, but there were none I considered acceptable. She did become a little frustrated, but I would not let her take up any occupation. I was responsible for her welfare and safety and intended to ensure she was not exposed to wrong elements. I was equally frustrated and often discussed the matter with my best friend, Hanna. Though she had a wider experience and knew a lot more people, neither could she come up with any suggestion. The resolution came in an unexpected manner, though I had some apprehension about it. Hanna's mother-in-law, who was a dear, and I had become friends in our own right. We had not seen each other for a while, so I decided to visit one afternoon. Her home, a large detached property sitting in its own extensive grounds, had been inherited from her pseudo parents. She was an adopted child. It was a pleasant summer afternoon, so we had lunch on the lawn. It happened Hanna, her husband, and sister-in-law were also visiting. If I had known, I would not have gone. I hate inconveniencing people. Hanna's husband was very attractive, with a good physique. He was also a nice person but not of strong enough character for Hanna. They were in the process of a divorce, but retained a degree of friendship. The sun was blazing, so he decided to strip down to his rather brief underpants and sunbathe in one of the deckchairs, which was interesting.

Nora, Hanna's sister-in-law, was not, to put it mildly, as refined as my friend. During the introductions, Hanna gave a brief history of how my niece came to be with us and what we were looking for. As soon as Nora heard of our search, she virtually grabbed May from me. It turned out she was looking for an au pair to care for her four children. All three women, Nora, her mother, and Hanna, considered my niece a potential employee. To be frank, I did not think much of Nora and was not sure I wanted to entrust May to her. Sadly, she and Nora seemed to hit it off. At an opportune moment, I took my niece aside and asked how she felt about the prospect of looking after Nora's four children. She was fairly positive, so, though still having reservations, I agreed to an initial meeting with the siblings. The following week, Nora collected us in her car, part of her divorce settlement, I assumed. The journey was rather nerve-racking. She was an erratic person, which was more than evidenced by her driving. My niece had always been fond of children, so the possibility of looking after some quite thrilled her. To my surprise, she and the children jelled in the short time we were there. May subsequently made it clear she would like to accept the position. Though I retained doubts about Nora's suitability, I agreed. She could always come back to me if it did not work out.

In later years, I came to regret the decision a little. I discovered Nora was rather promiscuous, often taking men home with her, rarely the same one. She was also very messy, dirty, totally lacking in hygiene, constantly used foul language, and believed in getting what she wanted by using people. Gratefully, though she took advantage of May, getting her to look after the house as well as the children, she never abused her, physically or mentally. Unfortunately, my niece was still of an impressionable age and adopted, for life, most of her employer's home habits, but thankfully not her promiscuity. There was an eventual upside. When the children were older and required little looking after, May obtained some professional training. It enabled her to acquire good employment for the remainder of her working life. Later, it helped her look after her seriously ailing husband and to send money back home when they needed it, especially after her father's death.

My niece had been working at Nora's for some months when the police came looking for her. In response to my inquiry, the officer in charge simply said she had overstayed and would not answer any further questions. In truth, he was quite aggressive. I certainly found his general attitude offensive and frightening. I feared they intended to deport her for some reason, though I knew her papers were in order. Also, as far as I was aware, everything else had been properly organised. Therefore, I did not understand what it was all about. Looking back, I now realise I had not got her a green card. When discussing the issue with May, not too long ago, she assured me all her documentation had been put in order using her new address. Computer systems were new technology at the time and tended to be stand-alone systems. Where they did exist there was consequently no means for the varied police forces to link them. Mail or telephone remained their primary means of communication. As there was no reason for them to connect May with the town where she now lived, there was no reason for them to contact the relevant force. The officer's attitude and approach, and refusal to give a straight answer, bothered me, so I decided not to cooperate. I told him she was out with friends and I had no idea when she would be home.

They left and I sincerely hoped that was that. How wrong! The officer, together with some constables, would turn up in the middle of nights and insist on searching through the apartment. They even looked under beds and in cupboards. The officer continued to treat me with disrespect and aggression and still refused to give a proper explanation. My son was home for some of the time and became very unsettled, telling me he could not cope with anymore. This naturally upset me, resulting in me shouting at the officer that May was not there. The harassment, what else can I call it, continued for a while and then just stopped. Why, I do not know. I may only speculate the officer was on some sort of mission or simply took delight in upsetting people. Whatever it was, I am surprised I was not charged with obstruction. No explanation was ever forthcoming, so I will never know what was going on.

All this upset made me scared to visit May. The police might follow me or intercept any communication. Though this was unfamiliar territory, I had seen enough news reports and documentaries, as well as fictional programmes, to have some idea of what could happen. However, after a while I began to worry. I had undertaken with her parents to be responsible for her welfare. Was everything okay? I needed to know. On one of my rare nights off, I carefully got the bus to the town where she was now living. It is a wonder my neck survived the constant looking round to ensure no one was following. Darkness had descended by the time I reached my destination. At least that gave me the chance to remain concealed. Again and again I checked I was not being followed. It sounds rather farfetched, like some television drama, but it is how it was. When I got to the house, I remained in the shadows. In response to my knocking, the elder boy's voice came through, asking who was there. I told him, but he just laughed, as did the other children. While still laughing, he said it could not be me because I was dead. You can imagine my shock. I told him not to be silly and to let me in. He would not open the door and all of them continued to laugh rather grotesquely. This continued for a while, leading me to conclude they were not going to cooperate. It appeared my niece was not there. You may wonder at such a response. Regrettably, I have to tell you they were never very nice. In subsequent years, May would refer to the elder brother as 'a right bastard'. It appears they were just as horrible in adulthood. My niece told me she was out. I am not sure if that was true. She never explained why, but for some reason seemed to have a strong dislike for me. Upsetting, especially in view of what I have done and tried to do for her.

I happened to mention the incident to a friend. Seeing how upset it had made me, he offered to take me as the journey, particularly under the circumstances, was not an easy one. Having explained my fears, he suggested I lie low on the back seat when leaving our town and when in the other. I felt like some criminal but considered it was the right thing to do. Five times he took me, and five times the same thing happened, but with increasing aggression. I have to say, though there is nothing to substantiate it, I believe May was behind the door with them. She did sometimes display a very nasty streak. My friend became increasingly annoyed, asking why I continued going as it was clear they did not want to see me. He told me to stop trying. I knew it was sound advice, but still wanted to fulfil my promise to May's parents. However, after the fifth time, I very reluctantly came to the same conclusion. As mentioned, my niece loved children and, though she knew they were not nice, did her best to present them in a positive light. But, later, even she tired of it.

May eventually married a much older man she met through her work. He was a divorcee with four adult children. She insisted on returning home for the wedding. I suspect it was to prove to the family she could find a husband. In view of his age and appearance, he was anything but attractive, it failed to impress. Not long after he contracted cancer and several other severe conditions. He also drank too much. In fact, he was an alcoholic. Both did their utmost to try and cover the fact up. Sadly, he was unable to produce children, so her long held hopes for a family were forever thwarted. She nursed him for years and it must be said it was only due to her care he lived as long as he did.

I am glad to say I saw more of May in recent years. It would have been sad to leave this life without having spent some time together. She still seemed to resent me for some reason, but I chose to overlook it. After all, she was my niece and life is too short to hold grudges.

31

Predators

The visit to my family had lasted longer than anticipated. I had therefore been a little worried my positions may have been filled and I would have to look elsewhere for alternative employments. I need not have worried. Everyone warmly welcomed me back, which was nice. At the club, they jokingly scolded me for being absent so long. Some customers had apparently stayed away because I was not present. That soon changed once they heard I was back. Though I had enjoyed visiting my relatives, in some ways I was glad to be back among colleagues and acquaintances and back to my own life, such as it was. It is nice to do different things and to relax for a while, but it is not the same as living your own independent life. I soon got back into routine with my adrenaline kicking in again, enabling me to deal with the tiredness. Nothing had really changed in my absence. Marriages and relationships had not improved or degenerated that much. Though, in the case of Mr and Mrs Badger, I cannot say they were at all happy.

Shortly after my return, some gentlemen from London came to the club and asked for the Badgers. It transpired they had a problem with the club's name. A name it had used for years. Apparently, these men owned a club in London that had been registered with the same name. Only recently had they heard of our establishment. Rather arrogantly, they considered they had primary right to the name, intimating unless ours was changed, there would be trouble. We got the impression, some of the trouble would not be exactly legal. Many London clubs were, and for all I know may still be, owned by rather unsavoury characters. London gangs often used them as fronts for their illegitimate businesses. My employers had been part of the nightlife world for many years and knew what 'trouble' could mean. They had seen others suffer. Therefore, without further discussion or argument, they agreed to the change. A change that was promptly carried out. Fears that the re-naming would lose clientele proved unfounded. Customers knew who we were and my own loyal following did not care about such a cosmetic alteration. If anything, it may have brought additional business. People were always on the lookout for fresh places to go. Though customers enjoyed having a regular venue where they felt at home, some variety now and then was welcome. The new name showing up in the press would have implied a new club.

While discoursing with my employers, the men from London had noticed me working. When business with the Badgers was completed, they approached and asked if I would be interested in working in their club. Hardly able to believe the arrogance of them trying to poach me from under the very eyes of my employers, I gave them a hard stare. However, unperturbed, they continued assuring me they would pay more, and it was a better establishment. As you are aware, seeking a satisfactory income was a constant with me. Therefore, despite the arrogance and as much as I dislike London, I decided it would do no harm to look. The substantial increase in salary had to be considered. I should have known better. On the agreed day they took me there in their car. The place certainly was very swish. The premises were far more extensive than in any other place I had worked, and the work would be similar to what I was already used to. When my tour was completed, I required the toilet. I was just checking myself in the mirror before rejoining my hosts when two women suddenly attacked me. I may be small in stature but was physically strong and therefore able to fight them off, despite their considerable aggression. It turned out they were lesbians who frequented the club and who had found me attractive. Why must they always do that, to me at least? Why not just strike up a conversation? As related elsewhere, I have encountered lesbian hostility, but, up to this point, had not realised quite how violent women can be towards another woman. They really had been violent. It quite put me off. If this happened on one short visit, I wondered what it would be like to be there full time. Despite the salary being far more and the premises very nice, I had been inwardly uncomfortable with the London atmosphere. Consequently, I had been undecided whether or not to accept. The toilet incident made the decision for me.

During my tour, a couple of good looking men were sitting at the bar. When I returned to the room, they made a distinct point of talking to me. They told me they were on their way to a nice place where I could earn far more money than was being offered here. Naturally, my ears pricked up. After all, it had primarily been the substantially increased salary that had brought me here in the first place. I am usually a very cautious person and very reluctant to go anywhere with people I do not know. Whether the incident in the toilet had thrown me off balance or whether it was the fact of having gone to London in pursuit of a job, or both, I do not know. They seemed pleasant enough, so I agreed to accompany them. It could do no harm to look. In my naïvety, I never seem to learn.

We drove to a house in a district I did not know. Not that I knew many except those we came across when my son and I lived in the hostel. They rang the doorbell but, before I knew what was happening, had jumped back into their car and driven off. I was astounded and obviously left in a quandary. What to do? Before I could decide, the door opened and I was ushered in with a warm smile. Now I was here, I thought I might as well have a look. If there was a good job going, I should see what it entailed and how much it paid. Once over the threshold, I was left on my own, again. I suppose I should have realised there was a reason for the odd behaviours. The house was full of people walking round, drinking, and cavorting. Thankfully, as mentioned before, I have a quick intellect and soon realised what sort of place this was. Some were half clothed. I recognised a well-known gentleman who was often in the news.

Later, when some scandals broke in the media, I also recognised two of the women who had been there. They turned out to be highly paid prostitutes. You may find the following anecdote amusing or sad, but I must tell you about it. The well-known figure had his penis hanging out that I must tell you was rather small. However, everyone looked and, out loud, would say, 'Oh my, what a big one.' It was clearly a response agreed upon by common consent. It does seem sad someone should need such blatantly false assurances. I had seen and heard enough. This was definitely not a place for me. I leave it to you to imagine how I felt. 'Contaminated' does not really do it justice. Without drawing attention, I worked my way back into the hall and quietly left. A further challenge now faced me. I had no idea where I was or how to get to the centre of the city where I should be able to get a train.

I walked about for a while but recognised nothing. I was thoroughly lost. I was also too nervous to ask anyone for help. It was dark, not a nice area, and I had heard many stories about the criminal elements of London. Eventually, I came across an underground station where the ticket man was very helpful. He explained how I could get to the mainline railway terminus I needed to get home. With much trembling and fear, I finally made it back, exhausted and frightened. I really had been silly and had exposed myself to dangers not thought of before.

Glad to have escaped unharmed, so I thought, I decided there was no point in telling people about the incidents. I simply went on working and living as usual. In my innocence, or perhaps naïvety,

I had not appreciated who or what the two men were. One dark evening, on my way to work, they suddenly confronted me at the corner of the High Street. I assume they found out the town I lived in from the men who had invited me to work in their London club. I certainly had not told them. Without a word, they beat me up and left me for dead in the gutter. Thankfully, some passers-by saw my comatose form and called an ambulance. I do not know what it is like now, but then the police always accompanied an ambulance on such calls. In response to their questioning, I said I did not know who had done it and assumed it was a general mugging, though those were not as common then as now. At last I had realised the men must manage prostitutes. It was well known pimps would kill girls who did not cooperate. I heard of one who was thrown from a speeding car. Another, whose body had been found in woods. I saw no point in endangering myself further when I could not tell the police very much about them. Besides, they might hear and come back to finish the job. Remember, I also had my son's safety to think of. They would not think twice of hurting a child.

When recovered, I returned to working as normal and kept to the mugging story. I naturally became nervous of dark roads and strangers for a while. Sad, because as I have said, these were generally safe times.

32

Disappointment

When my son finished his education, he decided to go straight into work. He wanted to do what he could to help with our finances. Initially, he was employed by a High Street retailer. Through his honesty, he built up his own loyal customer base. When a customer wanted something cheap and hard wearing, he would show them what was available in the store. At the same time he would direct them to other retailers who carried more the type of item they were interested in. When the customer required something of quality, they would return to my son. This meant, in effect, he was responsible for generating a good income for his department. The items purchased inevitably carried a higher price tag. I think he was happy there having made friends with colleagues as well as enjoying the challenges different customers brought. He has some amusing anecdotes about his experiences.

Out of the blue, so to speak, Terrance contacted me, saying he would like to see his son. I am sure, having read through our past history, you will appreciate what a true surprise this was. As you know, he had never shown any such interest before. In fact, as you also know, it was the opposite. Perhaps the unsatisfactory life with his new wife motivated this apparent change of heart. I had reservations. Understandable when you consider the past. However, upon thinking it through, I concluded it was only fair and right for my son to see his father, despite all the trauma he had inflicted upon us. I believe a child usually benefits from having contact with both parents. Though that obviously has to be assessed within the realities of the person's individual character.

During the visit, my ex-husband asked our son if he would like to work in his shop. He had established his own electronics business. My boy, with no input from me, was uncertain. In the end, he decided it was at least a chance to get to know his father. He had been very young when we divorced and though he remembered him, he did not know him. I do not think he really wished to give up his current employment, but decided spending time with his father was more important. As you would expect, I was not entirely happy but considered I should not object. It was only right and fair my son should have the opportunity.

As mentioned, Terrance had re-married. Their home and the shop were within a pleasant village too far away for my son to travel daily, but not so far he could not get back easily if necessary. He had to live with the family, which he found difficult. I have already told you none of the children were very friendly and, along with their mother, tended to be surly. Also, how dirty and untidy the house had been. Regrettably, none of this had changed since my stay. I have to admit to being constantly on edge while he was there. What if Terrance reverted to his previous ways? After two weeks my son had enough and came home. I must emphasise, this was his decision and in no way influenced by me, though I was grateful to have him safely back. Besides the discomfort, he said it had all been a waste of time. He never got to spend much time with his father. All that really happened was him being left to manage the small shop while his father went out on jobs. Usually for most of the day and often part evenings. It was almost as if he had wanted unpaid labour to man the shop. He was not to see his father again for fourteen years. Then it was but a brief visit arranged by Terrance's wife. My son told me how disappointed he had been with that visit. His father seemed to have absolutely no interest in him or his life. The timing, however, had been perfect. Later, he explained how he had been thinking of his father and what it would be like to meet him again, after all the intervening years. The visit provided the clear answer. Though disappointing, it eased his mind once and for all.

Still determined to bring money in, my boy applied for and got a situation in a five-star hotel. When visiting his original place of work, the manager unexpectedly appeared on the shop floor, which I understand was very unusual. He asked my son if he would return. It transpired he had been missed, and they had been unable to replace him. Reading between the lines, I think his customers had been asking for him. The hotel hours were anti-social, requiring him to be present morning, noon, and night, with just a couple of hours off in the afternoon. The pay was no better either, especially considering the hours. He agreed to return to the retailers. To his delight, he received an increase in salary shortly after.

Though he appeared happy enough, I was concerned he had not found a career job. He could continue in the retail business, but there were no real prospects where he was. I did not want him to have to struggle as I had. I had been racking my brains about what to do when a solution, perhaps it would be better to say an opportunity, was presented. You will recall I had become friendly with some television presenters. Among them were my small group of gay friends, many of whose colleagues often joined them for a drink. In passing I was musing over my concerns when one, who hosted a successful programme, suggested a career in television. I jumped at the idea. He said he would see what could be arranged, but in the meantime I was not to tell anyone, including my son. I cannot convey how excited I felt about this possible prospect for my son's future. However, to my consternation, this was not to be.

One day my boy came home and told me he had joined the commandos. I was shocked, surprised, and disappointed. He had not mentioned he was looking into such a career. The idea of him joining something so dangerous troubled me. Nor did I like the idea of him being far away. My disappointment was because my friend had just told me he had managed to get my son a position within the local television network. However, my son was determined. When I asked why the commandos, that is The Royal Marines for those who do not know, he said it was the challenge that attracted him. He had already considered the Royal Air Force and the Royal Navy.

It took several months for his entry into Her Majesty's forces to be approved. First, was the fact that although a citizen, I am not British born. Second, was the matter of finding Terrance, who had moved from the village. The bureaucrats required his agreement. I am not entirely sure, but you may remember, as part of the divorce proceedings, something like a residency order had been implemented. It was to subsist until our son reached his majority, that in those days was twenty-one. As I understand it now, the effect was he would not be allowed to live abroad without both parents' approval. The commandos wanted him to go overseas. They needed his father's agreement so they would not have to go to court constantly, to request permission for every posting. It took some time for the forces administrators to find Terrance. Though I would have rather he did not go, I did not want my son thwarted or disappointed in his expectations. I worried his father, just to be awkward, would refuse. Thankfully, his own service with the Royal Navy helped him approve our son's choice.

From the moment he left I worried. His upbringing had not prepared him for such a physical life. He, however, completed the demanding training with only a couple of minor injuries. I was still anxious about him being in such a dangerous profession, but at the same time very proud.

Now I come to a prelude that would see another unwelcome change to my life. For those who do not know. All military personnel take part in a passing-out parade to signify completion of their training and availability for active service. I was determined to be present at my son's. Besides the fact I love him very much, he had no one else. I did not want him to be the only one without someone in attendance. I asked to see the nice woman who had interviewed me for the laboratory job. She was the senior manager who we were not permitted to approach directly. I intended to ask for time off to attend the parade. Unfortunately, my supervisor was rather a bitch, excuse my language. She refused. So I asked her for the day off. Again she refused, but very abruptly this time. The refusal and attitude irked me. I had never requested a day off, had taken no sick days, and had one of the best attendance records. Though the steam had been rising within me, I managed to control it and in a civilised tone stated again my son had no one else and I needed to go. She still refused. In fact, she almost hit me with a broom that happened to be leaning against the wall. Thankfully, another member of the team noticed and inserted herself between us. I have to assume this boss of mine was jealous for some reason. She was never very nice to me. Perhaps the fact I had been given the job when it had not been advertised had upset her. Maybe it was because I was considered good looking. I do not know.

On the day, I simply telephoned to say I would not be coming in. As you are aware, that was something I had never done before. I repeated my son had no one else and I would be going to his parade. My destination was not an easy one to get to from where I was. It was in a rural location on the other side of the country. Somehow I negotiated the trains, freezing cold rural railway stations, how the wind blows through them, I can still feel it's biting touch, and the local buses. Despite it all, I arrived in time. I had begun to doubt I would. I was pleased and proud my son had achieved success in his training as he is not a macho type nor was he particularly athletic. My heart could not have expanded more as I watched him on the parade ground.

When I returned home I felt extremely unwell, looked awful and did not feel I could cope with seeing anyone. I think the strain from previous events had finally caught up. The incident with the supervisor had not particularly stressed me, however, it may have been the trigger for all the suppressed anxieties and worries to surface. I remember I kept repeating to myself, 'Cannot go on anymore.' 'Cannot go on anymore'. I did not return to work the next day and, in fact, never went back. I continued to feel unwell for several days, not even venturing out of the door. On one of those tiresome days I happened to look out of the window and saw a chauffeured limousine pull up at the curb. I immediately recognised it as one of the firms. The chauffeur got out and made for my block. With the dark tinted windows, I could not tell if anyone else was in the car. I still felt unable to cope with seeing anyone, so did not respond to his knock. Others had been sent before and after, but I could never bring myself to open the door. I really did not want to see anyone. I suspect some may have brought the salary due to me for work done. It is a shame I never answered. Not because of the money, but because of the nice woman who I did not wish to let down. It seemed obvious neither she nor any of the other managers or supervisors knew what had occurred. Naturally, my supervisor would have said nothing. Perhaps the other girls who worked in the laboratory did eventually tell about the refused day off. It was a good job with a reasonable salary and I hated to lose it. However, there was no doubt my supervisor and her friends would have made life more than a little difficult if I had returned. Had I not sufficient stress and worry in my life without adding to it?

Here we go again. I hope this is not getting too tedious for you. Now my day job was ended, I had to find some other source of income. I needed something quickly so went to the restaurant-pub where I had worked before. There was a lunchtime vacancy. As usual, the owner was thrilled to see me and offered for me to start straight away. So kind as it ensured I had some additional income immediately.

Upon successful completion of his training, my son had a short tour of duty with an active unit. If any of you have, or had, relatives in the forces, I think you will understand I was never at ease while my son was away on active duty. After he was posted to the Far East, where he formed part of a brigadier's staff. Sadly, he had his twenty-first birthday there, which meant we could not celebrate it together. A wonderful cake one of my friends had his ship's chef make, and some champagne went to waste. My son has never been one to make a fuss of his birthdays, so some colleagues and he simply went for a drink. They got drunk and wandered off, leaving him on his own. Not the ideal way to celebrate such an occasion. He said he had been glad they left and did not have to put up with their drunken antics. He enjoys a good time like everyone else but does not have patience with unnecessary stupidity.

While my son was in the Far East, Terrance unexpectedly called at the flat. It happened to be one of the infrequent times I was home. Seeing him on the doorstep surprised me, but you will not be surprised also made me apprehensive. However, he looked so dejected and downcast that, when he asked if he could come in, I let him. He stood silently for a while and then asked if he could stay the night. As you would expect, and despite his disconsolate state, I responded with a firm negative. I asked about his bandaged wrists and the other bandages and plasters I had noticed scattered over him. In a low, despondent voice, he just said, 'Never mind. Never mind.' After a further brief silence, he pleaded for me to let him stay. Again I refused. He continued to plead and I to refuse until his beseeching became quite pathetic. I began to feel sorry, as it was clear something was amiss. He definitely was not the Terrance I knew. In the end I did not have the heart to turn him away and agreed he could sleep on the divan in the front room. However, after all our previous history, I did not feel I could trust him, so locked myself in my bedroom for the night. In the morning he left without any breakfast and in parting said, 'Thank you. You most probably have, momentarily, saved my life'. Such a strange phrase. I never saw him again. Later, I found out his wife had been hitting him. Neither did she bother to hide, or deny, her infidelity. Though it cannot be proven, there is an inkling, after his untimely death, that she a trained nurse had slowly poisoned him. Maybe he had started to think it, and that was what he meant in his parting words. I need to point out this scenario was not of my making. Others have told me how she would tell them the day Terrance would die, as if she had the gift of insight or prophecy. He died that very day! Despite deserving to be treated harshly, after all he had done, I feel sorry Terrance should have ended up in such a state. I never stopped caring.

33

Finally

I longed to get away from the flat and estate, and if possible, buy our own home. Therefore, I continued to work round the clock. No longer having to pay college fees also enabled me to save far more. Those savings, along with the money my son and sister sent, mounted until I thought a house was within my reach. There were however, stumbling blocks. At the time, it was usual for husbands to be the earner and for wives to stay at home. Housewife was recognised and accepted as a normal occupation, but not a profession. That meant banks and building societies would not consider lending to a lone woman. They were thought to be too high risk. I only learnt this when applying for a mortgage. It was very disheartening and demeaning to be constantly rejected and considered less trustworthy than a man. In these days of comparative equality, some of you may find it hard to believe there was such a time in our society. But there was, and it continued for a very long time. I am sure you will understand how demoralising all this was and how it left me feeling rather dejected. Nevertheless, I was determined not to give up unless

I really had to. I searched round, with little hope, I admit. Then I heard, how I do not recall, that local councils offered mortgages. After the experiences with the more traditional lenders, I thought little of my chances but still decided to apply. An unsympathetic man interviewed me. I was getting very frustrated with his attitude when a woman intervened. She turned out to be his boss. Looking over my application, she noted all my jobs, and the combined income. She also appeared impressed I had saved enough for the required deposit. We talked a little and in the midst of the other information, she told me it was not the council's policy to lend to single women, but my application would be considered. I would be notified of the final decision in due course. At last, someone was prepared to consider me. I cannot express how this made me feel after all the rejections. I still held little hope, but it was a good feeling to be taken seriously.

After some weeks of nothing, I assumed, as expected, my application had been rejected. Then, without any warning, I received a letter asking me to attend at the central council offices. Upon arrival I was shown to the office of the lady who had intervened. She explained again it was not their policy to lend to lone women. At least she had the decency to tell me to my face. Most of my other rejections had been by short unsympathetic letters, sometimes no more than a note. She went on to say she had been following me in her own time. You may imagine my initial indignation. Before I could say anything, she appeased my resentment, to some degree. She continued to say how impressed she was with my hardworking and the fact I did not mess around with men. She also discovered

I was highly respected and considered reliable. In conclusion, she confirmed her willingness to grant me a mortgage. Then went on to say how, in some ways, it was a risk for her as she was sticking her neck out. However, she did not consider there was anything to fear and believed the council would never have any trouble with me. Reading between the lines, I think she was annoyed women continued to be treated with such disrespect. After all, she had achieved a responsible position as a woman. Gratitude is hardly a sufficient word for what I felt. Without this wonderful woman, I would never have been able to buy my own home. My self-respect had been damaged by the all the humiliation and rejection, now some of it had been restored. Can you imagine what would be the outcome if all this had happened in this day and age? Despite the constant refusals, I had continued to look round for a house. More in hope than anything else, I suppose. As a result, I had already seen one I liked in a nice central location. I would be able to walk to all my places of employment. With the unexpected mortgage, I was able to purchase this lovely detached four-bedroom house. Finally, we had a home of our own. I doubt you can fathom how excited I was. I knew there would be no problems with the repayments because I ensured they were within my income bracket. The fact interest rates then did not swing violently as they do these days helped. They went up at one point, but I had allowed some leeway. My finances were put under strain at one stage, but I still made the payments. I was determined not to default and for much of the time survived on one sandwich a day.

Slowly, bit by bit, I was able to afford soft furnishings. I love white and painted the house white throughout, inside and out. I also carpeted the entire house in white. When I found some curtain fabric I liked, I bought the whole bail which made my home unique. It took longer to buy the more solid furniture. That I bought piece by piece as funds permitted. Doing so did not prove problematic because society was far more settled then. Furniture fashion did not change rapidly. I was able to match all the furniture. Thankfully, there was a small front garden. I hate houses where the doors open directly onto a pavement. The back garden was a reasonable size, allowing me to indulge my enjoyment of plants and trees without it becoming a headache. To finish it off, I placed some planted wooden barrels on the paved side passage. At last I felt I had made some positive progress in my life. After all the negatives, it was almost overwhelming. I had to pinch myself at times to believe it really was true, it had happened, and I was now the proud possessor of my own home.

At first, I thought the neighbours on one side would become friends. Regrettably, I was wrong. The woman was little more than a whore. She would sleep with any man to obtain a favour. That included electricity, gas, tax, insurance, and council engineers and officials. Sex for money was also something she would not decline. She was also always looking for ways to cheat people. Her husband was a weak, indifferent man. He drank, took drugs, and would also have sex with anyone. None of this was in secret from the other. They even did it in the same or adjoining rooms. Besides drinking almost nonstop, she also constantly took drugs in an attempt to retain her figure. My metabolism meant, no matter how little or much I eat, my figure stayed the same. It proved a point of considerable jealousy. I soon learnt they were anything but friends.

Unfortunately, they frequented most of the clubs in town. Sometimes the ones I worked in. It was annoying, but I always retained a friendly disposition. First, it was my duty to them as customers. Second, perhaps more importantly, they were known to be very vicious with anyone they considered had crossed them. I try not to give into fear but at the same time know when to be wise. I never really understood why they stayed together, though I think he loved her. It was no surprise to learn recently they have separated. She, weasel that she is, kept the house and car. He went on to run his own public house, though most believe he is drinking away the profits.

My only other real contact within the area was the minister of the local church. He made a point of calling at all the houses in the parish, especially when someone new moved in. He was very nice and both he and his wife took a kind interest in my welfare. I have always believed in God and missed my home church. Whenever I could, I attended a service. Several of the church ladies also befriended me. It was nice to have a community that considered me a part of them without making undue demands upon the little time I had available. Community in my young rural home had been something we never really thought about. It was just there and part of us. Although I still did not fully understand English society, we got on fairly well. The church gatherings also provided pleasant, undemanding, relaxing times for me, and an opportunity to worship God along with others. Something I truly appreciated.

I continued to work hard, both in my employments and on the house. It may have been tiring, but it was worth it. You have read enough to appreciate how happy I was to have my own home at last. Overall, despite the occasional problem at my places of work, I enjoyed what I did. Life, for a change, was not too bad.

It was during this time I made some new acquaintances. Of these, I would particularly like to mention my insurance man and his wife. They were a lovely, down to earth, caring couple. Unlike most these days, he really sought the best suitable policy for me. One that gave the cover I needed without extortionate premiums. His wife was an invalid confined to bed for most of the time. She was a wonderful knitter and embroiderer and would not allow her condition to daunt her from pursuing these pastimes. Her stitching in both disciplines was unmatched, and she made a small living from commissions. Her life, by necessity, was quiet, but she did receive recognition. Having entered a competition to make clothes for the newborn of a famous public family, her details appeared in the national press, as one of the winners. We remained friends for a long time.

The long working hours with my later and later arrival home began to tell. It was now more often than not, three, four and occasionally five a.m. Coincidently, just as I was wondering what to do about it, some officers from a short-haul cruise company asked if I would consider working on one of their ships. They gave me the impression the pay was good and the work reasonably straightforward. There was nothing to lose by making a few further enquiries, so I did. The information appeared favourable, and I eventually agreed, in principle, to work for them. I would delay final acceptance until I had time to think it through properly. They offered me the management of a perfumery shop at the rank of lieutenant. The rank attracted a salary that outstripped the combined income from my existing jobs. You will understand how tempting that was, but after all my experiences I needed to be sure. After further consideration, I concluded it would be a worthwhile move. My son was serving away, so there was no barrier to me being absent from home. To their consternation, I submitted my resignation to all my employers. They did not want me to leave but understood once I explained about the salary. They knew they could not match it. The recruitment board had also assured me sole use and charge of the shop till. Time proved mine was the only one always accurate to the penny. I seem to have a natural talent for on-the-spot arithmetic. This was before the advent of tills that assess the change due back to the customer. The navy blue uniform with its gold lieutenant bars was rather flattering, especially as they were cut to fit our figures.

The cruise ship's ports of call were in Southern Europe and North Africa. Needless to say, many passengers spent much of their time in the bars. Consequently, a lot were often drunk by the time they came to make purchases. My bar experience paid dividends, as I have become an expert at dealing with intoxicated people. I have learnt how to pacify and prevent an escalation into aggressive behaviour.

On the contrary, they usually end up submissive and friendly. It was very busy work, but the time passed pleasantly enough. It will not surprise you to know, as had become normal in my previous work, I had to deal with unwanted attentions. Not just from the male passengers or crew. You have seen how my various encounters have taught me to take care, especially with lesbians, some of whom had proven very violent. Thankfully, I was able to handle these incidents without any altercations arising. I must say here, I do not have a problem with same-sex relationships of whichever gender. It is just I have had some unfortunate experiences.

I should mention one incident that occurred early on. One day, soon after my acceptance of the job, Mr Badger appeared on the ship while it was in port. He was in one of his, or should that be usual, drunk-high conditions. Shouting at the top of his voice, he demanded to see me and the captain. He accosted the captain with, 'She works for me, not you!'. My only shocked retort had been 'Mr Badger!'. I quickly explained to the captain who he was. A quiet order was given and my former boss was politely escorted from the ship. I felt rather embarrassed, but the captain told me not to be concerned. True to his word, neither he nor any of his officers mentioned the incident again. I have to admit to feeling very sorry for my ex-boss. I do not know what lay behind his drink and drug taking, but it was have been something painful and undermining. Overall, he had a nice family and a good position, so it was hard to conceive what was bothering him. We never really know what is at the root of someone's behaviour.

Being rather naïve, as I still am in some ways, I look back and wonder how I survived North Africa. Apparently, the white slave trade was in full swing then. I have no idea if it still is. Many women had been kidnapped, never to be heard of again. In the time I had ashore I usually went to the bazaars. The only time I had ever seen something similar was in those all too short early years with my beloved mama. Every October, what I may only describe as an annual fair came to our rural district. This was a great event. Besides the occasional church holidays, people rarely had time off. The agricultural nature of our livelihoods did not allow for it. However, everyone would make time to go to the fair. We always went as a family unit, though father would wonder off for a while with his friends and mama would chat to the ladies while the three of us, my sisters and I, ran off to take in all the sights. The brightly lit fair rides and colourfully costumed attendants and entertainers were, to us at the time, breathtaking. By today's standards it would be considered a very low-key, basic event, but for us it was marvellous. Our favourite rides were the ones that took us into the air, like the big wheel. It was the nearest we would ever come to flying. So we thought. The jugglers and clowns scattered around would have us all laughing for most of the time. Beside the fair, there were also multiple stalls laden with all sorts of goods, a bit like the bazaar I was now investigating. There were dresses, scarves, skirts, blouses, table linen, ornaments, kitchen utensils, tools, and so much more, much of it from foreign lands. This was where I saw my first cuckoo clock. My sisters and I wondered if our comic hero, Zoro, had such things in his home. When it was time to eat, we would gather back together. The food vendor's mouth-watering aromas having opened our appetites. Roasted piglet was a firm favourite, and I understand still is. It was also here I had my palm read. Most of the store holders and entertainers were from gypsy stock. The woman told me I had a long lifeline and would live to sixty plus. You need to bear in mind, at the time, sixty was considered old. Now, with the improvements in health care and medication, it is considered middle-aged. I passed sixty long ago. I still have the paper the palm reader gave me. Despite the transport improvements and therefore ability to travel further distances, the area primarily remains an agricultural, parochial district, with few going far on a regular basis, some never. The fair remains a highlight for the otherwise busy community. It may still seem basic for those of us accustomed to the technically enhanced entertainments of today, but it is still fun. In some ways, the less sophisticated amusements are more enjoyable, more human.

At the North African bazaars, I would bargain for home furnishings and occasionally a luxury. My son and I both have nice watches from there. These are the genuine article not some knock off that you hear about so much these days. There was one time when I wanted a number of items from the same merchant. He asked a ridiculous sum. I bargained until I got the lot for eleven pounds, despite him having asked that for just one of the items. This was when one pound went a long way. That is how I got many of my home's soft furnishings. I can be forceful, determined would be a better word, when occasion demands. That characteristic combined with the fact I am dark haired, whereas the slaver's customers preferred blonds, probably saved me from the fate of other women. While on one of these excursions, the captain saw me and was shocked I was on my own. Thereafter, he insisted I never went without an escort. He was afraid of losing me to the slave market. Hair can always be dyed. I still marvel at what I must refer to as my escape. It gives me shivers to think what could have happened.

Upon returning to our home port, the ship normally underwent a two-day maintenance schedule. It was rather nice to have a couple of days off between trips. It was also a revelation to see how much could be done in an uninterrupted day or two. I completed the house decorating, met up with my dear friend Hanna, and still had time for the garden. I even had time to sit and enjoy my new home. It was wonderful.

Naturally, as this was a cruise ship, the best cabins were retained for paying passengers. Ours were in the bowels of the ship. You know I am particularly conscious about hygiene and will therefore understand how grateful I was, as an officer, to have my own cabin. However, that fact did not help in the end. During one voyage, the toilet drainage system developed a blockage and sewage spilt out. Regrettably, the spillage was within the ship. Within the bowels were we had our quarters. Besides the awful pervading stink, we had to wade thorough ankle deep sewage to get to our workstations. I felt so contaminated and was forever retching. It was only strong self control that prevented me from vomiting everywhere. I used up many sample perfumes to eradicate the smell from myself and the shop. Unfortunately, the problem was not resolved until we returned to port. By then I had lost considerable weight. I had only been six stone at the start. I knew I could not cope with such an experience again and wondered what to do. The decision was made for me. I returned home to find the house had been broken into. Brief discussions with neighbours revealed some people knew my work would keep me away from home for a few days at a time. Most people find such an experience difficult. My hygiene hypochondria meant I felt violated. I definitely could not face the experiences of contamination and violation again. I resigned my commission. At least I would be going home each day. Hopefully that would deter burglars.

34

Ransom

When I told them I was leaving to work on the ship, Mr and Mrs Badger had not wanted me to go, but understood my reasons. They accepted they could not offer a similar salary. It had been the same with the management of my middle of the day job. All had insisted I contact them if I returned to shore for work. While the hours had been long and the pay not as good as it should have been, working at the club had been pleasant enough. Therefore, as I needed to be earning, I went back. This is becoming repetitive, but I also needed something else. The income from the club alone would be insufficient. Yes, you guessed, I went back to the restaurant-pub. The landlord had been delighted to see me and took me back without hesitation. So, here I was again, back into my routine of going from one job to the next with little break. I had secured another cleaning job for the in-between hours. At least the ten o'clock start alleviated some of the strain. I would miss those lovely days off between trips.

My life went on as usual. I continued to work hard and my previous clientele returned once they heard I was back. It was nice but also tiring as they insisted I always serve them and they enjoyed staying late.

A very handsome American started coming to the club. Rob was a gentleman in every sense, as well as intelligent and fun. He became a consistent customer, and we got to know each other well. When we went out he always insisted on taking me for dinner to elegant high-class restaurants and clubs. Evenings out with him were always special. I did not know for a long time that he was a multi-millionaire. His business interests were extensive, and his family owned houses all round the world. Though he often gave me lifts home, I never invited him in. I wanted to ensure there was no misunderstanding about our friendship. One year, on my birthday, he telephoned to wish me a Happy Birthday and told me to look out of the front window. Parked outside was a white Mercedes sports car with a huge white ribbon tied in a bow round it. It staggered me. Goodness knows what the neighbours must have thought. As you are aware, one of my rules is never to be indebted to anyone, particularly a man. Many truly wonderful gifts had been declined upon this premise. Yet again, I felt I had no choice but to refuse. Some of you may think me foolish to have declined such a wonderful gift, but, as you are also aware, I needed to be careful. He was understandably upset and told me it was nothing more than a present from a friend. I knew he was genuine and believed him. Nevertheless, I did not want to take any chances so made my refusal unambiguous. Looking back now, I think I was unduly hard but still consider it was the right decision. He gave the car to his mother, who was a wonderful person, if a little eccentric. She drove all her cars at speed and wrote this one off on a major road outside London. Thankfully, she was unhurt. Apparently, she had done the same with all her cars. It was simply she had been accustomed to excessive wealth all her life. She never gave thought to the loss of a car. Some may think this made her an uncaring, selfish person. On the contrary, I can assure you she was a lovely, warmhearted woman.

One evening Rob and I arranged to meet at my place of work, though I had the night off. Another gentleman, who was very keen on me, happened to be there. He was a wealthy farmer who also had separate business interests. Though I had never given him reason to think it, he considered he had a monopoly on me. It is tiring to have to deal with such attitudes on a regular basis. Why cannot people accept when someone says they want a friendship, they mean just that? I suppose, to be fair, some women like to play the game, but I am not and never have been one. He should have known that. Both had strong characters, so when Rob arrived, there was an unpleasant standoff. An iron band of tension tightened round my chest as the atmosphere intensified. I could see, unless something was done, there would be a fight. I was scared what the result might be as both were physically robust. I hate these types of situations. Have I not seen and experienced enough violence in my life? And this time, it was to be over me. I found the very thought of it horrific. That I should ever be the cause of violence is anathema. Believe me, though it is often portrayed as romantic to have men fight over you, it is anything but. It is ugly and frightening. To prevent any further escalation, I tamed my fear and told them I did not want any unpleasantness, suggesting the three of us go for a meal. Hopefully, some resolution could be reached in a more relaxed atmosphere. Thankfully, both respected me and usually listened to what I had to say. They agreed and at the meal I got them to shake hands. They would never be friends, but at least they parted without any further antagonism. I never saw the farmer again.

Until I met Rob, I never understood why rich people want so many houses. The family was very, very rich, leading to them having to put up with unwanted interest, often from unsavoury individuals. They were all very caring, always ensuring their staff and anyone who had a connection with them were looked after. When one of their butlers was kidnapped, they paid the ransom without question. They kept him close to hand thereafter. Regrettably, this was not their only encounter with kidnappers. Rob's sister was taken by a nasty gang who cut her earlobe off and sent it to the family with their ransom demand. Naturally they paid. She was never the same again. The family constantly moved from house to house without warning. It was their way of trying to stay ahead of the evilly inclined. They always travelled by private jet and dark windowed limousines. Once arrived, his sister never left the grounds of their homes, effectively becoming a prisoner. You may think that was okay because she lived in rich, comfortable surroundings. Not so. A gilded cage is still a cage. It is no way to live. From being a fun-loving, outgoing person, she became a very fearful, despondent, sad shell of herself.

I have to admit I started to have feelings for Rob. He was so different from anyone I had met, and not just because of his wealth. He was a genuine, loving person. Without any prompting or suggesting from me, when he proposed, he included his intention to adopt my son. For once in my life I was in a serious dilemma about whether to accept. Normally, I knew straightaway and would give a prompt refusal. This time I was very tempted because of my feelings and his genuineness. However, one point finally decided the matter. He told me, in view of what the family had already been through, he would employ bodyguards for both of us. Each member of the family, as well as all close associates, had been provided with one. The thought of my son being in jeopardy and having to live with the constant threat worried and horrified me. Sadly, I had to tell Rob I could not face such a life and was afraid to expose my child to such danger. He understood perfectly. If I was determined, he would respect my decision, but we would not be able to see each other again. The merest suggestion of a connection would endanger me and my son. Up to now our friendship had been very low key with him always taking care not to attract attention. This was one of the saddest refusals I have ever made. We never met again, and I heard nothing further of the family. I sometimes wonder if I should have taken the chance. In retrospect though, I think I made the right decision. Many aspire and long for such wealth, but it does have its drawback. Of course, I would have liked to have enough to be comfortable and not to have to worry where the next penny was coming from. But the cost to personal peace of mind and physical security was too high. It was a very real disappointment to lose Rob. One I felt deeply. My life thereafter continued in the usual vein, but without the pleasurable interludes he had provided. It took a while for my emotions to adjust. However, this was thankfully not the end of enjoyable company, though I never felt the same way about anyone else. You may think I made a big mistake in refusing, but I ask you, would you be prepared to place your loved ones in such danger, despite the wealth?

Every few months, Harvey, a chief engineer on an American oil tanker, would show up. He would come for lunch at the restaurant-pub and make a point of waiting for me to serve him. His ship only called in occasionally, so our friendship developed slowly over a long period. He was very open and honest about his life. He told me upfront he was married and had grown children whom he cared for very much. It is so nice when someone is so candid and clear. We got on very well and over time became very good friends. As always, I made sure he understood this was just a friendship. I am glad to say he had no problem with that. I cannot respect anyone who cheats on a partner, no matter how tenuous their relationship may be. Not that Harvey's marriage was. As far as I was aware, it was sound. He frequently spoilt me with lovely gifts from the various places his ship called, as well as meals in good restaurants and clubs. It was one of those rare friendships where we could completely relax in each other's company. We often laughed together, but could also sit quietly with no discomfort. With my busy life, it was in many ways a therapeutic friendship. I was aware he had eventually developed deeper feelings for me, but was very grateful he never attempted to move beyond being friends. Both of us appreciated the enjoyment of what we had.

There was an occasion when he only had a day or two in port and was disappointed we would only see each other once. His next port of call was in Italy, where the ship was due to stay for a week or more. He suggested I take a few days off and visit the same city. We could meet when he was off duty. He offered to arrange the hotel and pay for everything, including the flights. As you will guess, following my usual reserve, I was uncertain. However, by this time, we had been friends for several years and I knew he could be trusted. Nevertheless, I still hesitated. You are aware of how I hate to be indebted to anyone. Two factors finally persuaded me. First, I believed him when he said he really would like my company in Italy. And second, we would not see each other again for some time. He was due to return to America for a protracted period. Also, if truth be told, it was a time when I could do with a break. My work routine was telling again. There was no bar to going as my son was in the Far East. Anyway, he was now an independent adult and would have been able to look after himself.

When I arrived a waiting limousine took me straight to an excellent first-class hotel. Though not what you would call a wealthy man, Harvey was well paid and could afford the best of everything. He had provided his family with an excellent home and paid for his children to go through university. As I said earlier, I believe his marriage was okay, though the strain of not seeing each other for months at a time sometimes told. He had to work during the days but organised with the hotel for me to go on tours of historic sites and beauty spots. He did not want me stuck in a hotel room day after day. One afternoon, I found myself the only person on a coach trip. It would have struck me as strange but for the fact several of the other trips had been under subscribed. We went up onto nearby mountains from which there were fantastic views. The driver and courier were pleasant and treated me with considerable respect. In my naïvety, I thought I was being given special treatment with this selective tour. I became uncomfortable when we were still travelling round six hours later. Evening was drawing in and I wanted to get back before dark, and Harvey and I were due to meet up. I told them I had enjoyed the excursion but had now had enough. The men paid no attention, which disconcerted me. After the attention they had paid me earlier, their change of attitude raised alarm bells. That was until, all of a sudden, we headed back down the hill and to the hotel. As the coach came to a stop, two robust members of the hotel staff immediately appeared at the door. Each took an arm and virtually carried me into the lobby where the manager was waiting. He took me to one side and, after asking if I was all right, told me to take my rings off. I like rings and was in the habit of wearing several at a time. It rather took me aback until he explained. It turned out my 'special trip' had been a kidnap attempt. The men had thought I was a wealthy woman. Partly because of my jewellery and partly because of the high-class hotel. They had telephoned with a ransom demand. The manager, who thankfully was an experienced and sensible man, and accustomed to his country's woeful ways, had told them I had not been able to pay my bill. That was why they had suddenly returned me. You may imagine my gratitude. I consider myself very lucky. There had been several reported incidents of successful kidnappings by the Italian mafia. In many cases, they had killed the victim. I have no idea why I was simply returned and not harmed. The manager thought they were probably new to this type of crime and had panicked. He gave instructions I was never again to be allowed to go anywhere on my own, no matter how close the venue may be. For example, I used to have lunch in a restaurant across the road, but now had to be accompanied by two members of staff. When finished, the restaurant staff would telephone the hotel for someone to collect me. Naturally, Harvey showed his appreciation by paying them well for their protection and service. You will understand this was a very unnerving experience. I have never taken another holiday in Italy.

Eventually, Harvey, who was many years older than me, informed me he was to retire. He enjoyed his job and sailing round the world but the company policy was unambiguous. It was a sad time for us. In retirement, he would live with his wife in America and rarely, if ever, venture back to England. We both enjoyed our friendship so much, we had never thought it would have to end sometime. It seems whenever I find something good in my life, it is taken away, by one means or another. Our last couple of days were spent going out for meals and drinks in nice places. We said our tearful goodbyes and never saw each other again, though we occasionally wrote to each other.

A year or so later, I received a letter from his wife letting me know he had died. She obviously knew about our friendship and I believe, from the tone of her letter, knew it was exactly that. She thanked me for being a friend to Harvey during his absence from home and wished me the best. It was nice of her. I think most women would have been bitter and jealous, not understanding as she did the nature of our relationship.

35

Duped

In the past, gold was considered to be one of the best investments. Therefore, when finances permitted, I invested in some sovereigns. There was a jeweller I got to know, from whom I had purchased a few small pieces, a cross and a couple of rings. I felt he was someone to be trusted and, having bought a few sovereigns from him before, asked if he would get me more. My primary aim was to ensure my son would have financial security in the years to come. He confirmed he would, but before I could collect them he suffered a severe heart attack. Out of respect, I did not want to disturb his family at such a difficult time and therefore did not go to his shop straight away. When I did, I found the shop had closed. I never got those sovereigns. Looking back, I realise it was a bit naïve of me. His relatives were not really that caring. At least I may stand with a clear conscious even though I have missed out on what would have been a valuable investment. I did, however, receive a most unexpected gift from an admirer. Jack was a very wealthy man who could have lived a very comfortable, safe life. However, he and a friend loved the danger and thrill of being racing drivers. Undoubtedly, they could both afford the high octane cars, even if they got written off. One day he called into my place of work to see how I was. We had not seen each other for a while. Knowing I declined gifts, especially from men, he simply placed a sovereign on the counter and left before I noticed. I did not see him again. Why not, I do not know. It was very generous and, as I could not return it, I added it to my small collection that became very handy in later years.

Other than gold, property was the other investment people considered viable. I have always thought it so. Even more so later, as gold became subject to considerably greater fluctuations than it had used to be. I was therefore quite excited when an opportunity arose that enabled me to consider the purchase of a second house. It was on a road not far from the one I lived in. Still a lone woman, I knew a bank or building society mortgage would be impossible. I regret attitudes regarding the viability of single women had not changed yet. A second from the local authority was also out of the question. Not wishing to lose the chance through lack of funds, I, in the first flush of excitement and not giving it proper consideration, rushed to a moneylender. At the time, I thought these were similar to banks but just privately owned. I was about to learn the truth.

Having explained my purpose and financial position, a loan, in principle, was agreed. No papers were completed or signed. Returning home excited at the now possibility of fulfilling my desire, I finally sat down to think it through. The more I thought, the more I doubted the wisdom of borrowing more. As you are aware, except for my mortgage, I had always taken care not to be in debt. Now here I was considering a substantial, additional loan. The more I contemplated, the more uncertain I became. I did not want to lose the house, but at the same time did not wish to overburden myself. Reluctantly, the initial excitement having subsided, I concluded it unwise to proceed. The moneylender was, naturally, unhappy when I informed him. Remember, I had not made any firm commitment, and we had not signed any papers or agreements. Here comes my inherent, and appears eternal, naïvety and innocence again. He asked if I would pass the loan to a man who he knew required such a sum. They would make repayments direct to the company and I would have nothing further to do with it. From his account, it appeared the person really could do with some help. Therefore, out of the kindness of my heart, I agreed upon the understanding all would be as he had said. Naïve or what? You may feel exasperated by my continuing lack of worldliness, but I have always wanted to be able to trust people. That despite my experiences of constantly being let down. Neither then nor now do I fully understand such arrangements. Of course, I have a grasp of the basic principles but no comprehension of all the legal ins and outs. My mortgage is the only such contract I have ever been involved with.

You guessed! The man immediately defaulted. The moneylender then told me I was now responsible for the repayments. As you would expect, after all we had agreed, I was very unhappy, and initially argued the point. However, I made the repayments to ensure I did not create any problems for myself. I needed time to determine what might be done. The solicitor I consulted told me I could have the man who had received the loan taken to the bankruptcy court. I instructed him to do it. However, he was not prepared to go ahead until he met the moneylender to determine the facts. The outcome was, he advised, or rather told, me to carry on paying until the man got out of his problems. Throughout you have read about my earnings and will understand I could not afford the additional expenditure. The purchase of the second house was intended to be an investment that would provide an income. That would have covered all the outgoings associated with the property. As the purchase had not proceeded, I was not in receipt of any further income. Repayments had to be taken from my existing, very limited resources.

This state of affairs continued for sometime with no sign of the man getting out of his problems. I kept on telling the solicitor to take action, but he just did nothing. The ongoing situation depressed me. I had always been careful and now found myself struggling because of other people's exploitation. The whole affair was to last nine years! I had some savings but was determined they would not be touched. As you have seen, I never knew when some circumstance would require my son and I to have access to independent funds. Throughout those years, I remained in a constantly frantic state. I frequently fell to my knees, broke into tears and hit my head on the floor. It was punishment for being so naïve. Not only were the payments draining my meagre fiancees, but I was also afraid my home would become jeopardised by a lack of funds.

Despite the awful experience and my consequent condition, I still wanted to see if I could invest in another property. You may think me crazy, but I was not prepared to let these people deprive me of a valuable investment. Not only for myself but also for my son in the long term. At the time I knew many people who had bought homes in Spain and understood there were sound and secure schemes in place to help finance these purchases. If that was the case, at least my own home would be safe should I decide to go down that road. I frequently discussed with an agent I had been introduced to the possibility of buying a property there. This time, I wanted to make sure I understood all the implications. I mentioned to him what I had been through. Not my usual habit, but I think I just needed to get it off my chest, so to speak. 'You're still paying.', he said. I asked how he knew that. He did not answer. These sorts of people seem to know each other and generally have information about each other's business. He told me, as the loan was technically and legally in my name, the moneylender could put a second mortgage on my house. I did not see how this could be done, but the more I thought, the more worried I became. I went to the department that administered my mortgage to check if they had placed a second mortgage. The clerk looked out the papers and was able to confirm they had not. I breathed a sigh of relief. It was time to bring an end to this. I asked for the outstanding balance. He took a few minutes to calculate it and I saw I had sufficient to pay the total amount. 'That much!' he exclaimed. It was a reasonable amount for those days. I confirmed in the positive. Immediately, I went and got a cheque from the building society. Returning to the office I passed it over and waited for the formalities to be completed. I then received my property documents. At last I was the owner of my house with no one else having an interest. As I had the deeds, I understood nothing could now interfere with my right of ownership. This was prior to the formal governmental property registration system that is in place now. For the first time in many years, I felt a sense of ease.

The whole trauma with the loan was draining and tiring. Therefore, now my home was safe, I felt I could just about afford to take a break. To be honest, I felt it essential for my ultimate wellbeing. To pursue the idea of a property in Spain, I had to go there for a week or two, so off I went. Regrettably, my visit was anything but relaxing. A local agent took me to see several stretches of wild barren wasteland, telling me they were prospective building plots. I could pre-purchase a nice property based on an architect's drawing. To say I was not impressed would be an understatement. To add to this disappointment, one agent persistently tried to persuade me to sleep with him. I returned home very despondent, believing nothing would ever work out for me. I gave up the pursuit of a property in Spain. In light of subsequent events, where those who had made a commitment lost out, I am pleased I stopped.

The situation with the moneylender loan had not changed in my absence, adding to my heightened pessimistic feelings. Eventually, I could take no more. I got a razor and went to the solicitor's premises. Without ceremony, I stormed into his office and shut the door. I shouted, 'Take him to the bankruptcy court as I asked you to do at the beginning. I have sent letters to various people, so the truth will be known. I will commit suicide here and now (*I showed him the razor*) unless you sort this out now!'. He was visibly shaken. I was serious, and he knew it. He said he would telephone straight away. I told him to hold the receiver so I could hear who he was talking to. I suspected he may try to contact his staff to get help. He explained the situation to the moneylender who agreed to bring an immediate end to the affair. Why do people have to be so unreasonable? It took the threat of suicide to terminate something that should never have started. I had believed a sob story and out of the kindness of my heart had wanted to help. But, yet again, I found myself taken advantage of and abused. I wish I could become hardhearted, but even now my son despairs of me. I am still gullible. Prepared to believe anyone. As he says, we both like to see the good in people. He has learnt not to trust anyone, though he does find it very disappointing. It appears the solicitor and moneylender were in cahoots, but would have been hard for me to prove, besides which, I just wanted to be free of it all. I have simply outlined the facts rather than go into all the depths of despair I felt and the physical effects upon me. I will simply say, it was a very unhappy and desperate nine years I endured.

Though the majority of people I worked with, and customers were reasonably pleasant, I no longer felt I could sustain round the clock working. After so many years of burning the candle in every possible way, my health was starting to suffer again. I constantly felt strained, stressed, and weary. I was also tired of having to avoid or deal with unwanted attentions. Though I had paid the mortgage and had no debts, I would still need an income for day-to-day expenses and utility bills. I decided to open my home as a Bed and Breakfast establishment. A difficult decision for me because I consider my home sacrosanct and have never liked having people in my private space. However, needs must. Yet again, and for the last time, I submitted my resignations to Mr and Mrs Badger and the landlord of the restaurant-pub. They were sad to be losing me for good this time, but kindly understood how I felt. They all agreed I should take care of myself for a change.

I am not a businesswoman and was not sure how to attract custom. I did have the foresight to let a nearby local theatre have my details, which resulted in the occasional actor or ballerina staying. The local social security department found out I had set up my little business. I assume this was from my registration as a new concern. They contacted me to say they could provide suitable guests for extended periods. I did not realise then what sort of people they sought accommodation for. I soon learnt. Here are just a couple of examples of the people sent to me. A young man kept leaving the door open. I told him not to but he continued to ignore my instruction. When I asked him why, he said it was so friends could come in. One of my rules was no visitors. Something I always made clear from the start. I warned him, if he continued to leave the door open he would have to go. The matter was subsequently taken out of my hands. One evening, answering the doorbell, I was greeted by the sight of police holding the boy. He was naked, with only a blanket wrapped round. One of the policemen explained they had simply come to collet the boy's belongings. His naked state had shocked me and I could not help asking him what he had done. Adding that I had treated him as a mother and why could he not behave? I never knew what he had done and never saw him again. Terribly sad, he was not very old and I think could have been a nice person. Perhaps drugs or some other vice had got the better of him.

Then there was the rude, abusive, dirty, disrespectful young girl. I did try to persevere with her, but in the end had to acknowledge her a lost cause. She had no respect for anything or anyone in the house and I needed to think of the other guests to whom she was constantly rude. I should have realised she was a problem person when the social security insisted they pay me direct rather than let her have the money. When I told her she had to leave she became extremely violent and pushed me down the stairs. My shoulder struck a storage heater at the bottom very hard. Besides it being dislocated, I was bruised all over, particularly my back and was limping for sometime after. I understand after being relocated, she asked if she could return. I think, too late, the girl realised how well off she had been with me. Staff from the social security department came round with flowers and apologised for their 'clients' behaviour. However, matters did not cease there. There were other unpleasant people, situations, and events to the point I declined any further custom from them. Some managers or supervisors, I am not sure what their role was, came to discuss the issue, but I was adamant. They apologised again, saying they had tried to be careful who they sent, inferring these had been the better ones. I hate to think what the others would have been like.

The neighbours I told you about also ran their home as a bed-and-breakfast. Due to their drinking contacts and immorality, they were often full. On those occasions the woman would ask if I had a vacancy to accommodate those she could not. I would have preferred to refuse outright, but I needed the income. Nevertheless, I insisted upon meeting the person first and only agreed if I judged them to be reasonably okay. I say reasonably, because most of her clientele were very dodgy people. She paid me one pound per night. It was not until much later, when some friends told me I was being used, I learnt she was charging far more but not passing it onto me. One pound may seem a bargain to people today, but as I regularly point out, these were days when money had a greater and more realistic value.

Besides the troublesome people described, I had one long-term private guest. He was an elderly retired gentleman whose family did not want him with them. They constantly tried to put him into a retirement home, which he had made clear he did not want. How uncaring families can be. I did my best to ensure he had enough to eat and stayed warm. I kept the house and rooms very clean and provided a full breakfast for everyone. I also gave him, and any other guest who happened to be resident, Sunday lunch. Things became a little difficult when he formed more than a general attachment for me. I had to ensure, as gently as possible, he understood there would never be anything between us. He gave me lovely boxes of chocolates and wonderful bouquets, which he said were to show his appreciation for my care. I judged it was genuine, so continued to accept his gifts as long as they were appropriate. He remained with me until I ceased to operate as a bed-and-breakfast concern. He was very sad when he had to move. I think he rented a room somewhere else. I felt sorry for him. He was a refined gentleman who should have been able to enjoy a peaceful, settled retirement, but he was unwanted by his own.

On top of all these problematic situations, you will understand how I constantly felt vulnerable with strangers in the house. To try and counteract the fear, I implied to my guests I was not alone. I did this by calling out to a fictitious son and husband who were supposedly in the private rooms. Thankfully, it was never put to the test. After a year or so, it was apparent I was never going to make any real money out of the venture. I also constantly felt stressed and strained. Yet another disappointment. The venture was supposed to have made my life a little easier, but did anything but. I decided to abandon my business. I judged my savings, together with the money my son and sister were sending, would be sufficient for my needs.

36

Cheated

When my son returned from the Far East he was stationed in the West Country. Then, after completing his final tour of duty in a local barracks, he decided to remain there in civilian life. By this time, I no longer wanted to be, nor felt I could cope, on my own. I missed my son very much and decided, with the advancing years, I would like to be near him. Therefore, very reluctantly, I sold my home. You may imagine, after all I had been through to get it, I found parting with it a bit traumatic and confess to having cried when leaving for the last time. I still remember it with great fondness and affection. My son tried to find me a suitable house before my move, but after a year of searching had found nothing to my taste. He therefore arranged for me to rent a flat in the same building as his. Because he had his own life and friends, we would not live together, but intended to be within easy reach of each other. It took several more months before I found anything I would even consider. Housing in the West County was very different from what I was accustomed to. If I am honest, I was very upset we would not be sharing a house. However, I understood my son's wish to maintain the independence of his own home that he had accomplished since leaving the forces. We need to allow our children to find their own way in life, as much as it can hurt at times.

I lost one house because I felt the need to have a private building survey. The surveyor took so long to get his findings to me that the vendor accepted another offer while I was waiting. I was very cross. The survey had cost a substantial amount, leading me to expect a more efficient service. I had also quite liked the property. Without going through an unpleasant complaints procedure, there was little I could do. Perhaps I should have followed it through, but I was tired and just wanted to find a home. Anyway, the likely amount I could have recovered after costs would not have been very much. The hassle it would have involved just did not seem worth it. Eventually, I found a much smaller place in the centre of town. It had a garden that was completely surrounded by a twelve-foot wall. That provided a sense of security, especially as I would be living on my own in a strange district. It seems to be my lot that nothing should ever go smoothly. It transpired, the local authority had placed an order declaring the property unfit for human habitation until certain works had been undertaken. The vendor, who was a relative of the deceased owner, had already had the work done but had not obtained the release. In the end, my son and I traipsed round the ten storey local authority offices, following the relevant forms from one department to another. We succeeded in getting the release order, although we were both exhausted by the end. It was a tiny house making it difficult to get my furniture in. We managed, though the rooms were very overcrowded. Over time, I was able to make it reasonably comfortable, though I never really relaxed. I felt vulnerable all the time.

It was during this time I decided to visit my homeland for the purpose I outline in the following pages. You may or may not have gathered I have never recovered from my mama's passing. I still miss her terribly and would love to be able to embrace her again. I have sometimes dreamt we are together, laughing and hugging the way we used to. It is difficult to explain my emotions. I think because I was so young and so very attached to her, the shock of her sudden, untimely death imbedded itself into my being. I have never been able to say a final farewell. I long for her and think I will until the day I die, and probably thereafter if we do not meet.

I decided building some sort of memorial would be an ideal way to pay tribute to such a wonderful woman. You may consider me bias, and naturally I am, but you will come to see I am far from alone in my assessment. At first I thought of a chapel where mama would be honoured for the loving, caring person she had been. However, the diocese bishop was not particularly forthcoming. I had not been asking for mother to be beatified or canonised. I simply wanted her to be recognised for her goodness and kind works. This fell on deaf ears despite the fact I was prepared to pay for everything. Therefore, to at least have something, I decided to see if I could renovate the old family home. I would then add a monument to mama's memory. As I have said elsewhere, several people in the village still remember her goodness and beauty. Several have good cause to be grateful for her loving care.

Through the years, whenever my son and I went over, besides seeing Anna and Christopher in the metropolis, we also visited my eldest sister Helen, who still lived in the village. My son loved staying in their antiquated home. It has always been one of his favourite places. A traditional house of the period with no inside oven or toilet. The latter was at the top of the garden. Delightful in winter! Roasting was done in a clay kiln built in the garden. Wood was burnt until reduced to charcoal when my sister would put the tray of food in. There is nothing like the taste of food cooked this way. We both love it. My brother-in-law's wine completed these meals. He used his own grapes that were trodden by foot in the traditional manner. He then left the wine to ferment for a year in wooden barrels. I have never tasted anything that comes close. It truly enhanced all our meals. Villagers are proud of their own wines and always proffer theirs as the best available. However, they openly acknowledged there was none to compare with my brother-in-law's. Thankfully, drunkenness was never a social problem in those days. People only drank when they ate and never to excess. There was none of the British habit of trying to drink as much as possible within a limited space of time. I suppose, to be fair, this was assisted by the fact there were no licensing hours, as in the British Isles.

Although we visited my sister several times, we had never gone up to the family estates, which were within the highest regions of the village. I felt a visit to the place where I had lived my happiest years was long overdue. I also now had plans for it. Accordingly, I set out to find our old family home and estates on my own, as neither my sister nor her husband were able to accompany me. My sister could no longer walk far as her legs and feet gave her a lot of pain. My brother-in-law was becoming frail and consequently limited in his movements. Neither was my son with me on this occasion. Following the road up through the village, it surprised me how well I remembered the way and surroundings as I had been very young when last there. I even recognised houses which were now broken shells and wrecks, whose original occupants I could still recall. On the way up I met several people, many of whom were astounded at how accurate my recollections were. They had lived in the village all their lives but could not recall some things until I reminded them. From what you have read so far, you will appreciate I have a remarkably good memory. Thankfully, age has not diminished it.

Finally reaching the area, I became excited when I glimpsed our old house. It harboured so many memories of childhood and mama. I am sure, having read through my early history, you will appreciate what seeing it again had been like for me. Sadly, my joy was short-lived. Someone had taken adverse possession of the house and surrounding land. When I broached the point with them, they became very aggressive and almost physically violent. Time revealed them to be uneducated, basic (*almost animalistic*), and very rough people. I returned to my sister very upset. My intent to restore our home to its former glory was now thwarted. Helen told me neither she nor any of her family had been up there for many years. I was really cross. How could they have let someone take our home and lands? In fairness, I must acknowledge my sister had a lot of problems in her early married life. I mentioned these earlier on. She had struggled simply to exist. Our house and lands had therefore not been at the forefront of her mind.

The law authorised me, because I had lived outside the country, to reclaim our property. I could have the present occupier thrown out, and if I wished, the house bulldozed flat. The last thing I would have wanted. I am not a vindictive person, though I have to admit in this instance I did feel very bitter. It would have been within my rights to make these people homeless and see them thrown on to the streets. That would have been the result of any legal action on my part. I simply could not do that. It took a while, but eventually I managed to reason with the occupier. I would only take back the small piece of land where our clay oven and woodpile had originally been. It was much smaller than I would have liked, but at least it was where my mama had walked and worked. It was her memory I was determined to preserve more than anything else.

At the time, there was only one person who could authorise the building of a house in our district. He drew up plans for a nice, though small dwelling. The dimensions of my little plot decided that. Besides being a council official, he was also an architect. Once the area planning authority had approved the plans, I engaged him to build the house. In my historic naïvety, I had thought all such people were to be trusted, especially as he was responsible to the authorities. Later I learnt, in my land you have to be present every moment construction is underway, otherwise things are not done correctly, or honestly. I also came to understand, corruption and bribery are considered normal acceptable practices. I had obviously been away too long, and from a too early age, to comprehend my people's woeful habits. It hurt. The architect kept asking for more money, which I had to take out from England. Our meetings to hand over the cash became so frequent, staff at the hotel cafe, where we met, eventually asked if I was building a hotel. Building costs those days were low and they could not believe I was handing so much over for a house. I also became concerned about the amount, but too late, as work was nearing completion. There was also the fact that my people can be ruthless if you question them in their professional capacity. Reprisals can be very nasty indeed. Wishing to avoid any unpleasantness and not desiring to get involved in a court case, I said nothing. That sounds very weak, but I really needed to be careful.

To add to my stress and upset at the continuing demands for more money, on one of my currency delivery trips, I was robbed at the capital's railway station. They lifted my passport and a few thousand pounds from my handbag. I always paid the architect in cash. His request. The shock was terrible, especially considering that the city was then considered one of the safest, crime-free places to visit. The police's attitude, who were anything but helpful, made the situation worse. We, my son was with me on this occasion, were sent from one side of the city to the other. No one was in the least bit interested in helping. Naturally, we went to the British Embassy where the locally employed staff proved so rude and unhelpful I stormed out. It was not just their rudeness. Since escaping my son's father I had learnt to stand up for myself and expect to be treated with respect and consideration. I was not prepared to allow these bureaucratic mini officials treat me as a person of no consequence. In normal circumstances I may have challenged them, but by this time I was stressed, exhausted, and exasperated. I would not return when they shouted after me. Belatedly, they had realised their mistake in treating me so badly.

I apologise if this all reads like a list, but I do not wish to bore you with endless details and have therefore opted for simply highlighting the main event points. To cut a very long story short, I ended up with a very small, badly built house. All the trimmings and accessories shown in the architect's plan had been omitted. I was very disappointed with the end product. However, to try and rectify it would have meant taking out a lawsuit. In my country, even now, you do anything you can to avoid involvement with any legal action or the courts. Some people have spent their lives trying to sort out such matters. Often there is a concurrent ongoing feud that can take violent forms. I really had no choice but to accept the end result.

To make the house habitable, I bought some nice furniture for which the shop owners overcharged because they knew I lived abroad. In those days they seemed to think, if you came from another country you were very rich and therefore entitled to be cheated. I had always believed our people to be as sophisticated and decent as my family. Regrettably, I quickly discovered this was not the case. You have read enough of my story to know how upsetting this was for me. I had always been proud of my heritage and now had to face the unpleasant realities of modern day behaviours.

In remembering those precious days with mama, far too few, I was also interested to know what had happened to the baby mama had looked after. After mama's untimely passing, papa had concluded it inappropriate for us to keep him. After all, my sisters and I were still children ourselves. I am not entirely sure what my motivations were. For sure, I wished to know if he still lived, and if so, what he had done with his life. I admit, at the same time, I had felt a small degree of resentment. Of course, I knew it had not really been his fault mama had died early. He had been an abandoned baby who needed looking after. In case you are wondering, one thing I had been sure of is that I had no desire to exact any sort of retribution or revenge. It really had not been his fault. My dilemma was how to find him. There were few from the adult generation of the time still about, but I did know the old teacher still lived in the village. At first he thought I was my sister Anna, but then recalled when I reminded him how young I had been at the time. Upon asking if he knew the man, as he would be now, I was concerned to see a troubled, shadowy expression pass across his features. Looking straight into my eyes, he told me it would be best to leave things alone. I said I would just like to meet the man and see how he had turned out. I did not want anything else. He firmly told me his advice was to leave well alone. And, then added, that anyway he did not know him. An evident lie, but I sensed well meant. He repeatedly continued with his advice to forget. Then, presumably to change the topic, he was clearly determined not to say more, told me he had written a brief history of the village. Would I like a copy? My grandfather and father were both mentioned. They were both important characters in our society. When thanking him for the book, I asked if he was sure he would not tell me more. 'Leave it alone dear.' This time, there had been no mistaking the warning in his voice. It certainly left me with the distinct impression it would be dangerous to continue with my inquiries. I wondered what could possibly be wrong. Had he turned out to be such a bad lot? I asked the odd question of others in the village, but with no success. Neither did the little history book prove of any help. The teacher has since passed away. I still wanted to know who the baby became, but also sensed it would have been dangerous for me to continue. Not just for me, but also for my sister, who was still living in the village at the time, and perhaps even my son. I no longer ask and have to accept I will never know what became of the baby my mama had so lovingly cared for. He would most certainly have died without her.

My son and I still lived in the West Country, but I was not really happy there. I felt lonely and vulnerable. My son visited twice a week, which was great, but he had his individual life and friends and wished to continue living in his own house. I should mention he came close to marriage a couple of times, but things did not work out. After nine months, I saw no point continuing in this unsatisfactory state. I decided to go and live in my home village. Selling the house was easy as all the work had been done and I had made it an attractive, centrally appointed property. Leaving my son was my one concern, but he would visit from time to time. Life, I felt, would be preferable as, even now, people have no thought of being robbed or mugged. It just does not happen in this primarily rural district. People often leave keys hanging in door locks, irrespective of whether they are in or not. Just imagine what would happen in Britain should people take into their heads to act similarly.

Prior to returning to England from my last visit, I had agreed with the architect for the property to be painted inside and out. I returned to find they had sprayed the outside, but had left the inside in the same state as the plasterer had left it. A further result of me not being on the spot. In summer, there is always a lot of sand and dust. Therefore, before I could do anything, I needed to clean from top to bottom. I had been looking forward to painting the inside and making the house a home, but before I could, the weather changed. It became very cold and snowed heavily. Quite a phenomenon, as it hardly ever snows in this region. There was no heating, as we had primarily built the house for summer use. I was freezing. My sister, upon seeing the inclement weather, became concerned for my welfare and sent her elderly husband up the hill with a hot meal and some of his gorgeous wine. I felt really sorry for him as it had obviously been a struggle nevertheless, you will understand how grateful I was. In all honesty, I am not sure I would have pulled it through without that meal. The cold had me shaking violently. I suspect I would have developed hypothermia without the warming nourishment.

When the warmer weather returned, I continued with my original plans. The ceilings were a nightmare to paint. They are far higher than those we mostly encounter in England. To this day I do not know how my neck was not badly damaged. A recurring theme in my life. When the paint had dried, I added ornaments and paintings. The large painting I had been given in Southern Ireland had pride of place, high on the main wall. A further result of me not being on the spot was, while the house had been under construction, the builders had not been careful to secure it against wildlife. There are a lot and some, like snakes and scorpions, are dangerous. Some small lizards, which are rife in the area, had taken the opportunity to establish their home within the house. Spotting a few going behind the large painting, I stood on a trunk to reach them. I did not want them cohabiting with me. The painting came away and I fell heavily onto the solid floor, landing on my hip. I think I must have been unconscious for a while because I was in a daze when I became aware again. Amazingly, I was able to get up and walk. Thankfully, my hip appeared undamaged despite the heavy fall.

I will break for a moment to tell you of an incident that gratified me. One day, when walking through the village, a man I did not recognise suddenly rushed up and grasped me in a bearhug. He held me so close I felt the intense emotion reverberating within him. Much to my relief, he eventually released his grip and stepped back. He then told me, when he was a boy, he lived just above our house. The query in my eyes must have been obvious. Then I noticed his limp. In those long off days, especially in rural societies, folklore and superstition abounded. Any form of disability had been viewed as a punishment from God, or a curse for some wrongdoing. The locals believed any association with such a person, even a relative, would also condemn them. Consequently, those who suffered any such condition were ostracised. They had forced this poor boy to live in a small shack hidden within the edge of the forest. The shack had been no better than those used for goats or pigs. He went on to tell me, if it had not been for my mother he would have died. She had fed and clothed him as well as de-flea him. She cared for him when ill and taught him how to look after himself. I thanked him for remembering. My worries of no one doing so now alleviated. Because of her, he had lived a full life and even married. Most of these people had been unable to find decent employment or a life partner. He considered the fact he was now in his fifties nothing short of a miracle. By virtue of his wife coming into an inheritance, he had been able to establish a successful tree growing business. He gave me a lovely olive tree in memory of my dear mama.

I continued with my work round the house and, when needing a break from that, clearing the vastly overgrown garden. It was while doing this I discovered the mass of brilliant red germaniums mama had planted. The tall dry grasses had been hiding them from view. It thrilled my heart to see them, something mama and I had enjoyed together. Thankfully, this variety survives on its own, without the need for any human input. When digging the hard dry ground round them, I found their roots go deep and far, seeking out water supplies. Very successfully it seems. This was also when I introduced some trees and plants into the small garden. The olive tree has pride of place. As I am now not there often to nurture it, it only produces a few olives, but those it does are rich and tasty. After a planting session I went to the fully tiled bathroom to clean up. Some water must have spilt on the floor because I suddenly found myself in midair. It is not a large room, so I ended up bouncing from one item of bathroom furniture to another. I struck the side of the bath and then came down on the toilet basin mouth first. After, I bounced from the sink onto the hard floor. This time I was definitely unconscious for some while. When I came round, I was in a lot of pain and had great difficulty getting onto my knees, let alone my feet. My back, mouth, and shoulder hurt terribly. The mirror reflected a face of multiple colours, green, yellow, blue, red, pink, white, and more. I attempted to sort myself but realised something was seriously wrong. I therefore struggled to the only doctor in the village. He has since died and there is no village doctor. After applying some first aid he sent me to the nearest hospital. They said I had to go to the major hospital in a city some two to two and a half hour train journey away. Added to which there are only three or four trains a day. Remember, in my homeland, there was no national health service and the medical expertise was limited back then. Thankfully, this has changed in recent years. More and more doctors train overseas and then return. Though in considerable pain, I had to make the journey to a city I did not know on my own. Finally arriving, the doctors immediately ordered an x-ray of my shoulder. I had to wait some time during which I saw a dog brought out. When I challenged the staff about it, they became unfriendly and aggressive, denying having x-rayed the animal. There was little I could do, especially as I was a stranger on my own in an unfamiliar place. My x-ray confirmed the doctor's suspicion that my shoulder was dislocated. In order to reset it, he summoned four waiting patients and told them to hold me down. It brought back all my memories of the Gestapo, traumatising me further. I managed to overcome my fear long enough for the doctor to yank the shoulder back into place. The pain was excruciating. He then made me give each man money. With no health system, I had to pay for every consultation and treatment, but giving money to other patients for basically traumatising me was a bit rich. As you would expect, my arm and shoulder needed to be placed in a cast with a supportive bandage. I hardly believed my ears as he told me to go and buy the requisite materials. He could not have cared less when I said I did not know the city or where the chemists were. Belligerently, he simply repeated his instruction to go and get the materials. Just imagine if that happened in this country. I managed to find a pharmacy and also my way back to the hospital. After setting my shoulder in plaster, he told me I had to stay in the city for a few days. Again, I told him I was a stranger to the city and had nowhere to stay. He just told me to find a hotel. It is hard for us who are used to a national health service to appreciate the impact of not having one.

The unsatisfactory behaviour and concern about whether the right treatment had been given or if they had set my shoulder correctly led to my decision to return to England. I tried to telephone my son, but without success. In those days, the international telephone line was subject to timing barriers. If a call was not answered within a specified number of seconds, the line automatically cut off. With that and my son not often being home because of his busy life, I never got through. This was before mobile telephone technology was commonplace. In the end I decided to make my own way back. To add to my troubles, the airline would not honour my return ticket. It was one of those where the return date is fixed and under their rules cannot be changed. I explained my situation, which from my physical condition they could see for themselves, but they would not budge. Left with no alternative, I had to purchase a one-way ticket. Fares from my homeland then were considerably more expensive in comparison to England and other countries. The amount was extortionate and took what money I had remaining. The medical, travelling, and hotel expenses had been substantial. You have seen how I have always been careful with money. To be left yet again without any was almost incomprehensible.

My son had now bought his own house, to which he had given me a key. He was at work when I arrived, so I let myself in and waited in the hall, disconsolate and a little fearful. I was not sure if I would be welcome, having turned up without any warning. Looking back I realise how foolish that was. When he did not appear at the time I expected I became anxious. An hour or so later he arrived, having stopped for groceries on the way home. As you will comprehend, he was surprised to see me standing there. I burst into tears at the sight of him, someone I knew and loved. He hugged me and let me weep.

Eventually, my tears subsided, and I was able to explain. His new home was just down the road from the local hospital to which he immediately took me. The duty doctors confirmed my shoulder had been set properly and there were no other injuries they could see. In time, it came to light I had a hairline fracture through my spine and a vertically split tooth. The result of having struck the toilet basin.

Once rested and recuperated, I turned my thoughts to the future. As my new house in the village was to be my home, I decided to take those possessions I particularly wished to have around me. I carried what I could with me. With the limited weight allowance, flying was not really viable, though I made the journey a couple of times. Having considered various options, including the rail journey we had made in previous years, I settled on inexpensive coach travel. There was no limit on weight or how many pieces of luggage you could take. Despite all the difficulties encountered in these journeys, I made the trip several times. Rather than bore you with every experience, I will simply highlight some incidents. These will give you a general idea of what it was like.

One driver smoked non-stop. In itself unnerving as he continued to take out cigarettes and light them while driving. It was also very unpleasant for us non-smokers with the constant smoke haze. His driving also gave my fellow passengers and me the impression he was continually drunk. We became really frightened when the engine stalled and he started poking about in it with a lit cigarette hanging from his mouth. I shouted for him to move away. He was so stubborn, or thick, he did not move until I pointed out it was his face that would get burnt. Even then he had to be told to put the cigarette out before returning to the engine. Regrettably, in every trip, the drivers proved as ignorant and rude as this one. These were long journeys, lasting several days. Without the potential for proper rest, I chose to sit inconspicuously at the back, hoping for some degree of peace there. Many of my fellow travellers proved to be of low moral character, flirting and indulging in base acts with other passengers. On one trip, the driver was clearly looking for such interaction and insisted upon me siting in one of the front seats. I resisted as much as I could, but had to be wise because we were at the driver's mercy throughout the journey. The way he kept looking in the rearview mirror annoyed and concerned me. First, it was irritating, frustrating and embarrassing, and second, it meant he kept taking his eyes off the road. These trips were additionally exhausting for me. The general state of the toilets we stopped at, and my dislike of using public bathroom facilities, led to me eating and drinking as little as I could. Thankfully, I had a strong constitution and was able to wait until I got home. However, I joined my fellow passengers in open objection when one driver tried to stop us from having any food or drink on the coach. The period between stops was considerable, and it was often hot. If nothing else, we needed water. Even this hardened man could not resist such an open reaction. He had no option but to succumb to the democratic consensus. You may be wondering why I had not simply had my possessions shipped out. Quite honestly, it never occurred.

I sought to take us much as possible, which meant my suitcases were very heavy. This became a problem for the part of my journey that had to be undertaken by ferry. We were responsible for getting our luggage onboard, without assistance. On one occasion I did not know which was my ship and had stood on the dockside pondering. Finally, determining the correct one, I had to move my suitcases to it. This time I had really filled my larger ones and could barely lift them. I struggled to move one an inch, literally, and then another. I really could not lift them because, besides being heavy, I was by this time very rundown, tired, and undernourished. The ferry crossing occurs toward the end of the trip. Panic rose when I thought I would be unable to get to the ship before it sailed. I would have been in a right pickle then. Strange place, no accommodation, and not a vast amount of money. It turned out a senior police officer had been observing me, though I had noticed. He very kindly sent one of his constables to help. I was so grateful, but did not know if it would be in order for me to tip him or not. Quickly deciding, I tried to slip some money into his hand, but he politely pulled back, bowed, and said it had been his pleasure to help. Life can hold pleasant surprises at times.

One more event I would like to tell you about. On one of my return trips, to be my last, as it turned out, the driver unexpectedly told us to get off in the centre of a capital city. This was so there would be space for some friends of his. I was incensed and told him my ticket had been booked months in advance. My habit was to always buy a return ticket. He was clearly taken aback by this news. Apparently, most travellers purchased their tickets at the last minute. However, he still continued to insist I and the others disembark. We were next to a public park with no sign of a coach station or any other official building. Some of the men and a handful of the women had not been fussed about the random spot. This confused me until I realised, from the way they eyed each other, an indulgent night was anticipated. I was not having any of that, neither were the remainder of my female companions. We blocked the door and insisted the driver, at the very least, contact the firm's office. We also pointed out we had people waiting for us at our destination. One young man was blind and I ended up assisting him. Eventually, in response to the call we had demanded, someone from the company's local office turned up. Ultimately, after a lot of nonsense, they got us onto an England bound hovercraft. Why the hovercraft? Partly because there were no further ferries that night and partly to make up the hours lost during the fiasco.

At the other end, my son had become concerned because we were several hours overdue. He went to the travel office, but at first the staff did little. Frustrated and worried, he strolled round the coach station noting as he went others waiting. Enquiring first the coach or bus they were expecting, he gathered together quite a few awaiting our arrival, including the parents of the blind man. Confronted by so many people, the office staff had no choice but to contact their European colleagues. Initially, the coach driver could not even be found. After a few hours, during which my son kept badgering the firm's employees, he and the others were informed we were on our way. I cannot describe the relief everyone felt when we eventually pulled into the British coach station and saw our loved ones.

All this just gives you some idea of what it was like to travel with this terrible company. Both in Europe and the United Kingdom, when anyone endeavoured to highlight the problems, the staff were neither interested nor prepared to do anything. I have not travelled by this means again. Anyway, I doubt I would survive it now.

37

Menacing

Though I had carried many possessions to my new home, there were still others I would have liked around me. Memories, I thought, were now all that was left of my turbulent life. Little did I know there was more to come. How to transport those treasures became the issue. It was evident I could not move them travelling by conventional means. I was certainly not prepared to undergo the horrors of the coach journeys again. My son had stored my remaining belongings in his spare double bedroom, hall, and dining room. He had insisted on keeping the sitting room and kitchen clear, so there was somewhere to relax without being surrounded by packing cases, suitcases, boxes, and packages. He did some research and after discussing the matter, we decided to ship some articles. As said, this would enable me to have items around that brought back memories of my eventful life. They would also help make my home more comfortable. To that end, he contacted various shipping firms, eventually settling for one of the more well-known companies.

Regrettably, although the firm had an excellent reputation for both national and international transportation, it turned out to be one of the worst decisions for us. Perhaps it was just the branch we worked with, but we both agreed we would never use them again. We have not, though we have since had more items shipped out. My son carefully arranged the delivery date with the agents. This was so we could be at the receiving end to deal with customs clearance. In the meantime, I returned to the house to prepare for the arrival of my belongings. My son kept in regular contact with the agents and gave them a contact address and telephone number to use in the event of any changes. He was consequently furious when he found out, at the last minute, they had put our container on a different ship with a different arrival date. The agents had not bothered to let him know. If he had not regularly asked for an update, we would have been unaware of the change. When he went to confront the office personnel, they greeted him with indifference and a complete lack of concern. My son normally has a very placid disposition, but this was too much for him. He lost his temper big time. The female staff became scared and everyone moved to the other side of the office and stood with their backs to the wall. One had the sense to summon a supervisor. Once apprised of the circumstances, he appreciated the difficulty the unwarned of change had created. Thankfully, he was far more level-headed than his colleagues and spoke with my son in a sensible and helpful manner. When taking his leave, my son made clear he would direct any consequent problems or additional costs to them.

In the meantime, I had returned to the United Kingdom as, from the original information provided, we had not expected delivery for another month or so. The change of ship meant we quickly had to obtain air tickets and arrange a hotel in my homeland's capital. We could have both done with some breathing space in which to relax, but there was no time. We had to find the local shipping agent assigned to deal with our consignment quickly. It took some time. His office was hidden away on an upper floor of a large building in a downtown area we did not know. It was just as well we had not wasted time in finding him. When we had, he told us he had been given to understand, because of the different ship, my possessions had already arrived in the local port. At the time, strict customs clearance procedures prevailed. The legal owner had to be present, in person, to deal with the authorities. A member of the agent's staff and we immediately travelled to the port, which was some distance from the office. There was no such thing as the luxury of a car. We had to use public transport. I was still suffering with the hairline fracture through my spine, and the further aggravation caused by the jolting transport made the journey a painful one. Upon arrival, we discovered the shipping company had, yet again, misinformed us. The ship had not berthed. A couple of days later we were told it had now definitely arrived. We went to the agent to confirm and arrange for clearance and collection. In order to avoid another pointless trip, the waste of his staff's time, and further pain to me, we asked the man to telephone beforehand to ensure the container was actually there. He simply ignored us. I regret to say, my countrymen can be obstinate and very unhelpful. They certainly do not believe in stressing themselves. We pointed out it was not just our time that could be wasted but also his staff's, who he had to pay. I certainly had no desire to undertake another painful trip unless absolutely necessary. These people seem to think by displaying such disregard they are proving their superiority. Ignorant fools. He continued to ignore us until my son, in his frustration, lost his cool, and shouted at him in his own language. We had been speaking English up to then. It staggered me. First, because my son is usually mild-mannered and second, because I had not realised how much of my language he had gleaned. He had been fluent as a boy, but over the years of non-regular use had forgotten much. He now flowed in clear, and frighteningly fierce vocabulary. To our utter exasperation, the agent's response was simply to say okay and pick up the telephone. It was as well we had insisted, as the container had not been unloaded. When we left the office, I told my son I had not realised he could speak the language so well. He said he found it did flow when he lost his temper, but not otherwise. There were to be a couple of other occasions in the years to come when I witnessed it again. Perhaps the loss of temper removes his natural reserve.

Subsequent to this upsetting time, we needed to get back into the city centre to deal with other matters. Getting from and to the agent's office necessitated a lengthy walk through claustrophobic grimy, hot streets, which in itself was tiring. The combination of the two, upset and walk, left us feeling the need to unwind. Once our other work had been completed, we enjoyed a relaxing meal in one of the lovely open-air restaurants, which abound in a particularly attractive historic area of the city. However, our problem day was not yet ended. We returned to the hotel to discover the key to our room would not work. It was late at night. In the warmer climate it is normal practice not to eat until late on. A member of the night staff tried to open the door for us, but without success. He said we would have to stay in a different room until the morning when management could call a contractor. Reading between the lines, I think he did not want to be held responsible for the cost of calling someone out there and then. We refused point blank. All our possessions were in the room and we could not be sure whether someone had broken in. The situation became tense. We, however, stood our ground until he called a locksmith. I failed to explain this was a time before electronic locks. This hotel, like most at the time, still used traditional brass locks and keys. Thankfully, there had been no break in, but we felt exhausted again. Could nothing go right for us?

Just a little bit more about this hotel. It was one I had found when flying into the country on my own. At the time, the national airport had been in a city suburb. Convenient, you would think, and indeed it was if you had your own transport. However, the taxi drivers always argumentatively demanded excessive fares. It could get very unpleasant, especially for a woman on her own. Wishing to avoid any further such encounters, I had looked for alternative transport and discovered the airline provided inexpensive coach transfers to their city office. This turned out to be in another downtown district.

I had not felt up to carrying my luggage into the city proper, so looked for suitable nearby accommodation and noted a hotel just a little way up a side street. Though it was clear I was not the type of guest they were used to, the reception gentleman treated me with courtesy and respect. I had subsequently stayed there each time I flew. Owing to its downtown location I never considered it wise, as a lone woman, to venture out after dark, however, when my son was with me we would stroll up to the city proper and enjoy late night meals and walks through the historic districts. The cool of the night air provided a pleasant respite from the intense afternoon heat. Returning from one of these outings, along the now darkened, poorly lit streets, we noted a surprising number of people standing about. Most were tall, beautifully dressed, fully made-up women. Or so we thought. It had not been until we heard a couple of them speaking we realised they were men. To be honest, they would have put many women to shame. They looked so elegant. It transpired this was a district where transvestites gathered. When we entered reception we noted a couple of these 'women' nervously glancing at us. We had not realised the hotel, though accepting traditional guests, catered for the 'ladies' and their clients and friends. I have to acknowledge, as my son can attest from when he lived in the Far East, these men do wear fantastically beautiful outfits and look great. However, I became concerned about the possibility of disease. This was a time when sexually transmitted disease formed a consistent part of news headlines. The bathrooms always looked clean, though with my hygiene hypochondria, I always gave them a further scrub.

So, from that point of view, I felt okay. Nevertheless, the thought continued to play in the back of my mind. We therefore stopped using that hotel, eventually finding one nearer the city centre. I rarely flew in on my own thereafter.

When the container was finally ready, we went to the port with one of the agent's young men. He told us to wait to one side while he found the customs officer dealing with our consignment. We wondered what was happening when he had been away for some time and went to look for him. Upon seeing us, he quickly came and took us a little distance apart. He explained he would have to pay some further money if we agreed to cover the cost. We were unwilling to comply. My son had ensured all costs had been covered and paid at the start. As the conversation progressed, it dawned. He was talking about a bribe. It was common practice, and for all I know may still be, for officials to demand bribes simply to carry out their duties. It was clear, unless we paid, they would not release my possessions. I normally resist such abuse and seek to correct the situation, but we felt trapped. We were also exhausted. Reluctantly, we agreed. Hey Presto! The papers were stamped and my belongings loaded onto a lorry.

I previously pointed out my countrymen have a tendency to be lazy and unhelpful. The shipping agent, as contracted, had arranged for my goods to be transported to the village. The contract with the English company was for door-to-door delivery. I have also mentioned the house is in the highest point of the village and the road is therefore steep. The removal men could not be bothered to exert themselves for fear of breaking into a sweat. They simply dumped my belongings in the main street outside a cafe. Thankfully, I was on friendly terms with the lady owner. She sent up to let me know what had happened. I was furious. We had paid for delivery direct to the house. I rushed down only to find the men had made a quick getaway. Now left to our own devises, I went and found a man who I knew had his own tractor. He agreed to take my heavy trunks, some of which would have been near impossible to carry by hand. I gave him a considerable amount in gratitude, though it was obvious he was going to ask for less. Nevertheless, we were left with no choice but to carry the remainder up. I am glad to say, everything was crated so no one could help themselves. During the process, the cafe owner kindly kept an eye on things for me. It was summer and very hot. Therefore, most people usually have a siesta after lunch, but not us. There were several heavier and larger items which I could not handle. My son carried on working through the heat, carrying items on his shoulders. It was tiring, but he persevered so we would not have to leave things sitting in the street overnight. He must have lost a couple of kilos. Everything was up at the house before dusk, for which I was very grateful. We spent the next few days sorting and storing. My son had to return to work and I was left to get on as best as I could. Naturally, we complained to the British firm's chief executive and demanded some compensation. He was anything but helpful and basically said it was our bad luck. I think we would have persevered with our claim had we not both been heartily and thoroughly sick of the whole escapade. We just did not feel it was worth any further stress and exertion.

I slowly sorted and ordered the house into what I wanted and looked forward to a peaceful, natural, healthy life. Everything is so much more open in my homeland. However, peace would not be forthcoming. Instead of being grateful for my consideration and kindness in not taking them to court or having them thrown into the street, those who had stolen my family home became very aggressive. In particular, the father who lived in the house at the time. He constantly threatened me with violence and death. It would have been difficult to prove, but most villagers believe he and his son had beaten his wife to death. Why, I do not know, but have heard similar accounts where men are simply fed up with the wife or mother. To try and avoid further undue difficulties and to have a degree of privacy and security, I fenced my small plot. That proved an event in itself. The sister of the now occupier of my family home, had started screaming for the entire village to hear, that I was trying to take over the village. She had been a thoroughly unpleasant woman. I had even seen her defecating in the open while holding onto a fence or wall for support. It had obviously been intended to antagonise and offend. Her screaming such nonsense made me wonder if she was really that ignorant, mentally deficient, or just trying to make trouble for me. The latter I would suggest. The labourers had stopped working, unsure what to do. I told them to ignore her and continue. However, to prevent any further nonsense, I agreed to have the footings of longer fence supporting pillars embedded on my side of the ancient wall. Normal size ones were originally going to be placed on top of it. No one really cared for the woman, but being one of their own as opposed to me 'the interloper', it seemed wise to concede some ground.

You may recall, I described how I discovered a mass of geraniums mama had planted when I was a child. Besides them, mama had, as was traditional for rural communities, also grown produce we could use. Among them were a few vines. Sadly, except for the one I am going to tell you about, all have gone. The remaining one had its roots in my plot. From there it grew up the wall of my ancestral home. I assume mama trained it to do so. Prior to fencing my land, I had politely suggested to the uncouth man who now lived in our old family home, he may wish to move it to his side of the boundary. He had not bothered, though I had given him plenty of notice. It subsequently dawned upon me he may try to use its presence on my side as an excuse to enter my property. I was having none of that. His type of deviousness had eroded my longstanding desire to trust and believe. As a rural society of the time, where most relied upon whatever they grew, removing a plant was frowned upon. Nonetheless, there was no way I was going to allow him to use it as an excuse. As mama had planted it, I would have loved to keep it, but that was out of the question. I knew I had to cut it down, even though the very idea terrified me. What would his reaction be? I waited for a day when I was fairly sure he would be away from the house. Helen happened to be visiting. Though she had great difficulty with her legs and feet, she had enjoyed coming up and delighting in the views and memories evoked. Sometimes, a neighbour or friend who was going to their forest plots would give her a lift. At others, she just took her time and struggled up. Helen had held the plant steady while I, with trembling everything and shaking from head to foot, started to saw through the thick trunk. Constantly, the fear he may return at any moment played in my mind. I forced myself to continue. The wood was far tougher than I expected and therefore cutting through was taking longer than anticipated. Sweat poured off like some unrestrained waterfall while my blood pressure hit the roof. Finally, the saw cut through. Then, rather than be accused of theft, that he would more than likely try, I deposited the remains over the fence. I knew the tender shoots would grow if he properly cared for them.

He shouted and aggressively gesticulated when he returned. I could have remained hidden in the house, but I would have to face him sometime, unless I wished to remain a prisoner in my own home. Drawing upon my courage, I ventured out. Managing to keep control, I quietly and politely said I had given him plenty of opportunity to remove it. He tried to tell me I had no right to which I simply told him I had every right, as it was my land. Rather than accept the truth, he recurrently threatened to kill me and then to cut me into small pieces. These, he maliciously told me, he would throw into the rough surrounding countryside for the wild animals to eat. I am a sensitive person. Knowing him fully capable of fulfilling his threat, I lived in constant fear. My trepidation resulted in a persistent shaking and inability to sleep properly. My health quickly deteriorated. Though I considered myself fairly tough, I came to no longer feel it possible to continue without encountering serious consequences. The toll of having to fight for so much of my life, and my increasing age, were both starting to tell. Therefore, with yet again the sense of disappointment at another apparent failure, I decided to return to England to live. My son and I continue to use the house as a holiday home. Despite all the upsets, he loves the place and lifestyle. For me, I am just glad to be somewhere my mama had been, even if it is only for these short visits. I have nothing else to remember her by. All possessions from the original house have disappeared.

Another unsettling incident, I have not told you about so far, occurred during this period. I have already explained how much I enjoyed the openness of living in the village. Also, that a truly special component for me, is the memories it holds. In between sorting the house and creating the garden, I frequently went for walks along the old familiar paths, up into the forest and down into the small valley behind our house. These were places mama and I had enjoyed together. Tears inevitably came with each recall. They still do. During one walk, I became aware something was different. It took a few minutes before it dawned that it was unusually quiet. Standing with ears strained, I realised there was no birdsong. Then, a couple of loud bangs echoed off the rock face I was standing by. If you can, imagine a 'death wall', the sort motorcyclists at fairs and circuses like to pit themselves against. When a small child I used to run along this vertical wall, my body horizontal to the ground without ever falling. I had been a great athlete and, presumably because I was so young, without fear. The thought of it now scares the hell out of me. The wall is at the bend of the path, just before it starts to rise into the forest. Upon rounding the bend, I was greeted by the sight of a young boy holding a rifle. It had been as tall as him. The next thing I noticed horrified me. Hanging from a string tied round his tiny waist had been numerous dead sparrows. My appearance had obviously taken him by surprise. He had stopped in his tracks and stared at me, his expression less than pleasant. There had also been a darkness in his eyes that should never be seen in one so young. I could not help but ask him why he had killed the poor little things. Telling him we had not even done that when we had been starving in the war and adding that anyway, they could not be eaten. He just stood staring, making no response. I then watched, further horrified, as he raised the gun to his shoulder and aimed straight at me. An evil glare had then intensified the darkness of his eyes. To my further horror, I saw his index finger curl round the trigger. I told him not to be so silly. Again no response but to tighten his grip. I had seen the trigger slowly moving back. I glanced about for shelter, but there was none. Trying to make a run for it would have been pointless. He would have had a clear target before I had any hope of escaping. Just as I was giving up all hope, the thud of running feet penetrated the deafening pulsation in my ears. Through the mist of fear, I saw two shadowy outlines pass me. Shaking the fog from my eyes, I then witnessed a man and woman deliberately place themselves between the boy and me. The man ordered him to put the rifle down. The woman also pleaded for him to lower it. However, the boy did not move but just continued to stare. After what seemed an eternity, and to the relief of the man, woman, and myself, he eventually lowered the weapon. Turning to face me, but I noticed ensuring they remained between me and the boy, the two adults apologised, stating he had meant no harm and that he really did not know what he was doing. I had serious doubts about that. It turned out, though old enough to have been his grandparents, these were the eight-year-old boy's mother and father. Throughout, he had continued to stare at me in a most resentful manner. It was evident their pleas had primarily fallen on deaf ears and that they had little control over their child. I became concerned he may resume his earlier behaviour, and it appeared I was not the only one. His father had kept looking over his shoulder. They begged me not to tell anyone. They did not want him to get into trouble. In response to them telling me it was simply he liked shooting, I told them it should never be at little birds. Why did he not just satisfy himself with target practice at inanimate objects? I also said they should teach him how to behave and he really should not be allowed to go round with a rifle. Upon confirming I would let it go this time, they thanked me profusely and took their son back to the village. I had watched with some remaining degree of fear, worried he may yet turn the gun he was still holding back onto me. Once they were fully out of sight, I found a place to sit and recover. He had clearly been following the example of some village men who thought it made them masculine to shoot defenceless little birds. Idiots! When they killed almost all, they even turned their weapons upon butterflies. The small valley I have mentioned used to be full of very large, rare, beautiful butterflies. No more.

At another time, I had been on my way to visit an elderly lady who lived on her own. I had known her as a child. Rather than go the long way round I decided to cut down a tiny, vastly overgrown path. To be honest, it did not even justify that description. Hardly ever used the tall, arid grasses had overtaken it. My legs bore the scratch marks for days. Occasionally stopping to enjoy the views, I noticed what looked like a couple of discarded tyres. Though there were strategically positioned large dustbins round the village, many could not be bothered to carry their rubbish to them. They would just dump it in the surrounding countryside or forests. Regrettably, this mimics what is happening in this country now. Besides the smell, it attracted many unpleasant creatures, rats, snakes and stray dogs among them. And, of course, it damaged the environment. I tried pointing this out, but they simply got annoyed at my audacity to say anything. The more I looked at the black objects, the more convinced I became they were not tyres. Intrigued, I approached closer. They were dead snakes! Though I have an inherent dislike of snakes, I had felt compelled to move closer. There had been one large coil nearest to me with two smaller ones further down. Inquisitive to have a better look, I had bent down but then recalled one of the village men telling me to be wary of these snakes. How they were devious and would feign death to attract potential predators. They would then uncoil and strike. My heart almost stopped when I noticed the large coil I was bent over breathing. The man had also told me they were deadly, and once bitten there was little anyone could do. I then found I had unwittingly moved between the three. I virtually ceased breathing as the seriousness of my position dawned. With no alternative left me, I had forced my fear down and made a hop, skip and jump, and then ran with all my might. Discussing this later, with the man who had warned me, we concluded it must have been a mother with her two offspring. I really had been very lucky to escape, though my intense palpations had left my heart and ribs hurting for a while.

Now back to England. My son's house was not ideal for the two of us. In addition, he often had friends visiting, which I found difficult as I felt in the way. He therefore kindly looked for, and found, a separate house for me. It was a nice modern property on a small new development. My son arranged and paid for everything, including new furniture throughout. There was a small garden at the rear and, as it is with many modern estates, an open plan lawn and flower borders to the front. After all my terrible experiences, I find it hard not to have a strong fence or wall surrounding my homes. Nothing could be done at the front, as the deeds specified the open plan. However, at the rear, my son had the insufficient low wire surround replaced with a much higher solid wall. It was a lovely house, but sadly, not destined to be a happy home. It was the last property in a cul-de-sac that abutted local authority playing fields. At first I thought how nice it would be not to have neighbours on one side. However, the local children turned out to be nothing short of evil. We later learnt the local authority and police intentionally relocated the criminal, troublesome, and worst elements of the town to the council estate on the further side of the fields.

It was evident to all, I did not originate from such a society or background. Regrettably, though I dressed normally and avoided wearing jewellery, I attracted unwanted attention. I cannot adequately describe how awful daily life became. Both younger and older children made a point of playing ball against the high fence dividing the development from the playing fields. It was virtually attached to the wall of my house. I spoke to them intelligently, kindly and with respect, but only received jeering responses. These young people evidently lacked teaching, manners, and respect for others. In my trips to the shops, I frequently saw mothers with their toddlers and was greatly shocked at the way they shouted, hit, and generally treated them. There was no example of good, respectful behaviour. Therefore, in fairness to the children, there was little chance for them to develop social skills. Neither did the parents seem to care if their children were truants. When my son was young, I always talked to him and discussed things with him. I never saw the point in shouting or swearing at a child when they could not understand. It is not only upsetting for all, but does nothing to help the child learn. Though children should learn to respect their parents and do as they are told, it does not help to just shout at them to do as they are told and then hit them. You may think I am being unduly critical. That is not so. I am simply trying to paint a picture for you of how things were. I will admit though, I often felt sorry for the toddlers. Here is an example of how I discussed matters with my son. He wanted a particular motorised toy. There were two models. One better quality, but obviously more expensive than the other. We did not have a lot of money. We never had. Rather than make a scene in the centre of the shop, as many round us did, I took my son to one side. Kneeling down to be on eye level, I explained he could either wait for us to have enough for the quality one or he could have the less expensive one now. He knew from his own experience, less expensive products did not last. He thought for a while and then told me he would wait. I always made sure he was never let down, by me at least. When we had enough for whatever he had wanted, and I had agreed he could have it, I always bought it. A patient boy, he knew I always did what I promised. That is very important for children. A further example, my son has always loved books. However, he did not like borrowing them from a library. He preferred to own them. Still does. He also loved books which were considered by adults heavy and beyond his years. He read some by Walter Scott set in the Jacobean period while still quite young. There was a series of leather bound classics he particularly liked. He has also always valued good quality. I discussed with him, to afford one of these special books, I would have to save up for two or three months. If he chose, he could have a less expensive edition. I then left the choice to him. He decided it was worth waiting and, without any prompting, also saved his pocket money. Then, on one of my days off, we would go to the shop where he could take up to two hours to select the one he wanted. I think the wide range overwhelmed him. If he could, he would have bought the lot. Even after all the years, and several house moves, he still treasures those books. All, including his first reading books, are in excellent condition. No broken spines or dog-eared pages. Some think it is rather fastidious, but it simply reflects his respect for literature and books in general.

I would like to share a funny incident from one of these book purchasing expeditions. As you know, I wanted my son to have the best education I could give him. To that end, I thought he should have the complete works of William Shakespeare. When I asked the assistant for it, she just stood looking at me in a queer way. It was not until I had repeated my request a couple of times that she responded, 'Oh, Shakespeare'. I was a bit irked, saying that was what I had been asking for. Quietly, she kindly explained that with my accent I had in fact been asking for Sexspeare. No wonder she had been confused and a little embarrassed. Her face had gone rather pink. But I digress.

I think it has become clear I like to walk to a destination, whenever possible. While living in this new house, I regularly walked the long distance into the town for my shopping. On one of my return trips I noted a young, hooded man following. My experiences of unwanted attention have made me very aware. I constantly look about. My encounters have also taught me never to allow a stalker to know where I live and that most are cowards. The glimpse of a knife in the young man's hand however, made this a more frightening episode. I knew a run for it was out of the question. First, I was loaded down with multiple, overflowing shopping bags. Second, I was wearing high heels. Until much later in life I had always worn stilettos. It just seemed normal. Third, I doubted I could have outrun him. He looked quite young. It crossed my mind he would probably be as cowardly as the others I had encountered in my life. Disguising the concern pulsating through me, I turned my head and made clear I had seen him. I thought he was going to have a heart attack. He stopped in his tracks and looked as I imagine a petrified deer would. He had then drawn the knife back into his sleeve and ran off in the opposite direction. Not sure what I would have done if he had not run.

Matters at the house eventually deteriorated to the point I had to call for the police to intervene. The police sergeant said he would ensure he and his men put in regular appearances. Hopefully, that would calm things down. A few months later, during which matters had not improved, there was one evening when things got rather ugly. The pressure was too much and I collapsed. Bear in mind this had been going on for months. The police sergeant, who had been good to his word, happened to be there. He called a doctor and then telephoned my son and told him to come straight over. Several friends were visiting, but he left them to their own devises. The police sergeant and doctor told him if I was to survive, he must take me from the place. The sergeant had previously said he could do nothing further and I had better move. This admission shocked the young constable with him. How sad to see our society descend to such unruly depths. My son told me to gather whatever I needed for the night. He then telephoned his friends and asked them to leave his house. He would explain later. Though I felt safer in my son's home, I could not relax that night. Fear and trauma had taken hold.

The next morning, I insisted all my possessions, furniture and all be moved. I was scared someone would break in. My son felt I was over-reacting, but telephoned his office to say he needed to take a day or two off. He moved everything the same day. His house, not being overlarge and already storing my other belongings, became even more crowded. However, he still insisted we have some area to relax in without being overshadowed by boxes and such. He kept the sitting room and kitchen clear. The long hallway on the other hand was full. We had to turn sideways to get through the front door and along the hall. Thankfully, neither of us was oversized. We never have been. My only regret is my son, who enjoyed the company of his peers, had to cease inviting friends.

38

Despicable

My son realised living apart was not going to work. I was getting older and less able to cope with living alone. He looked for a house to suit us both that would still allow him his own space. We viewed several, including one that looked like a two up two down from the front. This implied it simply would not be large enough. However, it was a surprise once inside. Unseen from the front was a third lower floor. A further pleasant surprise was that it opened onto a south facing garden. This, in turn, was completely surrounded by neighbouring properties, with an ancient, historic stone boundary between each. I was quite taken with this feature as a prospective burglar would have great difficulty getting to the rear of the property. To cut a long story short, my son sold both of our existing houses. One before our move, the other after. This meant we did not have to rush to get in and had time to clean and redecorate before transferring our possessions. It took much of the customary stress out of the relocation.

We were reasonably content in our new home. I was grateful it was in an area that enabled my son to visit his friends easily. Many were within walking distance, which was good as he prefers, whenever possible, to walk rather than drive. The district also pleased me. There were some very nice grocery stores within a five-minute walk. Nor was it too onerous a task to walk to the town centre in fine weather. My son usually drove to his office situated in the outskirts but occasionally, when he had no meetings or appointments, walked the forty minutes it took. As I said, he has always preferred walking. Even in London he walks, only using the underground when under a time constraint or his destination is an unrealistically long way to go on foot.

As seems to be my lot, I was not to be freed from challenging problems. The first occurred one day when I suddenly felt dizzy and collapsed onto the kitchen floor. Thankfully, my son was home and, being unable to gain any response, summoned our doctor. He had considerately placed a cushion under my head before doing so. In my semi-conscious state it had felt as if an intense blackness was surrounding me, through which my son's concerned voice had penetrated. As always, I wanted to get to him. To protect him. I was worried his father was kicking him again. My confused mind had obviously gone back to earlier days. I felt heavy and fearful of my inability to see. I had to get to him. Eventually, finding the wherewithal to force my eyes open, I was so happy to see my son's face hovering over me. He was supporting me in his arms. In a mumbled voice, I asked what had happened. He told me I had collapsed and the doctor was there. After examining me, and in answer to my son's concern, the doctor concluded I did not need to go to hospital, but he would arrange for some tests. The consultant's confused expression, when we eventually saw him, worried me. I began to think it must be something serious and wondered if I was dying. I am sure you are able to imagine what was going through my mind. His response to my asking what was wrong, was that he was not sure. However, he thought, from the scratches on my back, I may be having some sort of fits at night. Inwardly, I argued 'I do not have fits'. It is probably a generation thing, but it felt shameful to admit to such a possibility. Up to this point, I had not mentioned to anyone I had often woken to find scratches on my back, in places I could not normally reach. Perhaps I had been frightened or ashamed, or both. Ashamed because, as previously explained, back in my early rural existence, such matters were considered a punishment from God for some wrongdoing or a curse. My son had been very cross because, as he put it, how would he know when something was seriously wrong if I did not tell him about such things. To my consternation, the consultant arranged for further tests. I did not want to undergo anymore prodding and poking.

One test required a large lighting unit, full of multiple rows of bulbs, to be lowered to within a couple of inches of my face. It had been quite claustrophobic. There had then been a series of exceptionally bright intermittent flashes. I had to undergo this unsettling experience several times. I presume the idea was to see if it would trigger a fit. It did not. My son, who was permitted to accompany into the tests, complained after that it had almost given him a fit. Thankfully, the other tests were not so obtrusive. A week later, back with the consultant who was going through the results, there was still no resolution. I asked if my condition could be the result of when the German officer had struck me in the head with his revolver. He conceded it a possibility, but clearly doubted it. He decided to categorise it as epilepsy and, to my annoyance, prescribed phenytoin. My doctors and son despair at my reluctance to take any sort of medication. I realise it is necessary, at times, but I have never been at peace doing so. The consultant made a further appoint for a month later. In the end there had been no clear diagnosis. However, presumably to get me off their books, they settled on epilepsy. I have never really accepted it. I remain convinced it had been the result of that German officer's actions. Even all these years later, I still suffer pain and discomfort in that part of my head. I took the phenytoin for a while but eventually stopped. It made no difference. The fits, if that is what they were, decreased and ultimately stopped. Although it had not been taken into account at the time, it may be logical to suspect the stress I had endured leading up to this event had played a part. It did take a while for me to recover from the fear those urchins on the estate had caused me to suffer. And, of course, that is not to mention the other abuses and difficulties I have endured throughout my life.

My collapse was just the start of our troubles in this house. One evening, May, my niece, telephoned to tell us my eldest sister Helen had died. The fact her children had not let us know she was ill made our shock even worse. They had failed to notify us when her husband had passed away, which had made me extremely cross. I told them then they must let me know if my sister ever became seriously unwell. She had coped with leukaemia for many years. I am not sure I will ever forgive them. Although Helen was now gone and the funeral, in accordance with the tradition I have already explained, had taken place, we still wanted to say our own farewells. Prior to going to the village, we stopped to visit my other sister, Anna, in the capital. We then continued with our unhappy mission. As we were going to be there, my son decided we might as well have some time in the house, so took a few weeks off. As soon as we could, we visited the grave. You will understand how distressing that was. Helen was highly respected and liked by all in the village. Her demise saddened everyone, and all offered their sympathies. It took a few days for the reality of her passing to sink in upon us both. My son was very attached to his aunt. Once it had, we got on with general maintenance and gardening. We also took some relaxation time, though our melancholy was, naturally, always present. We missed Helen and her husband very much.

All too soon, the time for us to return came round. My son had to get back to his office. Because we had not been sure how long we would be away, he had not booked return flights. This was against his usual habit, but we had not thought it would be problematic. In previous years we noted how people got flights whenever they wanted. True to my normal troubled life, this time proved the exception. Unable to get the flights we desired, we had no option but to take a late night one. I should mention we always flew scheduled. There was one year when we had been unable to get a scheduled flight so had to fly charter. An experience we both agreed never to repeat. Because of the late night flight, we arrived home during the early dark hours of morning. We were tired and still upset. Neither of us had really grieved for Helen yet. We were looking forward to cleaning up and getting to bed, but this was not to be. In our absence, we had been burgled. Just writing that turns my stomach and makes me feel nauseas.

We called the police, only to learn they had already been. A neighbour, when passing one night, had seen the front door open. Rather than bore you with what became a very protracted investigation, I will simply say the inspector in charge was useless. He was far more interested in, and excited by, what he had found for sale at car boot sales rather than in recovering our stolen possessions. They had been visiting those and secondhand shops to see if they could spot any of our items. His careless attitude throughout incensed us and we would have lodged a complaint, but for the fact we were already exhausted and stressed. Thankfully, the insurance adjuster was decent. Nevertheless, it took his superiors a long time to agree the settlement, so much had been taken. Much of it was unique and irreplaceable. They had been unable to find any similar items upon which to base a valuation. There was no choice but to accept our estimates, which I am sure we understated. We are not people who cheat. Sad to say, we knew who was responsible. There were some new arrivals among my son's acquaintances, all of who knew we would be away for a while. It transpired these new interlopers were in the habit of utilising one of their extended family's five-year-olds to crawl through windows. They would then open the front doors for the others. Unfortunately, there was no hard evidence, meaning nothing could be proven. We had no option but to let the matter rest there. Sadly, my son felt there was no option but to withdraw from regular contact with that group of acquaintances. He was as upset as I.

As I have mentioned before, I am rather hypochondriac about cleanliness. I understand many people who have been burgled feel violated but for me, with my hypochondria, it was much worse. The thieves had been throughout the house, evidently aware there was no urgency. My son's friends not only knew we would be away, but they also had a rough idea for how long. The despicable creatures had even stood on all the beds. For whatever reason, I cannot think. There were no cupboards or shelves above them.

Thereafter, I could not relax. I would sit at the top of the stairs each night, watching the door. During the days, I dashed from back to front and back again, ensuring no one was trying to get in. I know it sounds ridiculous, but a dreadful fear had taken hold. I could not control myself. Intense fear, no matter how unreasonable it may appear, is an awful, disabling thing. My son naturally became concerned. It was clear, if I was to remain sane, I could no longer live in this house, or the region.

Eventually, after protracted negotiations, he organised a transfer to his head office. That would enable us to move nearer to some relatives who would be on hand in case I needed them. My son could not be with me all the time. He had to work. Worryingly for me, he had to start at his head office before we had a chance to purchase a new home. We were too far for him to commute, so he stayed with May and her husband, who lived in a London suburb. From there he was able to get to his office in central London, with a combination of walking, rail, and underground services. Each week, when possible, he took a day or two off to look for a property in the area we hoped to live. I had no wish to live in London proper. He spent many tiring days and nights searching. The place where the relatives lived and the surrounding area produced nothing. My son therefore started looking further afield. He came home for weekends with his laundry and for a rest. His working schedule and house hunting tired and stressed him. He therefore felt it unsafe to drive the long distance and undertook the lengthy journey by train. I expect you are able to deduce what impact all this was having upon us both, especially me, while on my own in the house.

While boasting she never charged anyone else for staying, May made my son pay an extortionate amount. He also found the place very uncomfortable. My niece was never hygienic and her cooking was always full of fat and high levels of salt. Things my son cannot cope with. Remember also, her husband was unwell and an alcoholic. So as not to appear ungrateful or snobbish, my son made a point of staying in for one evening a week. He ensured he had activities to keep him away for the others. On those he just popped back for a half hour or so to change and collect whatever he needed.

He was actually only there for three or four full nights. While house hunting, he sometimes had to stay in a hotel overnight. Each week, he left on Friday mornings and did not return until late on Sundays. On the one evening he stayed in, he usually ended up going to his room after a couple of hours. May would make it obvious they did not want him with them any longer. She could be very unpleasant in underhanded ways. In addition to the excessive rent, my son had to feed himself each day and in the evenings he was out. My niece was very much a miser and could be mean spirited with relatives. She never offered sandwiches or anything else. He did his best to economise by only having inexpensive snacks and using economical travel routes. Reminds me of the years I lived on one sandwich a day, something I had hoped my son would never have to experience. Rent, food, underground and rail fares, petrol and hotels, when looking for a house, combined to make it a very expensive exercise.

It took a long time to find a suitable house. We were moving from an area with reasonably priced properties to a very expensive district. A property that did not shout wealth but would enable us to enjoy as much privacy as possible would be ideal. It also had to be one where I would feel safe when on my own. We eventually settled on a charming detached bungalow. Our original plan had been to move in and decorate as we went. However, the owner had emigrated and left the place in a poor state. A contractor had been engaged to rectify some of the problems, but he only completed the work the day before our purchase was finalised. Regrettably, the bathroom remained unfit for use and our plans had to be revised. Neither of us could manage without that facility. At the very least my son needed a working shower to ready himself for work. I therefore had to remain where I was and my son in London. You may imagine how that made me feel. We needed to get the bathroom in order as soon as possible so engaged the existing contractor. We bought everything beforehand. Bath, washbasin, toilet, shower, expensive shower backs, and tiles. All he had to do was fit and plumb it all in. Unfortunately, he proved unreliable. It turned out he was fitting the work between other jobs. He even boasted about it. In the end, what should have taken two days at the most took almost five weeks. Why did we do nothing about it? First, he had already started and it would have been difficult to dismiss him and get someone else to take over. Second, we did not wish to face any possible legal action. We were both stressed enough.

Involved with a number of projects, my son was unable to get away. There was consequently no choice but for me to travel up to clean and decorate. Other than the bathroom, all other areas were accessible. The train journey was long and difficult, which did not help my overall condition. I would stay overnight, sleeping on a camp bed, and travel back, exhausted, the next day. You should bear in mind I was now older and found all this difficult and fatiguing. For fear of what may happen while away, I never stayed more than one night at a time. I have to say, despite my struggles, I and my son were very pleased with the final outcome of all the cleaning and painting. Even though, not for the first time, the less than easy task of painting the ceilings had caused my neck to hurt unmercifully. My son eventually managed to get a few days off to help with carpeting the whole bungalow. We did it ourselves because we did not want the trouble of having other workmen about.

Not to bother you with unnecessary details, I will just say the whole move, that is finding a property, completion, cleaning, decorating, and new bathroom took nineteen months. My sanity was under constant strain, but, as you see, or perhaps you cannot, I survived intact. We moved in during the summer.

Disappointingly, that was not the end of our house troubles. I despair of it ever being otherwise for me. The hot water boiler proved inadequate, and the central heating did not work. A combination boiler seemed the answer. The change would also do away with the existing need for several water tanks. I never understood why the antiquated system needed so many. We contracted one of the major and supposedly reliable national companies. From the start, there were problems. When disconnecting all the now redundant water pipes, one was left uncapped. In the morning we discovered cascading water. Then the new boiler would not work properly. It became a bit scary because it would cut out without warning while the gas still flowed. The ignition mechanism was electric, so the thought of a spark igniting the whole played on our minds. To cut yet another very long story short, I will simply tell you, we had sixteen of the contractor's workmen to the house. That was until the area manager gave us his personal telephone number, telling us only to contact him. In addition, they had cracked two radiators when connecting the new supply. Our new Axminster carpets, in two of the main rooms, were saturated. Added to all this, some of the workers telephoned my son at his office, asking how the new timing system worked. They were supposed to be the professionals! Thankfully, my son had made a point of reading the instruction manual thoroughly. In the end, after two months of all this nonsense, we insisted upon a new boiler. We had paid several thousand pounds, thinking to get the best system available. We were therefore less than amused when it was suggested the boiler should be sent to the makers for servicing. Angrily, my son refused. We both demanded a brand new replacement, straight from the manufactures. Once the new boiler was installed we never called or contacted the company again. Gratefully, the boiler worked. I continue to conclude nothing will ever go smoothly for me. Now the bathroom and water system were up and running, my son, with great relief, was able to leave May's, and I was finally able to escape the terrors of remaining in the old house.

In earlier parts of my tale, I have mentioned my love for and affinity with nature. I was therefore glad the bungalow had its own gardens. A twenty foot one at the front and an eighty foot long one at the rear. An aged oak and several fir trees stood along the bottom boundary. The front garden had been given some basic maintenance and was therefore presentable, if not interesting. The rear was another story. It had not been cared for in the least. Brambles covered the complete area densely. Since my son was at work for most of the time, I cleared them myself. Not a task I ever wish to undertake again. I am surprised my wounds ever healed. Thankfully, the lawn hidden under the brambles was not in too bad a state. I gave it and the surrounding shrubbery some tender loving care and then added flowers, bushes, and more trees. When he had the time, my son built a shed, a greenhouse, and a summerhouse and laid paving to each. A large garage occupied about a third of one boundary. However, it was not the eyesore it sounds. The vines and creepers which grew over much of the brickwork helped it blend in the with surrounding flora. The existing garage roof however, leaked but was too fragile to remove without professional assistance. My son therefore, with a bit of a struggle, put a secondary one over the top. A conservatory had been built on the back of the building, to the side of which was a nice, sheltered patio. In summer the garden was in full sunshine for most of the day. We also fitted a pulley clothes line that enabled my washing to dry nicely in the sun and fresh air. So much nicer than having to dry it indoors.

Due to his long commute and the unreliability of the rail service, my son usually left home early morning, while still dark. He normally returned late evening, again when it was dark. Nevertheless, I have to say, except for my boy's long absences, I was reasonably contented.

Shortly after having got things into order I realised, with all we had been dealing with, it had been quite a while since our last visit to the village. I became worried about the bills, which we paid whenever we were there. My concern was exacerbated by the fact, if the bill remains unpaid for a long period, the electricity company would cut the supply. By cut, I mean they actually physically cut the cables!

I had been told if that happened, it could take months to get them to reestablish the supply. Thankfully, they have become a little more realistic in the last couple of years, and even offer assistance to those struggling financially. I had hoped we would go together, but my son was involved with several long-term projects and would not be able to get away for a while. He suggested we wait but I was very concerned about the bills. He therefore, though not entirely happy about it, agreed to me going on my own for a couple of weeks and made all the arrangements. Other than sorting the bills, I expected to have a peaceful time tidying the house and garden. Yes, you are correct, that was a forlorn hope. Why can my life not be as problem free as others? I arrived to find the back wall of the house looking as if it had been submerged. It was how I imagine the walls of buildings in Atlantis, if it exists, would look at low tide. There was a watermark three quarters of the way up the wall and the plaster had been left a brownish yellow. Thankfully, I had arrived in summer, so the intense heat had already started drying it out. I was grateful the unusually high backdoor step had prevented water from entering the house, though there had been an unhealthy damp atmosphere inside. That soon cleared once I opened the windows and doors. Why had it happened, and would it happen again?, became questions of concern. I confess, as you will probably have guessed, I again felt disconsolate. Why, Why, Why, must it always be like this?

The rear of our property is bounded by an at least two hundred and fifty years old wall. Above, in reality on top of it, is an old footpath, more of a track really. In my parent's day, and before, it had been in frequent use, but no longer, in fact, not for decades. The previous winter's rain, I was told, had been unusually heavy and consistent. Evidently, this had caused the soil to shift, allowing a deluge of mud and water to sweep over the wall and engulf our property. In addition to the damp walls, there had been a remarkable amount of sand on the rear passageway. Obviously, something had to be done. I could not leave it for another winter. Thankfully, as it was summer I had time. Venturing into the village a day later, I searched for a labourer with experience of cement work. I had concluded a solid concrete barrier would be more effective than one made from bricks. A middle-aged man volunteered and came to assess what would be required. He, to my surprise, gave a reasonable quote. After all the experiences of being overcharged, I expected him to be the same. Unfortunately, a couple, whose house was not too far down from ours, heard about my dilemma and my decision to employ the middle-aged man. I must tell you both were very much of a bullying disposition. They insisted the man could not be trusted to complete the work and that they would undertake the task. I wanted to object, but knew to be careful. These were known to be rather vicious if anyone crossed them. I was made to hand over money so they could order and have delivered the equipment needed. Cement, sand, metal grids, and so on. When the lorry arrived it was laden but only a small portion was unloaded. I assumed the supplier was making more than one delivery and thought no more of it. I was therefore confused when they asked for more money the next day. The man audaciously, not the right word, threateningly would be more accurate, looked me in the eye, while standing with hands on his more than ponderous hips. He was a mountain of a man. He must have realised I was about to question why, but before I had the chance, menacingly told me it was to purchase further cement. This despite the fact more had been delivered earlier the same day. To shorten yet another long account, I will tell you further requests, rather demands, for money followed to which I would have objected, except for the worry of how they would react. I eventually realised the additional surplus equipment was being delivered to the couple's home. Essentially, it was theft, but there was nothing I could do without endangering myself. I was glad to see the man I had originally engaged had been included in the workforce. At least he would get something, though it would have probably been precious little. The one thing that bemused me was how the couple regularly gave him a glass of wine. I later learnt he was a heavy drinker, if not an alcoholic. Perhaps these rough people had saved me. Apparently, a few of the self-employed men were known to take months to complete a job that should only take days, or sometimes not at all. I am grateful to report the additional retaining wall and gully to take water away, constructed behind it, have served their purpose right up to the current time. The constant demands for money however, drained me of all I had taken, which would have been more than sufficient for my needs without these people. I had to get my son to send more out.

You would think I would learn, but no, here is my historic naïvety again. The storeroom metal door that I had installed when first doing the house up, the architect had left the room without door or windows, had withstood the savages of wet winters and arid summers. However, the same could not be said of the windows. I had not appreciated the metal used for them had been of extremely poor quality. They had visibly rotted. The couple's son had been part of the workforce and thinking, perhaps more hoping, he may be a different ilk to his parents, I asked him if he knew a metalsmith who could make and install replacements. He did. I therefore further inquired if the man would be up to constructing roof access steps. The house had been built with a flat roof that would enable easier maintenance. However, the architect again, despite having robbed me of so much cash, had not bothered to provide any stairs to get up there. Even without the maintenance issue, I needed access. In those days the water supply mechanism had been very basic, to put it mildly. In order to obtain sufficient power for water to enter the household system, water storage tanks were placed on roofs or upon large supporting pillars. Ours was on the roof. I had been persevering with a heavy primitive wooden ladder I had a local labourer construct at the start. However, I had been finding it increasingly difficult to lift as well as to straddle the rather wide apart rungs. I was getting too old for the splits. The quote he came back with was extortionate. Upon my reaction, he, in a tone that allowed for no compromise, abruptly told me, 'That is how much it costs.' What could I do? I knew full well if I attempted to get quotes from others there would be two outcomes. The workmen would take advantage and no doubt demand more and, more importantly, the couple would take considerable umbrage which, as I said before, could, probably would, lead to very unpleasant results. For me! So much for him being better than his parents. 'Like father, like son' comes to mind. Because of the limited space, we agreed a spiral staircase would be most appropriate. Again, because of the space, I could not watch while it was under construction and therefore had no chance to inspect it until the finished product was in place. I was upset to find they had used thinner than expected metal and it was rather shaky. The stairs are still in use, but it unnerves me each time I go up or down. Because of the thin metal, my son has to paint the whole thing regularly with rust proof paint. Usually every time we go. The winter weather results in rust patches appearing and we worry, without the regular treatment these may wear into holes, making the thing even more unsafe. Thankfully, the windows were of far better construction and have lasted well.

All this shows how my life is never free from challenges. An understatement, you will appreciate.

39

Endless

Each year, my son took two extended vacations. These were usually between five and seven weeks. He worked excessively hard the rest of the time. Prior to departing he always ensured his projects were on target or completed. That meant our visits could not always be at the same time of year. We always went to the house in the village. Some people consider it narrow minded and boring to go to the same place each time. We never found it so. Our vacations always started with a visit to my sister Anna in the city. After that we enjoyed time at the house. When it was too hot to work on the house or garden, my son sat on the veranda and painted something from the beautiful panoramic views. He always had his watercolours with him. During our stay we would take a further seven to ten day break at a favourite seaside spot. Then we would enjoy further time at the house. Another brief stop in the capital visiting Anna would conclude our vacation. I always enjoyed those because we were ageing and did not know how long we had. As Anna put it, 'we were in the throat of death'. That may sound morbid, but on the contrary, we were able to laugh and accept the reality for what it was.

Regrettably, as seems to be my lot, and as you have seen, our visits were rarely problem free. Through the years it has honestly felt endless. Almost three months after my sole visit, when I had the roof stairs and storeroom windows fitted, my son finally completed the projects that had prevented him from accompanying me. He needed a good rest and thought we may as well go to the village. I was happy to do so again. My two-week visit had hardly been restful or productive from the housecleaning and gardening perspectives.

My son was pleased to see the work done appeared adequate and should prevent any further flooding, though he found it difficult to justify the cost. I apologised for not having had the wherewithal to resist the rough couple. He told me not to worry, fully understanding the situation I had been in. He knew the people. We settled into our holiday, hoping it would now be a peaceful time and there were no further problems to come. If only. One evening, a sudden noise from the back of the house disturbed our relaxation. My son slipped his outdoor shoes on. We always change shoes at the door because of the constant dust we do not want to drag into the house. Dark had descended and he could not see, but could hear something. I worried it may be a snake. We have some poisons ones, one quite small and therefore hard to spot. Thankfully, we had the foresight to have a light fitted above the back door that my son now turned on. I had nervously moved to be with him, thinking I might be able to help if there was any danger. Really! Naïve or what? My son turned to tell me it was a kid, a baby goat. It had fallen behind our fence. You will recall I had my entire plot fenced once the house had been built. To support the wire at the back, a series of very tall polls had been inserted. For stability, the tops had been fixed to the overhanging roof surround, meaning they were at a slight angle. This had created a small, narrow v shape between the wire and the old boundary wall. The poor thing was bleating incessantly while trying, unsuccessfully, to get a foothold. He became even more agitated upon sight of us, despite us talking in soft tones. My son tried to shift him up through the mesh but could not get a good grip. In the end he resorted to pulling the wire away from the bottom so as to get both his hands under and then holding the distressed creature by the back of his little neck got him out. We were constantly worried it would break a leg. If he had his owner, whoever that was, would have killed him. I say killed because most of the rough locals did not bother with the kindness of a vet putting their animals to sleep. Sadly, they can be quite brutal. The lovely kid, he was white, reminding me of my own pet when I was a child, settled once freed from the wire. He must have realised my son was trying to help rather than attack him because he then stood close to his legs and watched all he did. A bit as a pet dog would. We guessed the little darling must belong to a woman who had no land of her own and simply let her goats feed wherever she could find vacant undergrowth. There was plenty nearby, so my son, with the goat trotting beside him, went in search of its mother. I lost sight of them in the dark. A few minutes later he returned to tell me they had found the mother, who had a number of other young with her. That was probably why she had not responded to the kid's bleating. The baby only left my son's side when he saw his mother to who he ran. We worked out where the kid had found a gap and my son sealed it with further strong mesh wire the next day. Thankfully we have had no further incidents than that, though a few years later we discovered three snakes which had become trapped in some of the smaller mesh wire and died there. They were the poisons ones. Gives me the shivers as I write. I wonder how you would have felt? We rarely see snakes in this country and then there is normally little danger.

Because of the delay due to my son's projects, we had arrived later in the year than was our custom. The change from hot or mild to cold weather can vary by as much as three or four months in this region. Unfortunately, the change arrived earlier on this occasion. I contracted pneumonia, that with the constant coughing resulted in a hernia. Upon returning to England, I was referred to a consultant who deduced I needed an operation promptly. He considered the hernia too severe to leave unattended. Getting a bed was eventful in itself, but I will not bore you with the details. During the operation my blood pressure dropped drastically and I apparently died. The surgeons pumped me full of various drugs and fought for three and a half hours to save me. I am very grateful to them, as in my country they would probably have let me die. Annoyingly, the drugs used detrimentally impacted my natural metabolism. I have never been one for taking tablets or any medication, meaning my system had been, until then, drug free. I have never been the same since.

Nevertheless, despite suffering all sorts of side effects, I am thankful to still have time with my son.

Our next visit was even more eventful. Disastrous would be a better description. And that for more than one reason. We were coming in to land at my homeland's central airport when I noticed several men standing on the edge of the runway. A very unusual occurrence you will appreciate. As the plane taxied toward the terminal building, they all moved alongside. The concerned looks as they examined the undercarriage of our plane could not be mistaken. Naturally, I also became concerned, thinking there must be something wrong with the aircraft, though there had been no announcement. The way they continued to follow us until the plane came to a standstill unnerved me further, especially as my countrymen are reluctant to admit to something ever being wrong. My agitation escalated when I noted armed police congregated along the sides of the approach runway and round the terminal building. We had not really been aware that those were the initial days of terrorist threats against aircraft. Small scale then, but nevertheless serious. Despite the unease the sight of the armed police had caused me, I was very glad when my feet finally touched the tarmac. It eventually transpired, there had been uncertainty that the righthand undercarriage of our plane would support the weight as we landed. The incident brought back to mind a previous occasion when we had come near to death. I suspect this had been playing in the back of my mind.

That incident had taken place a year or two before, when we had been arriving after dark. Our aircraft had been descending toward the runway on a fairly steep incline. The enjoyable babble of fellow passengers anticipating arrival and the meeting of their loved ones and friends had filled the cabin. Suddenly, we felt a harsh throttle back and our aircraft shooting skywards at a most alarming angle. The violent motion forced us into the backs of our seats. Very unsettling. I have to admit to fearing we were about to crash. The, up to that moment, lighthearted ambience was immediately replaced by a very tangible, intense breathless silence. The nervous, fear laden atmosphere had not been helped by the lack of any announcement from the cockpit. The plane continued, still at an incredibly sharp angle, to shoot skywards for what felt an endless age. It gave me the impression of what it must feel like to be in a space bound rocket, especially at takeoff. The plane eventually levelled out, for which we were all grateful. However, the acute, fear inundated silence continued. I could feel the held in breath, palpable dread, struggles to keep tears and screams under control, and the unasked questions. It was awful. Slowly, still with no announcement, we felt our decent recommence. White knuckles, saucer wide eyes, drained faces, stiff torsos and legs, and indications of under-breath prayers abounded as we descended through the dark night. All watched with bated breath as the runway rose toward us. Then there had been the unmistakable sound of tyres on tarmac, followed soon after by the noisy thrust back of jet engines slowing the aircraft. Recognition of the fact the plane had remained upright brought loud applause, cheering, and many 'Thank you God's'. The dense atmosphere that had threatened to suffocate but a moment earlier dispelled. You will not be surprised at how grateful we had all been when we finally stepped on to terra firma. Apparently, a plane that had been preparing for takeoff had overshot the runway. Thankfully, our pilot had been observant and realised, if he continued with our approach, an inevitably disastrous collision would result. Rather worryingly, it seems the tower had not spotted what was happening. I admit subsequently there had always been slight concern in the back of my mind whenever we flew, especially when travelling with my country's national airline. Physiological I suppose. It really would not have mattered which airline, if the pilot had been unobservant. For reasons I will not bore you with, we no longer fly, preferring to travel overland in our own vehicle and hence our own environment. So much nicer, even if it does take a few days. Also means we have the connivance of our own car at the house. It has made a surprising difference.

As we often did during our breaks in the village, we liked to visit some of the little places I knew as a young child. When mama and I were still together. You may recall my description of a long running stream from which we fetched our water and to which we took our laundry. The small valley it is in is just a few meters from the house. As mentioned, it now, thankfully, has a proper road to it rather than the old narrow, excessively steep track we used. It really is a wonderful place. It also brings back many lovely, happy memories. Why could my life not have followed the peaceful path it was clearly meant to? Anyway, we had gone down to enjoy the views, recall memories, and fetch some drinking water. Because the spring is natural, the water tastes far nicer than that from the household tap. We were coming back up when, with no warning, I suffered a severe stroke. I have to say, I suspect this was in part due to the impact of the drugs administered in the prior incident. I am not accusing anyone or attributing blame, after all my life was saved. It is simply what I think. My son had to carry me up the very steep hill to get back to the house. Although it was a terrible time, we can look back now and laugh at his antics. Someone really should have been there with a video camera. I had lost use of my right side and my speech and could not therefore help. When we eventually got to the house, he had to prop me against the gate, holding me in place with his knee, while he unlocked it. He then dragged me to the back door and again had to prop me against the wall. It was then a case of getting me over the rather large step. With one leg on the top and the other on the ground, he tried, but it did not work. I fell against him, now effectively pinning him against the wall. I was a dead weight by this time. Eventually, taking the risk of damaging himself for life, he, with all his strength, heaved me over the step. Then, somehow, got me across the room and on to a bed. He let me rest for a while, but I did not improve. This was before we had a car at the house, so he had to walk, in the intense summer heat, the half hour it took to the nearest locality with a cottage hospital. A doctor came and examined me and then told my son to get me to the hospital in the district's market town. As there was no ambulance service he had to call a taxi. The outpatient doctors quickly assessed my condition and were prepared to administer appropriate medication as long as my son first confirmed he was prepared to pay. What if he had not the money? I will let you answer that. After the medication had been given, they admitted me to a ward. My ultimate four-day stay was terrible. At first, the ward was crowded. A bed was therefore slipped into a space between the windows, straight opposite the entrance. Rather public. Everyone entering would first have full sight of me. Unlike the British hospital system, there is very little order. Patient's families basically camp round their relative's bed, even sleeping on any unoccupied beds. They bring a lot of food and essentially have family picnics in the ward. Neither are there any dedicated nurses. Two or three would circulate round the wards, though I never saw the same ones from day to day. Several were very brusque and unsympathetic. They would even try to take my temperature without waking me first, which was very frightening. Eventually, I was the only one left in the ward. At night I felt especially vulnerable as there were no security staff and hardly anyone else during the late hours. We sometimes do not appreciate the service we get in England. Though it is not what it once was, it is still superior to those in many other countries. To cut my explanations short, when we returned our family doctor sent me to a consultant who confirmed I had been given the correct treatment. He simply adjusted the medication dosage because it had been upsetting my system. I recovered full use of my right side and eventually, though it took a bit longer, my speech. My son became an expert at interpreting my grunts. Many are amazed I do not have any lasting issues, as so many have. In fact, you would not know I ever had a stroke, especially such a severe one, nor the few that followed.

You would think these, combined with previous incidents, were sufficient for one life. I wish. As you have already seen and will again, I am destined never to be free. Why, I do not know. Only God has the answer to that. Perhaps I will find out one day.

40

Penned

Although we both liked our new English home, it had one drawback. My son's long commute. To get to his office, he had, in all weathers, a half-hour walk to the railway station. There was a supposedly manned carpark, however, it was known for break-ins and vandalism. The station staff did not appear to consider it within their responsibilities. One account we heard, described how the staff had stood in the main entrance watching as some youths vandalised a car, but did nothing. They did not even report it. This was during the day! Since, with his long absence, the car would be there all hours, including when dark, my son decided not to risk it. I do not drive, so could not help. The train journey was supposed to be one and one-quarter hours, but never was. He then had a twenty-five-minute walk across open, windswept terrain. His total round-trip commute should have taken four and a half hours. However, due to the declining rail service, it ended up a regular six and a half hours, sometimes even seven. He was surviving on four to four and a half hour's sleep. On several occasions, when a large project was in development, he worked nine to fourteen hours a day, seven days a week. I do not think I need tell you what a toll this was taking on him. And, of course, I was also seeing precious little of him.

My son is a resolute person and continued this regime for seven years. He wanted us to be in a place where I felt reasonably safe and content. On top of the commuting, he increasingly had to go away on business. On one occasion he was obliged to go straight from one regional office to another and divert midway to a three-day conference. He was extremely tired and exhausted upon his return, but had to commute immediately to his own office without time for a rest. All this gives you an idea of the demands upon him. Demands which never relented.

His commuting, countrywide travelling, and increasing absences left me on my own for long periods. I do not mind my own company, in fact, I am very happy with it, but I missed him very much, and there appeared to be no end in sight. We discussed the issue and eventually concluded it could not go on. As said, I missed him very much, but more importantly, was concerned for his health, physical and mental. Unwillingly, but rationally, we both accepted he needed to move nearer to his office. I have already mentioned I do not like London, but have to admit that in general I dislike cities. In addition, presumably because of my bad experiences, neither do I ever really feel safe in large towns. Parochial and rural areas suit me better. We did not want to spend endless days, weeks, or months looking for a suitable house again, so settled, as an interim step, upon a top-floor apartment in a nice suburb. Obviously, there was less room, so most of our possessions had to go into storage. The accommodation was not ideal but in the end I considered it safer to be in a top-floor apartment rather than a house in the city. My son could reach his office within forty-five to fifty minutes. There were also eighteen trains an hour, whereas there had only been one an hour in our previous location. He became far more relaxed and was able to meet up with friends more often. I was also happier. I saw him far more, and we were able to frequently go out together.

The combined effect of the drugs used to save my life, stroke medication, and increasing age led to my general health slowly deteriorating. I never told my son I was concerned and did my best to hide the symptoms. But he had been quietly observing. He told me off for trying to hide things from him. How could he know when there was something serious that needed attention rather than me just being rundown? He became increasingly concerned and ended up deciding to take early retirement so he could look after me.

His eventual retirement, it took a while to come through, meant we no longer needed to remain where we were. I have already mentioned how much my son enjoyed my homeland and the lifestyle. There is also the fact there is no fear of burglary, mugging, or general violence as there is in most of the United Kingdom. In view of both these positives, we decided to move to the village. My son spent a few months going through our stored possessions to see what would be of use to us over there. He then arranged for them to be shipped.

Needless to say, he employed a different company to the one we had used previously.

Just to return for a moment to the subject of break-ins and violence. People who live in the district, not just the village, have no concept of theft, burglary, or mugging. It was quite common to find business premises unattended while the owner has popped out for a newspaper or something. By popped out I mean, have got into their cars and driven some distance to the shops. Very often whole key bunches, with house, car, business, and who knows what others, are left hanging in door locks. Tills were also frequently left unattended. We have been to a building supplier where everything was out and could have easily been picked up, with no sign of anyone about. We could have helped ourselves to whatever we wanted. In some other instances, we have found tills left in the care of eight-year-old children while the parents are attending to something elsewhere. The attitude is not restricted to businesses. People often left their homes with wide-open doors and windows and keys just hanging or laying about. It is nice and almost unbelievable such a society still exists. Even better is the fact no one is robbed or mugged. Unfortunately, this can no longer be said of the metropolis. In recent times, there have been reports of robberies, muggings, kidnappings, and death. However, much can be accounted for by the new open borders policy. Culprits, when caught, invariably turn out to be immigrants from poorer and rougher countries, who tend to congregate in city areas.

Although the shipping agents proved much better than the previous, and less expensive, there were still delays and untruths told. However, these were not to the same extent, and they delivered our possessions to the gate. It was a pleasant surprise to find nothing, including glass items, had broken in transit. My son had carefully packed everything.

I wish I could say life was peaceful and pleasant thereafter. But, as you are aware, that would have been very strange indeed. Late morning one day, my son called to me from the garden. The urgency in his voice had been unmistakable. I assumed there was another snake. A couple of days earlier I had gone to prepare lunch on the patio table only to discover a huge, and I mean huge, snake sunbathing on the warmed concrete surface. It gave me quite a turn. As much as I do not like any animal hurt, including snakes, I knew we would need to do something. We could not just leave it there. However, the initial shock had frozen me for a moment, during which the creature had scarpered off. I am not sure what I would have done if it had not. It really was huge. Thankfully, though there are a few deadly ones, most snakes in the area tend to be cowardly. They prefer to sneak away rather than confront. That is as long as they do not consider their young are under threat or have been trodden on in the tall grasses. I went out to find him with fixed gaze by the gate. In response to my question of what was wrong, he pointed to the rough drive leading to our house. With utter disbelief, I saw that someone had erected a low wire fence round the entire drive. Perhaps I better explain. My ancestral home, as previously detailed, is near the top of a small mountain. Some may prefer to describe it as a large foothill. Whatever the description, it is high up and borders a forest. A nearby ancient meandering path enables villagers to reach the estates they have obtained, to use a kind expression, over the years. These are within the higher forest regions. Our house is set back from that path. The drive, as we like to call it though more of a rough broad pathway, has for generations been accepted, by all, as a public right of way. That although it really only leads to our property. An ancient wall bounds one side. We understand it is at least two hundred and fifty years old. Uncultivated land that drops below the drive's surface level bounds the other. There remains within the wall an old solid iron ring to which I, as a young child, my parents, grandparents, and previous generations, tied our horses. That gives you some idea of how long my family has used the drive for. Neither of us could believe what we were seeing. We had been completely fenced in, leaving us with no means of exiting our property.

My son wondered if a couple who had been after the uncultivated piece of land were responsible. I was not so sure. He then instinctively moved to remove the iron poles and wire. I stopped him. He was angry, saying no one had the right to block us in. However, I was aware of a law that prevents anyone from taking a fence down on their own volition. We would have to call the police. Not a joyous thought in my country. He still argued that it was a public right of way. I had now recalled the law, a peculiar one admittedly, that stated once erected a fence could only be removed by the person who had put it up. Whether it was justified or not, did not seem to matter. I have absolutely no idea what brought about such a bizarre law. We called the police and waited.

Two police officers, standing on one side of the fence while we stood on the other, asked who the land belonged to. I told them, no one as it is a public right of way to my ancestral home. I then pointed to my parent's home, now occupied by the uncouth man, adding as I did so that most people considered it belonged to my parents. They appeared to accept but said they would have to find who had put the fence up. I asked them to remove it as we had been about to go for some groceries. To my amazement, they said not even they were permitted to take a fence down. We would have to wait and, in the meantime, not take it down. If we did, we would be in the wrong. The whole situation was ridiculous, as we told them, but they just shrugged their shoulders. The two of them then left us to our own devises. An hour later, one reappeared. My people are not known for their sense of urgency. He said they were still looking, but thought they may know who was responsible. To my complaint of it taking so long, he simply said it was lunchtime. When it comes to food, few of my countrymen will allow anything to interfere.

It was afternoon, with the consequent summer heat, when my son spotted someone coming. We ventured out to find the two policemen with another man. As soon as he saw us, the other man started shouting the land was his. When I asked who he was, he gave a name I vaguely recalled, but could not place. He then continued shouting the land was his, even after I explained it was a public right of way. I struggled to retain a normal voice and not get drawn into a shouting match. The senior police officer present saw we were getting nowhere and intervened. He ordered the man to take the fence down, so we could get out, and told him ownership would have to be sorted another time. Faced with the authority of the police, he begrudgingly complied. Most do not respect the police, but are too cowardly to disobey an edict. Once he removed the fence, well sort of, he had simply thrown the poles and wire on to the edge of the drive, the police left. We abandoned our shopping trip.

We had been going about our business the next day when the man turned up at the gate. He shouted again it was his land and we would have to pay him to use it. I told him not to be so silly. It had always been the path to our house. He continued to shout, though we kept to a normal conversational tone. His shouting escalated to such a pitch we could not understand the words. We asked him to discuss the issue as a normal human being but he would not, so we left him at the gate. Thankfully, it had been locked. He would have no doubt come in otherwise and goodness knows what may have resulted.

Once inside, we debated what to do. The man was obviously not going to give up. We decided we needed legal advice. The police had made clear they could not, or would not, help further. We went to the lawyer who had first helped me with my parent's home. Though I really did not want to get involved with the courts, never a good idea in my country, he said there was little choice if the man would not see sense. However, he would not represent us. He was semi-retired, with full retirement not far off. He wanted to keep on friendly terms with everyone and enjoy a peaceful old age. It was a disappointment, but I understood. People can make life very difficult if they consider you have offended them. Because our lawyers do not generally have a good reputation, I was anxious about who we could engage. He must have noted because he told me not to worry, he would recommend someone. His recommendation turned out to be a friendly person who even introduced us to his wife and children.

He discovered the objectionable man had been to the courts but had not commenced an action. We would have to start the case. That annoyed me. We were the innocent party. Nevertheless, unless we took steps, nothing would be done. We had the option not to bother, but the man might just start it all over again. Some choice! Reluctantly, we agreed he get the papers drawn up and hoped he would not overcharge like so many before him. I hoped the fact my lawyer friend had recommended him would help reduce any potential greed. He then told us we would have to pay the court. I argued how ridiculous it was that we, the innocent party, had to pay. That, he said, was the only way to get a case started. He then quoted a shockingly substantial amount. We went with him the next day to sign the papers and hand over the money. It turned out to be more than his quote, with taxes and administration fees being added. We also had to pay him. Lawyers in my homeland insist upon being paid as they do things rather than submit a final invoice at the end. I understood. Many clients would do their utmost to avoid paying or would delay payment for ridiculous periods of time. On the way out he informed us the case would not be heard in the central court where we were, but in the circuit courthouse in the next village to ours.

At the appointed time, on the first day of the hearing, we arrived to find what looked like a school building. People were milling about in the courtyard, many rather disgruntled. The place was firmly locked, with no sign of anyone within. Typical of my people never to be on time. Even our lawyer. Some forty or so minutes later, someone finally arrived with a key. Once inside we were taken aback by the disorganised rabble surrounding us. Several cases were to be considered by the circuit judge, but no actual times appeared to have been allocated. All anyone seemed to know was their case was to be heard that day. To our further amazement, the courtroom doors were never closed. As a result, those waiting for their case to be heard crowded into the room. They sat wherever they wanted and talked, rather loudly. It was chaotic. It was also hard to hear any of the proceedings, though the sitting judge occasionally commanded for quiet.

We had felt a little uncomfortable because many kept looking at us. Well, truth be told, they were staring. As would be expected in this country, we had dressed smartly. However, many were in their every day, crumpled, often dirty, clothes. Many of the lawyer's suits were in no better condition. Sometimes it was difficult trying to determine who was the lawyer and who the defendant or plaintiff. The constant cacophony and childish arguments raging between legal representatives and individual parties added to the chaos. It was often hard to know which case was being heard. It was only when we saw our lawyer move to the bench we knew ours was next. You will appreciate I am condensing this account and therefore jumping straight from one relevant point to another.

Judging from what had been audible above the noise, we gathered several cases had been going on for years. Many were evidently very bitter, and some women were in tears. I worried ours may become protracted like theirs. We eventually came to understand, unlike the British system, cases are never dealt with in one hearing. It seemed almost on principle. Most required several hearings with at least two or three months between each. No wonder cases went on for years. Our lawyer had not clearly explained beforehand that this was only to be the first introductory hearing for ours. It is hard to convey how disorganised and unsettling the court atmosphere had been. I wonder how people would react in this country if they had to face similar disorganisation. Neither of us ever wanted to return, but, of course, we had no choice but to do so at various future dates.

One thing that had come out of this first hearing was a request, or rather requirement, for witnesses to the historic existence of the right of way. The court did not consider our testimony alone sufficient. A couple did offer, but virtually vanished when the case started. I was disappointed, but understood. They had a lot to hide, especially from the authorities. The despicable man who had taken my ancestral home on the other hand, offered to stand witness to the uncouth man's ownership of the land. How on earth he could do that, when he knew it was all a lie, is beyond me. What were we to do? Who would stand witness to the truth? Though villagers had known for generations, none were willing to attend the court. As I have said before, you do all you can to avoid the courts and legal actions in my homeland. Sadly, as you have seen, we had no choice this time. Not if we wanted to be free of the ridiculous situation. In the end, my nephew, Helen's son, volunteered. Unfortunately, his less than charitable wife frequently undermines his kind and generous attributes. However, on this occasion, he had been determined. I am so grateful. As a retired naval officer who was also very respected, the judge gave proper attention to his testimony. Still not quite satisfied it fully settled the matter, she decided to visit the physical site of the dispute. You will appreciate again that I am condensing the tale. The proceedings had, in fact, been going for many, many, long months. Our stress levels were excessive and neither of us could relax properly between hearings. I think, perhaps more than anything, it was the lies that upset us the most.

To form part of the evidence, we were asked to obtain a copy of the police report recording their visit. We went to the area police station in the next village, the same one as the circuit court was in. To say they were unhelpful would be a gross understatement. Initially, the underemployed female office staff, each related to one of the policemen, could not find any record of the incident. We continued pressing until someone, reluctantly, acknowledged it had taken place, but they had not completed a report. Despite this admission, they continued to say they could not provide a copy. Keeping our tempers became difficult. We continued to insist, and they continued to refuse. In the end, as instructed, should we meet with such a reaction, we told them to telephone our lawyer. They were reluctant, but I think realised the need to comply with a legal representative. I do not know what the lawyer said, but it had the desired effect. The officers' annoyance had been manifest. They would now have to do some work. It still amazes me how lazy people can be even in the completion of work they are being paid for. They told us to return the next day. I worried they were going to mess us about again, but thankfully, the report was ready and waiting. The dirty looks however, were a little unsettling. Getting on the wrong side of the police can be detrimental. They can be just as vindictive as other citizens.

The lies our neighbour, as I have to call him now, told when testifying on behalf of the man shocked me. I had not expected it. Over the preceding months, he had chatted in a reasonably friendly manner with me over the fence. However, it quickly became evident how two-faced and evil he really is. Nevertheless, for the sake of all, I always try to maintain an even keel. Admittedly, it can be difficult at times. I continue to speak with him, when necessary, in a civilised manner. My son despairs at what he terms as my ongoing innocence and naïvety. I just cannot change. Not I will not, but honestly cannot. Maybe I am foolish, but that is who I am, and I have no desire to become bitter, vengeful, or cruel.

On the day the judge was to visit, we waited with nervous anticipation. Life has taught me, no matter how justified and accurate a case may be, the resulting verdict is not always right or fair. While the judge was taking in the lay of the land, our neighbour told her there used to be steps up the wall for my family to exit the property. He was referring to the two hundred and fifty years old wall traversing the rear boundary of our property. My son and I stood with open mouths. Even my thoughts had frozen for a moment. I asked the judge to have a closer look to see there was no sign of any steps ever having been there. He, however, carried on with his lies. Despite being shouted out by the man and our neighbour, the judge retained her equilibrium. Just goes to show how uncouth these men were. I mean, who shouts at a judge in such a situation? My son and I, other than commenting when obvious lies were told, or answering direct questions, had remained quiet and out of the way. The judge finally stated it was clear the path had been there for years. The man, within earshot of the judge, had actually called her an idiot and restated the land was his. Really! The final verdict had been to dismiss the case and confirm the drive's historic recognition as a public right of way.

Subsequent to the ruling, the man had called at the house and admitted he had made a mistake with us. We confirmed him in that thought, reiterating we had been willing to discuss the issue sensibly. He then asked if we would like to buy the land. When we pointed out the judge had made clear it was a public right of way, he told us he meant the land below the drive. That was in fact his. He waved his hand across the large rectangular plot. It eventually came to light he actually only owned a small portion. There is a lot more to this, but suffice it to say, we bought the land and negotiated with the other owners for the remainder. Without delay we had it fenced and now use it as an orchard for a variety of fruit trees, and to grow vegetables. The whole event, court fees, lawyer fees, advocate fees, taxes, travel, and so on ended up costing tens of thousands. It hurt, but at least the final resolution should enable us to look forward to a degree of peace. So I hoped. Please God.

41

Memorial

I was grateful we had not purchased a property prior to my son's retirement. We had been looking because, at the time, we envisioned him working for many more years. I would have been reluctant to leave a property empty now that we were going to be out of the country for extended periods. Besides the last robbery, I had foiled two attempted burglaries in a previous house. There was also the issue of regular maintenance that, in the British climate, properties require. The decision, however, had the disadvantage of leaving us with nowhere to stay when we returned. Once aware of this, May, my niece, much to our surprise, offered for us to stay with her whenever we needed. Why surprise? Despite all I have done for her over the years, my niece did not appear to like me very much. Neither my son nor I understand why not. She was okay with him, but not me. Of course, she knew my son would make generous recompense. It may have been that which motivated her. I regret she was very greedy for money.

We had been staying with May when a close neighbour in the village telephoned to say a massive fire was raging in the forest behind our home. They thought it may move down into the village. Unlike his usual calm, could-not-care-less demeanour, he sounded on the edge of hysteria. It turned out his unusual concern was because excessively high winds were preventing the fire brigade from gaining control. Flames had been leaping from tree to tree and moving at speed down the mountainside. As our house is in the topmost regions, it was clearly in danger. It all depended upon which way the wind blew. Probably due to the corridors the mountain and forest create, it had not just blown in one direction but kept turning. I asked my son whether he thought we should abandon my appointments and get back. Our visits were primarily designed for medical check-ups and, when required, seeing consultants. He did not think there was much point in rushing back. There would be little we could do. We would just have to hope. Though we did not talk about it much, we were both quietly concerned. What would we do if the house was destroyed?

My appointments, far too many for my liking, with all the pulling about, left me tired and ragged, which exacerbated the unsettled state the concerns for our home had created in me. I had been very pleased when these ended and I was given the all clear, in all instances. There had been several concerns. We could now return, to who knew what.

I can barely describe the scene, or our emotions, as we headed along the bypass leading to our village. I have always taken great delight in the forested mountains with their proud cypress and coniferous trees. Not forgetting the deciduous ones when they are bursting with life. Now the sight of barren mountains covered with blackened skeletal remains greeted us. Distorted ebony effigies littered the panorama. Fear and trepidation occupied the space where my heart should have been quietly beating. My thoughts travelled back to those wonderful years of my early life. In my mind's eye, I saw us making our way through the forest to our mountain top estates. The joy my sisters and I had in the beautiful cherry trees we owned, where we would sing to our hearts' delight, and so much more. I had not been able to hold back the tears the sight before us now and my memories evoked.

With intensified trepidation, we drove up the steep road to our home, signs of fire damage all round. I could not wait to see and yet had desperately wanted to put off the moment. The final approach takes us along the boundary of where the forest and upper reaches of the village meet. My heart physically ached. Trees I had known all my life were no longer. My tears fell unrestrained. The wild grasses, which in summer heat have a dry arid brown tinge, were now black and soot covered. How may I describe our held breath, tense tight chests, throbbing temples, and the nervous undercurrents permeating through as we rounded the final bend? What would we do if it had gone?

Thank You God had been our unanimous cry. The house was still standing and from the road looked intact. The few trees surrounding it however, showed signs of the fire. Including the cypress I had planted when first living there. But at least it had not been completely destroyed. The fire must have got very close. While my son was unlocking the gate, I looked across the village and noted most houses appeared intact, though some trees in the centre showed signs of damage. Ash and soot covered our drive. It made me wonder if our wooden doors and windows still existed. My son told me to wait while he checked if all was safe. Thankfully, it was, though it was very evident the fire had come very close to the building. Upon entering, apprehension gave way to gratitude. The furnishings were undamaged, though a heavy burnt aroma filled the atmosphere. Closer inspection also revealed ash everywhere. Prior to cleaning up, we checked the part of the grounds not visible from the road. Signs of intense heat were all about, but nothing major had been destroyed. When starting the clean up, my son made the mistake of not wearing any facial protection. Ash got right into his system and I worried the resulting cough would last and may cause internal damage. Thankfully, it did not. Quickly realising his mistake, he put on one of his cement mixing masks.

The neighbour who telephoned us in England saw we had returned and came up. His house is a little way below ours. He told us how scary it had been. They had seen smoke on the mountains but it was not until the flames became visible they realised how serious it was. That realisation was exacerbated further by the wind that was blowing in all directions. He said it really had to be seen to appreciate the horror. A tone of which was still evident in his voice. When they realised the fire was going to come into the village, he and a couple of others had filled portable tanks with water and doused their homes. He told us how fortunate we were. At one stage they could see flames hovering over our roof, but the wind changed direction, though not before the trees suffered. Two houses in the village had been destroyed and one person killed. She had been a mentally disabled woman who refused to leave her home.

A distant relative, well I think his father was related to someone in my family, though it has never been clear, told us more. He had inherited a long established family cafe in the centre of the village. When they had seen the ferocity of the fire and strong winds blowing down toward them, they, along with most of the villagers, had abandoned their properties. They gathered on the bypass and watched as the flames surged across the mountains. None had expected their homes or possessions to survive. His visible, perceptible relief at the outcome mirrored that of most of the villagers we subsequently spoke with.

Even now, some years since the fire, it saddens me to see the charred, ebony hued tree trunks prone in the reviving undergrowth. Nature is amazing and besides the hardy grasses, some bushes have started to grow again. It is even possible to see a few young tree shoots, though they look weak and forlorn. There is no doubt nature will, albeit slowly, retake its full place. Most estimates suggest it will take at least thirty-five to seventy years for the forest to return to its former glory. Regrettably, far too long for me ever to see. At least, I have my wonderful memories from when my beloved mama and

I used to look upon and walk through the delightful forests and countryside.

From what I can gather, uncouth individuals who had wanted to build within the forest had caused the fire. The law does not permit building in such areas without specific, and very unusual, governmental authorisation. They apparently thought by underhandedly clearing the area, they could circumvent the law. The resulting devastation and loss of life can never be justified. Besides the woman in our village, several had lost their lives, many in a horrendous manner. There are a lot of small communities dotted round the mountains. The thought of it all still makes me shudder.

There is no negating the horror and sadness of this fire. However, during the recovery period, it resulted in an incident that some may consider amusing. It was not for me, though I can understand why people would think it so. When such devastation has been caused, the government in my country does its best to help citizens. They offer allowances toward house repairs or the building of a new home when there has been total destruction. This applies to fire and earthquake damage. As it is a rather mountainous country, earthquakes are a frequent occurrence. The aunt of the man who had telephoned us told me, if it had not been for me, she would never have got her house finished. You need to know that she and her husband never worked. They spent their whole lives begging. They had obviously been masterful beggars. Not only did they seem to survive well on it, but had also brought up three children. I was confused. How could I have been involved? By the way, I should mention their house was still in the process of construction when the fire struck. Unsurprisingly, there had been some fire damage. There should not have been, as none of the close by houses had any. However, on the one and only visit I made to their home, I had seen they were a filthy family with rubbish of all sorts spread across floors and piled in corners. There was no way the wind blown fire would not ignite something. Without the rubbish, they would have escaped, as their neighbours had.

Cheating, as always, she had decided to try and get a larger, more refined building out of the philanthropic process. Though she had been given money, she constantly withheld payments to the builder. She hoped not to have to pay him the full amount. To my consternation, she told me each time the builder wanted to stop she told him I was coming to tea. When I asked her why she told him that, she said he apparently had what is called a soft spot for me. I fought to control my temper. To even suggest I would comply with the idea made me very cross. She simply retorted that it had kept him going, and she now had her finished home. I told her it was very naughty, struggling not to use more eloquent language. I had not been able to subdue my blushes, but managed to stem my anger.

When we finished cleaning up and were enjoying a well deserved rest, I mentioned again the two men who had come to the house when I was living there on my own. I do not know why they came to mind at that moment. Perhaps it had been the near loss of our home, the land upon which it stands the one place where mama had walked and that was still mine. My son recalled my have mentioned it and asked what it was they had wanted. The men had wanted to make a remembrance for my mother. I had been concerned other than the gentleman mentioned earlier, the one who gave me the olive tree, people may have forgotten her and her kindness. This assured me they had not. They had not known who I was at first until I explained I was her youngest daughter. Then they recalled how very small I had been. They were incensed when I told them the family home had been stolen and wanted to do something about it. If they had been younger, I think they may have gone round. But they were very old now. I am glad they did not try. The outcome, whichever way it went, would not have been nice. It turned out they were two of the children my beloved mama had cared for. Without her, they assured me they would have died. And, without her education, they would never have got the jobs they did or enjoyed the quality life they had. They had been searching for others mother had cared for, in the hope of them wishing to contribute to the building of a memorial. They had traced quite a few, though most were now dispersed across the country and overseas. I never saw the men again. Presumably they got too old or frail. A memorial was therefore never constructed.

One Mother's Day my son greeted me with a lovely card and kiss and suggested, as it was a lovely morning, we enjoy it before it got too hot. On the terrace table a wonderful collection of plants filled my eyes. My son knows how much I love plants rather than cut flowers. I hate to see them die so quickly. He then told me to look further while standing back. He had evidently hoped I would see without his prompting. A very large, floor standing, white marble plaque greeted my eyes. Engraved upon it, in gold lettering, was a tribute to my beloved mama. It was wonderful and brought the tears to my eyes. I had wanted to do something for a long time but had not been able to think what. This was just right. He had also set two lovely figurines on each side. At last, if anyone came, they would have somewhere to show their appreciation. I really could not have asked for anything better.

42

Malicious

Since attending university, my middle sister, Anna, had lived in the metropolis. City life suited her. When flying in and out of the country, we had always stopped to see her, but it had now been a long time since we had met. Her visits to the village had been rare.

Her daughter-in-law unexpectedly telephoned. Neither of us were in the habit of telephoning. She told me my sister was not too well. Anna and her husband had truly loved each other and since his death she had not been in the best of health. Up to this point, it had not created any undue concern, though we knew she had a long-term heart condition that medication had kept under control. However, clearly something had altered. My niece-in-law, now told us my sister had suffered two strokes which had left her weaker. Apparently, there was little she could do now. Very sad, as she had always been a strong, independent woman. I told her I would speak with my son and see about going up to see them. Losing Helen before her time had been hard and now I faced the possibility of also losing Anna. My son agreed we would go as soon as possible. He loved his aunts, and we were both still missing Helen.

We finally got there a couple of days later, just after lunch. Anna said we should not have bothered as it was such a long journey, four and a half hours each way. I made clear I had wanted to see her. It saddened me to watch her moving so slowly, with obvious difficulty. She kept assuring she was all right, but her tired, weak voice said otherwise. I offered to help, but she confirmed her daughter-in-law was taking care of all she needed. We sat and chatted about a variety of things. In particular, reminiscing about people and events from our past lives. I struggled to restrain my tears when leaving. I had no wish to give my sister further concern. She obviously realised matters were not good. We remained in regular contact with my niece-in-law thereafter.

Eventually, it became necessary for someone to be with my sister constantly. Her daughter-in-law willingly undertook the task. This despite her concern about having to leave her own family each night, even though they only lived on the floor below. My sister had built a lovely three apartment building on the site of the original house you may remember Christopher, her husband, had built. Each apartment would eventually be a grandchild's inheritance. There are three boys. I offered to help, but my niece-in-law pointed out I would be unable to turn or lift my sister when required. And my sister would have been too embarrassed to allow my son to do it. In the end, my niece, Anna's daughter, May, volunteered to go over now and then. You will recall she lived in London. My son and

I quickly assessed the reason for her sudden willingness. She had involved herself with a neighbour's young family, with the result of the children being perpetually in her house. Having met them a couple of times, we knew how tiring they could be. Evidently not wishing to upset the mother, she must have seen visits to my sister as a means of having a break. True to that end, she spent most of her time sleeping rather than truly helping her mother.

We visited a few times while May was there. It was never pleasant. On the third visit, we found Anna confined to bed. When we asked why, May said, with a very cold tone, her mother had kept slumping over so she decided it better if she did not get up. I also noted the sly look. One I had seen many times before and that I always found unsettling. Sadly, this inconsiderate, mean, and to me unnecessary treatment resulted in Anna becoming bed ridden. The inactivity meant she became weaker, which in turn led to decreased awareness. Seeing her like that depressed me terribly. However, I was pleased to note she appeared to recognise my son and I. Subsequently, and to my thinking primarily due to the confinement, she suffered a few episodes. Some had her admitted to hospital. You may recall, my country does not have a good health system. Consequently, some families employ people to look after their relatives at night when in hospital. On one occasion, the paid for nurse had not bothered to turn my sister as directed by the doctors. Several severe, very painful bedsores developed. They got so bad it was possible to fit, dare I say it, a man's fist into each. Also, because of the bed confinement, she had to have a catheter. Another uncomfortable and unpleasant experience.

Life had not been easy for her thereafter. When staying, May took over the care of her mother. Not a prospect I would have welcomed. My niece was generally a heavy-handed person, however, she appeared to take delight in being extra brutal with her mother. I had seen the pain in Anna's face. As I have mentioned before, my niece has never liked me, but it was now proven she almost hated her mother. I am being kind by saying, almost. I had wondered before, but now there could be no doubt.

After witnessing the sadistic behaviour, I avoided staying in the room when May was attending to my sister. I would not have been able to stop myself from saying something. If I had been able, I would have willingly taken over the care. My son and I eventually avoided visiting when my niece was there. On one of those visits Anna had been able to tell me, albeit in a very weak voice, May had been hitting her, even round the face. How can someone be so cruel? Whatever has gone before, not that I think there is any justification for her daughter's behaviour, it does not warrant such treatment. Someone in such a constrained condition deserves kindness and respect. If nothing else, her age and inability demanded such.

Something told me to expect the worse when my niece-in-law telephoned a week later. Anna had died. I had been unable to say much for a moment. A misty haze clouded my mind while tears fell unrestrained. Allowing a little time for me to recover first, she then told me how Anna had taken bad again and the doctor said she had to go to hospital. Before leaving, Anna asked her to take her round the house to look over her life's treasures. She then told her, in no uncertain terms, never to take her back home. She had been very determined and made her promise. We agreed she must have known. After we ended our call, I remembered May would have been staying. I suspect my sister feared what her daughter would do if they had returned her alive or dead. Horrible to comprehend I know, but May had a vicious, some would say evil, streak. I am certain, without her daughter's cruel treatment, my sister would have continued longer and in a fitter state. I find it difficult to forgive May, though despite everything, I still cared about her.

There is a lot more I could tell, but will spare you. Though we got a little lost in the city's back streets, my son and I arrived in time for the service and funeral. It horrified me to see May heartily and openly laughing and joking with strangers outside the church. Immediately prior to her mother's funeral service. Need I say more?

***

You will recall we had not retained a property in the country and my niece having offered for us to stay with her. Despite everything, we decided to continue with the arrangement. There had never been any indication of how long we would need to stay while undergoing medical appointments. Also, constantly in the back of my mind had been hope. Hope that May's attitude toward me would change.

That we would be able to have a proper aunt-niece relationship. I know. I really can be naïve. But hope is hope and without it we are lost.

On our next visit, she could hardly bring herself to say hello. Within seconds, she had turned from the door and gone back in. I was slightly stunned because it had been some time since we had last seen each other. I had brought her to the country, worried by the apparently disinterested treatment she had been receiving at home. Without me she would have none of what she now possessed. We followed, my son struggling to get our cases through the door. Within little more than a minute, she suggested we go to our rooms. Her tone and demeanour left no doubt she already wanted us out of the way. At least she offered to make coffee when we came back down.

My room was cold and dirty. There was also blood on the sheet. May had never been hygienic, the idea of cleanliness appearing to be a foreign concept. She truly resented using water and washing powder. Part of her miserly nature, I suppose. The washing machine's quick twenty-minute cycle was the only one she ever used. Everything went in, no matter the colour or how dirty. That first evening she provided a meal over which we attempted a catchup on our respective bits of news. However, she had no interest in what had been happening with us. She constantly interrupted with extracts of her own mundane, day-to-day activities. We then settled to watch television, but it quickly became apparent she found our presence irritating. With my sensitive disposition, I had not been able to ignore and suggested to my son we go to our rooms. Thankfully, he had also noted and agreed. Matters were to progressively worsen. I wondered why she had even bothered to invite us if that was how she felt. Having said that, she did not seem to mind my son's presence. It was me. I still do not understand why. I had only tried to do my best for her.

Within days, it became increasingly evident she did not want us in the house. Besides breakfast that my son prepared, from ingredients he had paid for, and brought to our rooms, we hardly ever eat at the house. My niece had ceased offering meals. The only exception was an occasional, and it was only occasional, invite to Sunday lunch. I must acknowledge she excelled at those. However, it turned my stomach when she wiped the fat from the baking tray with a slice of bread and, while eating it, smacked her lips throughout.

We had been talking about how I thought May did not mind my son, but seemed to resent me being in the house. We had returned to our rooms almost immediately after lunch. My niece having again made it clear we were not wanted. This had been on a Sunday near the start of our stay. My son put forward the suggestion that she had probably been thinking about her future. With her medical training, she must have been aware she had damaged her own longevity. Besides the complete lack of hygiene, she had also been grossly overweight for years. He suspected she was thinking of him looking after her when the time came. Something he made clear to me he would not contemplate. Anyway, she had more than enough to pay for a carer. He then added, it was now obvious she did not want to feed us. We would have to go out after breakfast and stay out. When not at appointments, we would have to spend time in shopping centres and find places to eat. It was not fair, considering how much he was paying her. He added, in some ways it would be better for us because her excessive use of fat and salt made it difficult for us to cope with her cooking. Sadly, her mood and unwelcoming disposition never altered. We followed the routine of being out all the time for the whole of our stay, despite my ill health. The omnipresent filth had made our situation even more uncomfortable. To try and make things a bit better, my son borrowed the vacuum to clean our rooms and the landing. He almost vomited when outside May's bedroom. Piles of her now deceased husband's body hair lay all about. He had died five years earlier!

I developed a very bad, almost non-stop cough, but despite the cold weather, May refused to put the heating on. My son told me how one morning, when he had gone to make breakfast, he found her at the kitchen table with three jackets on, but still clearly shaking with the cold. As I have mentioned before, my niece was a miser. She stubbornly refused to turn any heating on even though my son was paying her a vast amount, and she had more than substantial means herself. I had started coughing blood and suspected a touch of pneumonia. However, I prevented my son from asking her to start the heating. She would not have liked it and could turn very nasty. Irrespective of my condition, we still had to go out each day. At least the shopping centre was warm. Even the staff got to recognise us. My son thought they may even come to think we were thieves casing the place.

Our diet of sandwiches and soup became monotonous, but we had to exercise some sort of economy. We had no idea how long our stay would be. My appointments had been numerous and though my son paid for some private ones, they had been spread far apart. In the end, he spent four thousand pounds just for parking and the light, so-called meals. That does not take into account petrol nor the couple of thousand pounds he paid his cousin. He also paid for much of the shopping, though we were not eating in. I am sure you can imagine how we felt. Perhaps we should have left, but we had constantly hoped the consultant, doctor, and treatment appointments would end quickly. However, even with the private ones, it all took far longer than anticipated.

Our passports were due to expire, so my son arranged to go to the passport office to renew them. The office was far from us, so he opted to use trains and underground rather than drive through the chaos of central London. That meant it was not really viable for me to accompany him. He was worried about leaving me in the house, but we could not see an alternative. In my unwell condition, it would have been unsafe for me to be out on my own. After his departure I closed my eyes, hoping to get some sleep, but it would not come. My coughing and the intense cold would not allow me to relax. I had said nothing to my son, but I was becoming increasingly concerned. I had been coughing blood again. After about three and a half hours, I began to feel I could do with a drink and something to eat. My niece was aware of how poorly I had been for days, but still refused to turn any heating on. All day and evening I remained in bed. Not once did she come up or even call up. I could have been dead for all she cared. Perhaps that is what she hoped for. My son was furious when he got back late that night. He was ready to confront her but, again, I stopped him. We really could not afford to upset her. Looking back, I see how foolish this must appear, but I truly wanted to avoid any confrontation. May continued to treat me with little consideration, irrespective of my obvious poorly condition. As I have said too often, I have no idea why. Nevertheless, I cared and never wanted there to be bad blood between us. There were times when I was tempted to speak my mind, but managed to refrain. Anyway, she would have denied any wrongdoing.

Out of politeness, when returning after each day's long expulsion, we would go to the kitchen to greet my niece. She spent most of her life sitting at that table. On each occasion she only bestowed a couple of words before making clear we were not to remain. We quietly persevered until all my appointments had been completed. Thankfully, I was again given the all clear. I confess it had been a struggle to be out every day. My son had done his best to find places of interest to visit, but for most of the time it had been tedious. Discovering places to eat economically had also been a headache. As you may imagine, all this had been tiring in itself. However, when combined with all the prodding, pushing, and pulling I had been subjected to, it left me worn and fatigued.

We gratefully said our goodbyes when the time to leave arrived.

We left with the realisation we would no longer be able, nor had the wish, to stay with my niece. Even if she had the grace to invite us again. Thereafter, my son hired holiday accommodation for each of our visits. It proved expensive and not always as comfortable as I would have liked. Ultimately, after a few years of doing this, we decided we no longer wished to go through the hassle of finding somewhere each time. Therefore, despite our previous reasonings and reservations, my son decided to purchase a small apartment. Security, especially in view of our long absences, remained a concern. However, on balance, we felt it was the right decision. It took a while, but we eventually found one tucked away in the rear of an apartment building. It would not be very obvious when we were not there. Sadly, my health deteriorated during the purchase process, resulting in us remaining in the country longer than anticipated. I had, again, to attend further appointments. We now spend prolonged periods here. Far more than originally envisioned. At least it is a place of our own. It was, and is, disappointing to be so tied, but at least I am still here and have more time with my son. May God grant it continues for many more years.

Some may have noticed how I keep referring to my niece in the past tense. Not very long ago, her neighbour's children, the ones she became involved with, found her collapsed in her hallway. It was eventually determined she had died from a massive heart attack. It is a shame we never saw much of each other in recent years, though she would occasionally telephone and talk with my son. I never understood the problem she had with me, but I have always cared about her and wish we had enjoyed a better relationship.

43

Shadows

Life in the apartment was not always peaceful. Then it rarely is where a variety of people are congregated, at least, not in my experience. My son frequently discovered dents and scratches on his car. He asked neighbours several times, politely, to have more care and to ask their visitors to be more considerate. Most of the time, there was little improvement. On one occasion, he went out to find a rear panel dented and completely covered in white paint. In fairness, we do not think that was caused by a neighbour but probably by some delivery van. He had to have the whole panel scrapped back and resprayed. There is also a neighbour who must fancy himself a do-it-yourself expert. That he clearly is not. The banging will sometimes go on, at sporadic times, for days. He never seems to complete a project in one go. Often, within short time, he returns to the same area, clearly trying to repair something he has already supposedly done. We have never complained because we do not want to have upset between neighbours. Besides, this does not go on for months, though it sometimes feels like it. Probably due to him never seeming to have completed the task properly.

Sadly, my health has continued to deteriorate. I have had a few very nasty falls with resulting black and blue bruising. In a couple, I struck my face, arms, back, and legs. The photographs my son took would fit well into some horror production. If only it had just been those falls, as painful as they were. I, for various reasons, ended in hospital a few times. In one stay, I was told I had a heart attack during the first evening. That is when the consultant discovered one of my heart's valves has severely narrowed. To help me comprehend, he described it as having become like a piece of wet string. Some analogy! There was nothing he could do as, in my weakened condition, any operation would be too dangerous.

During one of these hospital stays they left me in bed without any physical therapy and my muscles consequently atrophied. I had already been having some difficulty with my legs, but this now made it difficult to walk. My son had to purchase a wheelchair to take me home. He also bought a couple of walking sticks. I have never liked them and when out would, when necessary, hold on to my son's arm. I often wonder how I have not pulled his socket out. He assures me I do not lean heavily besides which I am now quite light, not that I have ever been heavy. Unfortunately, my legs have deteriorated to the point I cannot walk far and often have to use the wheelchair. I have always been a strong woman, and after having to fight for so much, an independent one. You may therefore imagine how using the chair makes me feel.

Arthritis has eaten much of the bone in one shoulder, which has restricted movement. In one of my heavier falls, onto a tiled floor, I fractured the other arm and shoulder. The consultant, who happened to be a fellow countrywoman, became excited when new bone started to grow. She put it down to the healthy food and climate we had enjoyed as children. Unfortunately, the new bone has grown awkwardly and now restricts full momentum. Again, because of my weakened condition, there is nothing to be done. Even scraping the bone is out of the question.

So you see, my life is still not problem free. As I have often said throughout this autobiography, I do not think it ever will be.

***

Due to the Covid 19 lockdowns, and my poorer health, we did not visit our home in the village for a few years. When the lockdowns were over, and I was feeling up to it, we made the trip. I looked forward to seeing my ancestral home again, as well as our little house. It was a very sad sight that greeted us. There had been another major fire. This time we had not escaped to the same extent as we had with the last one.

All our lovely fruit, olive, and cypress trees, and all our plants are gone. There is absolutely no sign of them. It is like a barren wilderness. Neither is there any sign of the greenhouse my son built, except for melted plastic in the concrete. The only pointer to us having had a terrace table and chairs is a handful of rusty, distorted screws. The heat was such that even the aluminium ladder is missing large parts. There is no indication we ever had the wooden one. The back wall of the house was black and the doors and window bore scorch marks. One of the water barrels in the orchard had melted, as had all the watering pipes. It brought tears to my eyes to see all I and my son have cared for and enjoyed are no more. For me it is worse, because I know I will not see the recovery.

The same person who had helped with the last fire told us how he, his son, and another man had gone around with water tanks on the back of their vehicles and doused theirs and our houses. They even had to douse themselves. I am so grateful. This time there is no doubt we would have lost our home if it had not been for him. My ancestral family home, the one that was stolen, was however, intact, with just some of the surrounding land having become victim to the flames. We later learnt, the man who occupies my old home lost his wife during the Covid pandemic. He is older and not good at looking after himself, so primarily lives with his son and daughter-in-law in a distant town. Apparently, he comes to stay every other weekend just to keep the grounds in order.

The kind man who saved our house subsequently helped my son clean away the debris and re-plaster and repaint our home. We made sure he was well recompensed. He also helped with one very frightening incident. One afternoon, just as our friend was leaving for the day, my son spotted a snake by our back door. Unfortunately, it got into the house before he could get it away. Not accustomed to dealing with snakes, and quite honestly neither of us being particularly enamoured with them, my son called out to our friend as he was making his way down the hill. It took a few minutes to find where the snake had gone. I had visions of it popping up when we were in bed. Gives me the shivers to think of it. It turned out to have hidden itself, in a coil, behind our kitchen dustbin. It surprised me to see our friend was also nervous. I had often seen him and his father, who had now passed away, dealing with very large snakes. It turned out this, though fairly small, was poisonous. He therefore did not want to get too close and used a pointed stick to attack it. I can still see the open jaws hissing. The poor thing was as frightened as we and doing what it could to defend itself. The struggle went on for a while, the little creature refusing to die. In the end, our man got the better and managed to crush its throat. He disposed of the remains in an outside plot where the wildlife would no doubt eat it. We were so grateful to him, yet again. Through the years he has been a good friend. Later, early evening, he returned with a bag full of snake repellant pellets. My son had seen another, different snake on our veranda the day before.

During our stay, we had a lot of headaches sorting out various papers with the authorities. I say we but in my now weakened state my son had to deal with most of it, all in fact. The law had changed, and we needed to register our property boundaries or chance having the land confiscated. My people have always sought to sidestep taxes, so the latest government had established a better, accountable system. A relative had given us the contact details of someone he said would help. We thought he was a lawyer, but in fact he was simply an engineer. Anyway, to cut yet another long story short, the man cheated us. We discovered the bill should have been a sixteenth of what he charged. He even offered to pay the tax for us each year, for the same fee, but my son had the foresight to sort that himself, much to the man's amazement and annoyance. Our authorities are not the easiest of people to deal with, but my son persevered. When we told him, in his office, we saw one of his staff smirk. It turns out he is known for overcharging, but not by as much as he had us. We never saw or heard from the relative who had recommended him. That, even though we knew he and his wife had visited their house in the village for one night. He knew I had not been well and this may be my last visit but did not even have the, what shall I call it, courtesy, not the right word but it will have to do, to just come and say hello for five or ten minutes. I assume he knew about the man's cheating and was too ashamed to face us.

We enjoyed a couple more weeks, eating at a favourite restaurant and enjoying cool drinks in a seaside cafe we have loved for many years. However, the heat began to intensify and I did not feel I wanted to stay further, though we had originally thought to be there for a further three or four weeks. My son was surprised, but quickly arranged for our journey back to the United Kingdom. Perhaps I had sensed something more, because my health grew worse once we were back.

***

As you have seen, throughout most of my life, I have been constantly deceived and lied to. Regrettably, this has never changed.

I had considered writing this, and the following chapter, as an epilogue, but sense, for you the reader, they are more appropriate as chapters. I will leave my son to, in due course, handle the eventual epilogue that must become appropriate at some point.

Besides the wonder of my son, my life has been a shadow of what it should have been. I was born into a loving, prosperous family, with the prospect of my life following a similar genteel, quiet path of family, fulfilment, love, and service to others. As you have seen, that was not to be. The actions of one lustful man catapulted me into a world of bitter cruelty and depravation. Thereafter, my life staggered from one brutal event to another. Of course, there have been those few, too few, lighter fun moments, but overall my life has not been nice.

My sisters also had their difficulties. Helen married the love of her life, but it was a life of financial struggle, and at first, with her in-laws treatment, cruel. Anna, of the three of us, did better, but in the first years also struggled financially, though she was clever and eventually achieved financial success. However, the early loss of her adored husband to cancer marked her forever. She was never the same again. Our parents were remarkable people who instilled in us a true sense of love, inner strength, courage, wonderful values, abilities, and so much more. It is their teachings, love, and care that helped the three of us survive so much. Me in particular, as my life was the most traumatic of the three. Without their input, I would have been removed from this world long ago. I so, so, miss my beloved mama. I always will.

I confess, my experiences have left me with a primarily negative outlook. As much as I have hoped and sought to believe and trust, people consistently let me down. Whenever anything positive has entered my life, it is quickly negated and destroyed. The pain in my emotional heart is great as I write this. Why could my life not have been otherwise? Or at least less severe? I will never know the answer. Well, not while in this lifetime here on earth.

One thing I can still delight in is that I continue to have the joy of my son. I can look back with gratitude for having been able to save him, providing him a decent education, and giving him as protected a life as I could. Though, he has also had his disappointments.

In this autobiography, I have shared many details of how experiences impacted me emotionally, psychologically, and physically. How many influenced my decision making and how they dictated my life's path. By doing so, I hope I have been able to instil some hope, comfort, and awareness for any who have, or are, experiencing similar challenges. To know they are not alone and there is the possibility of escape from brutal circumstances. Life after may not be as we would desire nevertheless, it is possible to go on to live a reasonable, if not entirely happy, life. I was able to create a home and bring up my beloved boy. I will miss him so much.

44

Closing

I write this because I know my end is near. We all know it will come, but are we ever truly ready? Now I am at the end, where do my thoughts go? What do I look back on as most precious?

The first precious memory, and one that has never left me, you will guess if you have read through this autobiography and not skipped to the end, is my beloved mama. We had such a close love. Not claustrophobic, but genuine, heartfelt, unfathomable love. Her passing in my arms is one of the terrible moments of my life. I would go so far as to say the most terrible. That despite the awful treatments I subsequently endured. I was not quite five, and here, the loving, caring world ended abruptly. At least it did for me. Throughout my life, the deep, heart-rending cry in my heart has always been for her. I do not know whether there is any truth in the thought we meet our loved ones again. If there is, how wonderful it would be. My life, existence, or whatever it should be called thereafter, would be with mama. I hope we do see each other again. I will hug and never leave you again. Please excuse the blotted ink marks if you can see them.

Second, of course, is my son. What would life have been like without him? Easier, no doubt, but I would not have that. My life has been about him. Yes, it was a struggle, but I can now stand back and admire a kind, gentle, caring man. I am so glad I was able to save him and provide him with a decent education and protected life. I realise I am repeating myself, but I really am so grateful to have achieved it. He has had his disappointments, but then most of us have. I could not love him more than I always have. My greatest sadness will be having to leave him. If only we could be together for all eternity, all three of us.

Third is having had the opportunity to, for a while at least, live and walk on the ground of my old ancestral home. Even though the house and surrounding land have been stolen, I can still enjoy the memories it evokes. Of course, this links to the first and prime precious time I had with my beloved mama.

Fourth would be the memory of having purchased my own home as a single woman. That was a true achievement, and one I have always been proud of. I have never forgotten it and, in all honesty, have missed it.

Fifth, is my lovely little budgerigar. He was a real character and loved me unconditionally. It may seem strange to talk of a budgerigar loving, but his behaviour and actions spoke to the truth of it. I missed my childhood pets, and he was the one and only pet I had thereafter. His passing was also a sad time.

What else? Those far too few moments, of which there really were too few. Especially those with my one and only real friend, so

I thought, Hanna. She was a real character, and we really did have a few hearty laughs together. More recently, there have been my fellow authors. Who have shown me great kindness and consideration, though we never met in person.

My life has been a challenge. As it is for many. I wish I could say the challenges had ended, but it seems I am not to be spared. However, by the grace of God, I have survived much and had some successes. I am also privileged to have more time with my son.

I have described this chronicle of my life as a reluctant autobiography. That is because I am essentially a private person and, as you have seen, dislike public exposure. It is also because I am ashamed of those events that reflect negatively upon some relatives, and of my weak timidity in the earlier part of my adult years. However, I do not think it would be right to depart this life without leaving some sort of record of my experiences. It has been difficult to write because it has stirred innumerable sad, painful, and hurtful memories, though many have never been far from my thoughts. I do not feel the book really does justice to all I have endured, nor does it truly convey the full strength of the emotions and fears. Nevertheless, I have done my utmost and believe it is the best record I could compose. As I have mentioned elsewhere, I have intentionally omitted some details and events. There is no justification for unnecessarily traumatising readers beyond what is required to make sense of some situations. The rest will pass into eternity with me. My primary aim, besides providing a history of my life and the times I have lived through, is to try to help and inspire those who, by whatever means, have suffered, or are suffering, in their lives.

I appreciate the above is a repeat of what I have already said in the prologue. However, I am fully aware some readers skip those and therefore wanted to ensure you understood both my reticence and eventual motivation for writing.

I hope the sharing of my life has shown you we are capable of withstanding events and circumstances we may have previously thought impossible. It has certainly shown how resilient our human spirits can be, even if we do not believe it at the time. We are able to overcome and move forward to reasonably successful lives. Even if they are not always as happy as we would like. We can live with the scares and still enjoy the memories from the happier, fulfilling moments.

For those who have, or are experiencing abuse, of whatever nature, know you do have the power and ability to escape and overcome. You can go on to live a fulfilled and successful life. Even if it still has its challenges. You do not have to remain in fear of your abuser, or anything else come to that. There are many organisations and websites which offer advice, support, and help. I wish they had been available for me. They were not, but I survived and so can you.

I wish each of you happiness and success in whatever you do and wherever your path may lead.

With all my best,

T. R. Robinson

Epilogue

It is with a very heavy heart I have to tell you my beloved mother has passed away.

We had planned on this, my mother's autobiography, being published before an epilogue became appropriate. It would have been included in a second edition. That mother will not see the finished book is a sadness and disappointment.

Mother would want me to finish her story by sharing the final events.

It will not be easy, but I will do my best.

Aware there was not a lot of time left, my mother wished to see her ancestral home one last time. I therefore made the arrangements. Though her strength and health had been progressively declining, we had no worries about her undertaking the journey. That was until her breathing became difficult when the doctor directed me to take her to the hospital. Investigations revealed her heart and lungs had weakened. End of Life support was put into place before her return home. Even so, she was still semi-active and was still determined to visit her family home. When I asked if she was sure, her response was to tell me she would walk it if she could. That rather answered the question.

Something changed a day or two before we were due to set off. However, she still wanted to go. Mother found the journey difficult. We have travelled overland for many years. I am disappointed to have to say, once we reached our home in the village, mother took to bed. Her breathing had become more difficult, and there was additional pain. After a few days, I became concerned and telephoned one of the nursing contacts in England. She said I should really consult a doctor. As my mother has explained in her, this, autobiography, that is not something you willingly do over there.

The result was her being admitted to the local hospital. Examination had shown her lungs were filled with fluid. In sharing her previous experiences of hospital in that country, mother has told you how bad it was. Things have not improved much. The only positive is that many of the consultants and doctors have since trained abroad. The nursing staff, however, were rather brutal. They treated mother as if she were a lump of meat rather than a frail, older person in need of gentle handling. There was little care, and I ended up staying in the ward with her twenty-four hours a day, seven days a week. I hate to think what would have been the outcome if I had not.

The rough treatment and her weakness led to her eating very little. She became weaker and increasingly depressed. After twenty days I decided to take her home. They were effectively killing her. The consultant and registrar were not happy, but I put my foot down.

Her condition did not improve greatly at home, but at least I could take care of her and she was spared the brutality.

Arranging the journey home proved far more difficult than I expected. We decided mother was in no condition for the overland journey back, so I booked a flight. I had spoken to the airline's medical unit beforehand to ensure there would be no difficulties. On the day, we undertook the four-hour taxi journey to the airport. There are no regional airports. The airport staff, despite my confirmation of having spoken to their medical unit, refused to let my mother board. It was very upsetting. In the end, we had to call our taxi driver back, and make the four-hour return trip.

I had no choice then but to book our overland travel. That also proved a challenge, but I managed to sort it for a couple of days later. Mother was very poorly all the way, but we made it, despite several delays on the way. To my shame, I have to admit, I do not think I fully appreciated how unwell mother felt.

The day after our return, mother was not at all well and I was told to call an ambulance. They spent a lot of time examining and taking tests but finally concluded mother was not stable enough to be moved. A hospice nurse came that evening and administered some pain relief. The next day, a Sunday, mother was still poorly and the hospice nurse who had called in again, summoned another ambulance. It took a while, and a second ambulance crew, but in the end they admitted mother to hospital. The doctors and nurses did their best, but there was little that could be safely done. The consultant and I agreed a forward plan that we thought would help improve matters. This had been on the third morning of mother's stay. It therefore annoyed me when later the same day we were told mother was to be moved. The hospital bed manager wanted her bed. I understood that but was cross when I found they had moved mother to an enhanced dementia ward. My mother has all her faculties. There has never been any suggestion of limited mental capability. It was awful. One patient was screaming nonstop. Another kept shouting, again nonstop, for a nurse. Others were mumbling or talking nonsense. I stayed for a while to give mother her evening meal but had no choice but to leave her there for the night. Mother has always been a sensitive woman, and I worried how she would cope. I hardly slept. I went back the next day determined to bring her home. It took a bit of sorting, but I got her home that evening.

A hospital bed was delivered the next day, but only with small handgrip rails. I found mother on the floor the next morning. I checked for any head injuries, but there was just a slight cut on her knee. As it was a weekend again, I had to buy temporary child rails to use until they delivered proper rails the following Monday. I took care of mother with hospice nurses only coming when I felt a need for them. It took a few days before we started to get mother's pain under control. I expected her to brighten up a bit and looked forward to having some more time with her.

Mother had always been proud of the fact I had never seen her unclothed. Her weakness, even before this latest change, meant I had to help her shower and clean her when it became necessary. That was very upsetting and robbed her of her dignity. I did my best not to be too intrusive. My mother has been a strong and independent woman for most of her life. I know that was not always the case in the early years of marriage to my brutal father, but once free of him, it was. It was therefore very difficult for her to have all these people intimately interacting with her, including me.

On the second Saturday, she slept more than usual. I spoke with a hospice nurse a couple of times over the telephone. We concluded she was just exhausted and needed the sleep. Nine o'clock that night I saw she had slid down more than usual and it was putting pressure on her lungs. As I often had to, I lifted her up in the bed, which is when she gave two loud, rasping breaths and passed away.

This is very hard for me. Other than the years of my military service, mother and I have been together for most of my life. There is only the two of us. I suppose that should be was, but.

Everyone who ever met mother always commented on how lovely and genuine she was. Indeed, she was one of those precious soles we rarely have the privilege to know. Yes, she never lost her innocence or naïvety, which could sometimes be exasperating, but I would not have had it any other way. To hope for, find, and see, the best in people was her constant aim. To have her in my life and to have benefitted from all her love and care has been far more than a privilege. It has been a genuine blessing.

I am very sad to say, the peace mother longed for, and we hoped she would enjoy, at least for a time before the end, never materialised. Her faith has always been strong and I hope she is now at peace in God's arms.

I miss her very much, and always will. My life will never be the same.

Peter Robinson

OTHER BOOKS

By T. R. Robinson

<u>Memoir</u>
Tears of Innocence
Negative Beauty
Lost Dreams
The Hammer
Broom Attack

<u>Novels</u>
Peter
Loving Maria

<u>Short Stories</u>
Her Next Door
Reverse Gear
Snake in the Grass
Off Balance
Felina
Manipulation
The Blonde Brunette

All are either entirely true or heavily based on real events.

www.ingramcontent.com/pod-product-compliance
Lightning Source LLC
Chambersburg PA
CBHW060544080526
44585CB00013B/445